Why are some places in the world characterized by better social service provision and welfare outcomes than others? In a world in which millions of people, particularly in developing countries, continue to lead lives plagued by illiteracy and diseases that can be easily prevented or cured, understanding the conditions that promote social welfare is of critical importance to social scientists and policy makers alike. Drawing on a multi-method, subnational analysis of the stark variations in educational and health outcomes within India over the course of the past century, this book develops a novel argument for the power of a shared solidarity as an impetus for welfare policy and outcomes. Combining comparative historical and statistical analyses, this book shows that Indian states that witnessed the emergence of a shared subnational solidarity, or subnationalism, were more likely to institute and maintain a progressive social policy and, relatedly, witness better developmental outcomes. This argument marks an important break on the one hand, from existing theories about social welfare, which emphasize the importance of economic development, social democratic parties, the nature and extent of electoral competition and ethnic diversity, and on the other hand, from the dominant negative view of the implications of identity for welfare.

Prerna Singh is Mahatma Gandhi assistant professor of Political Science and International Studies at the Department of Political Science and faculty fellow at the Watson Institute for International Studies at Brown University. Prior to joining Brown, she was assistant professor at the Department of Government at Harvard University. Singh has received numerous awards and fellowships, including from the American Political Science Association, Harvard Academy for International and Area Studies, the Center for Advanced Study for India (CASI) at the University of Pennsylvania, the American Institute of Indian Studies and the Charlotte Elizabeth Procter Honorific Fellowship from Princeton University. Her articles have been published in several journals, including *Comparative Politics, Comparative Political Studies, Studies in Comparative International Development, World Development* and *World Politics*. Singh is the co-editor of the *Handbook of Indian Politics* (2013).

This book has been awarded the Woodrow Wilson Prize by the American Political Science Association for the best book published in politics and international relations, and the Barrington Moore prize by the American Sociological Association for the best book published in comparative historical sociology in 2015. Her article 'Subnationalism and Social Development: A Comparative Analysis of Indian States' was awarded the Luebbert prize for the best article published in Comparative Politics in the last two years; the Mary Parker Follett prize for the best article published in Politics and History in the last year, both by the American Political Science Association, and the outstanding article prize in the Sociology of Development by the American Sociological Association.

Advance praise

"This is a magisterial book that takes on one of the most important questions of all times – why do some places develop more inclusive welfare regimes and deliver better social outcomes than others? Singh highlights the role of communal cohesion and shared affective bonds in producing the sense of mutual obligation that is at the root of progressive, redistributive policies. Along the way, Singh carefully shows where existing explanations fail to explain the puzzle of subnational variation in Indian social policies and development and takes the reader on a theoretically informed and empirically rich journey through parts of India from the late 19th century onwards. This book is a joy to read and is based on a rigorous combination of qualitative and quantitative research."

Melani Cammett, *Professor of Government, Harvard University*

"In this outstanding book, Singh examines the question of what drives social development. Based on a comparative subnational and longitudinal analysis of Indian states, she mobilizes an extensive amount of evidence to show that social development depends in large measure on the sense of shared identity within a community. Theoretically innovative and carefully researched, this superb study is likely to influence comparative scholarship on welfare outcomes for a long time to come."

Giovanni Capoccia, *Professor of Comparative Politics, University of Oxford*

"Why are levels of social development in some Indian states so much higher than in others? Prerna Singh locates the source of this variation in the degree of shared identity – the sense of "we-ness" – among the state's citizens. Where solidarity within the subnational political community is strong, as in Kerala and Tamil Nadu, citizens put the collective good over individual welfare and support progressive social policies that generate marked improvements in health and education. But where subnational solidarity is weak, as in Uttar Pradesh, Rajasthan until the 1990s, and Bihar until the mid-2000s, such common purpose is absent and public policies are significantly less developmentally oriented. This is a novel and important argument, and it is supported by a rich array of qualitative and quantitative evidence. *How Solidarity Works for Welfare* is a must-read for anyone interested in understanding the sources of social welfare improvements in developing nations, and a welcome antidote to the tendency to view social attachments strictly as impediments to development."

Daniel N. Posner, *James S. Coleman Professor of International Development, University of California, Los Angeles*

"As famously argued by Gosta Esping-Anderson, the West European and North American politics of welfare is based on three arguments: market imperfections, religion, and class. The US and UK represent the first type; France and especially Germany drew upon the Catholic tradition of help; and Scandinavian countries tapped into the rise of social democratic parties to construct a welfare net for all. An entire generation of scholars working on welfare states has taken Esping-Anderson's view as a founding imagination for further exploration – for or against. Prerna Singh's manuscript radically departs from this comparative wisdom. The key for Singh is the notion of community, not class, religion or markets. Relying on Indian materials, Singh argues that when a public sphere internalizes the idea of community, mass literacy goes up significantly and the physical health of the masses also does. A truly novel and arresting argument."

Ashutosh Varshney, *Brown University*

Cambridge Studies in Comparative Politics

General Editor

Margaret Levi *University of Washington, Seattle*

Assistant General Editors

Kathleen Thelen *Massachusetts Institute of Technology*
Erik Wibbels *Duke University*

Associate Editors

Robert H. Bates *Harvard University*
Gary Cox *Stanford University*
Stephen Hanson *The College of William and Mary*
Torben Iversen *Harvard University*
Stathis Kalyvas *Yale University*
Peter Lange *Duke University*
Helen Milner *Princeton University*
Frances Rosenbluth *Yale University*
Susan Stokes *Yale University*

Other Books in the Series

Ben W. Ansell, *From the Ballot to the Blackboard: The Redistributive Political Economy of Education*

Leonardo R. Arriola, *Multi-Ethnic Coalitions in Africa, Business Financing of Opposition Election Campaigns*

David Austen-Smith, Jeffry A. Frieden, Miriam A. Golden, Karl Ove Moene, and Adam Przeworski, eds., *Selected Works of Michael Wallerstein: The Political Economy of Inequality, Unions, and Social Democracy*

Andy Baker, *The Market and the Masses in Latin America: Policy Reform and Consumption in Liberalizing Economies*

Lisa Baldez, *Why Women Protest: Women's Movements in Chile*

Stefano Bartolini, *The Political Mobilization of the European Left, 1860–1980: The Class Cleavage*

Robert Bates, *When Things Fell Apart: State Failure in Late-Century Africa*

Mark Beissinger, *Nationalist Mobilization and the Collapse of the Soviet State*

Nancy Bermeo, ed., *Unemployment in the New Europe*

(continued after the index)

How Solidarity Works for Welfare

Subnationalism and Social Development in India

PRERNA SINGH
Brown University

CAMBRIDGE
UNIVERSITY PRESS

CAMBRIDGE
UNIVERSITY PRESS

University Printing House, Cambridge CB2 8BS, United Kingdom

One Liberty Plaza, 20th Floor, New York, NY 10006, USA

477 Williamstown Road, Port Melbourne, VIC 3207, Australia

4843/24, 2nd Floor, Ansari Road, Daryaganj, Delhi - 110002, India

79 Anson Road, #06-04/06, Singapore 079906

Cambridge University Press is part of the University of Cambridge.

It furthers the University's mission by disseminating knowledge in the pursuit of education, learning and research at the highest international levels of excellence.

www.cambridge.org
Information on this title: www.cambridge.org/9781107697454

© Prerna Singh 2015

First published 2015
First paperback edition 2017

A catalogue record for this publication is available from the British Library

Library of Congress Cataloging in Publication data
Singh, Prerna.
How solidarity works for welfare: subnationalism and social development in India / Prerna Singh.
    pages   cm. – (Cambridge studies in comparative politics)
ISBN 978-1-107-07005-9 (hardback)
1. India – Social policy.   2. India – Social conditions.   3. India – Politics and government.   4. Subnational governments – India.   5. Nationalism – India.   I. Title.
HN683.5.S4957   2015
306.0954–dc23   2015004868

ISBN 978-1-107-07005-9 Hardback
ISBN 978-1-107-69745-4 Paperback

For Nani, whose endless love sustains me

Contents

Figures and Tables

FIGURES

TABLES

Acknowledgments

The process of writing this book has been a testimony to its central argument about the constructive potential of solidaristic communities. I have been fortunate to be part of intellectual communities, across the United States and India, that have sustained and enriched my ideas and writing. Atul Kohli's writings attracted me to Princeton, and into the world of US academia. I am grateful to have had his counsel, wit, kindness, and gentle but firm commitment to asking big questions with stakes for the lives of people across the world, serve as a beacon for my journey so far. From the very first time I became interested in questions of identity politics and welfare, Deborah Yashar has served as a critical sounding board, throwing my arguments back at me, pushing me to hone and sharpen them with each iteration. I have grown to rely on Mark Beissinger's guidance and companionship on the road of ideas and have greatly valued his leading me to think both deeper and more broadly about questions of ethnicity and nationalism. Evan Lieberman encountered far more unruly versions of these chapters and their author, and to him goes the credit of patiently and committedly disciplining both within political science. I am thankful to Evan for consistently setting, and pushing me towards higher bars of scholarly rigor. Beyond these model thinkers and teachers, whom I was grateful to have as a dissertation committee, I benefited at Princeton from exchanges with Chris Achen, Nancy Bermeo, Angus Deaton, Kent Eaton, Amaney Jamal, the late Smitu Kothari, Zia Mian, Philip Pettit, Jonas Pontusson, Grigo Pop-Elcheses, Gyan Prakash, Joshua Tucker, as also the often intense and always lively conversations with my fellow graduate students – Will Barndt, Barbara Buckinx, Ja Ian Chong, Leo Coleman, Antonis Ellinas, Matteo Giglioli, Bruce Gilley, Jennifer Lieb, Noam Lupu, Quinton Mayne, Gwyneth McClendon, Dinsha Mistree, Kanta Murali, Andrew Owen, Valeria Palanza, James Wilson, and Natasha Zharinova. Their presence, together with that of Louis-Pierre Arguin, Grunde Jomaas, Cynthia Nazarian, and Ian Parrish greatly enlivened my years at Princeton. And when I was ready to leave, Aaron Goodfellow, such a truly good fellow, helped me make the trip.

During twenty two months of field research I had the privilege of learning from literally hundreds of hours of conversations with scholars, political leaders, bureaucrats, civil society activists, local development workers, teachers, nurses, doctors and citizens across Tamil Nadu, Kerala, Uttar Pradesh, Rajasthan, and Delhi, who gave so generously and graciously of their time and thoughts. The argument of this book grew in clarity when I was able to take what I had learned from these conversations, to a range of textual material in the (mercifully) cool, dark sanctums of archives across India. I remain deeply grateful to the staff at the Kerala State Archives and the library of the Center for Development Studies in Thiruvannanthapuram (a stunning Laurie Baker construction, and certainly one of the most charming libraries in the world); Tamil Nadu State archives in Egmore, and legislative assembly archives in Fort St. George in Chennai; Rajasthan State Archives in Bikaner and legislative assembly archives in Jaipur; and at the Central Secretariat library, Nehru Memorial, Parliamentary library, and the National Archives of India, in New Delhi, with a special note of gratitude to Dr. Pradeep Kumar at the National Archives. I am also thankful to Yogendra Yadav, Sanjay Kumar, Himanshu Bhattacharya, and Kanchan Malhotra at the Center for Study of Developing Societies (CSDS), Delhi for sharing some of their data. For thought-provoking conversations and for making available the oasis of serenity that is Center for Policy Research in Delhi as a retreat to think and write through my extended field research, I am grateful to Pratap Bhanu Mehta. It was a great privilege to spend some time with the legendary doyens of India studies, Susanne and Lloyd Rudolph, during my research in Jaipur. It was a big boost to my confidence to hear them concur with my incipient thoughts on Rajasthani subnationalism and beyond. I also learned a lot during my field research from conversations with the late Anil Bordia, R. Govinda, Sharda Jain, Mr. Methi, Partha Mukhopahyay, Sudha Pai, and Michael Tharakan. I remain indebted to Rudra Gangadharan, Shanta Sheela Nair, and Madhav Nambiar for their help with the logistics of field research in Tamil Nadu and Kerala.

This book has benefited at different stages of its evolution from feedback from Frank Baumgartner, Mark Blyth, John Carey, Kanchan Chandra, David Collier, John Donaldson, Peter Evans, Peter Gourevitch, Antoinette Handley, Jonathan Hartlyn, Yoshiko Herrera, Evelyne Huber, Niraja Gopal Jayal, Stathis Kalyvas, Ravi Kanbur, Erik Kuhonta, David Laitin, Michele Lamont, Taeku Lee, Raul Madrid, Alison Post, Biju Rao, Andrew Reynolds, Graeme Robertson, Matthew Rudolph, Ben Ross Schneider, Aseema Sinha, Jeff Spinner-Halev, John Stephens, Matthias vom Hau, Michael Walton, Andreas Wimmer, and Jason Wittenberg. I am especially grateful to Akshay Mangla, Irfan Nooruddin, Hillel Soifer, Steven Wilkinson, and Adam Ziegfeld for reading and providing detailed comments on different parts of this manuscript. My work has been strengthened for being part of a terrific community of scholars of my generation working on India, including Rikhil Bhavnani, Jennifer Bussell, Simon Chauchard, Francesca Jensenius, Akshay Mangla, Dann Naseemullah, Tariq Thachil, Gabi Kruks-Wizner, and Adam Ziegfeld.

I remain deeply indebted to Devesh Kapur for his incisive suggestions and for the gift of a year of peaceful writing in the stimulating environs of the Center for Advanced Study for India at the University of Pennsylvania in Philadelphia. I received many helpful suggestions when presenting my work at Yale, MIT, UC Berkeley, Dartmouth, UNC Chapel Hill, Sanford School of Public Policy at Duke, and the Annual Meetings of the American Political Science Association and the Midwest Political Science Association. I am delighted to acknowledge a special debt of gratitude to Sarah Chartock, Rachel Beatty Riedl, and Maya Tudor; what germinated as a weekly writing group at Small World Coffee in Princeton has continued beyond, and deepened to become a solidaristic community that I rely on for much more than feedback on written work.

The Government Department at Harvard University under the helm of Nancy Rosenblum and Tim Colton provided a fertile ground for the growth of this book. For their constructive engagement and support I am grateful to Bob Bates, Dan Carpenter, Gregorz Ekiert, Peter Hall, Fran Hagopian, Jennifer Hoschild, Nahomi Ichino, Steve Levitsky, Liz Perry, Susan Pharr, Ken Schepsle, and Daniel Ziblatt. I owe a special debt to Jorge Dominguez, under whose leadership the Harvard Academy for International and Area Studies provided a refuge for an important set of thought and revisions. I am also grateful to my graduate and undergraduate students who engaged with parts of the manuscript in successive iterations of my Politics of India class and the graduate research workshop in Comparative Politics. I am especially grateful to Volha Charnysh and Chris Lucas, in collaboration with whom I was able to test an extension of the argument presented in this book, about the pro-social effects of the increased salience of an Indian national identity. The Center for Government and International Studies was made that much brighter by the luminosity of Steven Bloomfield, as also the presence of Frankie Hoff, Kathleen Hoover, Bruce Jackan, Sharon Jackson, Joanna Lindh, Tom Murphy, Larry Winnie, and Diana Wojcik.

This book owes much to the able research assistance of Jyoti Agarwal, Daniel Alfino, Harsh Chandra, Kunal Gautam, Tara Hariharan, Jonah Hill, Saksham Khosla, Anubhav Mohanty, Jonathan Philips, Alexander Sahn, Priyanjali Sinha, Tess Wise, and especially Jordan Sessler and Adi Dasgupta. I am grateful to Sonia Bhalotra, Suraj Jacob, and Rohini Somanathan, for sharing their data. A big thank you to Raymond Hicks for his help in cleaning and compiling these data as well as in thinking through model specifications. For over a decade, I have been fortunate to have Pranav Garg as my go-to person for all manner of statistical queries. This book provided me the opportunity to get to know the wonderful Wangyal Shawa who has created the maps reproduced here. For getting in touch with the person, whose name he invariably saw listed before his in the record of requisitions in the National Archives of

India, I am grateful to Gyanesh Kudaisya. It is a source of much gratification to me that our independent engagements with the same archival material led us to congruent conclusions. I am grateful to Ms. Yamuna Shankar, General Manager and Trustee of Children's Book Trust, New Delhi for her kind permission to use Shankar's cartoon. For scouring, and emerging with some gems from, the archives of the *Hindu* publication group in Chennai (as also for dragging me awake and out of our room during the fire at the annual meeting of the American Political Science Association in Washington D.C. in 2014), I am thankful to Kanta Murali. The research for this book was greatly facilitated by the generous financial support of the American Institute for Indian Studies, the Princeton Institute for International and Regional Studies, University Center for Human Values and the graduate school at Princeton University.

The pages ahead bear the imprint of the incisive criticism and genuine intellectual excitement that I received at a book workshop chaired by Kathy Thelen that brought together on a sunny spring day, Melani Cammett, Ron Herring, Dan Posner, Lily Tsai, and Daniel Ziblatt in Cambridge and Pradeep Chhibber virtually from Berkeley. My gratitude to this amazing group of scholars is matched only by my admiration for their research. I thank Emily Clough for her assiduous note taking during this workshop. It seems only appropriate that this book has been completed within the portals of an especially solidaristic scholarly community at the Department of Political Science and the Watson Institute for International Studies at Brown University. For bringing me into, and playing a key role in energizing this community, and for his inspiring mentorship, I am grateful to Rick Locke. In Ashutosh Varshney and Patrick Heller I feel fortunate to have as new colleagues, exemplary scholars whom I have long been inspired by and learned from. I would also like to take this opportunity to acknowledge the incisive and helpful suggestions I received from the reviewers for this book, and to thank my editor at Cambridge University Press, the legendary Lew Bateman. For initiating me into the study of politics I remain grateful to my teachers, Geoff Hawthorn and John Dunn at the University of Cambridge. My years in New Hall were made that much more memorable by the companionship of Sveta Alladi, Emily Ferenczi, Nicola Olesiuk and Sam Sparrow.

One of the highs of this project has been to see reflected, or perhaps it would be more accurate to say, to be able to project, the argument about the power of nested identities in the fierce delicacy of the art work of Bharti Kher. Insofar as the artist's generosity means that "The Deep Abyss" (bindi on board) is now the visual gateway into this text, I very much hope this book will be judged by its cover.

For opening up their homes and hearts to me during the research and writing of this book, I am grateful to Otima and the late legendary Anil Bordia; and Indu and Colonel Fateh Singh in Jaipur; Shantanu and Poonam Consul; Shukla and Rajinder Chatrath; Neeru, Shashi, Sidhant, and Nitya Thakur; Akriti, Abhinav, Anjana, and my beloved late uncle Anil Sharma in Delhi; the Cyriacs in Kochi; Rani and James Thanickan in Ernakulam; Peter and Amrita Jhanjee in Virginia; Arvind Chintamani and Anju Jeswani in New York city; and the Kakkar family, especially my cousin Amit; Naeem, Mehvesh and Faiz Ahmed; and through happy happenstance, my Delhi comrades, Ranjani Mazumdar and Ravi Sundaram, in Princeton. I am also grateful for the support of my family in Beijing – Mengwei Chen, and Drs Liu and Chen.

I have been sustained, even from afar, by the creative energy and camaraderie, of Pooja Bhartia, Rana Dasgupta, Ankur Khanna, the Raqs Media Collective (supremely talented creators of kinetic solidaristic communities, wherever they may land), Rajesh Thanickan, and Parismita Singh, who deserves a special note of thanks for being the spirited, if often unwitting, companion in so many adventures in thought and on the ground. I have come to rely on the intensity of thought and aestheticism of Clara Han and Maarten Ottens. The wonderful friendship of Andrea Caceras, Pooja Chandra, Michael Hooper, Quinton Mayne, Michael Rutberg, Sandra Shuman, and Carina Wendel, leaned the scales of the lived experience of my official status in the United States while completing this book, more towards resident than alien.

Over the years I have been so lucky to have Asha and Maya Singh as sources of good cheer and sustenance on frequent trips to Delhi. For the special bond of sisterhood, for her creative vision and artistic eye that illuminate my intellectual concerns as much as they enrich our lives, and for bringing the delightful Ankur Tewari into our lives, I am grateful to Prarthna Singh. This book stands on the bedrock of the integrity and sacrifice, and the unconditional love and support of my parents, Sanjivani and Abhimanyu Singh, who stand as personal, intellectual, and moral inspirations. I realize now, that in their deep social conscience, and occupational itinerancy as part of the Indian Administrative Services, lies the heart of my commitment to studying questions of welfare and wellbeing, and to learning through the method of comparison. I feel blessed, for the past many years now, to have had by my side my fellow traveler, the beautiful, caring, and wise Bhrigupati Singh, who continues to remind me, in equal measure, the significance of why we do what we do, and of the importance of having fun while doing it. It is my ardent hope that Uma Jaan, whose joyous arrival marked the final stages of the completion of this book, grows up in a world that affords better and more equal life chances for her and her peers. I can only hope that this book might play some part in a greater recognition, and harnessing, of the power that solidaristic communities can play therein.

I

Subnationalism and Social Development:
An Introduction

The quality of life that a person leads depends critically on *where* she leads it. It is well known that the residents of Scandinavian countries enjoy a far higher standard of living than the citizens of countries in Central Asia or Latin America. More puzzling is the fact that people living in countries in the same region of the world also lead dramatically different kinds of lives. An infant is over three times more likely to die before his first birthday if he is born in Bolivia rather than in adjoining Argentina. A woman in Iran is nearly twice as likely to be literate as her counterpart across the border in Pakistan. A person in Niger is expected to live about twenty years less than an individual in neighboring Algeria. What is most striking is that variations of this kind persist even within national boundaries. The chances of growing up illiterate are more than twice as high for a Chinese who lives in Qinghai or Tibet as compared to Beijing, Liaoning, or Jilin. In the United States, in South Dakota, a resident of Bennett County is expected to live twelve years less than someone in Moody County. Why do people in different parts of the world, in neighboring countries, and even within the same nation, experience such dramatic divergences in their levels of well-being?

The question of variation in social welfare regimes and developmental outcomes has animated a rich and long-standing body of social science research. An influential strand of this literature emphasizes the significance of regime type. Until recently, there appeared to be scholarly consensus that democracies instituted a more progressive social policy and were characterized by higher social development outcomes than autocracies (Besley and Kudamatsu 2006; Boix 2001; Brown and Hunter 2004; Brown and Mobarak 2009; Lake and Baum 2001). However, important challenges to this view have now emerged (Gerring et al. 2011; Rothstein 2011; Shandra et al. 2004). Another important set of works has argued for the primacy of state institutions. Huber et al. show that aspects of constitutional structure that disperse political power and offer multiple points of influence on the making and implementation of policy, for example, federalism, presidential government, strong bicameralism, and single-member-district systems, are inimical to the institution of social policy (1993: 735, 722). In a similar vein, Gerring and Thacker (2008) argue that "centripetal" institutions that centralize authority but are also broadly inclusive such as unitary sovereignty, a parliamentary executive, and a closed-list PR electoral system, are the optimal constitutional structures for social development. Immergut (1990) proposes an analogous argument to explain the variations in healthcare systems across Western Europe in terms of veto points in state institutional structures that render them vulnerable to interest groups. A distinct scholarship emphasizes the significance of the legacy of colonial rule for contemporary social welfare policy and outcomes. Colonization by the British, for instance, has been argued to be associated with better postcolonial developmental outcomes because of the nature of the legal institutions that they implemented (Hayek 1960; La Porta et al. 1998; North 2005) as well as the liberal economic model adopted as compared to the Spanish mercantilist model (Lange et al. 2006; Mahoney 2010). An important work by Acemoglu, Johnson, and Robinson (2001) focuses less on the characteristics of the colonizing power and more on whether or not European colonists could safely settle in a location, the argument being that settler colonies were characterized by less extractive institutions that were conducive to the enforcement of the rule of law and investment and which have persisted to the present date. Yet another set of scholars, following Weber (1948), have stressed the importance of the state bureaucracy for development (Heclo 1972).

But how do we explain the often stark variation in social welfare policy and outcomes among subnational units within a single country, characterized by the same regime type and virtually identical legal, financial, and electoral institutions; a broadly shared history of colonialism and a centrally trained and recruited bureaucracy? A subnational comparison within India, a federal, bicameral, parliamentary democracy with a uniform single-member electoral system, history of nonsettler British colonialism,[1] and a highly regarded national civil service, provides a rich context for an analysis of this puzzle. Indian states (or provinces) have been characterized by a striking degree of subnational variation in the nature of social policy, and relatedly, levels of social development (see Figures 1.1 and 1.2).

While certain states have attained levels of social development, conceptualized in terms of the education and health of the population, approaching those enjoyed by middle-income, industrialized countries, other states have fared worse than countries in sub-Saharan Africa. In a country the demographic size of India, these divergences translate into dramatic differences in the quality of life for millions. In the 1950s, residents of Bihar (which has a larger population

---

[1] In Chapter 2 I discuss the important differences in the nature of colonial institutions across British India and the implications for social welfare policy and outcomes.

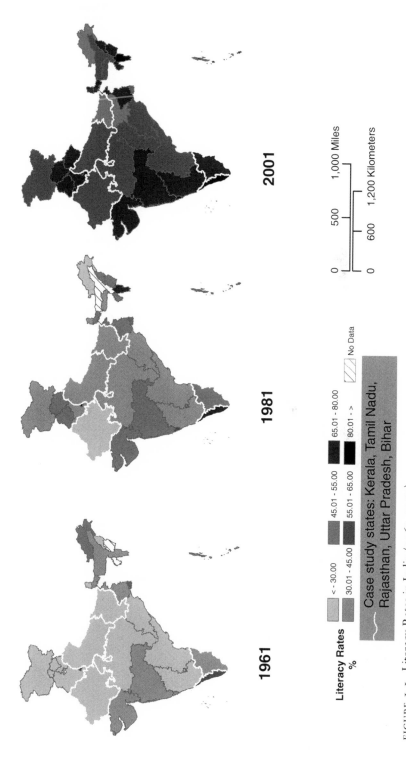

Literacy Rates
%

< - 30.00	45.01 - 55.00	65.01 - 80.00
30.01 - 45.00	55.01 - 65.00	80.01 - >

No Data

Case study states: Kerala, Tamil Nadu, Rajasthan, Uttar Pradesh, Bihar

1961   1981   2001

0   500   1,000 Miles

0   600   1,200 Kilometers

FIGURE 1.1. Literacy Rates in India (1961–2001).
Source: Census reports of India

3

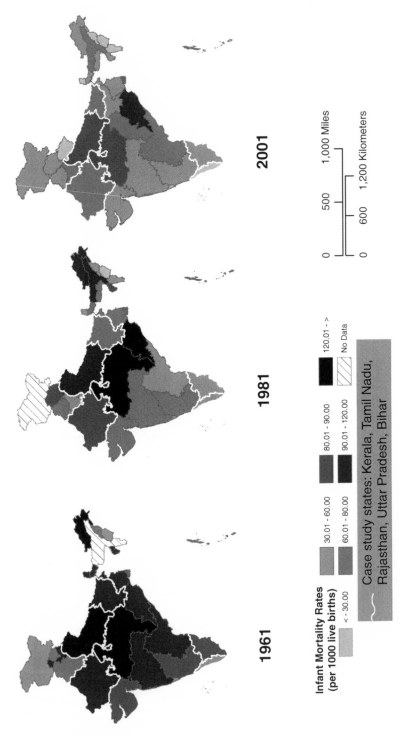

FIGURE 1.2. Infant Mortality Rates in India (1961–2001).
Source: Sample Registration System of India

4

than France) were less than half as likely to be literate as people in Himachal Pradesh. In the 1970s, women in Orissa (which has a larger population than Argentina) were expected to live, on average, over twelve years less than women in Punjab. In the 1990s, children born in Madhya Pradesh (which has a population just a little lower than Turkey) were five times less likely to survive through infancy than those born in the state of Goa. Even today, women in Maharashtra (demographically equivalent to Mexico) are four times less likely to die during childbirth than their counterparts in Assam. What explains this variation?

The answer to this puzzle, this book suggests, lies in understanding how the shared solidarity that emerges from a collective identification can generate a politics of the common good. Such an argument marks a departure from both the traditional emphasis on the role of class (Esping-Andersen 1990; Heller 2005; Kohli 1987) as well as from the dominant view of the negative implications of identity for welfare (see Singh and vom Hau 2014 for a review). In contrast, this book seeks to show how differences in the strength of affective attachment and cohesiveness of community can be a key driver of subnational differences in social policy and welfare. A shared identification fosters a communal spirit and solidaristic ethos and encourages a perception of not just individual but also collective interests. Bonds of oneness promote a sense of mutual obligation. Elites bound by such solidaristic ties are more likely to push for progressive social policies that further the welfare of the subnational community as a whole. State emphasis on the social sector is a necessary condition for, and a primary driver of social development. Solidarity with the political unit in which people reside also tends to foster greater sociopolitical consciousness and engagement on their part, which increases the likelihood of their involvement with the social services provided by the state. Such popular involvement can supplement the effects of a progressive social policy on social welfare. Among the political units in a country that have primary jurisdiction over social policy, those with a stronger collective identification are therefore more likely to institute a progressive social policy and have higher welfare outcomes than political units that are characterized by a relatively fragmented subnational identity. Relatedly, the primary implication of this book is that there should be a match between the political-administrative unit that has jurisdiction over social policy and the locus of collective identification. Units – national or subnational, whether they be provinces, cities, municipalities, or villages – are more conducive to the institution of a progressive social policy and the realization of welfare outcomes if they are a source of shared identity and solidarity.

Indian states, the subnational political unit that is vested with constitutional authority over social policy vary greatly in the strength of the solidarity of their political community. These differences in *subnationalism* have played a critical role in generating differences in the progressiveness of social policy and levels of social development, conceptualized here in terms of the education and health of the population. This book delineates the mechanisms through which

TABLE 1.1. Socioeconomic Indicators across Case Study States (1960–2010)

	Rural Poverty (%)	Rural Inequality	Population Growth Rate (%)	Scheduled Castes (%)	Scheduled Tribes (%)	Muslims (%)	Religious Fractionalization
Tamil Nadu	57.3	30	1.5	18.2	0.87	5.5	.21
Kerala	56.2	33	1.4	9	1.2	22.9	.56
Uttar Pradesh	46.3	29	2.4	20.9	0.7	17.1	.28
Rajasthan	53.6	34.4	2.6	16.5	12.2	7.9	.19
Bihar	64	27.5	2.0	14.2	7.8	13	.28

Note: Averages of indicators from 1960 to 2010. Religious fractionalization is calculated based on the Ethnolinguistic fractionalization index (ELF). See table 6.7 for more details.

TABLE 1.2. Economic Development across Case Study States

	1960s	1970s	1980s	1990s	2000s
Tamil Nadu	797.7	870	1221.6	2069.7	2920.6
Kerala	688.3	786.2	998.9	1467.1	2123.8
Uttar Pradesh	766.2	817	1022.8	1199	1433.6
Rajasthan	668.5	774.7	817	1184	1442.1
Bihar	555.7	571.7	707.28	774	914

Note: Real net state domestic product deflated by consumer price index for agricultural workers (Rs per capita).

subnationalism influences social welfare by presenting a comparative historical analysis, from the late nineteenth-early twentieth centuries to the present date, of the neighboring states of Tamil Nadu (TN) and Kerala in the deep South, and the two adjacent provinces of Uttar Pradesh (UP) and Rajasthan, as well as a briefer study of Bihar, in the North-Central Indian heartland. It then tests the validity of this argument against prominent theories that would explain such subnational variation in terms of levels of economic development; the importance of class-based formations, notably the strength of social-democratic parties; the nature of political competition; or the extent of ethnic diversity, through a statistical analysis of all Indian states from the 1960s to the 2000s.

The provinces of Tamil Nadu, Kerala, UP, Rajasthan, and Bihar are typical Indian states on a number of key economic, sociopolitical, and demographic dimensions (see Tables 1.1 and 1.2). They also exemplify the striking subnational variation in social outcomes within the country referred to earlier. Kerala has adopted one of the most progressive social policies of all Indian states and been characterized by social development indicators that put it not only substantially above the rest of India but on par with the top 30 percent of all countries in the world. While less celebrated and not yet equivalent to those of Kerala, the social achievements of the neighboring state of Tamil Nadu have also been quite remarkable. Successive state governments in Tamil Nadu have devoted substantial budgetary resources to welfare provision, which has

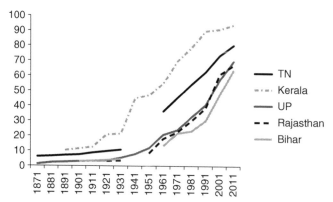

FIGURE 1.3. Literacy Rates in Case Study States (1911–2011): Total Literacy Rates.
Source: Census reports of India

allowed the residents of the state to enjoy a far better level of social development than their counterparts in most other parts of India. If Tamil Nadu was an independent country, it would be ranked about a dozen places higher than the Indian average in a global ranking of literacy and more than two dozen places higher in a ranking of infant mortality rates. In contrast, Uttar Pradesh, Rajasthan, and Bihar have been marked by deep social backwardness. At the end of the colonial period, almost 90 percent of the population in all three states was illiterate, and one in every ten children born was expected to die before his or her first birthday. Even as late as the 2000s, just a little less than half the female population of these states was illiterate, putting them, if they were independent countries, in the bottom 15 percent in a global ranking.

It is important to note, however, that these differences have not been as long-standing and deeply entrenched as they are often made out to be (see, for example, Sen 1990). Even as late as toward the end of the nineteenth century, Kerala and Tamil Nadu did not have a significant lead in social welfare outcomes over UP, Rajasthan, or Bihar (see Figures 1.3–1.6).[2] Around this time, UP was widely hailed as a "model province" (Pai 2007: xvi), an example of good governance for other directly controlled areas of British India (Kudaisya

[2] During the colonial period, the states of Tamil Nadu, UP, and Bihar were under the direct control of the British. Tamil Nadu was a part of Madras presidency. Present day UP corresponded to the North-western provinces and Oudh, which was known after 1902 as the United Provinces of Agra and Oudh, and after 1935, simply as the United Provinces. Bihar was part of the Bengal presidency until 1912, when, along with Orissa, it was carved into a separate province. Kerala and Rajasthan, on the other hand, were indirectly ruled by native kings, under the overall suzerainty of the British. The present day territory of Kerala is composed, for the most part, of the two princely states of Travancore and Cochin and also the northern district of Malabar, which was a part of Madras presidency, while Rajasthan, known during the colonial period as Rajputana, is a conglomeration of more than two dozen princely states. For stylistic simplicity, the territories that constituted Tamil Nadu, Kerala, UP, Rajasthan and Bihar in colonial period and before the reorganization of states in 1956 have been referred to by their postcolonial appellations in all the figures.

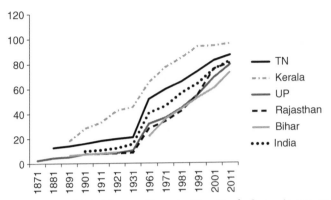

FIGURE 1.4. Male Literacy Rates in Case Study States (1911–2011).
Source: Census reports of India

2007: 8). It was home to the "finest and most industrious of the native races," endowed with rich natural resources and a well-developed system of roads, railways, and irrigation facilities (Crooks 1897: 3). In contrast, the princely state of Travancore, which corresponded to a bulk of the territory of the present day state of Kerala, was characterized by recurrent budgetary deficits, a corrupt and incompetent administration, poor infrastructure and odious social customs based on one of the most rigid and repressive caste hierarchies of Indian states. As a result of this misgovernance, the state of Travancore faced the threat of direct interference and even outright annexation by the neighboring Madras presidency throughout the 1850s (Jeffrey 1976: 64; Tharakan 1984: 1961). It should therefore come as no surprise that Kerala was not characterized by higher social outlays or better development indicators than UP or other Indian provinces during this period. Until the 1870s, the state of Travancore took little interest in and made no organized attempt to promote the education and health of its people (Singh 1944: 398). During the mid-1870s and early 1880s, the female literacy rate in the princely states of Travancore and Cochin was virtually as minuscule as in the United Provinces.[3] Even toward the end of the colonial period in 1930, a man in the territories that constitute present day Kerala was expected to live, on average, less than thirty years. Similarly, both in absolute terms as well as relative to other Indian provinces, social development in the Madras presidency was far from advanced at the end of the nineteenth century. From the 1850s to the early 1900s, the Madras presidency and UP were equivalently placed on a number

---

[3] In 1875, female literacy rates in Travancore and Cochin were 0.5% and 0.4% respectively (Ramachandran 1996: 257). According to the Census of India for 1881, the female literacy rate in the United Provinces was 0.1%. In these years male literacy in Travancore and Cochin was 11% and 8.4% respectively, as compared to 4.5% in the United Provinces.

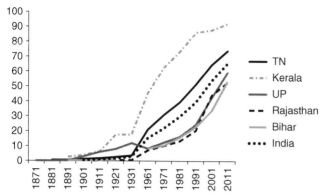

FIGURE 1.5. Female Literacy Rates in Case Study States (1911–2011).
Source: Census reports of India

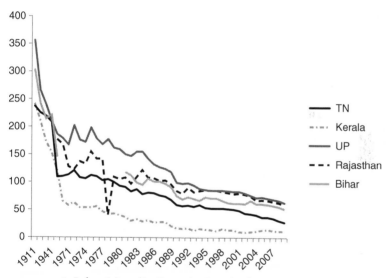

FIGURE 1.6. Infant Mortality Rates in Case Study States (1911–2010).
Source: Bhattacharjee (1976); Sample Registration System of India (1971–2001);
Registrar General of India (2010)

of social indicators, including education expenditures and infrastructure, with
UP even enjoying a marginal lead in some years (Risley and Gait 1903: 166).
In 1881, 99.2 percent of the female population of the Madras presidency was
illiterate, as compared with 99.8 percent in the United Provinces. In 1901,
female literacy rates in Madras (0.9%) were only slightly higher than those in
UP (0.3%), Rajputana (0.2%), and Bihar (0.2%).

Not only was social development in the Southern states virtually equivalent to that of the North-Central states in the late nineteenth century, but within the Southern region, Kerala did not yet have an edge over Tamil Nadu. In fact in the 1870s and early 1880s, both male and female literacy rates in the Madras presidency were higher than in Travancore and Cochin. Through the closing years of the nineteenth century, public expenditures on the social sector in Travancore and Cochin were about the same as those in Madras presidency as well as other princely states such as Mysore, Baroda, or Hyderabad (Singh 1944: 406). Madras was also in a relatively superior position with regard to public health. The network of medical facilities was better developed and the health status of the population was higher in Madras as compared to Travancore and Cochin. In 1870–71, the chief medical officer, for example, reported that the mortality rates in Trivandrum, the capital of Travancore, "compared most unfavorably with similar towns in the Madras Presidency" (Singh 1944: 432).

Finally, it is important to highlight, within the overall context of North-Central Indian backwardness, the surprising lack of a significant developmental lead on the part of UP over Rajasthan or Bihar. In British India UP was regarded as "one of the best governed of all Indian states" (Pai 2007: xvi); On the other hand, the princely states of Rajputana were widely viewed as bastions of deep economic, political, and social backwardness (Markovits 2002: 406). Bihar was widely viewed as one of the most backward of the directly ruled areas of the country; the colonial government's per capita expenditure on the region was the lowest compared to any other part of British India. These three states entered the postcolonial period with UP enjoying a distinct advantage in terms of its economic situation and the quality of its political and administrative institutions. However, from the 1950s onward, despite facing a precarious budgetary situation, Rajasthan has adopted a more progressive social policy, earmarking substantially higher budgetary expenditures to social development than UP. In comparison to UP's location in the heart of the fertile Indo-Gangetic plains, Rajasthan's location in the most arid part of the subcontinent – the state is a vast desert or sub-desert zone – has made it a land of endemic food and drinking water shortages, constantly confronting the danger of famine. Yet UP, Rajasthan, and Bihar have been characterized by roughly equivalent levels of social development, with Rajasthan and Bihar even enjoying a lead in health outcomes. During the 1990s, Rajasthan made substantial improvements in social development, particularly education, registering in 2001 the single largest jump in literacy rates of any state in India since the beginning of the collection of literacy data in the Census of India in 1871. While absolute levels of some developmental indicators still remain below those in UP, Bihar has also witnessed a major developmental turnaround since the mid-2000s, registering the sharpest rate of improvement in educational and health indicators of all Indian states, a development that prompted its being hailed as a "model" for overcoming social backwardness.

Why, despite having similar starting points in the late nineteenth century, have the states of Kerala and Tamil Nadu achieved a massive developmental lead over UP, Rajasthan, and Bihar? Why, despite being in a marginally worse position than Tamil Nadu in the 1870s, did Kerala overtake its wealthier neighbor to become a global model of social development? Why have the states of UP, Rajasthan, and Bihar been caught in a general pattern of social backwardness? Why, despite a number of potential advantages, has the state of UP not been able to gain a substantial developmental edge over Rajasthan or Bihar? Why has Rajasthan instituted a more progressive social policy than UP or Bihar since the 1950s? Why did Rajasthan make important social gains only as late as the 1990s? What explains the dramatic social improvements in Bihar from the mid-2000s? In this book I seek to demonstrate that these variations in social policy and development both *across* as well as *within* these different provinces over time are best understood in terms of differences in the strength of their subnational identification.

The cases of Tamil Nadu and Kerala show how the glue of subnational solidarity can play a critical role in facilitating social development. In both states, subnationalism emerged as the result of the strategic calculation of interest-maximizing elites locked in a competition for sociopolitical power. Once established, however, a cohesive subnational identity fostered a shared solidarity, perceptions of shared needs and goals, and a sense of mutual obligation. Elites came to redefine their welfare not only in terms of advancing individual or group interests but also collective subnational welfare. Elite support for public welfare pushed the governments of these regions to prioritize social development through substantial increases in the budgetary outlays on education and health. This was a necessary condition for subsequent gains in social development. In addition, the spread of subnationalism to the Malayali and Tamil people at large through sociopolitical movements and organizations spurred them to a greater degree of sociopolitical engagement. This increased the likelihood of popular involvement in the day-to-day functioning of government schools and hospitals, in turn raising the probability that state social expenditures translated into accessible and efficient public services. In this way, a powerful subnational solidarity triggered a progressive social policy which, supplemented by societal engagement, combined to generate key improvements in social development in Tamil Nadu and Kerala.

Until about the mid to late nineteenth century, both Tamil Nadu and Kerala were characterized by the absence of a subnational identity. Tamil subnationalism began to emerge among elites in Madras in the early 1900s and spread to the people by the 1950s and 1960s. Malayali subnationalism, on the other hand, began to take root among elites in the last decade of the nineteenth century and became popularly rooted in the first few decades of the twentieth century. I argue that it was because of this earlier emergence of subnationalism that Kerala began to make important social gains and to gradually gain a significant lead over Tamil Nadu through the early decades of the twentieth century.

The cases of UP, Rajasthan, and Bihar, on the other hand, draw out the broad trajectory of how the absence of subnational solidarity dampens social development. UP has historically been characterized by the prominence of ethnic or national identities. Elites correspondingly pushed for the advancement of their religious and/or caste groups, or focused on issues of national interest. In the absence of any sense of subnational identification, there was virtually no conception of the welfare of UP as a state. Consequently, successive governments in UP did not introduce a comprehensive social policy for the state. Instead, at different points in time, they initiated policies targeting the development of specific religious or caste groups or simply followed the federal agenda, which, until the mid-1980s, did not prioritize welfare. In the absence of any allegiance to the political unit in which they resided, the residents of UP were less likely to come together to monitor government schools and health centers and, as a result, even the limited expenditures that the UP government allocated towards basic social services yielded minimal developmental gains.

Within this overall pattern of backwardness, the case studies of Rajasthan and Bihar show how an increase in the cohesiveness of subnational solidarity in a political unit can generate an improvement in social indicators. During the colonial period, there was little to no conception of a shared subnational community, nor of common interests or ethical obligations among the people of the regions that came to constitute Rajasthan. As a result, there was an almost complete absence of state or societal action in the social sphere. During the early years after Indian independence, in a process similar to that which occured in Kerala and Tamil Nadu, elite competition sparked the beginnings of Rajasthani subnationalism. Motivated by a concern for Rajasthani welfare, elites in the state pushed for greater governmental emphasis on the social sector. Yet Rajasthani subnationalism remained confined to an elite stratum and did not resonate with a majority of the residents of the state, who retained strong loyalties to their former native kingdoms and fiefdoms. The absence of a popular subnationalism meant that people were less inclined to take an interest in the sociopolitical life of the state, and to be involved with the public services provided by the state, limiting the potential gains of the relatively generous government allocations to the social sector. Beginning in the late 1980s, generational change and the rise of a subnationalist party in turn initiated the process of the spread of Rajasthani subnationalism to the people at large. This encouraged increased involvement with schools and health centers, thereby promoting important improvements in welfare. Rajasthani subnationalism is, however, far from rooted in the popular psyche, and the maintenance of the pace of social gains remains uncertain. Similarly, during the colonial and much of the postcolonial period, the state of Bihar was characterized by an almost complete absence of any sense of subnational solidarity and was instead characterized by substate regional and caste-based identifications, which led to social welfare being demanded and provided along these lines. In the absence of any kind of broad-based social policy, developmental indicators in Bihar remained abysmal. In the mid-2000s, however, a challenger elite began to construct and broadcast a Bihari identity as a tool in their attempt to wrest power from an established elite. Once it had been evoked through this elite competition, Bihari subnationalism rapidly took root among a large cross-section of political, economic, and social-cultural elites and has been an important impetus for a striking turnaround in social policy such that welfare has progressed from barely being on the policy agenda to becoming one of the government's top priorities. The state's attempts at fostering the spread of a Bihari identity among the people at large through embedding it in a range of different institutions appears to be reaping rewards and this popular Bihari subnationalism has in turn begun to encourage greater involvement with the public services in the state.

The remainder of this chapter begins by defining social development and discussing why the question of explaining variation in levels of social development is worth asking in the first place. It then specifies the research design used in the book. Finally, it provides an overview of the other chapters in the book.

DEFINING SOCIAL DEVELOPMENT

The scholarship on social development is characterized by the salient underlying theme that purely economic dimensions of development, such as GDP per capita, do not adequately capture the human experience. A "truer" assessment of the level of development of a state and the standard of living of its citizens necessitates a move beyond purely income-based indicators to take account of social factors.[4] I conceptualize social development in terms of two key attributes of a population – education and health outcomes. Of the cluster of features associated with social development, education and health have been the most prominent. The annual Human Development Report published by the United Nations Development Programme defines the social dimension of its Human Development Index (HDI) in terms of achievements in education and health.[5] Drèze and Sen (2002), seminal contributors to the field of development economics, have also conceptualized social development in terms of the education and health of the people. Insofar as education and health are believed to be good predictors of, or sensitive surrogates for, other dimensions such as the availability of clean water, overall status of women, and the condition of the

---

[4] These include, for instance, the distribution of income, levels of poverty, the availability and quality of education, the status of healthcare and medical services, the availability of housing, levels of sanitation, access to potable water, the nature of labor laws, the status of women, availability of unemployment wages, child support, pensions and other benefits.

[5] The HDI is a composite of variables capturing attainments in three dimensions of human development – economic, educational, and health. These are captured by per capita monthly expenditure adjusted for inequality, literacy rate, and intensity of formal education, life expectancy at age 1, and the infant mortality rate.

home environment (Morris 1979: 95), this study's focus on education and health is likely to enable claims about social development more generally.

THE IMPORTANCE OF STUDYING SOCIAL DEVELOPMENT

Access to basic public goods and services has a profound influence on the quality of people's lives across the world. In a world in which millions of people, particularly in developing countries, continue to be dogged by illiteracy and plagued by ill-health caused by vaccine-preventable diseases, understanding the conditions that give rise to high or low social development is of critical importance to political scientists and policy makers alike. The provision of basic social services such as education and healthcare is widely regarded as one of the primary responsibilities of democratic governments. An enlightened and productive citizenry is in turn considered to be a prerequisite for the effective functioning of a democracy. The efficacy with which a democratic government provides social services has repercussions for its legitimacy and durability. Many of the developing countries in Asia, Africa, and Latin America that have difficulty providing basic public goods are also the ones struggling the most to build effective states and maintain regime stability (Tsai 2007: 355). An analysis of social development can therefore further our understanding of how democratic states can better fulfill their duties to their citizens, and by doing so, can function more effectively and with greater legitimacy and stability. Following T. H. Marshall's influential formulation, most scholars have emphasized the provision of social rights as an essential condition for "full citizenship" of a polity.[6] Social development has also come to be seen as constitutive of human freedom and capabilities, and can help shed light on how individuals can lead "richer and more unfettered" lives and become "fuller social persons" (Nussbaum 2001, 2006; Sen 1999: 14–15).

It is also useful to highlight the particular significance of an investigation of social development in the empirical context of India. The establishment and maintenance of democratic institutions in India in the context of low levels of economic development and high levels of ethnic diversity has been widely studied and lauded (Kohli 2001; Varshney 1998). Yet, while India has been relatively successful in guaranteeing civil and political rights, it has failed miserably in ensuring even a minimal range of social rights for its citizens. Social rights figured prominently in the political and intellectual debates of the Indian nationalist movement (Jayal 2013).[7] However, despite their periodic

---

[6] T. H. Marshall's influential formulation set up the notion that citizenship involved not only civil and political rights, but crucially, social rights that allowed citizens to lead a "life of a civilized being according to the standards prevailing in the society ... The institutions most closely connected with it are the educational system and the social services" (1964: 72).

[7] Niraja Gopal Jayal (2013) discusses how the right to education, for instance, was included in 1925 in the Commonwealth of India Bill prepared by a committee chaired by Annie Besant and supported by forty-three Indian political leaders from different political parties and submitted to the British House of Commons. It also figured in the Nehru Report in the 1920s, which

articulation in political forums, documents and endorsement by political leaders including Gandhi and Nehru from the 1920s through the 1940s, and intense debates in the Constituent assembly itself, social rights did not make it to the legally enforceable set of fundamental rights in the Constitution of India. They were instead relegated to the Directive Principles of State Policy, which are meant to guide policy but are not justiciable in a court of law. In his famous "Tryst with Destiny" speech on the eve of independence from British rule in 1947, India's first prime minister, Jawaharlal Nehru, had declared the eradication of "ignorance and disease" as one of the most crucial tasks facing the country. Yet through the Nehruvian period and successive decades, India has been characterized by frugal allocations to the social sector, even relative to other developing countries. Today, six and a half decades of democratic rule and more than two decades of robust economic development later, levels of social development in India, measured along virtually any dimension, remain abysmal. Perhaps the starkest indicator of this is that almost *half* of Indian children under five are classified by the WHO as suffering from moderate to severe stunting. This is the highest proportion of children in *any* country in the world. The infant mortality rate in India (42) is more than three to four times its BRIC counterparts. Brazil (12.3), Russia (9) and China (11). The infant mortality rate in India is also substantially higher than almost all other countries at its level of economic development. Within its own neighborhood, for instance, countries in South Asia, such as Bangladesh and Nepal, and in Central Asia, such as Tajikistan and Uzbekistan, which have equivalent or higher incomes to India, all have lower infant mortality rates. The maternal mortality rate in India is almost double that of Iraq. In terms of life expectancy, India is ranked at 145 among a total of 197 countries. A woman in India today, on average, lives 20 years less than her counterpart in Hong Kong. India is also home to the largest number of illiterates in the world.

According to the 2011 census, 74 percent of the population is literate, which is equivalent to that of countries such as Guatemala and Uganda. A particularly worrisome portent for the future of Indian education is that the youth female literacy rate (percentage of females aged 15–24) is in the bottom 15 percent of all countries in the world. In the composite rankings of the HDI, India is ranked 135 out of a total of 187 countries, just below Tajikistan and above Bhutan.

prefigured the Constitution of India adopted in 1950 in many important ways. According to the Nehru Report the right to free primary education was to be made enforceable regardless of caste, class and ethnic distinctions "as soon as due arrangements shall have been made by competent authority." It also urged the Parliament to draft laws for "the maintenance of health and fitness for work of all citizens." 'The Resolution on Fundamental Rights and Economic Changes' presented to the Karachi session of the Congress in 1931 included, in addition to civil rights, a range of social and economic rights including the right to education. Social rights were also central to a number of the "alternative constitutional imaginings" that were published during the 1940s (Jayal 2013: 137–143).

An attempt to understand how in the overall national context of low social development, some Indian states have approached levels of social development equivalent to middle-income countries while other regions have fared worse than some of the most poorly performing low-income countries, promises to yield insights for scholars not only of India but also of comparative politics, the politics of welfare provision and the political economy of development.

METHODOLOGY

In this section I will discuss the methodology of this book, highlighting the rationale for the adoption and advantages associated with the use of a subnational research design and mixed methods.

Subnational Research Design

As noted at the beginning of this chapter, the unit of analysis in this book is the Indian province. A subnational research design characterizes some of the classic works of comparative politics (see, for example, Putnam 1993) and is also increasingly popular today (Tsai and Ziblatt 2012; Giraudy et al. 2014). The study of the welfare state, however, has remained dominated by the national unit of analysis. And yet, as I detail below, the move to a subnational unit offers distinct empirical, methodological and theoretical gains.

Sociopolitical phenomena rarely occur uniformly across the territorially defined subnational units of a political system. National averages can often conceal significant subnational variation. A country that is classified as "developed" based on national indicators could include within it regions of substantial backwardness. A subnational research design better equips us to handle the spatially uneven nature of processes such as social development (Snyder 2001: 94). Most leading studies of the welfare state have focused on Western European countries, which tend to be smaller and characterized by a far greater degree of equality in welfare policies and outcomes within their national boundaries, as compared to most other parts of the world. The study of social welfare in developing countries, on the other hand, appears to push, arguably even necessitate, a focus on subnational units. Large developing countries such as India, Brazil, South Africa, China, Pakistan, and Indonesia, to name only a few, are characterized by striking variations in social policies and outcomes within their national boundaries. Differences in the provision of social services and welfare outcomes across cities, provinces, or regions within these countries are sometimes as large as or even larger than differences across national boundaries in Western Europe. A comparison of subnational units allows one to look beyond the common-place characterization of a country such as India as "socially backward", to recognize and theorize cases of substantial development and egregious backwardness that are concealed by this national characterization.

Moreover, across the world, primary jurisdiction in a number of critical areas, including but not limited to economic growth, welfare policy and the provision of public goods and services, language, and cultural policies, rests with subnational rather than national administrations. Subnational governments, at different levels, are the prime movers, controlling the allocation of expenditures and making key policy decisions. In some federal countries the constitutional division of powers has historically been such that subnational rather than national governments have primary jurisdiction and exercise almost complete administrative control over social policies. This is the case with social policy in India. Under the Indian Constitution the primary responsibility for developmental policies has rested with states rather than the national government.[8] States play the key role in the formulation and execution of policies regarding both education and health, and account for nearly 90 percent of total government expenditure on these issues (Mehrotra 2006: 32). In other places, subnational units are gaining increasing control over social policies through processes of decentralization. As such subnational units are clearly the appropriate unit of analysis for scholars interested in understanding the politics of the formulation of social policy. Further, examining social policy at the subnational level can provide a useful analytical window into national welfare outcomes, which under the conditions of the subnational governments' control over social policy are not only aggregations but also products of subnational politics.[9]

In addition to this empirical rationale, it is also analytically advantageous to focus on the subnational unit on methodological grounds insofar as it allows for the construction of controlled comparisons. In particular, this allows for the holding constant of a range of potential explanatory variables such as regime type and the nature of state institutions that have been shown to be

---

[8] Article 246 of the Indian constitution divides policy areas among three lists – the Union, State, and Concurrent lists. The Union and State lists consist of subjects under the exclusive purview of the central and provincial governments respectively, while the Concurrent list is composed of subjects upon which both levels of government have jurisdiction. Health is on the state list. Education was shifted from the state list to the concurrent list by the 42nd Amendment of 1976. A former education minister observed that prior to 1976, "Whether it was primary education or secondary education or university education, the states if they were so inclined, could do what they liked without the Center having any voice in the legislation they passed or in the administration of the system" (quoted in Basu 1995: 221).

[9] There have been some analyses by economists of public goods provision in India with districts as the units of analysis (see, for example, Banerjee & Somanathan 2004; Banerjee, Somanathan, & Iyer 2005; Betancourt & Gleason 2000). Such studies do have the advantage of access to a much larger dataset – India has more than 600 districts but only 28 states. However, insofar as districts are purely administrative units devoid of all economic or political power, they are not meaningful units of analysis for understanding the formulation of public policy. Moreover, it is notable that all of these studies find state fixed effects to have a substantive and statistically significant impact on public goods provision, indicating that unobserved characteristics of states, such as subnationalism that vary across states but not across districts within a state explain a large part of the variation in social services.

key determinants of the national welfare state, but which are the same across different subnational units within national boundaries. In this way systematic within-nation comparison increases the probability, relative to cross-national studies, of obtaining valid causal inferences in small-N research (Snyder 2001).

Relatedly, on a theoretical level, studying the welfare state subnationally provides an opportunity not only to move beyond well-known national-level explanations to uncover hitherto understudied factors that are more visible and/or work specifically at the subnational level but also, as will be discussed at some length in the conclusion, to provide a fresh analytical lens to illuminate welfare policy and outcomes at the national level. Theories derived from the inductive study of the subnational welfare state offer a potentially productive route toward furthering our understanding of the causes and ways in which we think of addressing problems of underdevelopment at different units of analysis.

Mixed Methods

With an eye towards maximizing analytical leverage, this book combines qualitative and quantitative methods through a "nested research design" in which the intensive within- and cross-state case study analysis of five Indian states is *nested* in a statistical cross-state analysis of all Indian provinces (Lieberman 2005: 435). I inductively build a theory of the way in which subnationalism influences social development through a comparative historical analysis of the cases of Tamil Nadu, Kerala, UP, and Rajasthan, along with a briefer study of Bihar. Like other works in this tradition of research, my main aim is to provide a systematic and contextualized comparison of these five states over time to identify the ways in which subnationalism influences social development (Mahoney and Rueschemeyer 2003: 10). In each case, I undertake "process tracing" (George and Bennett 2005), beginning from the mid-nineteenth century or the turn of the twentieth century into the 2000s, to delineate the causal mechanism, that is, key events, processes, and decisions over time that link subnationalism to social development, as well as to examine the relevance of competing explanations. Such a historical analysis reflects an understanding of social policy as a process that unfolds gradually, as a result of fundamental, slow-moving factors, rather than simply as a product of triggering or precipitating factors, such as the choices of actors at particular moments in time (Pierson 2004: 42). In contrast to the "snap-shot" analyses that have dominated recent social science scholarship books such as this, that "place politics in time" can greatly enrich the explanation we offer for social outcomes of interest (34).

The temporal analysis of the cases is structured around an "institutional origins" design (Lieberman 2001: 1020). In order to demonstrate that a powerful subnationalism generates improvements in social development, it is necessary to show that higher levels of social development were not already in place prior to the emergence of subnationalism. I therefore divide and analyze the historical record of all five states in terms of periods prior to and subsequent to the emergence of elite and mass subnationalism. Drawing on a combination of archival analysis, in particular an examination of government documents from the colonial and postcolonial periods, newspapers, the record of legislative assembly debates, as well as field research, including more than two hundred structured open-ended elite interviews, focus group meetings, and participant observation at schools and health centers, I establish a clear chronology in which the emergence of a cohesive or fragmented subnational identity precedes improvements or stagnation/deterioration of social indicators. This specification of a clear historical sequence provides a powerful basis for making causal inferences (Lieberman 2001: 1017). I then test the validity of the subnationalism argument, which emerges as the salient explanatory framework through the case study research, against prominent alternative explanations through descriptive and statistical analyses of all major Indian states from the 1960s until the 2000s.

This combination of qualitative and quantitative research methods reflects a belief in the complementarities of these methodological approaches and the synergistic value of employing both in conjunction. The main advantage of such a mixed-methods research design is that the qualitative and quantitative analyses offset each other's weaknesses and are mutually supportive. The small-N case study research bolsters the regression analyses, first, by identifying a range of factors that might influence social development, thereby facilitating the specification of more complete, theoretically informed models, and second, by guarding against potentially spurious correlation. The medium-N statistical analysis, in turn provides enhanced analytical leverage over the comparative historical study by increasing the degrees of freedom, thereby allowing for the testing of the influence of subnationalism vis-à-vis a range of other explanatory variables. The regressions are also critical to assessing the external validity of the subnationalism argument insofar as they allow me to check whether, controlling for various socioeconomic and political variables, subnationalism can explain variations in education and health expenditures and outcomes in a larger universe of cases. In addition to compensating for the limitations of either approach taken in isolation (Lieberman 2003: 237), a mixed-methods research design also allows for integrated causal inference that would not have been possible through the use of a single method. I will now elucidate the rationale for the selection of my case study states.

Case Selection

The single most plausible and prominent determinant of social development is arguably, economic development. In development policy circles as well as in popular discussions it is widely believed, based implicitly on the Rostowian model (Rostow 1990) where economic growth is the impetus for passage through various stages of development, that the wealthier the political unit, the higher its levels of social development (Filmer et al. 1997). A scatter plot

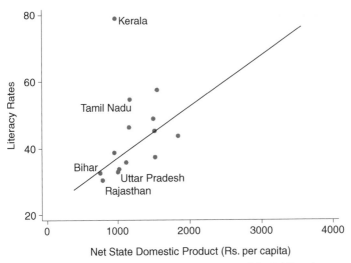

FIGURE 1.7. Relationship between Economic and Social Development in India: Literacy and Per Capita State Domestic Product (1985).

based on a regression analysis of education and health outcomes on economic development for Indian states does indicate an overall positive relationship for all years in the post-Independence period. But it also presents a number of outliers. Figures 1.7 and 1.8 show scatter plots with a fitted trend line for the relationship between per capita state domestic product and literacy and infant mortality rates respectively for 1985, the median year in our statistical analysis. From such "off-the-line" states, whose welfare outcomes are not well-predicted by levels of economic wealth, I selected four states for case study analysis that allow for the greatest variation on the outcome variable.[10] Specifically, I chose two cases above the line – Tamil Nadu (TN) and Kerala, which have far higher levels of literacy and lower infant mortality than would be predicted by their

---

[10] It is important to note that while my research design is broadly in line with the Model-building Small-N analysis (Mb-SNA) followed by a Model-testing large-N analysis (Mt-LNA) approach to nested analysis specified by Lieberman (2005: 437), it differs in one critical way. Lieberman recommends starting with a well-specified model; only if this model is not robust should one move on to the Mb-SNA, which should entail an examination of cases that are not well predicted by the model. However, as Rohlfing (2008: 1497) points out, it seems paradoxical to select case studies based on the residuals of poorly performing regression models. Therefore, contrary to Lieberman's suggestion, I begin with a deliberately underspecified large-N analysis, specifically designed to help me move on to the Mb-SNA. The preliminary large-N analysis includes only the explanatory variable that is widely believed to exert the single most decisive influence on social development. I chose case studies that are off-the-line because they allow me to explore which factors, in addition to this prominent explanatory variable, influence education and health outcomes. Because of its extremely low developmental indicators, Bihar also adds to the variation on the outcome variable.

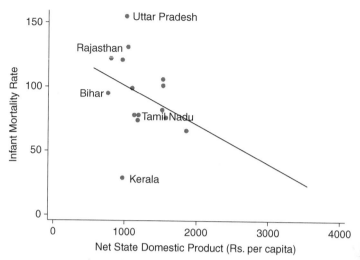

FIGURE 1.8. Relationship between Economic and Social Development in India: Infant Mortality Rate and Per Capita State Domestic Product (1985).

level of wealth, and two below the line – Uttar Pradesh (UP) and Rajasthan, both of which have fared more poorly than their economic status would suggest.[11] While these cases do move around depending on which time period one looks at –Tamil Nadu and Rajasthan are generally "lesser" outliers than Kerala and UP, and in later time periods, all states cluster closer to the line – these are, in general, to use Gerring's (2001: 221) terminology "disconfirming crucial cases" that allow for an exploration of the determinants of social development beyond differences in economic development. The case of Kerala also fulfills Gerring's other criterion of a "paradigm case" that is chosen "because it has come to define, or at least to exemplify a concept of theoretical outcome," in this case, social welfare (2001: 219). In addition, while the case study states are deliberately chosen to maximize variation on the outcome variable, Kerala's levels of education and health outcomes render it an "extreme case" (217). Such an extreme case, according to Gerring, is particularly useful in elucidating the mechanisms at work in a causal relationship because, as William James noted, "moments of extremity often reveal the essence of a situation" (ibid.). I follow Heller's reasoning that the "exaggeration" produced by a case such as Kerala

[11] Bihar was chosen for analysis after this initial case selection for the insights that its remarkable recent turnaround on social policy and dramatic developmental gains offer for the argument of this book. Bihar does fit with the overall case selection rationale insofar as it is, as shown in Figure 1.7, an "off-the-line" case for education outcomes, displaying lower literacy than would be predicted for its level of per capita state domestic product. For health outcomes, however, in part because through much of the post-Independence period, Bihar was the very poorest state in the country, the province has done marginally better than would be predicted by its meager per capita state domestic product (see Figure 1.8).

should not be interpreted "simply as a distortion of the 'typical' case, but as a clarification, just as the addition by a computer of 'extreme' colors to a remote scanning device does not distort but 'enhances' the photograph by improving the visibility of the phenomena we are interested in" (cited in Heller 1999: 6). In contrast to the vast scholarly and popular literature, much of which portrays the state's development in singular terms as the product of various "unique" factors, I attempt to demonstrate that Kerala's educational and health achievements can essentially be explained by a more acute manifestation of the same constellation of causal factors that are at play in the development experiences of other Indian states. Combining the insights from the extreme paradigmatic case of Kerala with Tamil Nadu, Uttar Pradesh, and Rajasthan, as well as Bihar, I hope to develop an argument that taking account of the full range of social development in India is imbued with maximum theoretical robustness as well as scope for empirical generalizability.

OVERVIEW OF THE BOOK

The primary objective of this book is to explain variation in education and health outcomes both across Indian states and within a state over time and to use this to develop a more general theoretical framework for understanding spatial and temporal divergences in social development outcomes.

The book is structured as follows. I begin in Chapter 2 by clarifying the concept of subnationalism and then move to specifying the theoretical mechanisms through which it is hypothesized to influence social policy and development. I focus primarily on the critical top-down mechanism of state action, that is how subnationalism fosters the formulation of a progressive social policy but I also delineate the supplementary bottom-up mechanism of societal action of how subnationalism fosters popular involvement with the delivery of social services. I then explicate the direction of causality by previewing evidence from my case studies that improvements in social development occur only subsequent to the emergence of subnationalism. The chapter also lays out the set of conditions under which subnationalism might be expected to lead to social development.

Before moving on to explicating how subnationalism influences social development in subsequent chapters, in Chapter 3 I seek to establish both the reasons why, and the ways in which, Tamil Nadu and Kerala have been characterized by a more powerful subnationalism as compared to UP and Rajasthan. A close examination of the histories of each of these states shows that the emergence or absence of subnationalism is a product of the strategic choice of interest-maximizing elites. In all four states, at different points in time between the late-nineteenth and early- to mid-twentieth centuries, a set of exogenous modernizing influences triggered an intense competition for sociopolitical power between elites who chose whether to evoke subnational symbols (as in the case of Tamil Nadu, Kerala, and Rajasthan) or some other identity, such as religion (as in the case of UP), depending on which was more likely to maximize their advantage in this contest. Elite subnationalism percolates to the people at large through sociopolitical movements and associations. In addition to exploring the factors that give rise to subnationalism, this chapter also provides a rich narrative assessment of the cohesiveness of subnational identification across Tamil Nadu, Kerala, UP, and Rajasthan. This account is deliberately structured around the same indicators and should therefore be read in conjunction with and as a "thicker" complement to the subnationalism index that is developed in Part I of Chapter 6.

Chapters 4 and 5 present a comparative historical analysis of social development in my case study states. The paired juxtaposition of Tamil Nadu and Kerala with Uttar Pradesh and Rajasthan, as well as a shadow study of Bihar, facilitates the delineation of the mechanisms though which cohesive and fragmented subnational identities give rise to high and low levels of social development respectively. Further, the comparison of Tamil Nadu and Kerala highlights how differences in the timing of the emergence, nature, and strength of subnationalism (for example, whether it has percolated from elites into the popular realm) gives rise to differences in social policy and societal action and, as a result, in levels of social development. In addition, the longitudinal analyses of Rajasthan and Bihar showcase how the move from a weaker to a more powerful subnational solidarity can generate important social gains but also, in the case of Rajasthan, how the lack of popular embeddedness of a subnational ideology can limit the pace of development.

Chapter 4 focuses on the "positive cases" of Tamil Nadu and Kerala. I establish that the celebrated social gains of Kerala and the less prominent but substantial achievements of Tamil Nadu are a reflection of an essentially similar process of subnationalism-generated synergy between the progressive social policies of an activist state supplemented by the collective monitoring of public services by a politically conscious citizenry.

I analyze the case of Tamil Nadu in terms of four time periods corresponding to the absence of subnationalism, the emergence of elite subnationalism, the strengthening of popular subnationalism, and the development of a cohesive subnational identity. In the absence of any sense of a shared Tamil identity, until the 1900s there were few demands for, and consequently little attention by the state to the social sector. Development indicators were low but incidentally not lower than neighboring Kerala. The emergence of Tamil subnationalism among urban, non-Brahmin elites at the beginning of the twentieth century brought education and health onto the governmental agenda, but in the absence of popular identification with the Tamil subnation, residents were not active in utilizing and monitoring public services, and the increased social expenditures could, therefore, yield only limited development gains. It was the spread of Tamil subnationalism to the masses during the 1950s and 1960s that triggered important improvements in education and health outcomes. I show how, from the 1970s onward, a powerful Tamil subnationalism, firmly rooted

in both the elite and popular consciousness, has led to sustained improvements
in social development.

I analyze the case of Kerala in terms of three time periods corresponding to
the absence, emergence, and strengthening of Malayali subnationalism. I show
that until the 1890s, in the absence of any sense of a shared subnational solidarity, the government paid minimal attention to the social sector. The state
was consequently characterized by rates of illiteracy and mortality that were
high not only in absolute terms but also relative to Tamil Nadu and other
Indian provinces. A progressive social policy was introduced and an increase
in education and health indicators occurred only after, and as a consequence
of, the emergence of a powerful subnational solidarity both among elites as
well as in the popular domain in the late nineteenth century. As a result, by the
1920s–1930s, Kerala had gained a discernible lead over Tamil Nadu and other
Indian provinces. I highlight how from the 1950s onward, a powerful Malayali
subnationalism has generated consistently high social expenditures as well as
active societal monitoring of schools and clinics, which together have generated Kerala's substantial social achievements. Insofar as the so-called 'Kerala
Model' has attracted considerable scholarly attention, I also critically analyze
some of the most prominent alternative explanations for Kerala's development.

Chapter 5 discusses the "negative cases" of Uttar Pradesh and Rajasthan, as
well as Bihar, tracing the broad links between a fragmented subnational identity to weak governmental commitment to the social sector and limited political consciousness and mobilization in favor of social services, which together
give rise to low levels of social development. Through the beginning of the
twentieth century into the first decade of the twenty-first century, UP has been
characterized by the absence of subnational solidarity – the primary locus of
popular identification has been either below or above that of the subnation.
I examine three time periods corresponding to the prominence of religious,
national, and caste identities respectively. From the 1900s to the 1940s, popular demands for education and health and consequently, the limited social
policies of the British government in the United Provinces were framed in terms
of the welfare of Hindus or Muslims rather than the people of UP as a whole.
From the 1950s to the 1980s, the question of the national good rather than
the development of UP animated the provincial policy agenda. Since the early
1990s, demands and policies for social welfare have been framed in terms of
the advancement of particular castes. As a result of this emphasis on either sectional or national welfare rather than on the welfare of UP, the state has been
characterized by low social expenditures and a lack of popular involvement in
public services, which together have resulted in consistently low development
indicators.

This chapter also illustrates the mechanism of change through case studies of Rajasthan and Bihar. I demonstrate how the move from a very weak to
a more consolidated subnational solidarity among elites in the postcolonial
period prompted the adoption of a more progressive social policy in Rajasthan

and how the beginnings of popular subnationalism in the 1990s triggered an increase in development indicators. Until the 1950s, in the absence of any conception of a Rajasthani identity, the princely states of Rajputana were characterized by a lack of attention by the state to the social sector and consequently abysmal social indicators. The emergence of Rajasthani subnationalism among elites in the early post-independence years pushed the state to devote substantial budgetary outlays, greater than other North-Central Indian states, to the education and health sectors; however, the absence of popular subnationalism meant that there was little monitoring on the part of the people of the education and health services provided by the state, which limited the gains from a progressive social policy. From the 1990s onward, the beginnings of the percolation of Rajasthani subnationalism to the people at large triggered greater societal involvement with the social sector, which helped translate the generous social spending into important social improvements, especially in education. Popular Rajasthani subnationalism, however, remains an incipient phenomenon and as a result, the pace of social gains in the state are far from certain. Reflecting the overall relatively weak subnationalism, social development in Rajasthan also remains much below that of Tamil Nadu or Kerala. The briefer, shadow case study of Bihar further illustrates how the emergence of a sense of subnational solidarity can serve as a trigger for breaking out of long-standing social backwardness. Until about a decade ago, Bihar had been characterized by a near absence of any sense of subnationalism. Through the colonial and post-independence periods, the state was instead characterized by powerful identification and mobilization around substate regional and caste-based lines, which led to the demand for and provision of social welfare along these lines. In the absence of an encompassing welfare agenda, limited social policies targeted toward specific substate regions and caste groups could yield only very meager gains and the state came to be synonymous with the worst of India, a poster child for underdevelopment across the world. The emergence of a Bihari identity among elites since the mid-2000s and gradually also among the people of the state at large has, however, led to a dramatic turnaround with the Bihar state government adopting an ambitious and inclusive welfare agenda characterized by unprecedentedly large budgetary outlays and a host of innovative social schemes. While the state obviously still confronts enormous challenges as regards access, provision, and quality of, education and health services, and developmental indicators remain dismal in both absolute and relative terms, the state has made a break and is rapidly shedding its global image as an "area of darkness" (Economist 2004). Whether and at what pace the improvements continue will depend among other factors on how deeply a sense of subnational solidarity is embedded in elite and popular consciousness. But this chapter suggests that there are reasons to be optimistic about Bihar's developmental future.

Chapter 6 seeks to test the broader validity of the subnationalism argument developed through the comparative historical analyses of Chapters 4 and 5. In order to do so, Part I develops a valid and reliable measure of subnationalism. I draw on the definition of subnationalism outlined in Chapter 2 to construct an indicator based on language, specifically the existence of a single, common, and distinctive language; along with three observable manifestations of subnational consciousness – the existence of a popular movement for the creation of the state, the absence of a separatist movement for the division of the province, and the presence of a subnationalist political party. These individual indicators are aggregated into a composite index of subnationalism, which ranges from 0 to 4, where 0 indicates a very weak and 4 represents a very powerful sense of subnational solidarity. I present the scores for all Indian states on this subnationalism index. Part II of Chapter 6 presents descriptive data and estimates a series of Ordinary Least Squares (OLS) regressions to assess the impact of the strength of subnationalism, as measured by this index, on social development outcomes. The statistical study shows that controlling for levels of economic development, the presence of social-democratic parties, the nature of the party system, the closeness of political competition, the degree of ethno-linguistic fractionalization, inequality and poverty rates, and using a range of different statistical models, the strength of subnationalism is positively associated with both education and health indicators as well as expenditures for the fifteen major Indian states from the 1960s to the 2000s. This statistical support for the findings of the case study research serves to provide further support for and enhance our confidence in the subnationalism argument.

Chapter 7 begins by exploring the extensions of the subnationalism argument. It then draws out the broader scholarly and policy implications of this study. It also examines the relationship between subnationalism and national identity and the potential feedback loop from social development to subnationalism.

2

How Solidarity Works for Welfare: The
Subnationalist Motivation for Social Development

The previous chapter established the central animating puzzle of this book and specified the research methodology that will be employed to tackle it. This chapter how solidarity promotes social welfare. It begins by clarifying the concept of subnationalism and then moves on to delineating the mechanisms through which subnationalism influences social policy and development. It will also discuss the conditions under which subnationalism can be expected to influence social policy and development.

SUBNATIONALISM

Conceptualizing Subnationalism

In recent years there has been a huge surge of scholarly interest in the concept of subnationalism or substate nationalism as it is more commonly termed (see, for example, Banting 2000; Beland and Lecours 2008; Breuilly 1993; Catt & Murphy 2003; Erk 2005; Forrest 2004; Guibernau 1999; Harty 2001; Keating 2009; Knight 2010; Kymlicka 2002; McEwen & Moreno 2005; Moore 2003; Sinha 2005; Tiryakian & Rogowski 1985). In line with the existing scholarship, subnationalism is conceptualized in this book as the identification with, or aspiration for, a self-governing homeland located within the boundaries of a sovereign country. The ideology and movement of subnationalism incorporate both cultural and political dimensions – people with a belief in a shared past and a common culture, based often but not necessarily on language, who identify with, or desire the creation of and control over, a political-administrative unit within a sovereign country that corresponds to a territory they believe belonged to their forebears. Such a conceptualization maps closely onto some of the most influential understandings of nationalism (Anderson 1991; Connor 1978; Deutsch 1966; Geertz 1963; Gellner 1983; Hobsbawm 1990; Stalin

1954; Weber 1948).[1] Both nations and subnations may be seen, in a sense, as forms of "imagined" political-cultural communities (Anderson 1991). The fundamental feature that unites subnationalism and nationalism and provides an important criterion for differentiating them from other types of collective identities is the centrality of the association with political self-determination. What separates subnations and nations from ethnic identities such as race, religion, caste, tribe, as well as from gender or class identities is the attachment to or desire for control over the political institutions of a putative historic homeland. What distinguishes a subnation from a nation, however, is that while the political demands of nations necessarily involve sovereign statehood, subnations either explicitly aspire to or are willing to settle for control of a political-administrative unit within a sovereign country.

A number of scholars do not make this distinction, subsuming what is delineated here as subnationalism within the language of and discourse on nationalism. Indeed the boundary between nations and subnations is permeable. Group demands are shaped by the political context in which they operate; groups might alter their demands for independence versus an autonomous homeland depending on what seems expedient or realistic at the time. Despite this potential fluidity, however, it is both empirically and analytically useful to distinguish subnationalism from nationalism. The origins of nationalism are commonly traced to the fall of absolutism and the birth of mass national states in North America and Western Europe in the latter half of the eighteenth century (Hutchinson and Smith 1996: 7). This is not to suggest that nationalism has ceased to be important. Indeed, the breakup of countries in Eastern Europe and of the former Soviet Union in the 1990s are testaments to its continued potency. Yet the contemporary international system with established national states with entrenched external boundaries appears to be more conducive to the existence of subnationalism. There are today empirically at least as many movements for political-institutional units within a sovereign state as there are groups engaged in a struggle for sovereignty (Minorities at Risk Project 2009). In addition, in recent decades more and more countries and virtually all Western democracies have worked toward accommodating subnationalist movements within their borders through various forms of federal autonomy arrangements.[2] From an analytical point of view, recognizing subnationalism

---

[1] Corresponding to this conceptualization, I measure the strength of subnationalism across Indian states in Chapter 6 in terms of an index that includes language, specifically the existence of a single, common, and distinctive language; and three observable manifestations of subnational consciousness – the existence of a popular movement in support of the creation of the state; the presence of a subnationalist political party and the absence of a movement by a group *within* the province for a separate, breakaway province.

[2] Kymlicka (2002) argues that there has been a trend through the last century across Western democracies of a move away from suppressing subnational movements to accommodating them through a "multination federalism." He points out that in the beginning of the twentieth century only Switzerland and Canada had adopted some form of autonomy arrangements in response to

as a distinct phenomenon allows for an understanding of the potential differences in the consequences of movements for autonomy as compared to separatism. This book will show a shared subnational identity to be a force for the common good; yet group identities, especially nationalism, are infamous for their historic association with chauvinism, xenophobia, and violence. The association of subnationalism with a more limited claim and/or institutional settlement than sovereignty has important implications for its creative versus destructive potential as a group identity. As will be discussed further in a later section on Scope Conditions, either the explicit demand for, or willingness to settle for, autonomy within the existing constitutional-legal framework depresses the negative potential of subnationalism as compared with, for example, nationalist movements for a sovereign state.

The Emergence of Subnationalism

As will be discussed in detail in the next chapter, based on a comparative historical analysis of the case study states, subnationalism is theorized to emerge as a product of elite choice in the course of political competition. This emphasis on elite choice follows in a long tradition of scholars, including but by no means limited to Gellner (1983), Kedourie (1966), Greenfeld (1992), Hobsbawm (1990), and Anderson (1991), who grant a pivotal place to elites in their analyses of the origins of nationalism. A combination of exogenous, socioeconomic influences creates a challenger elite who seize the opportunity created by administrative or electoral reforms to gain access to greater political power. This brings them into competition with the dominant elites who in turn attempt to maintain their preeminent position. In such a competition the challenger elites seek strategies that will strengthen their claim to political power vis-à-vis the dominant elites. In particular, challenger elites attempt to adopt symbols that allow them to come together in a minimum winning coalition that also 'others' the dominant elites. A collective challenge is seen as a more effective strategy to counter the hegemony of the dominant elite than different groups of challenger elites each acting on their own. Challenger elites therefore seek a set of symbols that allow them to coalesce into a single, minimally sized, superordinate group. In order to maximize the likelihood of success, it is important that the symbols chosen not only bring together the challenger elites into an "in-group"

subnational movements but since then the list has expanded to include Swedish-speaking Åland Islands in Finland after the First World War, South Tyrol in Italy and Puerto Rico in the United States after the Second World War, Catalonia and the Basque Country in Spain in the 1970s, Flanders in Belgium in the 1980s, and Scotland and Wales in the United Kingdom in the 1990s (2002: 4). In 2001, France, which was an exception to this trend in its refusal to grant autonomy to Corsica, finally granted Corsica limited autonomy in the form of law making power and the extension of Corsican language teaching in an attempt to end the separatist violence on the Mediterranean Island (The New York Times 2001).

but also help cast the dominant elites as an "out-group." Subnationalism emerges if the challenger elites perceive the espousal of subnational symbols such as a common history, memories, myths, culture, and language to be the most advantageous strategy in their quest to wrest political power from the dominant elites. This is more likely to be the case if subnational symbols can serve to both unify the challenger elites into a single front and also distinguish and distance them from the dominant elites. For example, subnational symbols can allow challenger elites to come together as "sons of the soil," rightfully entitled to hold positions of political power in the province, in opposition to the "outsider"/"foreigner" dominant elites with no legitimate claim to power. The challenger elites' adoption of subnational symbols is by no means determined by the underlying ethnic demographics and is much more a product of this instrumental calculation.

In contrast to scholars who theorize an automatic, chronological progression from elite to popular nationalism (Hroch 1985: 23), I argue that the spread of popular subnationalism is a deliberate and not inevitable process that rests, in particular, on the espousal of subnationalism by popular movements and/or organizations. A number of scholars have identified popular movements and associations as the primary instruments for the communication of elite nationalist ideologies to the people at large (Brass 1974; Hroch 1985). Political movements and parties have also played a critical role in virtually all nationalist and subnationalist movements across the world. In order for subnationalism to spread among the people, it is therefore necessary that it be espoused by a powerful, broad-based sociopolitical movement or organization. The spread of elite subnationalism to the people depends on the effectiveness and reach of the sociopolitical movements and associations as well as on the extent to which the subnational symbols evoked by the challenger elites resonate with the people. Subnational symbols are likely to have a greater mobilizing appeal if they hold historic significance and have subjective meaning. However, as noted earlier, elites can also rediscover, rework, and reinvent myths, values, memories; the key condition is that they should, in Hobsbawm's words, be "on the wavelength to which the public is ready to tune in" (Smith 1998: 129).

Subnationalism can be sustained through the purposive actions of elites and subnationalist movements or organizations; it stands strongest, however, when it is undergirded by an institutional foundation. A subnational identity is most likely to be maintained when it is institutionalized, for example, in a single language policy state-sponsored subnational festivals and art forms, as well as the establishment of arts, literary, and cultural academies. A subnational identity that is deeply institutionalized is most likely to be maintained, but this is by no means inevitable. Subnationalism can weaken or disintegrate in the face of various challenges. It might, for instance, be weakened by the rise of ethnic identities as evidenced by the prominence of ethnic leaders and increased ethnic mobilization via ethnic social movements and/or political associations that deliberately act outside or against an overarching subnational solidarity.[3] This rise of ethnic identification might be related to a similar dynamic as that through which subnationalism emerges – a new set of challenger elites find it useful to draw on ethnic symbols in order to counter the dominance of a more established elite – or it might be a product of other factors, a theorization of which is beyond the scope of this book.

THE SUBNATIONALIST MOTIVATION FOR SOCIAL DEVELOPMENT

Having clarified the concept of subnationalism and delineated how it emerges, in this section I will sketch out a theoretical schema for how the strength of subnational solidarity influences social development. The vast majority of the social science scholarship on welfare focuses on the actions of the state.[4] Welfare states have been shown to be the key providers of social services across Western Europe and other advanced, industrialized countries (Esping-Anderson 1990; Huber & Stephens 2001; Lynch 2006; Mares 2003; Pierson 2001). States in developing countries, while obviously "weaker" than their counterparts in the developed world, have also been the primary actors in the provision of public goods and services. In fact, one of the salient features of politics in the developing world in general has been argued to be the decisive importance of state action (Horowitz 1985: 201; Veliz 1980).[5] There has, since the 1980s, been an increased involvement of nonstate actors with the provision of welfare in the developing world (Cammett and Maclean 2011). This is still, however, relatively limited compared to the size and impact of the state. A review of an influential body of political economy literature on public goods provision, mostly but not exclusively on developing countries, concludes that social services are a product almost entirely of top-down state

---

[3] It is important to clarify following the influential scholarship on multiple identities that ethnic identities are by no means inherently opposed to or necessarily pose a challenge to subnational identification. Ethnic identification can coexist comfortably with and even bolster subnational identification (Sidanius et al. 1997, Dowley and Silver 2000).

[4] This is in contrast to the political economy scholarship on public goods provision, which has problematically focused predominantly on the provision of social services through collective action on the part of local communities (see Singh & vom Hau 2014 for an extensive critique).

[5] In his discussion of the so-called third world policy process, Horowitz points out that the share of resources both invested and consumed by the state is typically larger in developing as compared to advanced industrial societies (1985: 201). He also argues that while compared to developed countries, "the state structures of developing countries may be weak, their legitimacy doubtful, their capacity to bring about change imperfect at best; yet what the state does may nevertheless be inordinately important for the developing society" (ibid.). This is similar to Claudio Veliz's (1980) theorization of the "centralist" Latin American state, which intervenes in virtually every aspect of social life.

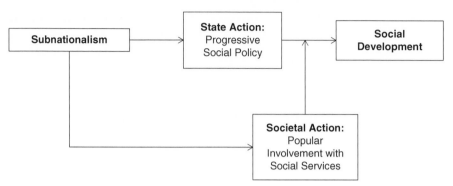

FIGURE 2.1. The Subnationalism Argument.

interventions and have much less to do with bottom-up community mobilization than most theoretical models in that scholarship predict (Banerjee,
Iyer, & Somanathan 2006, 2008; see also fn 28 in this chapter). In line with
this, the focus here is on how subnationalism encourages state prioritization
of the social sector. The institution of a progressive social policy is argued to
be a necessary condition for improvements in social development. Popular
involvement with social services facilitates their effective functioning. Societal
action can therefore be an important supplement in realizing the full benefits
of a progressive social policy (see Figure 2.1).

   As noted in the previous chapter, primary jurisdiction over social welfare
in India has rested with the provincial rather than the national government.
Provincial governments in India, many of which are equivalent in size to
some of the largest countries in the world, are in charge of a number of
critical sectors including law and order, agriculture, social development, and
communications. Of all the many conceivable subjects or problems to which
they could be paying attention at any point, however, state officials focus on a
smaller set of issues, the "policy agenda" (Kingdon 1984: 3). So the key question would seem to be – How does an issue make it onto the policy agenda?

   The policy agenda has been argued to be influenced both by the "participants" such as political elites as well as "political processes" such as
public opinion (Kingdon 1984: 16). In order for an issue to make it to the
policy agenda, it must be "seized upon" and backed by political actors
(Hansen & King 2001: 259). The most powerful of these political elites
have been shown to be elected officials (Kingdon 1984: 19) though the role
of career bureaucrats can also be critical.[6] An issue has also been hypothesized to be more likely to rise to agenda prominence if it is congruent with
public preferences and ideology (Erikson, Wright, & McIver 1993; Manza &

---

[6] In India since the 2000s, activists, researchers, and civil society organizations have also played
   an increasingly important role in the passage of important legislation notably the Right to
   Information Act (2005), the National Rural Employment Guarantee Act (2005), and the

Cook 2002; Page & Shapiro 1983) or the "national mood" more broadly defined (Erikson, MacKuen, & Stimson 2002; Kingdon 1984). Recent studies, however, have shown that the effects of public opinion on public policy in the United States have been significantly overestimated (Burstein 2006; Page 2002). The role of the public in influencing the policy agenda is likely to be even more modest in developing countries where the means to gauge public opinion, such as opinion polls, media, meetings with advocacy groups, are typically more limited and patronage politics is more prevalent. In general, social policy is therefore most likely to make it onto the policy agenda if and when it is supported by political elites particularly in developing countries such as India. This is a necessary condition for the introduction of a progressive social policy. The rise of social services to agenda prominence might also be aided by support among the public, though this is neither a necessary nor a sufficient condition.

In this section I draw on scholarship across the disciplines of social psychology and political philosophy to argue that a collective affective identity such as subnationalism constitutes a powerful motivational basis for political elites to support a progressive social policy. In particular, I build on social identity and self-categorization theory in social psychology, as well as the liberal nationalist school of thought in political philosophy, to argue that identification with a shared subnational community generates a sense of "we-ness" and triggers a perception of common interests and ethical obligations among members of different subgroups. Recategorization into a superordinate group, such as a subnation, can help transcend subordinate group boundaries and correspondingly shift the focus away from the exclusive pursuit of subgroup or individual interests toward collective welfare of the group. Elites that perceive a shared subnational solidarity are therefore more likely to push for the prioritization of policies, for example, the provision of social services that further the welfare of the community as a whole.

The powerful consequences of group identification have been well-established (Allport 1954). Laboratory as well as field experiments in social psychology have consistently and robustly demonstrated that once people feel part of a group, their affect toward that group and its members becomes more positive (Transue 2007: 9).[7] Studies in the so-called minimal

---

ongoing National Food Security Act (2011). This is, however, a recent development. The influence of policy experts or activists on legislation was very limited prior to the early 2000s.

[7] The perception of an in-group requires contrast with an out-group. But a number of studies have shown that in-group identification and loyalty does not necessarily entail outgroup discrimination or hostility. Baumeister and Finkel (2010) review a sizable body of evidence from a range of laboratory experiments and field studies that show that variations in in-group positivity and social identification do not systematically correlate with degree of bias or negativity toward out-groups. On the basis of this they assert "despite widespread belief that ingroup positivity and outgroup derogation are reciprocally related, empirical research demonstrates little consistent relation between the two" (539).

group paradigm have shown that this preferential evaluation and treatment of in-group members occurs even when the basis for the initial categorization of individuals into groups is arbitrary (Tajfel 1970). A branch of social identity theory called self-categorization theory has gone a step further to show the powerful effects of manipulating the typically fluid, multiple identities that individuals may hold (Kramer & Brewer 1984; Tajfel & Turner 1986). One of the central findings of self-categorization theory, and of the Common Ingroup Identity Model (CIIM) in particular, is that recategorization into a single overarching identity is an important unifying mechanism, prompting individuals to transcend their subordinate groups and perceive a superordinate identity. Groups that were previously seen as "them" are folded into a larger conception of "us." It is important to clarify here that the development of a superordinate identity does not require the elimination or abandonment of alternative identities. Individuals invariably possess multiple identities. As historian Linda Colley writes in her influential book about the forging of a British identity, "identities are not like hats. Human beings can and do put on several at a time" (2005: 6).[8] The CIIM explicitly recognizes that individuals may conceive of themselves as belonging to the superordinate group as well as to one of the subordinate groups included within the new, larger group (Dovidio & Gaertner 1999: 103). This is particularly important for intergroup relations, as Transue (2007: 79) points out, because it is often more feasible for individuals to emphasize and/or adopt a new category than to stop identifying with or using an existing identity.[9]

A host of studies have conclusively shown that once members of different groups are induced to conceive of themselves as members of a single, superordinate group, their attitudes and behavior toward former out-group members become more positive through processes involving pro-in-group bias, and they begin to think in terms of the welfare of the group as a whole (Dovidio and Gaertner 1999: 103). This has been hypothesized to occur because "Inclusion within a common social boundary reduces social distance among group members, making it less likely that individuals will make sharp distinctions between their own and others' welfare. As a result, outcomes for other group members, or for the group as a whole, come to be perceived as one's own"

---

[8] Colley goes on to state, "I am not suggesting for one moment that the growing sense of Britishness ... supplanted and obliterated other loyalties. It did not ... Great Britain did not emerge by way of a 'blending' of the different regional or older national structures contained within its boundaries as is sometimes maintained, nor is its genesis to be explained primarily in terms of an English 'core' imposing its cultural and political hegemony on a helpless and defrauded Celtic periphery ... the Welsh, the Scottish and the English remain in many ways distinct people in cultural terms ... Britishness was superimposed over an array of internal differences" (Colley 2005: 6).

[9] There is considerable evidence that identification with sub-group identities is not only compatible with but might also reinforce identification with superordinate identities (see for example Wells 1998, McEwen and Moreno 2005, Moreno 2001, Sidanius et al. 1997 and Dowley and Silver 2000).

(Kramer and Brewer 1984: 1045). There is a perception of common interests and goals and a prioritization of collective rather than purely individual or sectional welfare (Brewer 1979; Tajfel & Turner 1986). One way to think about it is that it is not that individuals cease to behave strategically but instead that a sense of belonging to a superordinate identity leads to a "transformation of motivation" whereby self-interest at the personal or subgroup level is redefined at the collective level (De Cremer & Van Gugt 1999). Favorable outcomes for other group-members are related to favorable outcomes for oneself (Tyler & Smith 1999).[10] This blurring of individual and collective interest increases the value that people place on public goods. Individuals bound together by a common identity are more likely to support and work for public goods (DeCremer & Van Gugt 1999). Interestingly, these positive behavioral effects for the group-identity manipulation have been found to occur consistently even when the basis for superordinate group identification was "seemingly trivial" (Kramer & Brewer 1984: 1056). It is therefore not surprising that in-group favoritism has been found to be particularly strong when the basis for the superordinate group identification is a powerful, emotionally resonant national or subnational identity (Charnysh, Lucas, & Singh 2015; Robinson 2012; Sachs 2009).[11]

In a distinct but related body of scholarship, studies in political theory in the "liberal nationalist" paradigm have emphasized how a shared national identity can foster support for collective welfare through an additional channel, that of ethical obligations. When individuals perceive themselves as members of a nation, or subnation, they prioritize and work for the common good also because of the "deep and important obligations [that] flow from identity and relatedness" (Tamir 1993: 99). The crux of the argument is the power of what Tamir has termed "The Magic Pronoun: 'My' " (95). The obligations owed to those we consider as our own are different from and more wide-ranging than those we owe others. A sense of belonging together leads to the transcending of purely reciprocal compromise, on which interpersonal relationships in general, might be said to be loosely premised, and triggers prosocial behavior. Individuals who view themselves as compatriots, belonging to a national or

---

[10] This is very similar to the idea of a "linked fate" described as the acceptance of the belief that individual life chances are inextricably tied to that of the group and that what happens to the group in question will also affect what happens to the individual (Dawson 1994). According to Dawson (1994), strong notions of a linked fate with members of their racial group led to a situation in which wealthier African Americans, rather than acting on the basis of their class interests, instead found it most efficient to improve their own individual positions by pursuing the common welfare of the group.

[11] In what is perhaps the most directly relevant study for this book, in an online survey experiment, my co-authors and I found that recategorization within a shared national identity prompted our Indian respondents to extend monetarily costly prosocial behavior across a deeply divisive ethnic boundary (Charnysh, Lucas, & Singh 2015). See also the discussion on extensions of the argument in the concluding chapter of this book.

subnational group, meet "not as advocates for this or that sectional group, but as citizens whose main concerns are … the pursuit of common ends" (Miller 1998: 48).

Bringing together and building on this diverse body of scholarship, I argue that an attachment to an overarching subnational identity encourages a perception of shared interests and a sense of mutual commitments on the part of individuals from divergent subgroups, who are therefore more likely to support policies, such as social welfare, that further the collective good of the subnational community as a whole. It is important to reiterate here that identification with the subnational community does not require the elimination of identification with or mobilization around other cleavages, such as ethnicity. Even when ethnic identities are strong, perceptions of a superordinate connection have been shown to enhance inter-ethnic trust and acceptance (Dovidio & Gaertner 1999: 103). Gaertner et al. (2000: 184) put it succinctly, "If people continue to regard themselves as members of different groups but all playing on the same team, or as part of the same superordinate entity, intergroup relations between these subgroups would be more positive than if people considered themselves as members of separate groups only." They go on to cite a number of studies (Huo et al. 1996; Smith & Tyler 1996) that show that the positive effects of a superordinate identity remain stable even when the subordinate identity remains just as strong (Gaertner et al. 2000: 195). Subnationalism thus offers a way for individuals to transcend, but not necessarily abandon, their subgroups, such as ethnic groups, to also perceive of a collective identity and support the public good.[12]

Elites bound by a shared subnationalism are therefore more likely to push for the inclusion of social policies that benefit the subnational community as a whole, such as the provision of primary education and basic healthcare onto the policy agenda. If subnational identification has also taken popular root, their constituents are more likely to be in favor of public goods, and this is likely to serve as an additional, though not necessary, impetus for political elites to back social policy.

In contrast, in states that are not characterized by a superordinate subnational solidarity, the positive effects of in-group bias do not extend to all members of the subnational community but only to members of their subgroup. Individual perceptions continue to be structured in "us" and "them" terms; there is little conception of a more inclusive "we." Individuals evaluate

---

[12] Miguel (2004), for example, finds that ethnically diverse communities that perceive a stronger national identity in Tanzania are able to achieve far greater success in fund-raising for the provision of public goods in particular primary schools, as compared with similarly diverse communities that did not share a superordinate national identity just across a randomly imposed colonial-era national boundary in Kenya. Transue (2007) shows that when self-identified whites in America perceive a shared American identity, they are more likely to support a tax increase for public schools that benefit both Whites and African-Americans.

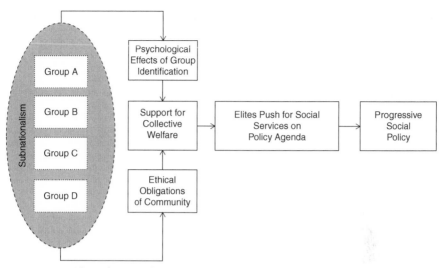

FIGURE 2.2. The Subnationalism Argument: The Top-Down Mechanism.

distributional decisions from the perspective that only one group will benefit and they will want that group to be their own (Transue 2007: 80).

Political elites tend to push for policies that further the interests of their subgroup, for example, elites from dominant agricultural castes are likely to push for favorable prices for agricultural goods and subsidized inputs such as irrigation and fertilizers; elites from mercantile castes are likely to push for economic and fiscal concessions and state protection; elites from backward castes will push for policies such as affirmative action targeted toward their caste brethren. Social welfare is not likely to figure prominently on the policy agenda. If and when social policies are introduced, they are more likely to be targeted toward subgroups, for example the distribution of benefits such as free textbooks or bicycles and the reservation of seats in schools and colleges for members of particular ethnic groups, or the prioritization, in a context of widespread illiteracy, of secondary or higher over primary education that will benefit the rich and/or more educated sections of society. In the absence of universal policies, such as literacy campaigns or vaccination drives, aimed at the welfare of the subnational community as a whole, these targeted policies are likely to yield, at best, very limited gains. This top-down mechanism is summarized in Figure 2.2.

The prominence of social welfare on the policy agenda is a necessary condition for higher levels of social development. It is difficult to imagine a region that has high social development in the absence of state attention to the social sector.[13] It is possible, however, that while a progressive education and health

---

[13] This is by no means to deny important instances of social service provision by local communities and civil service organizations. India's neighbor to the East, Bangladesh, for example is a

policy is critical, it might not in itself always be sufficient for ensuring developmental gains. In India, as well as in other developing countries, the state establishes schools and health centers, but these are frequently characterized by the absenteeism of service providers, shortage of supplies such as teaching materials, medical equipment, and drugs; and faulty or inadequate infrastructure, including dilapidated buildings and the absence of toilets in schools that renders them semi- or nonfunctional (Banerjee, Deaton, & Duflo 2004; Kremer et al. 2005). Popular involvement with the social services provided by the state can play a key part in ensuring their effectiveness. Societal action can in this way be an important supplement to state action in generating higher levels of social development.[14]

A powerful subnational identity can play an important role in fostering societal involvement with the social services provided by the state. In particular, it can help overcome some of the factors, notably a low degree of awareness of, and participation in, the political sphere that might limit people's involvement with public services, and by doing so, limit the potential gains from a progressive state social policy.

There is a large and important scholarship on the instrumental bases for political behavior (McAdams 1982; Olson 1965; Verba, Schlozman, & Brady 1995). As Rahn (2004: 21) points out, all these rational-choice inspired models recognize the significance of non-instrumental motivations for political and civic involvement, notably a shared identity, whose impact usually exceeds that of more instrumentally oriented variables such as political knowledge or skills. A number of studies have shown that group solidarity, in particular attachment to a superordinate political identity, such as a nation, is associated with a greater degree of political attentiveness and participation in electoral and non-electoral spheres (Huddy & Khatib 2007; Rahn 2004). One of the mechanisms through which this has been hypothesized to occur is that commitment to an identity generates emotional arousal, which fosters an interest in politics and consequently, a propensity toward political action. As Rahn puts it, "Politics is more interesting to people who are committed to some kinds of collective identities ... because the self is more emotionally invested in objects that have a public, or political nature" (2004: 22). In a similar vein, political

---

case where a NGO, BRAC (Bangladesh Rural Advancement Committee) is the primary social, especially educational, provider in the country, but it is important that, like in many other cases of social service provision by NGOs across the world, BRAC works with the explicit consent of, and in collaboration with, the state. Some might even say that BRAC sets and implements state social policy in Bangladesh.

[14] It is important to note here that even though intuitively as well as from a normative point of view, we imagine that mobilized communities enhance the developmental efforts of a state, the evidence on this is mixed. While a number of studies find that societal mobilization has positive effects on the functioning and quality of public services (Bjorkman & Svensson 2009; Duflo et al. 2007; Evans 1997; Tendler 1989), other studies including one in India find little to no effect (Banerjee et al. 2010; Olken 2005).

theorists stress that it is only if citizens have a sense of belonging together that they will value participating together politically (Mason 2000: 117). A shared identification is seen to be critical in fostering an "activist idea of politics" (Abizadeh 2002; Miller 1995: 10). This inherent potential of a sense of community to incite political interest and involvement may be intensified by the activity of political associations that are premised expressly on a shared identity. As noted earlier, subnational movements and parties can play an important role in fostering popular subnationalism. In addition, broad-based movements for the formation of a subnational political unit and/or the activities of a party based explicitly on a subnational identity tend to bring people into the political arena through campaigns, manifestoes, and public meetings and rallies.[15] Both through their emotional arousal of a sense of a shared community as well as their mobilization capacity, subnational movements and parties are therefore likely to boost sociopolitical consciousness and participation. An enhanced awareness of, and proclivity to participate in, the public sphere increases the chances that people will approach state representatives, for example to provide inputs about the public goods provided by the state. Such interactions between public agents and engaged citizens may be seen to constitute a "state-society synergy" (Evans 1997), which has been theorized to be critical for the efficient delivery of public services.[16]

In states with a powerful popular subnational identification, individuals tend to show greater awareness of and involvement with public life, and consequently are more likely to be involved with the provision of public services. By ensuring that public services function more effectively, societal involvement can therefore augment the effects of a progressive state social policy. In contrast, in states where there is little popular subnational solidarity, people will tend to be less emotionally aroused or mobilized, and consequently less inclined to take an interest in and be involved with the political life of the province. As a result, it is unlikely that people will organize or approach state officials to provide feedback about potential inefficiencies in public service delivery. The absence of popular involvement with public services might in this way limit the gains of a progressive social policy. This bottom-up mechanism is summarized in Figure 2.3.

---

[15] Scholars have argued for the exceptional mobilization capacity of parties "employing culturally thicker appeals to community" (Subramanian 1999: 323). Subramanian, for example, writes that such parties used "methods of mobilization which reached deeper down into post-colonial societies. Such methods were particularly fruitful where such forces tapped the prior solidarity of socially capable groups" (ibid.).

[16] The concept of state-society synergy has usually been associated with the interaction between state institutions and civil society, but the underlying idea that civic engagement strengthens state institutions should hold even when the source of the "intimate entanglement" (Evans 1997: 7) of public officials and private citizens is a shared identity rather than civil society organizations.

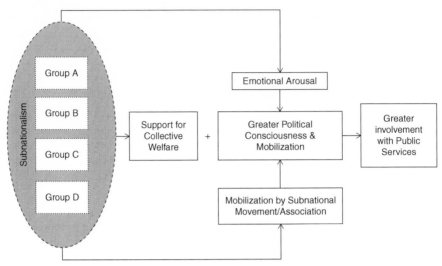

FIGURE 2.3. The Subnationalism Argument: The Bottom-Up Mechanism.

In summary, states with a powerful subnational solidarity on the part of both elites and the people at large, tend to be characterized by a progressive social policy as well as popular involvement with the public goods provided by the state, the situation that is most conducive to social development. The presence of a powerful subnationalism among elites is sufficient to ensure state prioritization of social welfare, but the absence of a subnational solidarity among the population might limit popular involvement with social services and impede the maximization of the potential benefits of a progressive state policy. States characterized by an absence of subnational identification among both elites and the people are unlikely to witness either the institution of a consistent and committed social policy or active societal supervision of the limited public services that are provided, and as a result social development is likely to be low.

EXPLICATING THE DIRECTION OF CAUSALITY: SUBNATIONALISM
WORKS FOR WELFARE RATHER THAN VICE VERSA

The previous section set out the theoretical framework of how subnationalism fosters social development. It is important to consider, however, whether the direction of causality might in fact be reversed. Improvements in social development can lead to conditions that encourage the growth of subnational solidarity. The provision of social services and improved social development can enhance the legitimacy of, and consequently loyalty, to and identification with, the state. The provision of services such as healthcare, housing, education, and income security can be seen to contribute to social solidarity and to reinforce the ties that bind citizens to state or substate political communities (McEwen 2002). The social institutions of welfare provision can themselves also emerge as important symbols of identity, representing as they do a "common heritage, a symbol of shared risks and mutual commitment, and a common project for the future" (Moreno & McEwen 2003: 8). In the UK, for example, the welfare state, which was established in large part as a consequence of the solidarity generated by the Second World War, gradually came to replace the rapidly dissolving Empire as a symbol of national identity. Moreno and McEwen (2003: 13) point out that the social institutions established were distinctively British and offered a new reason to feel a sense of belonging and attachment to the British state. This is clearly brought out by Gordon Brown's statement on the fiftieth anniversary of the NHS that "when people talk of the National Health Service, whether in Scotland, Wales or England ... here national is unquestionably British" (Beland & Lecours 2008: 106). It is also evident in the prominent place accorded to the NHS in the 2012 Summer Olympics opening ceremony in London entitled "Isles of Wonder," which was widely seen as a "love letter to Britain" (Dawson 2012). Similarly in Canada, in the absence of a foundational myth, the idea of a generous and comprehensive welfare state became a source of Canadian identification and unity, and a key element in the distinctiveness of the country vis-à-vis the United States (Beland & Lecours 2008: 53). States can also explicitly and deliberately use social services to construct a collective political identity, most notably by using mass schooling to systematically inculcate nationalist ideas (for the classic statement on this, see Weber 1976; see also Darden 2014; Darden & Grzymala-Busse 2006).

While the possibility of a reversal of the direction of causality specified in this book, that it is in fact welfare policies and outcomes that drive subnational solidarity, is therefore clearly theoretically plausible, a close empirical analysis of Indian states does not support such a conclusion. First of all, the emergence of subnationalism temporally precedes the introduction of a progressive social policy and rise in social indicators. The previous chapter pointed out that prior to the emergence of subnationalism at various points in the late nineteenth and early to mid-twentieth centuries, Tamil Nadu, Kerala, UP, Rajasthan, and Bihar were characterized by roughly similar levels of social backwardness. Subnationalism emerged in Tamil Nadu and Kerala in a context of abysmal levels of social development. In the next chapter I attempt to clarify, through an examination of disaggregated welfare indicators, that it was not the case that elite subnationalism was driven by improvements in the welfare, especially literacy for particular groups, or that the spread of popular subnationalism is a product of developmental gains among lower castes.

Any fears that perceptions of pride associated with the development of their province might be behind the rise of subnationalism are dispelled by evidence that at the time of the emergence of Tamil and Malayali subnationalism, elites in both Tamil Nadu and Kerala by no means saw their respective provinces as "developed" (Koshy 1972: 53; Sundararajan 1989: 2). Take the case of Kerala, for example, wherein the signatories of the Malayali Memorial of 1891, one of the first clear indicators of the emergence of Malayali subnationalism, argued that Malayalis were underdeveloped as compared to other parts of India.[17] At the turn of the century, Kerala was described as "a body that was seldom washed and was full of dirt and filth" (Koshy 1972: 53). In the 1930s, in a work entitled the "The Future of the Malayalees," noted Malayalam journalist Kesari A. Balakrishna Pillai wrote that "the Malayalee's position, when compared to that of others, is very backward" (cited in Devika 2002: 55). Even the States Reorganization Commission (SRC) voiced reservations in recommending the creation of a single Malayali state in the 1950s, despite overwhelming popular demand in support of its formation, because of fears of its "unviability."[18] The SRC eventually supported the formation of a unified Kerala. However, the then chief minister of Travancore-Cochin, Panampilli Govinda Menon, while expressing his approval for this move, felt compelled to write to Prime Minister Nehru to forewarn him that the new state is likely to be a "'problem state' among the many proposed states."[19]

Second, subnationalism emerges through a process that is independent of state social policy or social development outcomes. As will be discussed at length in the next chapter, subnationalism emerges as a product of elite choice in the course of political competition. The rise of the elites who evoke subnationalism was, for the most part, unrelated to improvements in welfare. Instead, the decisive factor was the change in the socioeconomic status of particular groups associated with events, which were independent of social policy and development. Further, political competition between the challenger and dominant elite was triggered by administrative and/or electoral reforms, which were the result of a diverse set of developments, but in each of the cases, none that bore any discernible relation to the outcome variable of social welfare policy and outcomes.[20]

Third, education and health make it onto state policy agendas only *as a consequence of* the emergence of a subnational solidarity. In Chapters 4 and 5, I delineate how when progressive social policy was adopted in Tamil Nadu,

---

[17] Comparing Travancore and Malabar, the Memorial claimed that "there is little or no difference as to the extent to which education has spread in the respective countries" (Koshy 1972: 84), whereas the Census records of 1901 indicate that literacy in Travancore was in fact discernibly higher than in Malabar.

[18] The Report of the SRC stated that "There have been some suggestions that considering its size, the density of population, which is the highest in India, and the menacing problem of unemployment, it would be best for the whole of Kerala area to be united with Madras to form a South Indian state. A further argument in favour of this proposal is that Travancore-Cochin, deprived of its Tamil taluks and yoked with economically backward Malabar, would not constitute a viable unit" (States Reorganization Commission 1955: 86–87).

[19] Letter from Panampilli Govinda Menon to Prime Minister Jawaharlal Nehru, dated November 3, 1955. Views of the Government of Travancore on the Report of the States Reorganization Commission. National Archives of India, File number 20/1/55 SR.

[20] For a more extensive discussion of this, see in particular the conclusion of Chapter 3.

Kerala, Rajasthan, and Bihar, this was after, and a consequence of, elite subnationalist motivations.

Finally, I show a strong and robust statistical association between the strength of subnationalism and social expenditures and indicators over time. In Chapter 6, I present time-series cross-sectional analyses, which show a strong statistical association between the subnationalism variable and education and health spending and outcomes in a subsequent time period.

It is important to note here that I am not denying that a progressive social policy and high levels of social development may strengthen subnational solidarity in Indian states. The provision of a range of welfare services and substantial social achievements in Tamil Nadu and Kerala have likely enhanced the legitimacy of the state governments and, concomitantly, the strength of identification with the provinces. Once subnationalism has been in place for many decades and generated important improvements in social development, a potential feedback loop from social development to subnationalism might well exist. The next three chapters however, seek to delineate a clear historical sequence in which a subnational solidarity emerges prior to, and drives improvements in social development.

SCOPE CONDITIONS

In this section I will briefly highlight the scope of the applicability of the subnationalism argument. I anticipate that subnationalism is most likely to generate social development firstly, where subnational units have at least some autonomy, and ideally, substantial discretion over social policy and secondly, where these subnational units are located within an established central authority and are subject to some institutions of national oversight. Insofar as the primary dynamic of subnationalist political elites putting in place a progressive social policy can only come into play when a subnational unit has at least some jurisdiction over the social sector, this first scope condition is self-evident. The emphasis on the existence of an effective center that subnational units are accountable to requires a little more justification.

This book presents subnationalism as a benign and constructive force. Yet, as noted earlier, I recognize subnationalism to be a Janus-faced phenomenon that also has the potential to be destructive and destabilizing. Despite the existence of a significant body of research cited earlier, that shows that group identification is much more closely identified with in-group favoritism than out-group hostility and might not entail any out-group antagonism, subnationalism, like other group identities, tends to arouse concerns about its potential for violence. In general, subnationalism and other forms of group identity provoke fears about two types of violence – external violence against an out-group notably the national government, and internal violence against minorities located within subnational boundaries. The chances of both of these kinds of violence, which are likely to be very disruptive of social development, are minimized

when there is a consolidated central authority to which subnational governments are accountable.

Strong subnational solidarities are often seen as harboring the potential to
threaten national unity by eroding national allegiances and generating centrifugal tendencies.[21] An established central authority is critical to ensuring that
subnational identification and mobilization do not prove to be destabilizing
for the national state. Power needs to be consolidated before it is redistributed.
If central authority is weak, the emergence of strong subnational movements
could certainly prove dangerous. However, if a powerful center has already
been established, the existence of subnational attachments and mobilizations
need not prove destabilizing. In fact, the accommodation of subnational sentiments can placate potentially secessionist movements. As long as there exists a
strong center, subnationalism need not threaten and may even further the unity
of the nation. To illustrate, the fear that powerful subnational identities might
threaten the unity and stability of the nation has been especially strong in India.
Nehru was concerned that the rise of linguistic subnationalism in the 1950s
could destabilize a newly sovereign India and therefore deliberately dragged his
feet and stalled the creation of new states for as long as was possible. Nehru's
apprehensions were echoed by other political leaders as well as external observers. Scholars such as Selig Harrison (1960) went so far as to predict that linguistic subnationalism would lead to the breakup of India. This specter has been
raised each time the question of creating new states in response to powerful
subnational movements emerges. However, none of the three major phases of
state formation in India – linguistic subnationalism of the 1950s, the creation
of new states in response to the subnational movements by tribal groups in the
North-East, or the carving out of the three states of Uttarakhand, Jharkhand,
and Chattisgarh in 2000 – have threatened, and many have argued have in fact
strengthened the unity and sovereignty of the Indian state.

Further, the presence of a clear established national government allows for
the possibility of dual identification with both the national and subnational
community. A number of scholars have stressed the compatibility between
national and subnational identities (Colley 2005; Moreno & McEwen
2003). Most people likely hold dual (if not multiple) identities (Colley
1992). Opinion surveys clearly indicate that subnationalism and nationalism can sit well together. The example of Spain is illustrative. Moreno (2001)
shows that through the 1990s, often seen as a high point of subnationalism in Spain, in all seventeen Spanish *Comunidades Autónomas* (substate
regions and nationalities), a vast majority (approximately 70%) of respondents expressed some form of dual self-identification with both their subnational community (for example, Andalusian, Basque, Catalan) as well as Spain.

---

[21] Yet, as will be discussed shortly, this need not be the case. Strong subnational solidarities can
sit comfortably with, and even shore up, national identification (Wells 1998; Moreno 2001;
Moreno and McEwen 2003; Colley 2005; Stepan, Linz and Yadav 2010).

Similarly, in the National Election Studies post-poll survey conducted in India in 1996, only 21 percent disagreed with the statement that they should be loyal to their own region first and then to India, but in the 1995 round of the World Values Survey, 91 percent of respondents also claimed that they were proud to be an Indian. In an analysis of worldwide surveys such as the International Social Survey Program (ISSP) and the World Values Survey, Dowley and Silver argue that one should not assume that "where strong subnational identities are allowed to flourish, loyalty to the state will erode. In fact, our evidence suggests that the opposite may be true" (2000: 370). Dowley and Silver find that "Turks, Roma, Francophones, Basques and Catalaons who express that they feel very close to their ethnie are slightly more patriotic to the larger state than those of their group that are not especially attached to the group ... attachment to their dominant ethnie leads to higher levels of patriotism for the state as a whole in all four countries" (Dowley & Silver 2000: 368). Similarly, Sidanius et al. (1997) find that the stronger the attachment to their ethnic group, the stronger their national identity for Latinos in the United States.

While the existence of a consolidated central authority dampens the potential for external violence against the nation, the existence of institutions of accountability and/or a constitutional commitment to liberal values, which are most often but not necessarily associated with democratic governments, is essential to reducing the likelihood of the incidence of violence against groups such as minorities who reside within the boundaries but are excluded from understandings of the subnation. The presence of liberal, democratic norms about the treatment of minorities as well as the availability of institutions by which minorities can make demands and ask for the redress of any grievances are likely to be important factors in dampening the potential of violence by the subnational state against them.

Moreover, it is important to highlight that within the boundaries of a consolidated state with institutions of accountability, the destructive potential of subnationalism is lower as compared to nationalist movements. Central governments tend to be more willing to negotiate with and accommodate movements for autonomy as compared with demands for secession, which are often met with violence, triggering a retaliation and putting in place a cycle of conflict.[22] The likelihood of violence against an external "other," such as the central government, is likely to be far lower in the case of subnationalism as compared to nationalism. In addition, the chances of internal violence against minorities are also relatively lower in the case of subnationalism. Even

---

[22] As noted in footnote 2, there has been a growing trend through the twentieth century, across national especially western democratic governments, of accommodating, rather than suppressing, subnational movements. Switzerland, Canada, USA, Finland, Spain, Belgium, UK and even France have entered into different institutional arrangements to fulfill the demand for autonomy on the part of subnational movements. Stepan, Linz and Yadav (2010) in fact propose a classification of countries such as India, Spain, Belgium and Canada that have been constructed through accommodation with subnational movements as "state nations rather than nation states."

if subnational governments have considerable autonomy, they are subject to at least a minimum amount of oversight from the center. This means that aggrieved minorities who feel that the subnational government is not responding to their concerns can appeal to the national government, which in turn can intervene on behalf of the repressed or discriminated minorities – either pushing subnational governments into taking action or overruling offending policies. Insofar as national governments do not in general have a similar institutional mechanism of oversight – international agreements, norms and pressure do not bind national governments to nearly the same extent as the dictates of the national government compels subnational authorities – the likelihood of internal violence is also likely to be lower in the cases of subnations as compared with nations.

ALTERNATIVE EXPLANATIONS

This section examines the plausibility of the subnationalism argument against the most prominent rival explanations of the determinants of education and health outcomes. As noted earlier, the research design of this book – a comparison of subnational units, which share a common legal, administrative, financial, and electoral structure – allows for the control for a range of powerful hypotheses including regime type, the constitutional structure of decision-making, the nature of electoral laws, and the quality of the bureaucracy. This section briefly discusses arguments that explain social development in terms of economic variables, notably levels of economic development; political variables, including rule by a social democratic party, the nature of the party system, and political competition; demographic variables such as levels of ethnic diversity; historical variables such as the nature of colonial rule, and sociocultural variables such as civil society and the prevailing political culture. Insofar as the statistical analyses in Chapter 6 examine how a number of these variables, particularly economic, political and demographic variables, influence social expenditures and development outcomes, this section also foreshadows these findings.

Economic Development

Economic growth is widely believed to lie at the core of social development. Skocpol and Amenta point out that Wilensky's view that "economic growth is the ultimate cause of welfare state development" has predominated among comparative social scientists (1986: 133). Modernization theorists emphasized economic development as the prime mover of improvements in the social sector. Economic growth was believed to automatically and inevitably lead to concomitant improvements in the political and social realm. Parsons (1951), Lipset and Rokkan (1967), and Smelser and Lipset (1966), for example, argued that with economic development all less developed countries would shed the characteristics associated with traditional societies, such as an illiterate, emaciated population and an authoritarian political culture, and acquire instead the characteristics of modernity, that is, an educated, healthy populace and a democratic political culture. More recently, studies in development economics have found income to be a robust and strong determinant of social outcomes. Filmer, for instance, writes that "National income is strongly associated with child mortality and primary school completion" (2003: 6–7).

A number of other studies, however, point to the inadequacy of economic factors in explaining social development. Economic development is found to be unable to predict the timing of the adoption of social insurance programs by twelve European nations between the 1880s and 1920s (Flora & Alber 1981) and across fifty-nine countries between the 1880s and 1960s (Collier & Messick 1975). Castels (1979) finds that neither the level of economic development nor rates of economic growth can explain changes in social sector spending among democratic capitalist states in the 1960s and 1970s (cited in Skocpol & Amenta 1986: 133–34).

There is also considerable evidence that calls into question the adequacy of a purely economic explanation for social development across Indian states. Dutt and Ravallion (1997) point out that through much of the initial post-Independence decades, literacy rates were higher and infant mortality rates lower in the poorer states of India such as Kerala. Murti et al's findings (1995) about the limited influence of both income and poverty on development outcomes corroborates other research for the "weak" and "slow" effect of income on social welfare. Joshi (2007) finds that across Indian states from the 1980s to the 2000s, the contribution of economic development to human development has been less than that of "good governance" defined in terms of leadership priorities, state capacity, and policy implementation in the social sector. The statistical analyses of all Indian states from 1971 to 2006 presented in Chapter 6 confirms the insufficiency of economic development, variously conceptualized, as an explanation for social development. It is certainly the case that higher income is associated with an improvement in social indicators – Net State Domestic Product (NSDP) per capita has a positive and often statistically significant impact on literacy and education and health spending and a negative impact on infant mortality rates (IMR) – but the size of the impact in most models is minimal.[23] Moreover, even controlling for levels of economic development, subnationalism is found to be a powerful determinant of social development and expenditures.

---

[23] Further evidence in the statistical analysis in Chapter 6, for the inadequacy of economic development as an explanation for social development is the finding of a positive association between rural poverty and social expenditures and outcomes, as also the lack of a consistent negative association between inequality and social expenditures and outcomes.

Rule by a Social Democratic Party

Varying levels of social development have also been traced to differences in
the nature of the ruling political party. A popular variant of the argument,
which is equally as a representative of the broad category of explanations
termed "class politics," is related to the presence of social-democratic parties. The argument, widely cited in the welfare state literature on Western
Europe, is that states in which social-democratic parties are in power are
likely to incur higher levels of expenditure on social services and to experience greater social development (Hibbs 1977; Korpi 1983; Shalev 1983).
One of the most influential statements of this argument in the Indian context is by Kohli (1987: 10) who identifies an ideological and organizational
commitment by the ruling regime to include the property-less classes, such
as on the part of the Communist party in West Bengal, as a key factor
in the redistributive performance of state governments. In a similar vein,
Herring (1988), Franke and Chasin (1989), and Heller (2000) trace the
social achievements of Kerala to the strength of the labor movement and
the Communist party.

Rule by a social-democratic party, while clearly an important contributory
factor, cannot fully account for the empirical variation in social policy and
development both across states as well as within the same state over time. For
example, West Bengal has had the longest and most sustained experience of
Communist rule of all states in India. Yet its educational and health achievements are lower not only than Kerala, which has had a shorter and more inter-
mittent history of Left rule (Desai 2007), but also lower than states such as
Tamil Nadu, Maharashtra, and Gujarat, in which social democratic parties
have remained very weak and have been unable to come to power. In Kerala,
the Communist party undoubtedly played a pioneering role in the social gains
of the state, but as discussed further in Chapter 4, this has at least equally, if not
more, to do with their embeddedness in and espousal of Malayali subnationalism as their Communist ideology. Moreover, through the post-Independence
decades, Communist commitment to the social sector in Kerala has been virtually matched by that of Congress governments. There is no statistically significant difference between social spending by the Communist and Congress
governments in the state. As an observer of Kerala's politics puts it, "The defining feature of the (Kerala) paradigm is the centrality of political agency, *irrespective of the fronts that occupied office*, in the development process" (Lal
2006).[24] Similarly, another analyst points out that "Investment in education and
health infrastructure has been a consistent policy of all elected governments in
Kerala, *whatever their political leaning*" (Kutty 2000: 103, emphasis added).
The statistical analysis in Chapter 6 confirms that rule by a social-democratic
party has a generally positive impact on literacy and negative impact on infant

[24] "Growth with Welfare," Amrith Lal, Editorial Opinion, Times of India, June 22, 2006.

mortality across Indian states from the 1970s to the 2000s, but this effect only rarely achieves statistical significance.

Nature of the Party System

Another school of thought argues against viewing the role of a particular party in isolation from the electorally competitive climate in which it operates. They argue that the party system has a substantial influence on the policies adopted by any party irrespective of its ideology or constituency. Chhibber and Nooruddin (2004), for example, argue that in a single majority system, whether the party system is characterized by two-party or multiparty competition has an effect on the provision of public goods. Specifically, they claim that political parties engaged in two-party competition are more likely to provide public goods than those in a multiparty environment. This is because when there are only two effective parties competing in an election, each needs to win a majority to win the seat. Excessive reliance on any one group can isolate other groups from supporting the party and therefore, in order to stand a chance of winning the election, the parties must build broad, cross-cleavage coalitions by providing public services accessible to all groups. In contrast, where there are multiple effective parties competing, the proportion of votes needed to win a seat is less and parties consequently appeal to "vote banks" and specific groups through the distribution of club rather than public goods. In addition to being theoretically plausible, this hypothesis is also supported empirically in the statistical analysis in Chapter 6, which shows that the move from a multiparty to a two-party system leads to a statistically significant increase in education expenditure and a decrease in nondevelopment expenditure. It is notable, however, that the statistical analysis also shows that, even after controlling for the nature of the party system, subnationalism has a consistently statistically significant and positive influence on social development and expenditures.

Political Competition

The intuitive hypothesis, rooted in democratic theory, is that a more competitive environment will encourage political parties to be more proactive in the provision of public goods as compared to a noncompetitive environment in which they have little fear of being voted out of power. The classic formulation of this association between higher levels of political competition and progressive social welfare policies is by V. O. Key (1949), who argued that political competition induces all parties to cater to the needs of the "have nots", but in the absence of political competition, the status quo of an emphasis on the preferences of the "haves" remains. Key's study triggered an active research agenda, which has generated an impressive body of cumulative research but a mixed bag of answers. A spate of empirical research on American states in the 1960s indicated that the relationship between interparty competition and welfare expenditures is largely spurious, and that the two variables are instead both dependent on the level of socioeconomic development, which is the real driver of social policy (Dawson & Robinson 1963; Dye 1966). However, other researchers such as Sharkansky (1968), Sharkansky and Hofferbert (1969), Lockard (1968), and Barrilleaux (1997) have employed different data and methodological techniques to demonstrate that there is in fact a significant link between party competition and welfare expenditures even after controlling for various socioeconomic factors (Carmines 1974: 1118). Studies on the relationship between political competition and public goods provision in other parts of the world, especially China and Latin America, also provide similarly contradictory findings (Packel 2008). In China, Manion (2006) finds a clear positive relationship between competition, measured by the ratio of candidates to positions on village committees, and trust in elected officials; while Wang and Yao (2007) find increased competitiveness, measured by the existence of popular nomination procedures, to be linked to lower levels of public expenditure. In Mexico, Hiskey (2003) finds that less competitive municipalities, that is, where the dominant PRI (Institutional Revolutionary Party) won all elections in a five-year period with a vote share of more than 65 percent, had poorer records of public service provision than more competitive municipalities in which the PRI lost at least one election during the same period and had an average vote share of less than 60 percent. Other scholars of Mexico find no discernible relationship between competition when it is operationalized as the margin of victory and public goods provision (Cleary 2007; Moreno 2005) and government performance (Grindle 2007). Similarly, in a cross-national statistical study of nearly four hundred municipalities across four Latin American countries – Mexico, Brazil, Chile, and Peru – Kauneckis and Andersson (2006) find that competition, measured by the margin of victory in the last mayoral election, had no discernable influence on the provision of natural resource management services. The statistical analysis in this book does provide some support for the importance of political competition. In Chapter 6, increased competitiveness, measured by the margin of victory of legislative seats, is shown to boost literacy, dampen infant mortality, and increase education and health expenditures, and these effects often reach statistical significance at conventional levels.

Ethnic Diversity

Since the late 1990s, ethnic diversity has emerged as a prominent causal factor in studies of public goods provision and developmental outcomes. A large body of research posits a negative relationship between ethnic heterogeneity and the provision of public goods (Alesina, Baqir, & Easterly 1999; Alesina, Glaeser, & Sacerdote 2001; Baldwin & Huber 2010; Desmet, Weber, & Ortuño-Ortin 2009; Easterly & Levine 1997; Easterly, Ritzen, & Woolcock 2006; Hopkins 2009; Jensen & Skaaning 2015; Khwaja 2009 Miguel & Gugerty 2005). In a seminal article, Easterly and Levine (1997) show that ethno-linguistic diversity is negatively associated with indicators of public goods, including numbers of telephones, percentage of paved roads, efficiency of the electricity network, and years of schooling across countries in sub-Saharan Africa. Alesina, Baqir, and Easterly (1999) find that a variety of public goods – roads, schools, trash pickup, libraries – worsen or receive less funding with higher ethnic diversity in a sample of U.S. cities. In a study of community management of infrastructure in northern Pakistan, Khwaja (2009) finds that more homogeneous communities performed better than heterogeneous ones. Miguel and Gugerty (2005) find that more diverse communities are able to raise less funding for the upkeep of primary schools in Western Kenya. In the Indian context, Bardhan (2000) shows that ethnic homogeneity (in the form of 75% or more of the farmers belonging to the same caste group) is positively related to the successful maintenance of irrigation systems in South India. Banerjee and Somanathan (2004) and Banerjee, Iyer, and Somanathan (2005) similarly show that Indian districts that have a higher degree of caste heterogeneity also have lower access to a number of public goods, including public transport, electricity, and schools and health centers. Banerjee, Iyer, and Somanathan (2005: 639) have gone so far as to term the negative impact of diversity on public goods provision, "one of the most powerful hypotheses in political economy."[25] And yet there are serious conceptual shortcomings with, and associated empirical limits to this thesis (see Singh & vom Hau 2014 for a thorough review).

This study seeks to move beyond the conceptual limitations of the political economy scholarship in two primary ways. The critique of the political economy scholarship's measurement of ethnic diversity via the Ethno-Linguistic Fractionalization index[26] on the grounds that it violates key constructivist findings about the fluid, multidimensional, and socio-politically manufactured nature of ethnicity is by now well-known (Chandra & Wilkinson 2008; Laitin & Posner 2001; Lieberman & Singh 2012). What is less emphasized is that the "Diversity Deficit thesis" (Gerring et al. 2015) is derived, for the most part, from an excessively narrow focus in terms of agency – who provides the public goods – that stands at odds with the global historical reality of public goods provision. Most studies that show a negative relationship between diversity and public goods provision focus on the provision of public goods through

---

[25] Such has been the "consensus" that ethnic heterogeneity dampens public goods provision that scholars working in this research tradition have now sought to take the "next step" of exploring the micro-logics of this connection (Habyarimana et al. 2009, pp. 5; Baldwin & Huber 2010; Lieberman & McClendon 2013).

[26] The ELF is calculated as a decreasing transformation of the Herfindahl concentration index:

$$ELF = 1 - \sum_{i=1}^{I} \left(\frac{n_i}{N} \right)^2$$

N is the population, I is the number of ethnic groups, and n is the population in the ith group. It reflects the likelihood that two individuals chosen at random will be from different ethnic groups.

the collective action of local communities (see, for example, Algan, Hémet, & Laitin 2011; Bardhan 2000; Khwaja 2009: Miguel & Gugerty 2005: Fearon & Laitin 1996; for a notable exception see Alesina, Baqir, & Easterly 1999). In their summary of this scholarship Habyarimana et al. (2007) write that "[a] central question in political science is why *some communities* are able to generate high levels of public goods" (p. 709, emphasis added). While collective action by communities, for instance, to raise funds for schools, collect garbage, repair roads, clear drains and maintain other infrastructure projects is clearly important, as noted earlier in this chapter, across most parts of the world, the provision of public goods has been and remains primarily the responsibility of the state. That their theoretical models, which mostly ignore the state, are at odds with the empirical reality of public goods provision, has recently been recognized as a major shortcoming within the political economy scholarship itself.[27] This study, therefore, focuses squarely on the provision of social services by the state.

Moreover, this study seeks to move beyond the conceptual "mismatch between measure and mechanism" (Posner 2004: 850) that plagues the political economy scholarship. As mentioned earlier, some of the most seminal studies that established the diversity-development deficit thesis suggest that the way in which ethnicity works to undermine public goods provision is through ethnic polarization and conflict (Easterly and Levine 1997: 1204–05, Alesina, Baqir, & Easterly 1999: 1243). Yet they pay very little attention to whether, even within the limitations of the ELF index, the ethnic cleavage that they chose to measure diversity along is a source of polarization and conflict, or indeed even "politically relevant" (Posner 2004). In this book I measure ethnic diversity in a way that is arguably more consistent with the dominant underlying mechanism in most political economy studies, by identifying and focusing on the ethnic cleavage in India that has been found to be the most polarizing and conflictual. Ethnic groups have been widely conceptualized in terms of Horowitz's (1985) definition as all groups based on ascriptive group identities such as race, language, religion, tribe, or caste (Varshney 2001: 365). Across the different ethnic cleavages in India, Wilkinson (2008) finds on the basis of a dataset on collective mobilization from 1950 to 1995, collated from news reports in a major Indian newspaper of record, the *Times of India*, that mobilization around religion seems to have a much stronger association with conflict

---

[27] In a review of this literature, Banerjee, Iyer, & Somanathan (2006) observe that "a large part of the variation in access to public goods seems to have nothing to do with the "bottom-up" forces highlighted in these political economy models and instead reflect more "top-down" interventions" (p. 1). In a revised version of the paper published in the *Handbook of Development Economics* (2008: 3118) they tone down the claim to say that "access to public goods is often better explained by "top-down" interventions rather than "bottom-up" forces highlighted in the collective action literature. In both papers, most of their examples of successful top-down interventions are state interventions including prominently the case of Kerala.

and deadly violence than mobilization around other ethnic identities, such as language or caste. The statistical analyses in Chapter 6 thus examine how state social expenditures and development outcomes are influenced by ethnic diversity measured in terms of religious diversity (Wilkinson 2008).

Across Indian states from 1970 to 2001, as presented in further detail in chapter 6, ethnic diversity measured using data on religious groups is found to not undermine, and in fact have a positive statistically significant, and often substantial effect on social expenditures and outcomes. This finding, which at first blush appears surprising, is in line with a growing body of work that points to the empirical limitations of the conventional wisdom that ethnic diversity undermines public goods provision (Miguel 2004; Bouston et al. 2010; Hopkins 2011; Rugh & Trounstine 2011; Trounstine 2013; Foa 2014; Mirza 2014; Darden and Mylonas 2015; Gao 2015; Gerring et al. 2015; Metz-McDonnell 2015; Soifer 2015; Wimmer 2015; McQuoid n.d.). It is interesting to note in particular that my findings join disconfirming evidence for the diversity-development deficit thesis, on the one hand, specifically for the subnational unit of analysis and on the other hand, for the religious cleavage. In a statistical analysis of a global sample of countries Gerring et al. (2015) found that ethnic diversity, measured through a wide range of measures and across different cleavages, did not reduce a variety of development outcomes at the subnational level. Similarly, ethnic diversity has been found to not dampen the provision of social services across cities in the United States (Bouston et al. 2010; Hopkins 2011; Rugh & Trounstine 2011; Trounstine 2013), villages in Africa (Miguel 2004; Glennerster et al. 2013), India and Pakistan (Mirza 2014), Jordanian municipalities (Gao 2015), and Russian regions (Foa 2014). It is also notable that in almost all analyses, ethnic diversity measured along religion, does not dampen, and might even be positively associated with, social services and welfare outcomes. Scholars have pointed to how the increase in religious pluralism associated with the Protestant Reformation in early modern Europe (ca. 1500–1750) led to the extension of the quantity, quality and access to social services, such as education and health care, that were then provided predominantly by different churches (Chaves and Gorski 2001: 272). In a seminal work within the political economy scholarship, Alesina et al. (2003) examined the effects of ethnic diversity, calculated both in terms of fractionalization as well as polarization (Montalvo and Reynol-Querol 2002) measured along different cleavages, on a range of outputs including economic development and governance, and found that neither religious diversity nor religious polarization had a significant negative impact on economic development and in fact bore a positive relationship to a range of measures of good governance including controlling corruption, preventing bureaucratic delays, tax compliance, transfers, infrastructure quality, lower infant mortality, lower illiteracy, school attainment, democracy, and political rights. A host of other studies including Jackson (2007), Balasubramanian et al. (2009), McQuoid (2011) and Mirza

(2014) do not find support for the assertion that religious diversity impedes public goods provision.[28]

A number of different explanations have been proposed for why ethnic, and especially religious, diversity does not undermine the provision of social and public goods provision services. At its core, however, the absence of a negative relationship between ethnic diversity and public goods provision is indicative of the more general point that ethnic *demographics* need not map directly on to ethnic *politics* (Posner 2005; Singh 2011; Singh and vom Hau 2014). The existence of more people of different religious affiliations does not mean that there will necessarily be religious polarization or conflict, which might dampen public goods provision.[29] I argue, in line with work by Glennerster et al. (2010) and Miguel (2004), that one of the conditions under which objective ethnic diversity need not dampen public goods is when there is a subjective sense of a superordinate identity such as nationalism or subnationalism. Experimental studies shed light on the micro foundations of such a dynamic by showing that a shared national identification triggers prosocial attitudes and cooperative behavior between members of different ethnic, specifically religious and racial, groups (Charnysh, Lucas, & Singh 2015; Gibson & Gouws 2002; Robinson 2011; Sachs 2009; Transue 2007), which can, in theory, help overcome problems of collective action associated both with community provision or the petitioning of the state for the provision of public goods.

It is important to clarify here that there is no necessary pattern of association between national or subnational solidarity and the underlying ethnic composition of a country or region. Following the seminal work of scholars such as Anderson (1991) and Gellner (1983), nationalism (or subnationalism) is "imagined" and "invented" and this can occur under very different ethnic demographics. While ethnic homogeneity can be a powerful impetus for subnationalism, a powerful subnational solidarity does not require ethnic homogeneity and can be forged across different ethnic groups. As will be discussed in further detail in the next chapter, subnationalism emerges across Indian states as a result of an instrumental calculation on the part of elites in an attempt to gain greater political power; the emergence of subnationalism is by no means determined by or associated with ethnic homogeneity.

Miller (2000) believes that nationalism can be an inclusive, overarching identity that incorporates subgroups with distinctive religious and cultural traits. As has been analyzed in Singh (2011), Kerala is one of the most religiously

---

[28] It is interesting to note here that McQuoid (2011) and Mirza (2014) are both studies which attempt to use exogenous measures of religious diversity. This is important in light of the concerns, voiced within the political economy scholarship itself that the robustness of their correlations between public goods provision and measures of ethnic diversity are endangered by the potential endogeneity of the measure of ethnic heterogeneity and relatedly the possibility of reverse causality (Banerjee, Iyer, & Somanathan 2008: 20).

[29] In the case of India, the Varshney-Wilkinson database (1950–1995) shows that it is not the case that states with larger Muslim populations have a higher incidence of Hindu–Muslim conflict.

diverse states in India, yet it also has one of the most cohesive subnational communities and the highest levels of public goods provision. The homogenizing nineteenth-century French-style model of the monocultural nation-state might be expected to reduce ethnic diversity (Weber 1976), but an alternate, equally influential model of the multicultural "state nation" (Stepan, Linz, & Yadav 2011) exemplified by eighteenth-century Britain (Colley 2005) and contemporary India, Belgium, Spain, and Canada (Stepan, Linz, & Yadav 2011) recognizes that individuals can hold multiple identities and that ethno-cultural identification is not a threat to and in fact might even strengthen superordinate allegiances (Guibernau 2008; McEwen and Moreno 2005; Moreno et al. 1997; Moreno 2001; Wells 1997). This "unity in diversity" model of nationalism would thus not be expected to reduce and might even encourage ethnic diversity.

Civil Society and Social Capital

Since the 1990s, the twin concepts of civil society and social capital have experienced an enormous theoretical rebirth and are an important focus of research in both academic and policy circles. Membership in associational networks and norms of reciprocity and social trust have been shown to contribute to the effective functioning of democratic institutions (Putnam 1995),[30] maintenance of inter-ethnic peace (Varshney 2002), and economic performance at an individual (Narayan & Pritchett 1999) as well as at a cross-country level (Knack & Keefer 1997). There is also some evidence that civil society organizations promote public goods provision, such as state irrigation programs in Sri Lanka (Ostrom 1990) and waste management in Indian and Bangladeshi cities (Beall 1997; Pargal et al. 1999).

In many ways civil society and social capital arguments may be read as complementary to the argument presented in this book. In fact, the mechanism through which social capital operates, that is the promotion of political consciousness, social solidarity, and amelioration of collective action problems resonates with the argument about how subnational solidarity fosters a sense of collective welfare, promotes political awareness and participation, and encourages popular monitoring of public goods. However, while civil society theories and the subnationalism argument share an emphasis on the power of connectedness, they differ crucially as regards the identification of the basis and nature of the connecting bonds. For most civil society theorists the source of solidarity is structural, usually dense associational networks. They are not typically concerned with the affect that people attach to these networks.[31] In

---

[30] An important dissenting view is that of Berman (1997), who shows how civil society networks worked to scuttle democracy in Weimar Germany.
[31] Notable exceptions in this regard are Heller (1996) and Tsai (2007) who stress the solidaristic aspects of social capital produced by class mobilization in Kerala, India and by village temples and lineage groups (what Tsai terms 'solidary groups') in rural China respectively.

the argument presented here, on the other hand, the font of cohesion is affective, namely a strong subnationalist identification.[32]

Further, evidence from the Indian case raises doubts about the validity of civil society theories. Data from repeated rounds of surveys in India highlight the country's weak associational life. Chhibber writes, "In 1991, only 13 percent of all Indians belonged to an organization, the lowest figure for all of the democracies on which comparable data is available" (1999: 16). The 1996 National Election Studies survey indicated that 96 percent of respondents said they did not belong to any social organization. Even in Kerala, a state described as having a vigorous associational life (Heller 2000: 497), only 12 percent of the people surveyed reported being a member of an organization. Additionally, there is evidence that in contrast to the conventional explanations of civil society either as a product of autonomous private initiative or of antecedent civic practices (Putnam 1993; Varshney 2002), the emergence of civil society organizations in the Indian context was endogenous to the development of political parties. Heller (2000) shows how the Communist party in Kerala strengthened itself through entrenchment in civil society organizations. Subramanian describes how the ascent of Dravidian parties was closely associated with the growth of formal and informal intermediate associations, such as debating fora, reading rooms, and film fan clubs in Tamil Nadu (1999: 44). The distinctly political origins of civil society raise concerns about whether civil society in India has the autonomous impact posited by theorists, or whether its influence is instead contingent on and channeled through powerful, and in the case of both Kerala and Tamil Nadu, subnationalist political parties. The political roots and overall frailty of associational life in India limit the causal power of civil society arguments.

Nature of Colonial Rule

As noted in the previous chapter, an important body of scholarship emphasizes the importance of the nature of colonial rule, specifically the identity and characteristics of the colonial power, for postcolonial developmental outcomes (Hayak 1960; Lange et al. 2006; La Porta et al. 1998; Mahoney 2010; North 2005). Within this scholarship there is an intense debate on the developmental legacies of British colonialism.[33] As has been widely pointed out, British colonialism was far from uniform. The British ruled their vast overseas empire

---

[32] This resonates with Weber's point that there is no action and social relationship without meaning and recent network analysts who have observed that the social connectedness of a society is not specified simply by the structural properties of networks, such as their density or even the instrumental functions they serve, but by the meanings those networks produce and convey (Hall & Lamont 2009: 9).

[33] Ferguson (2004) and D'Souza (2002) argue for a positive developmental legacy of British colonialism while a number of other scholars including Davis (2001) emphasize its destructive consequences.

through two very different systems of control – direct rule, which involved the dismantling of preexisting political institutions and the creation of a centralized, territory-wide administrative apparatus controlled by colonial officials, and indirect rule, which involved collaboration with indigenous intermediaries who maintained their control over preexisting regional political institutions (Lange 2009: 4). In India, for example, toward the end of the colonial period, some parts were directly ruled by the British. The vast amount of territory, however, consisted of five hundred large and small princely states under the control of Indian rulers who were under the overall suzerainty of the British crown but retained considerable autonomy over internal matters. In India as well as in most other British colonies, both directly and indirectly ruled areas were integrated into a single uniform administrative structure at the time of independence. A number of scholars have argued, however, that the legacy of direct versus indirect rule has had lasting developmental consequences. Hechter (2000) sees direct rule as a disruptive force that generates conflict including nationalist violence. Mamdani (1996, 2001), in contrast, argues that indirect rule created and deepened ethnic divisions, which were at the root of the Rwandan genocide (2001) and entrenched the rule of local autocrats, which has impeded the developmental capacity of African states (1996). Similarly conflicting views characterize the impact of direct versus indirect rule for contemporary welfare outcomes in India. In a study of all British colonies including a case study of India, Lange (2009) finds that directly ruled British colonies have greater legal-administrative capacities and thereby superior developmental records. In contrast, controlling for selective annexation into directly controlled British India using a specific policy rule, namely the Doctrine of Lapse, Iyer's (2010) econometric analysis shows that areas that experienced direct rule have significantly lower levels of access to schools, health centers, and roads in the postcolonial period. Bannerjee, Iyer, and Somanathan (2005) also find that districts that had been under British control in the colonial period had less access to public goods, including education, health, transport, and communication facilities, than did districts that had been part of princely states.[34] In a similar vein, Drèze and Sen (2002) suggest that Kerala's higher levels of social development were in large part a product of its legacy of princely rule. They argue that Travancore and Cochin's status as princely states contributed to their higher levels of education and health insofar as it allowed the kingdoms an autonomy over public policy that directly ruled provinces did not enjoy, and insulated them from overall British antipathy to social welfare. According to them, Travancore-Cochin had "no need to bring ... policy initiative in line

---

[34] Banerjee and Iyer (2005) also find that districts in India where proprietary rights in land were historically given to landlords have significantly lower agricultural investments and productivity, and also investments in education and health in the post-independence period than areas in which these rights were given to the cultivators. For an important critique see Iversen, Palmer-Jones and Sen (2013).

TABLE 2.1. *Historical Legacies of Colonialism and Case Study States*

	Predominantly Ex-British States (Directly ruled)	Predominantly Ex-Princely States (Indirectly ruled)
Higher Social Development than Predicted by Per Capita Income	Tamil Nadu	Kerala
Lower Social Development than Predicted by Per Capita Income	Uttar Pradesh (Bihar)	Rajasthan

with what was happening in the rest of India, under the Raj ... They were not subjected to the general lack of interest of Whitehall officialdom in Indian elementary education" (Drèze & Sen 2002: 99).

Detailed historical research by scholars such as Tharakan, however, indicates that through the nineteenth and early twentieth centuries, the social policies of Travancore-Cochin in fact "broadly conformed to those prevailing in British India" (1984: 1919). Tharakan systematically traces the "the rather sudden outburst of government interest in education" as well as specific changes in education policies, for example, the promotion of vernacular schools, by the princely states of Travancore and Cochin to the directives of the Government of India (1984: 1960). Moreover, as Table 2.1 shows, my decision to undertake a paired comparison of the relatively high-performing states of Kerala, which consisted primarily of the two princely states of Travancore and Cochin, and Tamil Nadu, which was ruled directly by the British as a part of the Madras Presidency, on one hand, with the low-performing states of UP and also Bihar, which were ruled directly by the British, and Rajasthan, which was composed predominantly of myriad ex-princely states, on the other, allows for an exploration of factors that effect social development, while controlling for the nature of the colonial legacy.

Political Culture

A popular explanation, commonly propounded by political elites and bureaucrats I interacted with in the field, accounts for variations in social development in terms of differing political cultures. Top-ranking civil servants in the Ministries of Education and Health in New Delhi, for instance explained the divergent levels of education and health outcomes among Indian states in terms of whether or not they had a "culture of social welfare." However, such an argument is impossible to test insofar as it tends to conflate cause and effect. The explanatory variable – a "culture of social welfare" – is defined precisely in terms of the outcome of interest – high or low levels of social development.

It is difficult to take culture conceptualized in this way seriously as a potential determinant of social development.

More sophisticated understandings of culture treat it as a "mind-set" – composed of shared values and beliefs "which has the effect of limiting attention to less than the full range of alternative behaviors, problems and solutions which are logically possible" (Elkins & Simeon 1979). The individual preferences created by culture foster particular kinds of behavior and lead to certain outcomes (Wildavsky 1987). In its emphasis on how a shared affective identification generates a perceptual framework, which in turn gives rise to certain types of political actions, the subnationalism argument may be encompassed within a family of certain cultural approaches. However, while founded on a similar ideational base, the argument of this book is distinguished from many cultural explanations inasmuch as it seeks to *measure and test* rather than simply *assume* the existence and influence of a "culture of subnationalism."

An influential study that suffers from the aforementioned methodological Achilles' heel of cultural approaches is Weiner's (1991) important and thought-provoking analysis of low levels of primary education in India. Weiner argues that India's low per capita income and economic situation is less relevant as an explanation for low educational outcomes than what he terms "the belief systems of the state bureaucracy," defined as a set of beliefs that are widely shared by educators, social activists, trade unionists, academic researchers, and more broadly by members of the Indian middle class. According to him, at the core of these beliefs is the caste system, the Indian view of the social order, notions concerning the respective roles of upper and lower social strata, the role of education as a means of maintaining differentiation among social classes, and concerns that "excessive" and "inappropriate" education for the poor would disrupt existing social arrangements. This view of education as an instrument for differentiation, rather than a fundamental obligation of the state toward its citizens, means that those who control the education system are remarkably indifferent to low enrollment and high dropout rates among the lowest social classes and consequently India has one of the highest illiteracy rates in the world (1991: 5–6).

Weiner's thesis is provocative and certainly plausible but his lack of attention to the conceptualization and measurement of his primary explanatory variable – "the belief systems of the bureaucracy" – and to the testing of his hypothesis, renders it far less persuasive than it might have been. Weiner presents the beliefs and values of elites in contemporary India through vignettes of select interviews with elites at a single point in time. We remain unclear about what precisely constitutes a casteist view and how widely and intensely such a belief needs to be held and by which kind of elites (government officials at central, state, or local levels; activists; or educators) to adversely impact educational outcomes. Moreover, the caste-based beliefs and values of Indian elites are treated as a constant. Weiner does not attempt to show how these might vary in intensity and extent across space and over time, and how those changes might in turn influence literacy and child labor rates. For example, we have no way of knowing whether Weiner's study, which is national and to some extent cross-national in scope, could also account for the striking divergences in literacy levels in India at the subnational level. The absence of a clear conceptualization and measurement of "India's political culture" and specification of a procedure to test and falsify the hypothesis that this culture leads to low educational rates therefore prevents Weiner's very important insight from being a satisfying causal story.

CONCLUSION

This chapter has sought to set up the theoretical underpinnings for the subnationalism argument by specifying how subnationalism can serve as an important trigger for state prioritization of social welfare and relatedly for improvements in social development. The argument will be illustrated empirically through a comparative historical analysis of the successful cases of Tamil Nadu and Kerala and the relatively backward provinces of UP, Rajasthan, and Bihar in Chapters 4 and 5 respectively, and in Chapter 6 with a statistical analysis of all Indian states.

Building on the evidence for the central role of the state as an agent of social development across the world and especially in developing countries such as India, I focus on how a subnational identity can foster a progressive social policy. Subnational identification is theorized to be a powerful motivation for elites to support the collective welfare of the subnational community as a whole and consequently to back social policies, such as those for primary schooling and basic healthcare, which have a strong redistributive component. Such a formulation might strike some as a (much too) rosy view of elite, and more generally, of individual motivations and behavior.

Yet it is important to point out here that we are surrounded by instances of people deviating from strictly rational interest-maximizing behavior and in particular of accepting often substantial costs to behave pro-socially. In fact, if anything, "what is odd ... is the desire to derive everything from self-interest as if that were a natural or necessary starting point. It is a peculiar feature of the sociology of the present-day economic profession that this odd ambition should be so prevalent" (McPherson 1984: 77–78; cited in Etzioni 1988: 51). Most people honestly pay their taxes despite very low probabilities of detection and small expected penalties. Most people vote, even though the probability of casting the decisive vote is miniscule. Many people contribute generously to a range of charitable causes and/ or volunteer often large amounts of their time.[35] Most people take the trouble

---

[35] According to Meier (2006), estimations for the United States show that in 1995 more than 68% of households contributed to charitable organizations. In 1998 these private households donated more than $134 billion. In the same year, more than 50% of all adult Americans did

of mailing back "lost" wallets with the cash intact (Hornstein, Fisch and Holmes 1968). An overwhelming majority of busy passers-by in New York city assist individuals they think are in distress (Pilliavin, Rodin and Pilliavin 1969). Experimental studies show that contrary to Olsonian predictions, even in the presence of substantial incentives to free-ride, most people in fact cooperate (see, for example, Marwell 1982). Many phenomena, such as the production of open-source software, are difficult to explain by relying on strict self-interested behavior (Meier 2006). Most critically from the perspective of this book, there is considerable evidence for politicians being driven by pro-social motives. A review of the data about the behavior of politicians concludes that "approaches which confine themselves to a view of political actors as egocentric maximizers explain and predict legislative outcomes poorly" (Kalt and Zupan 1984: 279; cited in Etzioni 1988). It is not the case, as Downs (1957: 28) famously stated, that political elites "never seek office as a means of carrying out particular policies; their only goal is to reap the rewards of holding office per se." Political elites, and individuals more broadly, are clearly driven by a range of motivations other than narrowly defined interest maximization (see, for example, Fenno 1973; Kau and Rubin 1982; Mansbridge 1990).

The subnationalism motivation for social welfare proposed in this book may in this sense be seen as building on the distinct and influential scholarly traditions that have highlighted the role of values, affect and ideas in decision-making. Interestingly, Adam Smith, a key figure for neoclassical economists, while most prominently associated with his advocacy of self-interest in his book, *The Wealth of Nations*, did not himself believe that human beings are driven purely by selfish motives. In his first book, *The Theory of Moral Sentiments*, which it is believed he himself considered to be the superior work (Rae 1895), he wrote, "How selfish so ever man may be supposed, there are evidently some principles in his nature, which interest him in the fortune of others, and render their happiness necessary to him, though he derives nothing from it, except the pleasure of seeing it." A number of scholars have pointed to such moral sentiments as being an independent and more tenacious basis for behavior than cost-benefit calculations. Behavior that maximizes economic interests but violates one's moral values has been widely shown to bring on negative feelings including stress, guilt and regret (see studies cited in Etzioni 1988). The argument for subnationalism as generating a sense of closeness and ethical obligations towards members of one's subnational community and thus, a "normative-affective" basis for action also has important resonances with the communitarian paradigm, which sees "individuals as able to

---

volunteer work amounting to 5 million full-time equivalents. While the extent of charitable contributions and the engagement in volunteer work is smaller in Europe, it is still substantial. On average, 32.1% of the population of the ten European countries considered, volunteers. Taking hours volunteered into account, this amounts to 4.5 million full-time-equivalent volunteers.

act rationally and on their own, advancing their self or *"I"* but their ability to do so is deeply affected by how well they are anchored within a sound community and sustained by a firm moral and emotive personal underpinning – a community they perceive as theirs, as a "We," rather than as an imposed, restraining "they" (Etzioni 1988: ix).[36] Relatedly, the argument fits with the growing recognition of the importance of "hot processes" rather than only "cold," deliberative, reason-based thinking in the scholarship on judgment and decision-making. Historically hot processes had been relatively underemphasized by scholars of decision-making in large part because they were viewed primarily as biased and leading to irrational choice behavior. However, over the past couple of decades this has been a burgeoning research agenda with scholars now speaking of "affective rationality" (Peters et al. 2006). Concrete evidence for the critical necessity of this move is provided by neurologists. Patients who suffer damage, either through accident or illness, to parts of their brain that are believed to process emotion and feeling, but leave their cognitive skills intact, are still unable to engage in decision-making activities, leading the neurologists who have studied them to conclude that pure reason is not in itself sufficient for an individual to arrive at a decision; the ability to "feel" is an essential component of decision-making (Damasio et al. 1994). Further, one might also think of the argument that subnational identity is a motor for elite perceptions and actions as being in complement with the so-called ideational turn in political science, which recognizes the central role of ideas, in this case, ideas related to identities, in shaping actors' policy and institutional preferences (Beland & Cox 2011; Blyth 2003; Campbell 2002; Jacobs 2009).

It is also important to note that the perception and prioritization of the collective welfare that a sense of subnational identity is hypothesized to generate, in fact fits with conceptions of rationality that are broader than the by-now widely criticized lens of neoclassical economics. It fits in particular with Max Weber's famous conceptualization of substantive rationality as goal-oriented rational action within the context of ultimate ends or values; in the context of this book this larger goal would be the promotion of the welfare of the subnational community as a whole (Elwell 2013).

Interestingly, not dissimilar to the way in which neoclassical economists tend to absorb moral and ethical considerations within a utility-maximization model, some social psychologists may be read as framing acting for the collective welfare as self-interested behavior. There is simply a recasting of interests beyond the individual to include the interests of the group, in this case the subnational group. A shared sense of belonging leads to a shift in identity "from

---

[36] It is notable that the subnational community as conceptualized in this book fits both criterion of a community as laid out by Etzioni (2003) – first, it is a "web of affect-laden relationships among a group of individuals" and second, it is characterized by "a shared history and identity – in short, a particular culture."

the personal level towards the higher, more inclusive group level ('me' becomes 'we'-identity)" (De Cremer and Van Gugt 1999: 887) and this in turn increases the weight placed on collective outcomes in individual decision-making (Brewer 1979: 322). This is also in line with the arguments propounded within the larger scholarship on the importance of ideas, which suggest that the ideas held by individuals affect how they define their interests in the first place (Blyth 2002; Campbell 2002).

In addition to developing the subnationalism framework, this chapter also discussed some of the most prominent alternative factors, namely economic development; political factors including rule by a social democratic party, the nature of the party system and political competition; demographic variables such as levels of ethnic diversity; historical variables such as the nature of colonial rule; and socio-cultural variables such as civil society and the prevailing political culture, that might explain the progressiveness of social policy and development outcomes in a state. It is important to clarify that I am by no means suggesting that these factors are inaccurate or irrelevant; as the statistical analysis of social spending and outcomes across Indian states in Chapter 6 shows, some of the variables associated with these alternative explanations are found to be statistically significant predictors of education and health expenditures and outcomes. Instead my contention is that these factors, each taken individually as well as together, constitute an incomplete account. The main aim of this book is to shine the analytical spotlight on a hitherto underemphasized explanation – the power of a shared sense of identification, which as shown in Chapter 6 has a strong and statistically significant effect on social spending and outcomes even after taking into account a range of alternative factors. Any account of social welfare that ignores the role played by the "we-ness" that arises from a collective identification is therefore an impoverished one. This book's showcasing of how subnational identification can encourage state prioritization of social welfare and improvements in development outcomes advances, on the one hand, the scholarship on public goods provision and social welfare by drawing attention to a novel variable. On the other hand, it pushes against the scholarship which points to the destructive potential of collective identities such as nationalism.

3

The Origins of the Differential Strength of Subnationalism

Before moving on to test the theory about the influence of subnationalism on social development set out in the previous chapter, it is important to understand the causes for, and nature of, the differences in subnational identification across my four case study states. This chapter seeks to establish both the reasons why and the ways in which Tamil Nadu and Kerala have been characterized by a more powerful subnationalism as compared to UP and Rajasthan. I trace the emergence of subnationalism, as discussed in Chapter 2, to the espousal of subnational "symbols" by elites in the process of a competition for sociopolitical power. Elite subnationalism is spread to the people at large through a popular movement and/or an organization, such as a political party. Subnationalism can be sustained through the purposive actions of elites and/or subnationalist movements or organizations but is strongest when it is enshrined in institutions.

In all four states, at the beginning of my analysis, a set of dominant elites – the Brahmins in Tamil Nadu and Kerala, Muslims in UP, and Rajputs in Rajasthan – exercised overwhelming socioeconomic and political dominance over the region. At different points in time between the late nineteenth and mid-twentieth centuries, these regions witnessed a number of important, exogenous socioeconomic changes, which encouraged the emergence of a set of elites from then nondominant groups. Some combination of changes in agriculture and patterns of land ownership, an expansion of trade, a weakening of the caste system, the availability of unprecedented but very limited opportunities for English education, migration to cities, and growth of means of transportation and communication led to the emergence, or in some cases a resurgence, of a set of elites from the non-Brahmins in Tamil Nadu; the Nairs, Syrian Christians, and Izhavas in Kerala; the Hindus in UP; and Brahmins, Mahajans, and Jats in Rajasthan. Administrative and/or electoral reforms instituted in these provinces around this period opened up access to positions of power and provided these elites unprecedented opportunities for political advancement.

As the "challenger" elites took advantage of these opportunities, they came into conflict with the "dominant" elites who sought to maintain their political hegemony. In the course of this competition, challenger elites were likely to select and emphasize, from among the different symbols available to them, the ones that were most likely to strengthen their position vis-à-vis the dominant elites.

It is important to note that the selection of symbols by the challenger elites was an entirely strategic decision that was independent of the underlying ethnic demographics of the state. Ethnic diversity did not in any way determine the types of coalitions that subnational elites needed to or could build. The challenger elites evoked subnational symbols if they saw them as useful in advancing their stakes in their bid for political power. This was the case in Tamil Nadu, Kerala, and Rajasthan, where the adoption of subnational symbols was an attractive strategy insofar as it allowed challenger elites to coalesce into a single, minimally-sized "us" and distinguished them respectively from a Brahmin and Rajput "them." Challenger elites in these states belonged to different ethnic, caste and religious groups and realized that adopting a shared, superordinate identity that would allow them to mount a single, united challenge increased their chances of displacing the dominant elite as compared to each group acting on its own. Subnational symbols, in contrast to symbols of religion, caste, or class, allowed the challenger elites in these to adopt such a common identity and present a collective challenge. In addition, a subnational identity allowed the challenger elites in Tamil Nadu, Kerala, and Rajasthan to cast themselves respectively as Tamil, Malayali, and Rajasthani indigenes making a rightful bid for political power against dominant elites who were portrayed as outsiders who did not have a legitimate claim to power. In UP, on the other hand, the adoption of subnational symbols was not an appealing strategy for the challenger elites. This is because, rather than distinguishing them, it would have brought the challenger elites into the same subnational in-group with the dominant elites that they were seeking to displace from political power. The identity that was found to be more useful was religion. Challenger elites chose religious symbols that allowed them to come together as Hindus in opposition to the dominant Muslims.

The percolation of elite subnationalism to the people at large depends critically on its espousal by sociopolitical associations or movements. This espousal can be triggered by historically contingent factors. For example, the imposition of Hindi as the national language by the federal government in the late 1930s and the prospect of the formation of linguistic states in the early 1900s created the opportunity for the espousal of subnationalism by sociopolitical movements and associations in Tamil Nadu and Kerala respectively. A combination of material advantages (for example, the benefits associated with one's own linguistic state including opportunities for education and employment in one's native tongue and access to positions of political power) and emotional reasons (for example, the desire to live in a state of one's own, be able to work and have one's children educated in their native tongue) led the Tamil national-ist movement and the DMK party in Tamil Nadu and the Aikya Kerala move-ment and the Communist Party in Kerala to champion and disseminate Tamil and Malayali subnationalism respectively. The strength and organization of these movements as well as the fact that the subnational symbols chosen by the elites were deeply embedded in theses states' cultural and historical traditions meant that Tamil and Malayali subnationalism spread rapidly to and reso-nated powerfully with the masses in Tamil Nadu and Kerala respectively. In Rajasthan, the absence of a powerful, well-organized movement or party that could effectively communicate elite subnationalism to the masses impeded the spread of subnationalism to the people at large. The espousal of subnational-ism by an increasingly powerful political party, the BJP, together with gener-ational change, appeared to initiate the idea of a Rajasthani identity into the popular consciousness in the early 1990s, but this remains an incipient and incomplete process.

In addition to analyzing the reasons for the presence or absence of subna-tionalism, this chapter also seeks to systematically delineate the differences in the strength of subnationalism among my case study states. Subnationalism in Tamil Nadu, Kerala, UP, and Rajasthan is analyzed with respect to the fol-lowing elements, identified in the previous chapter as the key constituents and markers of subnationalism – a common culture, in particular a common lan-guage, and a shared subnational consciousness reflected in the existence of firstly, subnational mobilization in favor of the creation of a province, secondly, a subnationalist party, and thirdly, the absence of a separatist movement for the division of the state. These elements also form the basis for the construction in Chapter 6 of a subnationalism index, which is used to assess the cohesiveness of subnational identification across all major Indian states, including Tamil Nadu, Kerala, UP, and Rajasthan, from the 1960s to the 2000s (see Figure 6.2).

This chapter consists of four sections corresponding to each of my four case study states, in which I highlight, in turn, the historical chronology of factors, summarized in Figure 3.1, that have led to the differences in the strength of subnationalism, summarized in Table 3.1.

TAMIL NADU

Brahmin Dominance

At the beginning of the twentieth century in the Madras Presidency, Brahmins constituted approximately 3 percent of the population but exercised dispropor-tionate control over the political, economic, and social life of the province. But this region that came to constitute the state of Tamil Nadu had not historically been characterized by a strict Brahminical caste system. Prior to the twentieth century, the distribution of honors in Tamil society was not determined purely on the basis of one's position in the ritual hierarchy but instead reflected the

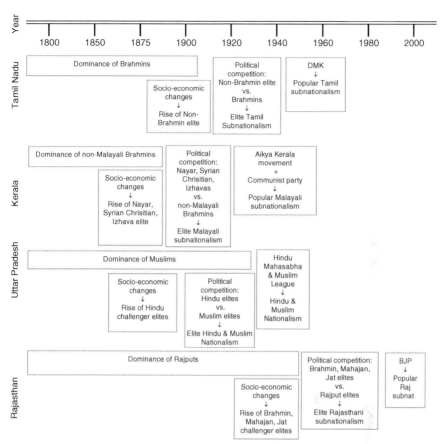

FIGURE 3.1. The Emergence of Subnationalism in Tamil Nadu, Kerala, UP, and Rajasthan.

achievement of wealth and power (Washbrook 1990: 243). Brahmins did not enjoy an exalted status in relation to other castes; rather Brahmins, especially poor Brahmins, were obliged to show deference toward lower castes of a sufficiently high economic status (Barnett 1976: 25). As early as the fourteenth century, land-owning *Shudra* castes shared local authority with Brahmins. Members of these wealthy cultivator castes enjoyed a "special relationship" with, and structural position close to, Brahmins (16). The gradual strengthening of British control over the Madras Presidency during the nineteenth century, however, disrupted this traditional power sharing between Brahmins and wealthy non-Brahmins.

British rule provided Brahmins the opportunity to acquire political, economic, and social dominance, particularly in urban areas. The expansion of the British administrative apparatus created a new urban profession. Radhakrishnan (1992) notes, "With their scribal background, Brahmins were

TABLE 3.1. *The Strength of Subnationalism in Case Study States*

	Tamil Nadu	Kerala	UP	Rajasthan
i. Language	Tamil	Malayalam	Hindi (many dialects), Urdu	Hindi (many dialects), Rajasthani
a. Single language	Tamil was one of the primary languages of Madras Presidency. 1950s: Tamil is the only official language of Tamil Nadu.	Malayalam was the only official language of the princely states of Travancore and Cochin. 1950s: Malayalam is the only official language of Kerala.	1837: Urdu replaces Persian as official language of United Provinces. 1900: Hindi and Urdu granted equal status. 1951: Hindi declared only official language of UP; Urdu stripped of official status. 1989: Urdu granted official language status after decades of protests; controversial decision; legal challenges continue.	Different dialects of Hindi (for example Marwari, Mewari, etc.) were official languages of different princely states of Rajputana. 1950s: Hindi is the only official language of Rajasthan. Efforts under way to designate Rajasthani as the official language.
b. Common language	85%	93%	72% Hindi, 9% Urdu	58% Hindi
c. Distinctive language	Tamil is the official and majority language only in Tamil Nadu	Malayalam is the official and majority language only in Kerala	Hindi is the official and majority language of 3 other Indian provinces. Urdu has official language status in one other Indian province.	Hindi is the official and majority language of 3 other Indian provinces. Rajasthani is unique to Rajasthan.
ii. Subnational Mobilization	Tamil nationalist movement (1940s–60s)	Aikya Kerala movement (1920–1950s)	X	X

iii. Separatist Movement	X	X	Movement for carving out of separate state of Uttarakhand from the hill districts of UP since 1920s. Successful in 2001. Proposal in UP legislative assembly in Nov 2011 to divide state into 4 new states (Awadh Pradesh, Poorvanchal, Budelkhand, and Pashchim Pradesh)	X
iv. Subnationalist parties	DMK, AIADMK	Communist Party of India (Marxist)	X	BJP (since the late 1980s, early 1990s)

the first to realize that under the colonial dispensation, English education was the key to government employment." As a result of their "eager acquisition" of a Western education, Brahmins flooded the state service, and as these positions increased in importance with the consolidation of British rule, so the Brahmins' political power was augmented (Radhakrishnan 1992: 4). The extent of the Brahmins' political supremacy is evidenced by the fact that in 1855, they constituted 90 percent of all district chiefs and occupied 78 percent of all district administration positions. In 1911, they held 70 percent of all government jobs (ibid. 19). The Brahmins also came to dominate the Congress party, which in the late nineteenth and early twentieth centuries emerged as one of the premier political organizations in the Madras Presidency. In addition to this increased political authority, changes in property laws strengthened Brahmins' economic position by giving them "an independent material base" and thereby breaking "their dependence upon the patronage of politically dominant non-Brahmin groups" (Washbrook 1990: 243). British law, which was heavily influenced by the notion of a uniformly Brahminical Hindu culture across India, also drastically altered the nature of intercaste relations in the Madras Presidency by fixing Brahmins at the apex of a historically contested and fluid social hierarchy (Washbrook 1990: 242).

Socioeconomic Changes Encourage Resurgence of Challenger "Non-Brahmin" Elites

At the turn of the twentieth century, Brahmins therefore occupied a position of singular political, economic, and social privilege. However, insofar as Brahmin political power was concentrated in cities and landowning non-Brahmins continued to wield control over rural areas, these two groups had distinct spheres of influence and did not directly compete with each other. This changed in the early 1900s when in response to a combination of "push" and "pull" factors, elites from wealthy non-Brahmin castes began to migrate to cities in search of political power. The nineteenth century was a period of economic buoyancy in the Madras Presidency. Agriculture was marked by an expanding productive base and increasing profitability. The opening up of Southeast Asia through imperialism had provided unique earning opportunities for more than 1.5 million Tamilians who worked there as laborers, bankers, and merchants in the late 1890s and early 1900s (Washbrook 1990: 244). These developments resulted in an improved financial position for a number of laboring castes who began to purchase land, usually from landholding non-Brahmins (Kumar 1998: 53). The decrease in the size of their landholdings through sale and/or partition among family members served as an impetus for wealthy non-Brahmin castes to move away from the countryside. They were also pulled to the cities because of the infiltration of modern occupational preferences to the countryside and, crucially, because of the enactment of policies by the British government to encourage recruitment of members of non-Brahmin castes to government service in light of growing concerns over Brahmin monopoly (Barnett 1976: 28).

Beginning in the 1850s, the British gradually became aware of the danger of the concentration of all administrative power in the hands of Brahmins. In the 1870s, the Census Superintendent of Madras W. R. Cornish "counseled the government that politically it was not to its advantage to view every question connected with the progress of the country through 'Brahman spectacles' and that its true policy would be to limit their numbers in official positions and encourage a larger proportion of non-Brahmin Hindus and Muslims so as to allow no special preeminence or great preponderance of any particular caste" (Radhakrishnan 1992: 7–8). In 1879, the Collector of Tanjore wrote, "It is one great misfortune of our administration that we should have already made such men our masters to a great extent" (cited in Irschick 1969: 19–20).

Through the closing years of the nineteenth and early years of the twentieth century, the Board of Revenue passed orders that aimed to loosen Brahmin control over government positions by reserving positions for non-Brahmins.[1] As a result, there was a surge of members of wealthy, non-Brahmin castes who moved to urban areas in pursuit of political power. City life, however, came as a rude shock to non-Brahmin elites, who suddenly found themselves socio-politically subservient to Brahmins with whom they had historically enjoyed a position of equality and often superiority in the countryside. Unexpectedly lumped into a large, undifferentiated category of ritually impure castes, these "proud, orthodox" elites from non-Brahmin castes came to realize their relatively disadvantaged position and therefore the need to strategize in their attempt to wrest political power from the dominant Brahmins (Barnett 1976: 25).

Political Competition between Challenger Non-Brahmin versus Dominant Brahmin Elites Triggers Elite Tamil Subnationalism

Members of wealthy non-Brahmin castes who had left rural occupations in pursuit of political power in the cities had traditionally identified themselves only in terms of their specific *jatis*, such as Vellalas, Nairs, and Chettiars, and had competed, often acrimoniously, with each other (and with Brahmins) for local control in the villages. In order to effectively stake a claim to greater administrative and legislative power and counter the common threat to their sociopolitical status posed by the dominant Brahmins in the cities, however, these challenger elites found it useful to mobilize around the encompassing, "symbolically synonymous" identities of non-Brahmin/ Dravidian/ Tamil

[1] In 1851, a Standing Order of the Board of Revenue was issued stating that a proportion of local revenue officers in every district be recruited from non-Brahmin communities (Irschick 1986: 30). In 1909, the Board of Revenue informed the Registrar of Cooperative Societies that "not more than one half of the total number of senior appointments in an office should ordinarily be held by Brahmins" (Radhakrishnan 1992: 16).

(Barnett 1976: 22).[2] The first clear instance of this is the formation of the Justice Party and its issuance of the Non-Brahmin manifesto in 1916. A superordinate subnational identity allowed the challenger elites not only to present a unified front of deserving "sons of the soil" but also to distinguish themselves from an undeserving, "foreign" dominant elite. The Non-Brahmin manifesto, for example, demanded increased representation for "the indigenous elements of the population" against the entrenched privilege of "foreign" Brahmins (Irschick 1986: 35). The challenger elites' decision to mobilize as Non-Brahmin/ Tamil was also influenced by the explicit endorsement of this identity by colonial administrators who, as noted earlier, were increasingly concerned by, and sought to curb, Brahmin power by promoting non-Brahmins.[3]

In their espousal of a Tamil/ Dravidian identity, the challenger elites drew upon shared symbols such as a common culture based crucially on a shared language and a rich literary heritage. *Tamilakam* is a word signifying the home of Tamil language, culture, and/or people that conveys "the internal psychic/ emotional unity of all Tamils" (Pandian 1987: 55). It has been in use since at least the first century BC and is argued to constitute the "earliest evidence of a Tamil people bearing a unique culture" (55, 25). This unique Tamil culture was rooted deeply in the Tamil language, which is one of the two longest-surviving classical languages in India. Tamil literature claims an "antique purity"[4] and

---

[2] For analytical convenience I have used the term "non-Brahmin" in the preceding discussion. It is important to note, however, that historically the term was not a relevant category. An administrative category of non-Brahmin was given sanction through British usage beginning in the mid-nineteenth century (Irschick 1986: 34). However, it was only with the emergence of the non-Brahmin/ Dravidian/ Tamil ideology and movement in the early twentieth century that this category was imbued with social and political meaning. Prior to this there were "no 'non-Brahmins' in South India," only distinct *jatis*, such as Mudaliars, Chettis, etc. (Barnett 1976). For instance, in response to the Non-Brahmin Manifesto of 1916, the *Times of India* commented that "To begin with, there is no such community as the non-Brahmin" (Pandian 2003: 1).

[3] I have noted how growing fears about excessive Brahmin influence prompted the British to institute preference policies in higher education and government employment for a non-Brahmin category beginning in the latter half of the nineteenth century. By the early twentieth century there had been little reduction in Brahmin presence in the state services. In addition, they had taken the lead in the electoral arena through the nationalist Congress party. This only exacerbated the unease of the colonial administrators, who redoubled their efforts to promote non-Brahmins in an attempt to rein in the Brahmins. Irschick writes that "All who could prove that they were 'non-Brahmin' were likely to be rewarded" (1986: 59). The influence of colonial policies on the mobilization around the non-Brahmin cleavage is evident from the fact that the Non-Brahmin manifesto quoted British bureaucrat Alexander Cardew's statement before the Public Services Commission in 1913, in which he drew attention to Brahmin dominance of the administration and stressed the necessity of increased non-Brahmin representation (Irschick 1986: 30).

[4] The Sangam literature, a body of more than 2,000 poems composed by almost 500 male and female Tamil poets from 300 BC to 600 CE, is described as "the earliest evidence of the Tamil genius" (Ramanujan 1967: 115). In fact the widely recognized literary scholar A. K. Ramanujan writes that "there is not much else in any Indian literature quite equal to these dramatic Tamil poems" (1967: 115).

continued to flourish for more than 2,000 years, but by the eighteenth century the palm-leaf manuscripts of many classic Tamil texts had been buried in private, mostly religious libraries (Pandian 1987: 47). In the nineteenth century, Christian missionaries, especially Robert Caldwell (1819–1891) and G. U. Pope (1820–1907), developed an interest in Tamil language and culture.[5] They translated, disseminated, and valorized Tamil classics and developed the theory that in pre-historic times Tamils spoke *chenthamil* (pure Tamil) and were characterized by *Saiva Sidhanta*, a philosophical and spiritual system based on the principles of universalism and social egalitarianism and opposed to religious orthodoxy. This indigenous Tamil culture, the Missionaries claimed, was destroyed by Aryan, Brahmin colonists who promoted their lingua franca, Sanskrit, and imposed a ritualistic and orthodox Vedic form of Hinduism, according to which all Tamilians were classified as "impure" and were ranked at the bottom of the caste hierarchy. The Justice Party and its successor, the Self-Respect league, drew heavily on this idea of foreign Brahmin oppression of a glorious, egalitarian Tamil/ Dravidian civilization, setting out the twin, interconnected goals of the revival of a "pure" Tamil culture and an immediate end to Brahmin dominance in the sociopolitical realms (Hardgrave 1965: 17–18).[6]

Growth of Popular Tamil Subnationalism

For the first three decades of the twentieth century, Tamil subnationalism was confined to a very tightly knit, closed clique of non-Brahmin elites. The Self-Respect movement of the 1920s led by the charismatic E. V. Ramaswamy, or Periyar as he was affectionately known, did draw in more people than its predecessor, the Justice Party, which functioned more like a gentleman's club, but it was the compulsory introduction of Hindi in schools by the Congress-led provincial government in 1938 that provided the historical opening for the emergence of a popular Tamil identity (Barnett 1976: 51). This policy was seen as an emotional affront – Hindi is a direct derivative of Sanskrit and the predominantly Brahmin government's move to make its instruction mandatory was interpreted as yet another attempt to impose "Northern Aryan Sanskritic culture over Southern Dravidian Tamil culture" (Arooran 1980: 210). It also carried a tangible, material threat of putting Tamilians at a disadvantage vis-à-vis Hindi-speaking Northerners in the competition for positions in the state bureaucracy. Periyar's able deputy, Annadurai, led an intense agitation against this policy, which mobilized thousands of disaffected urban youth who had been streaming into the cities either because they had lost their jobs overseas

[5] One of the primary reasons for this was to demonstrate that the egalitarian Christian values that they were preaching were all to be found in ancient Tamil literature (Irschick 1986: 81).

[6] The resurrection of Tamil language and culture provided non-Brahmin politicians with a rhetoric that helped them promote their political aspirations (Pandian 1987: 62). The destruction of Brahmin dominance and the ascendancy of non-Brahmins to power was in turn viewed as a vehicle for the promotion of Tamil culture.

or because their positions in the agrarian economy had been squeezed out by the Great Depression (Washbrook 1990: 244).

In 1944, under Periyar's directive, the Justice Party and the Self-Respect Union merged to form the *Dravidar Kazhagam* (DK), and in 1949, Annadurai broke away to establish a separate organization called the *Dravida Munnetra Kazhagam* (DMK).[7] The formation of the DMK marked a watershed in terms of the strength and reach of the Tamil subnationalist movement. The new organization championed the cause of a separate, independent political homeland of "Tamilnad for Tamilians" that had emerged in the wake of the anti-Hindi agitation.[8] It drew extensively on the realms of literature, public oratory, and cinema to revive/ invent legends of Tamil splendor, glorify Tamil heroes, and construct an overall narrative of a resplendent Tamil heritage, which proved to be very potent in mobilizing the populace (Price 1996: 372).

DMK leaders were key conduits for the dissemination of Tamil subnationalism. Many were very popular authors and between them published thousands of books, pamphlets, and journals "elaborating on the theme of the greatness of Tamil culture and Tamil language" (Pandian 1987: 65). The leaders of the DMK were also trained Tamil orators and transformed platform speech (*Maedai Paechu*) into a "dramatic art" (Pandian 1987: 65) that delivered powerful subnationalist messages to massive audiences, especially in rural areas which had not been penetrated by the Justice Party, the Self Respect movement, or the DK.[9] Another critical medium by which DMK leaders spread the subnationalist message was Tamil cinema, which had become the primary source of entertainment in Tamil society by the 1940s. Virtually all the top officials of the DMK were involved with the silver screen in some capacity (actors, directors, producers, script writers, music composers) and they deftly employed this unprecedentedly powerful means of communication, which reached large swaths of both the urban and rural Tamil populace, to extol Tamil values, glorify Tamil deities, and showcase the splendor of Tamil language and culture.[10]

---

[7] Subramanian notes that there was some debate regarding the use of the word "Dravidian" or "Tamil" in the party name but the former label was retained because of its evocation of a "great tradition" in contradistinction to and more glorious than Aryan civilization (Subramanian 1999: 138).

[8] It is interesting to note here, following Subramanian, the subtle modification to the name of the organization – the *Dravidar* Kazhagam referred to a group of people (the Dravidians) while the new name *Dravida* Munnetra Kazhagam referred to a country (Dravidam), and exemplified the vision of a linguistically defined, territorially rooted nation (Subramanian 1999: 142).

[9] An informant of Price recalled that "The DMK leaders were young, curly-haired, spoke in beautiful Tamil. When they heard Anna calling 'You, the self-respecting Tamil! Rise and come on!' everyone wanted to [follow] behind Anna" (1996: 373).

[10] The most notable in this regard was MG Ramachandran, an important figure in the DMK, who broke away to form the Anna DMK (ADMK), named after Annadurai in 1972, and is widely regarded as the most popular of Tamil film heroes and politicians. MGR's films were lush with subnationalist slogans, for example, in the blockbuster *Nadodi Mannan*, MGR's character sings, "Not to be afraid is the passion of Dravidians ... And our duty is to protect the (Tamil) nation."

Scholars concur that through the 1950s and 1960s there was a "mass internalization of Tamil identity" (Barnett 1976: 89). In the early 1950s, the DMK spearheaded a subnationalist movement for the creation of a Tamil-speaking state of Tamil Nadu, which "strengthened the political salience of linguistic bonds and solidified linguistic identities along Tamil Nadu's borders" (Subramanian 1999: 159). There was widespread popular involvement with this movement – thousands showed up to public meetings and scores of memoranda were submitted to the States Reorganization Commission. The extent to which subnationalism had taken root among the masses is also evidenced by the scale and intensity of the agitations – at least a dozen protesters immolated themselves – led by the DMK against the declaration of Hindi as the official language of India in the 1960s. It is notable that the DMK's renunciation of the secessionist demand and its almost seamless shift to the objective of increased autonomy for Tamil Nadu within the Indian union during these years did not diminish its popular appeal.[11] Just a decade after it made the transition from a subnationalist movement to a subnationalist political party and joined the electoral fray, the DMK won an overwhelming victory in the state elections of 1967.

Since its assumption of political power, the DMK, and in later years, its splinter subnationalist party, the Anna DMK (ADMK), have played an important role in sustaining popular Tamil subnationalism through the institutionalization of policies that lionize Tamil culture and also the espousal of demands for greater autonomy. One of the introductory acts of the DMK when it first came to power was to change the name of the state from Madras to Tamil Nadu (the land of the Tamils) and translate the motto of the state government from Sanskrit into Tamil. The government followed a self-declared policy of "Tamil everywhere and at all times." Quotes from Tamil classics were displayed prominently in public places, all signage was mandated to be in Tamil, and names of places were 'Tamilized' (for example, All India Radio became Madras Vanoli Nilayam) (Narain 1976: 433). In 1968, the World Tamil Conference was organized with great fanfare and provided a perfect opportunity for an "aggressive flaunting of the Tamil ego" (Spratt 1970: 78).[12] In 1970, the DMK instituted a poem in praise of Tamilttay, the "Goddess of Tamil," as the state "prayer song" (Ramaswamy 1993). The exaltation of Tamilttay was part of a trend of the

[11] Annadurai explained the dropping of the secessionist demand in terms of the need for national unity in the wake of the Chinese aggression in 1962 (Narain 1967: 468), but most scholars see this as a convenient justification insofar as the demand had begun to be gradually but steadily deemphasized in earlier years. Spratt notes that "some observers have indeed suspected that the demand for secession was never entirely serious; it was an expression of emotion, not a considered political proposal" (1970: 47).

[12] This conference went on to become a key arena where the DMK and ADMK competed to present their subnational credentials. To this date each party attempts to outdo the other in the pomp and splendor with which the greatness of the Tamil civilization is showcased at this gala conference.

state government's celebration of mythical or historical Tamil figures, such as the poet-philosopher Thiruvalluvar.

Both the DMK and the ADMK have been consistent and committed advocates of greater rights for the provinces. During the 1950s, the DMK had moved away from Periyar's militantly anti-Brahmin and atheistic formulation to a more inclusive, theistic articulation of the Tamil subnation, which emphasized the equal membership of all Tamil-speakers irrespective of caste or religion (Subramanian 1999: 136). The focus of opposition was gradually and deliberately moved away from Tamil Brahmins to the central government. Tamil Brahmins were now less Brahmins and more Tamil; New Delhi, which was portrayed as seeking to subvert a glorious Dravidian culture with corrupting Aryan influences, such as the introduction of Hindi, replaced the Tamil Brahmins as the new "other." Despite, or perhaps because of their abandonment of the secessionist demand, from the 1960s to the 1980s Tamil subnationalist parties were fierce espousers of state autonomy from New Delhi.[13]

Tamil subnationalism is today firmly embedded in both elite and popular consciousness and clearly visible in the media, popular literature, the rhetoric and action of political leaders, and in the signage, slogans, statues, and symbols in public spaces. In recent years, with the fragmentation of the national political system and the growing importance of regional parties, both the DMK and ADMK have at various times been in coalition with national parties but this has not dampened their subnationalist edge. Even when they have been part of coalition governments in New Delhi, DMK and ADMK politicians have acted as representatives of Tamil Nadu and the Tamil people. In 2008, for example, the DMK threatened to withdraw its support from the Congress-led coalition government in New Delhi that it had been part of from 2004 because of the issue of the perceived lack of a strong censure, on the part of the national government, of the Sri Lankan state's atrocities against Tamils in their attack on the LTTE (Economist 2008). In the state elections in Tamil Nadu in 2001, the DMK's membership in a national government that condoned the mistreatment of Tamils was one of the main issues on which the ADMK had campaigned against and eventually defeated the party (Rajan 2013).

Further, it is important to place Tamil subnationalism in the context of recent mobilization in the state by *dalit* organizations, on the one hand, and the Hindu right on the other. There is some debate between scholars who emphasize the pluralist, inclusive nature of the Dravidian movement[14] and those

---

[13] In 1969 the then Chief Minister Karunanidhi appointed the Rajamanar Committee to examine the question of center-state relations, which recommended that state governments be given full responsibility for all issues except defense, foreign affairs, communication, currency, and inter-state relations. In 1970, the DMK went on to organize an "Autonomy Fair," which among other things demanded a separate flag for Tamil Nadu "to secure a distinctive identity for the state in the federal set up" (Narain 1976:435).

[14] Subramanian, an important representative of this view, for example, writes that "Although the backward castes were important in the DMK's discourse and support base, the party differed

that point to the Dravidian movement's perceived prioritization of backward caste interests and discrimination against, and violent oppression of *dalits* as an important cause for the rise of *dalit* mobilization since the 1990s. What is notable, however, is that while on the one hand, the *dalit* movement has, like in UP, espoused a radical rhetoric and engaged in symbolism such as the installation of Ambedkar statues, it has also on the other hand, unlike in UP, mobilized *within* rather than against Tamil subnationalism. *Dalit* parties have portrayed themselves as the true defenders of Tamil subnationalism, which the Dravidian parties are indicted for having betrayed. In a speech quoted in Gorringe (2005: 17), for instance, an important *Dalit* leader cited the *dalit* movement as the "true heirs of Periyar" and criticized the DMK for abandoning the secessionist demand for an independent Dravidian land and for not doing enough for the promotion of the Tamil language. Both *dalit* mobilization and the engagement and response by the dominant backward castes has occurred within the overarching idea of an equally valued, imagined community of Tamils. Similarly, the recent attempts of the Hindu right to gain a foothold in Tamil politics have revolved centrally around their appropriation of Tamil subnationalism. Commentators have been quick to point out the "new-found love for Tamil language, history and icons" being evinced by the BJP and its volunteer wing, the Rashtriya Swayamsevak Sangh (RSS) (cited in Gnanagurunathan 2015).[15]

KERALA

Brahmin Dominance

Around the mid-nineteenth century, Kerala was characterized by a pattern similar to that of Tamil Nadu at the beginning of the twentieth century – Brahmins, in particular non-Malayali Tamil Brahmins, constituted just over 1 percent of the total population but exercised overwhelming social, economic, and political

significantly from 'backward casteist' organizations aiming to promote the interests of particular castes or caste coalitions, such as caste associations and parties like the Socialist Party in Bihar and UP until the 1970s, and the Janta Party, Samajvadi Janta Party, and Rashtriya Janta Dal in these states later. The DMK differed from such organizations as it incorporated caste and other categories within a vision of a popular community, which gave it a broader potential base and more strategic flexibility, and therefore greater and more durable success. It had an ambivalent relationship with Tamil Nadu's backward casteist organizations and enjoyed limited early success in regions where it emphasized appeals to particular backward castes" (1999: 142).

[15] In 2014 BJP MP Tarun Vijay, the former editor of the RSS mouthpiece, *Panchajanya*, asserted that "India will be incomplete without Tamil." Vijay called for the celebration of Thiruvalluvar Day as a national holiday and demanded that "biographies of revolutionary Tamil poet Subramaniya Bharathi and Thiruvalluvar should be made compulsory in colleges and schools all over India and read by every Indian" (cited in Gnanagurunathan 2015). In 2014 the BJP and the RSS also announced a year-long celebration to mark the 1,000th anniversary of the coronation of great Tamil king Rajendra Chola.

authority in the region.[16] In contrast to Tamil Nadu, however, Brahmins occupied an unquestionably supreme position at the apex of what was widely regarded as the most rigid and oppressive caste hierarchy of all Indian states (Cherian 1999: 476). This entitled non-Malayali Brahmins not only to high veneration and complete social subservience but also to a range of more tangible benefits, such as free meals and exemption from capital punishment or rigorous imprisonment – extended by a Hindu state to its most holy class (Jeffrey 1976: 112–13).[17] Non-Malayali Brahmins also tended to be economically privileged, with a number of them involved in the lucrative professions of trade and money lending.[18] Finally, and most critically, the non-Malayali Brahmins dominated the highest echelons of power in the princely states that were united to form Kerala.

Up until the mid-eighteenth century, most military and administrative positions were occupied by members of the Nair caste.[19] The non-Malayali Brahmins rose to power when the king Martanda Varma launched a ruthless and successful campaign to crush rebellious Nair chiefs. Unsurprisingly, in his new administration Varma promoted "dependent, dependable" non-Malayali Brahmins over the refractory Nairs (Jeffrey 1976: 3).

In addition to their knowledge of English and the workings of the British administration, non-Malayali Brahmins were doubly useful to a state ruled in trust for a Hindu deity insofar as they could perform religious functions and accompany the Maharaja to temples, which Nairs, who were *Sudras* and therefore carried a degree of contamination to Brahmin priests, could not (Jeffrey 1976: 8). The Dewanship, the highest administrative office in the state, which had traditionally been the stronghold of the Nairs, was held by non-Malayali Brahmins continuously from 1817 to 1877 (Jeffrey 1976: 6).

[16] The native Malayali Namboodiri Brahmins numbered "no more than a few thousand" and in stark contrast to the non-Malayali Brahmins resident in Kerala, remained almost entirely immersed in the preservation of their ritual status (by many accounts the highest of all Brahmins across India) and took "little part in public life" (Nossiter 1982, p. 27). As late as 1982, Nossiter (27) noted that "perhaps no caste in India has proved so resistant to change, preserving its ritual status in disregards of its material privileges." A notable exception to this was EMS Namboodiripad.

[17] In the 1880s, thousands of Brahmins ate for free daily in the 42 *uttupuras* or feeding houses provided by the state. The management of the *uttupuras* was considered one of the most important functions of the state and in 1864–65, for example, the Travancore government spent as much as 7.6% of the total state expenditure on this (Kawashima 1998: 24).

[18] According to Jeffrey, a third of the Trivandrum merchants listed in the Travancore Almanac for 1881 were non-Malayali Brahmins who dealt primarily in rice, cloth, and tobacco (1976: 112).

[19] Bayly (1984) points out that the Syrian Christians also held posts as warriors, brokers, and office-holders in the state bureaucracy during the eighteenth century and enjoyed a high social and ritual position equivalent to a high Nair subcaste; this position, however, declined during the early nineteenth century.

Socioeconomic Changes Encourage Rise of Challenger Nair, Syrian Christian, and Izhava Elites

Around the mid-nineteenth century, the region witnessed a range of key socio-economic changes (Jeffrey 1976) – in the social realm, a material and ideo-logical challenge to the caste system, and the availability of opportunities for western education, both in large part due to the activities of the Christian missionaries; in the economic sphere, changes in agriculture and trade; and in the political domain, the introduction of merit, rather than ritual status, as the key criterion for recruitment in the state administration. These social, economic, and political changes fostered the resurgence, from the Nair and Syrian Christian communities, and rise, from the Izhava community, of a set of "challenger" elites, who came to challenge the established dominance of the non-Malayali Brahmins.

The activities of Protestant Christian missionaries who had arrived in the region in the early nineteenth century were key to the undermining of the caste system. First, the missionaries' propagation of the idea that all were equal in the eyes of God struck at the creedal bedrock of the caste system and paved the way for the questioning of this religiously sanctioned hierar-chy. In addition to laying the foundation for such an ideological challenge, the missionaries actively espoused lower caste causes, such as the abolition of slavery, and fueled lower caste rebellions, notably the agitations by Nadar women for the right to cover their breasts. The relentless campaigning by the missionaries gave the Travancore state "a bad name" with the British administration in the neighboring Madras presidency (Jeffrey 1976: 265). By the 1860s, Travancore was "notorious for its misrule" and faced a very real threat of annexation by Madras (Kawashima 1998: 35). Further, the government of Travancore itself began to regard the conversion of the low-est castes to Christianity as a grave threat to the stability of the Hindu state (Kawashima 1998: 153). Consequently, the Travancore state embarked on a set of "modernizing efforts" under a young and revolutionary new Dewan, Madhav Rao, from the 1860s onward, which resulted in the gradual abolition of a number of caste-based restrictions, including slavery, forced labor, restrictions on the lifestyle choices (clothing, housing), and access to courts of law and public roads (Jeffrey 1976: 265). As a result of opposition from upper castes, especially non-Malayali Brahmins, some of these poli-cies remained a dead letter, but scholars concur that caste-based disabilities gradually diminished toward the end of the nineteenth century, though they still prevailed in many places (Kawashima 1998: 153).

In addition to weakening the hold of a centuries-old, ritual hierarchy on the minds of lower castes and reducing the state-sanctioned disabilities that they had historically faced, Christian missionaries also provided lower castes with their first access to a "western education." Missionaries established the first English schools in the region, and in contrast to state schools, which were mostly restricted to upper castes at this time, they opened the doors of these schools to all students irrespective of caste (Jeffrey 1976: 144). This access to English education was an important factor in the emergence of an elite from lower castes such as the Izhavas.

These developments in the social sphere were paralleled by key economic changes, particularly in agriculture and trade. The abolition of caste-based agrestic slavery; the "*Pattam* proclamation" of 1865, which granted the predominantly lower caste tenants ownership rights over 200,000 acres of state-owned *pattam* land; and the swift move from subsistence to commercial farming, fostered unprecedented economic mobility across caste lines. Lower castes, especially the Izhavas, witnessed the emergence of a landowning class and Syrian Christians became "increasingly affluent" (Kawashima 1998: 6). The second half of the nineteenth century was also marked by a rapid rise in foreign trade. Due to the growing European demand for products such as coir and coconut oil, the value of exports of coconut products more than doubled between 1870 and 1890 (Jeffrey 1976: 139). This upswing in the international trade in coconut products was matched by a hike – according to Jeffrey (141), a doubling – of the domestic trade in toddy and arrack, indigenous alcohols brewed from coconuts. The tending and tapping of coconut palms was the traditional occupation of the Izhavas. They were, hence, particularly well placed to take advantage of these developments. By the closing decades of the nineteenth century, a substantial amount of money had flowed to the hands of the Izhava community (Wilkinson 2004: 179).

These social and economic changes impacted different groups in different ways. In general, however, they gave rise to an English-educated, upwardly mobile elite from across the three most numerous communities of the state – the Nairs, Syrian Christians and the lower caste Izhavas – who now began to aspire to positions of political power. The administrative reforms in the 1860s, initiated as part of the modernizing efforts that were undertaken in response to the pressure from the colonial government of the Madras presidency, mentioned earlier, presented precisely such an opportunity. The new recruitment policy emphasized educational qualifications rather than one's position in the caste hierarchy as the criterion for selection to the state administrative service. For the first time in the history of the state, political power was now potentially accessible to members of all castes and communities. Elites from various groups, notably the Nairs, Syrian Christians, and Izhavas, vigorously staked their claims.

The leading contenders were the Nair elites who sought to reestablish their political preeminence. The social and economic changes of the mid-nineteenth century had been a double-edged sword for the Nairs. While many members of the community did gain access to a western education, social changes such as the spread of western values and economic changes – crucially, the granting of ownership rights to tenants – disrupted the Nairs' traditional matrilineal way of life and collective control over property. To counter their relative decline in prosperity, Nairs therefore "more than ever needed to find extensive employment in the government" (Jeffrey 1976: 154). Syrian Christians had traditionally enjoyed many of the social and ritual privileges of the Nairs, and from the fifteenth till the late eighteenth century, had also played a central role as warriors and officeholders in the functioning of the state. They, however, lost this privileged position during the early nineteenth century and were transformed instead into a "body of outsiders" shunned as ritually polluting and virtually excluded from government service in the Hindu state (Bayly 1984: 201). The Syrian Christians were, in general, a wealthy group – their origins were commercial and they continued to specialize in maritime and hinterland trade, benefitting monetarily from the development of a cash economy; they had also historically enjoyed a higher standard of education. They thus sought a political position commensurate with their educational and economic status. The third main set of elites who competed for the new administrative openings belonged to the Izhava caste that had historically been explicitly banned from the government service because of their "polluting" status. By the late nineteenth century, in large part due to the activities of the Christian missionaries, the Izhavas had managed to end most socioeconomic caste-based disabilities traditionally imposed on them, and some had acquired a western education. Changes in agriculture and trade had led to a rise in the financial resources of the caste as a whole, and the prosperity of some members. Izhava "pretensions, assertiveness and frustration were growing" and they were vociferous in demanding representation in the state services (Jeffrey 1976: 145).

Political Competition between Challenger Nair, Syrian Christian, and Izhava versus Dominant Brahmin Elites Triggers Elite Malayali Subnationalism

Nayar, Syrian Christian, and Izhava elites' pursuit of positions of political power brought them into competition with each other. These elites mobilized around caste and religious identities, competing zealously and at times bitterly for positions in the government service. Very soon, however, these challenger elites realized that the most effective strategy to gain greater political power was to come together under a superordinate identity that included all of them as "in-group" members and also simultaneously allowed them to "other" their common, powerful enemy, the non-Malayali Brahmins. A Malayali identity was found to be especially useful in this regard. The challenger elites' espousal of a Malayali identity as a means to strengthen their position in their political competition with the non-Brahmins was facilitated by the prominence of common cultural and linguistic traditions. The geographic isolation imposed by the Western Ghats, the mountain range that cuts off Kerala from the Tamil and Kannada-speaking areas in the east, had historically fostered the development of a shared and unique Malayali culture (Jeffrey 1976). The challenger elites drew on and used these subnational symbols including a myth of common

origin; shared heroes; Malayalam literature; and art forms[20] – toward the creation of a "cohesive, named" 'Malayali' community (Arunima 2006: 75).[21]

This process is exemplified by the "Malayali Memorial," a joint petition
by more than 10,000 Nairs, Syrian Christians, and Izhavas for greater native
representation in the civil services submitted to the Travancore government
in 1891. Each of these sets of elites had previously submitted petitions as representatives of their individual caste and/or religious groups that had for the
most part been ignored by the Travancore government. They calculated, correctly, that a collective, subnational Malayali challenge on the part of elites
from the most prominent communities, together representing more than half of
the state's population, would be far more difficult for the government to ignore
(Jeffrey 1976: 168).[22]

[20] The legend about the creation of Kerala that became popular at this time is that the sage
Parasurama flung his axe into the sea; the water receded and the land of Kerala emerged
(Aiya 1906; 210–12). The art forms of Kathakali, Koothu, Theyyam and the martial art of
Kalaripayattu were promoted as cultural forms "distinct from other parts of the world but as
common for the people of Kerala" (Thanickan 2006). Kathakali, for instance, was seen as integrating "rituals extending from south Canara to the southern Kerala and even the Christian
and Muslim elements ... to become a national art form transcending ... caste-bound ritual-
ism" (Cherian 1999). Namboodiripad, a leading subnationalist who also went on to head the
Communist party in the state, wrote evocatively about the "national literature" of Kerala. The
Kerala Mahatmyam and *Keralolpatti*, two works of the seventeenth century "which mix history,
mythology and speculation are usually taken to indicate the birth of a 'national' or regional
consciousness" (Nossiter 1982: 13). Referring to the rich Malayali traditions of painting, archi-
tecture, vocal and orchestral music and theatre, Namboodiripad went on to write that "the
artists who developed these art forms and the audiences attracted by them, have together created through generations, a sum total of cultural sensitiveness that has come to be a part of the
distinctive psychological make-up of the Malayali" (1952: 56).

[21] Until the 1870s, the term Malayali was used to refer only to members of the Nair caste. Arunima
notes that the Malayali Social Union, founded in 1877 in Trivandrum (which later gave way to
the Malayali Sabha and brought out a newspaper called Malayali), was seen as a Nair organization (2006: 75). During the closing years of the nineteenth century, there was a broadening of the
scope of the term from an exclusively caste appellation to a broader linguistic identity (Arunima
2006). The activation of a national Malayali identity in opposition to "foreign" Sanskritic
Brahmins fostered a language purification movement that sought to "cleanse" Malayalam of an
excess of "polluting" Sanskrit words. Arunima notes that as early as 1892, C. D. David, a newspaper columnist, called for increased pride in the language, writing that "Malayalam language
is the equal right of everyone in the *Malayala rajyam* ('nation of Malayalis') ... and must be
treated as a community wealth" (2006: 71).

[22] Such elite calculations are brought out clearly by Jeffrey's description of the way in which the
Nairs, the initiators of the Malayali Memorial, went about gathering support from the Syrian
Christians and Izhavas: "Given the need for numbers, for signatures, for leading articles and
eventually for public meetings, it became imperative to have allies and present the appearance
of a 'national' movement. A memorial presented by ... Nairs, complaining about the exclusion
of Nairs from public service would have been unconvincing and easily brushed aside ... (they)
therefore, went out to capture allies. In Madras P. Palpu, the young Izhava medical graduate was
recruited ... In the same way (they) assiduously courted ... Romo-Syrians" (1976: 167). Jeffrey
goes on to note that the "trick" was to "make the signatories appear representative of a large

In addition to invoking and valorizing a unifying Malayali identity, the challenger elites also sought to portray foreign Brahmins as the enemies of all Malayalis. Jeffrey's survey of regional newspapers through the 1880s brings out the discrediting and demonizing of foreign Brahmins – the general argument ran that not having to worry about subsistence owing to the free feeding houses, the non-Malayali Brahmins "devoted all their energies to surpassing and exploiting Malayalis"; the Madras Standard, for instance, described the Brahmins as "sucking the life blood of the country" (1976: 114). The local press was replete with complaints about the employment of "deceitful and treacherous" foreigners over honest, deserving natives in public service (Jeffrey 1976: 111, 4).

It is important to note here, in line with the constructivist literature on multiple identities, that this incipient elite Malayali subnationalism coexisted with identification and mobilization around caste and religion. As a scholar of Kerala notes, caste and religion and a broader Malayali identity "were not oppositional, neither did one erase the other" (Arunima 2006: 75). Nair, Syrian Christian, and Izhava elites invoked a subnational identity but did not give up their caste or religious allegiances. Shortly after the Malayali Memorial, in 1896 the Izhavas submitted a separate petition protesting discrimination against members of their caste. In 1903, in what Wilkinson (2004: 179) terms the "most important single act of lower-caste mobilization," the Izhava social reformer Sri Narayan Guru founded the Sri Narayana Guru Dharam Paripalana Yogam (SNDP), which worked for the reform of regressive caste rules and fought for greater sociopolitical rights for the community, including notably the right to enter temples. Izhava mobilization was matched by the Nairs, who set up their own caste association, the Nair Service Society (NSS), in 1914. The closing years of the nineteenth and early years of the twentieth century also witnessed the politicization of the very lowest castes in the region, the "untouchable" Pulayas and Parayas, who organized under their leader Aiyankali, for an end to a range of outstanding disabilities.

These movements, especially those by the lower castes, may be seen as representing, in Anderson's terms "a weakening of the belief that society was naturally organized hierarchically or centripetally," which, according to him was necessary for "the very possibility of imagining the nation" (1991: 36). Caste mobilization may thus be seen as facilitating subnational mobilization by enhancing the receptivity of the people to the idea of an equal, horizontal political community of all Malayalis. The existence of a subnational identity at the elite level in turn reined in the potential for conflict inherent in caste and religious mobilization. There was intercaste and inter-religious competition and, occasionally, conflict in Kerala, but this was greatly limited, as compared

---

and aggrieved Travancore majority, yet to exclude non-Malayali Brahmins like Rama Rao, the Dewan, who had been born in Travancore and lived most of their lives there" (1976: 168).

with similar mobilizations in other parts of India, because elites from these different communities also identified with an overarching Malayali subnation.[23]

Growth of Popular Malayali Subnationalism

Until the late 1920s, Malayali subnationalism was strongest among elites. The increasingly likely prospect of the creation of linguistic states in postcolonial India served as the historical opening for the spread of Malayali subnationalism to the people at large.

The Congress party, which had supported the principle of linguistic states since the beginning of the twentieth century, signaled a strong commitment to the policy by discarding British provinces as its organizational unit and restructuring itself on linguistic lines in 1921. It reiterated its commitment through official endorsements in subsequent decades. Around this time, the transition from colonial to Congress rule at the all-India level was also looming ever larger on the political horizon. As in the case of Tamil Nadu, the prospect of the formation of a Malayali state was appealing to a range of elites because of its potential benefits, notably greater access to positions of political and administrative power. But, as is evident from the memoranda submitted to the SRC, which will be discussed further in the next chapter, it was appealing at least equally because of the powerful emotional desire to see all Malayali-speaking people who were at the time divided across three different administrative units, the princely states of Travancore, Cochin and British controlled Malabar, united within a single homeland. The demand for a single Malayali-speaking state was spearheaded by a powerful subnationalist movement, the *Aikya Kerala* or United Kerala movement, which emerged in the 1920s and gained strength in subsequent decades. The *Aikya Kerala* movement was characterized by the passage of resolutions and the organization of public meetings[24] as well as the publication of histories and poems and composition of anthems glorifying the Malayali nation and demanding the creation of a "United Keralam."[25] A range

---

[23] For a distinct but related study that I have conducted of how identification with an encompassing Indian national identity can encourage inter-ethnic cooperation, in particular pro-social behavior on the part of Hindus towards Muslims, see Charnysh, Lucas and Singh 2015.

[24] In April 1928 a State Peoples' Conference in Cochin passed an *Aikya Kerala* resolution. Through the 1920s and 1930s, the Kerala Pradesh Congress Committee (KPCC) passed resolutions requesting the central Congress leadership to work toward the institution of Kerala as a separate province in the constitution of independent India. The KPCC passed resolutions in favor of a United Kerala in Malabar in 1928, Vadakara in 1930, and Kozhikode in 1935. Since its formation in 1941, the Cochin State Praja Mandalam emphasized the need for a United Kerala in each of its annual meetings. There was a slight lull in the movement during the years immediately preceding India's independence but it picked up shortly thereafter. A massive *Aikya Kerala* meeting, inaugurated by the Maharaja of Cochin and attended by more than 7,000 people, was organized at Trichur in 1947. In the following years, similar conferences were held at Alwaye and Palghat to press for the demand.

[25] In 1924, K. P. Padmanabha Menon published his scholarly *History of Kerala*, covering the history of Travancore, Cochin, and Malabar. In 1927, the Kerala Society for scholarly discussion

of sociocultural associations which were not directly involved with the *Aikya Kerala* movement, such as the All Kerala Theeya Youth League, Kerala Kalidasa Memorial Society, Kerala Literary Conference, Kerala Women National Service Society, All Kerala Women's League, and even the Kerala Hindu Maha Sabha, deliberately adopted, as is evident from their names, a 'Kerala identity.' Periodicals published from places as distant as Kozhikode in the north, then in the district of Malabar, and Thiruvananthapuram in the south in the princely state of Travancore, also came to call themselves as *Kerala Patrika, Kerala Chintamani, Kerala Kesari, Bhaje Keralam, Malayala Rajyam, Kerala Kaumudi.* All of this played a key role in the wide dissemination of Malayali subnationalism (Thanickan 2006: 4–5).

The *Aikya Kerala* movement was a nonpartisan movement with support from both the Congress and the Communists.[26] By the 1930s, however, the Communists took over as the vanguard of the *Aikya Kerala* movement (Harrison 1960: 193). From its beginnings in the early twentieth century, a Malayali identity was an important component of left mobilization in Travancore and Cochin. Class-based organizations were organized on a pan-Kerala basis, with the Kerala Women's Teachers Association, All Kerala Labor Conference, All Kerala Trade Union commission and Kerala Students Federation being prominent examples. In Malabar in the 1930s, the socialists in the Indian National Congress – the Congress Socialist Party (CSP), who later formed the communist party in Kerala – "represented a local reaction against national identity, in view of the subordination of local politics to the exigencies of the national party" (Menon 1994, 120; cited in Devika 2010: 801). The Communist party was itself established on an explicitly subnationalist basis, with its main leader E. M. S. Namboodiripad describing it as Kerala's "national party." According to him, "from its very inception (the party) put before itself the objective of a new, united, democratic and prosperous Kerala" (Harrison 1960: 195).[27]

The disciplined and well-organized Communist cadres were important vehicles for the spread of popular Malayali subnationalism. The records of the

---

on the region's history was established. Bodheswaran's collection of poems published in 1928, *Swatantra Keralam* (Independent Kerala), included the famous *Kerala ganam* (the Kerala anthem). P. Bhaskaran's powerful poem, *One Language, One Nation*, read:

Over the fields, singing aloud, let us move,
To sound the horn of united Keralam to the world.
In our new battles, in our sacrifices,
The new Keralam that we create is beautiful.

[26] The subnationalist periodical *Mathrubhumi* (Motherland) was founded by Congress leader Keshava Menon in the 1920s. In its very first editorial he wrote, "Although Keralites, who speak the same language, share the same history and myths and follow same customs and practices, are now under four separate regimes, it is necessary for these people who live in different parts of Kerala to be kept united. Therefore, *Mathrubhumi* will continuously strive for achieving that objective."

[27] As noted earlier, EMS was himself by all accounts a staunch subnationalist with a strong interest in Kerala's history and culture. One of his first major works was *Keralam: Malayalikalude Mathrubhumi* (Kerala: The Motherland of Malayalis) published in 1948 with a revised version in English, *The National Question in Kerala*, published in 1952.

States Reorganization Commission, the body appointed to assess the demand for linguistic states in the mid-1950s, indicate that more than two hundred organizations and individuals submitted memoranda in support of the formation of a unified state of Kerala.[28]

Subnationalism has remained central to the Communists' ideology. During its terms in office beginning in the 1950s, the Communist party and also, though to a lesser extent, the Congress, with which it has been in close competition, have played an active role in further strengthening subnationalism in the state. They have done this primarily by institutionalizing the promotion of Malayalam language and literature and Malayali arts and culture. In the early 1960s, the state government declared Onam, a festival that is unique to Kerala and celebrated by all Malayalis irrespective of religion and caste, to be the "national festival" of Kerala. Since then the state has sponsored an elaborate annual celebration of this festival "for promoting emotional integration among the different sections of the population."[29] In 2005, the Kerala government, which has "always had the unique distinction of being a generous patron of art and culture," for example, allocated a whopping Rs. 15.75 crores for projects including support for the state's three colleges of music, the establishment of an Artists' Welfare Board, a building grant for a Cultural Research Centre, and the construction of a museum and commemorative tableau in honor of the "great patriot" Keralavarma Pazhassi Raja.[30]

Kerala has been characterized by a strong perception on the part of the people of themselves as "different from the rest of India" (Achutanandan 2006: 5; Namboodiripad 1952: 31). Historians claim that "The Kerala culture ... has got its own peculiar traits which mark it off from all other Indian regional cultures ... (it is) a different cultural region that set itself apart as much from the north Indian cultures as from the other south Indian cultures" (Cherian 1999). Malayali identity defines itself in exclusion to other cultures but has, within itself, been extremely inclusive across a range of potentially divisive cleavages. Malayali subnationalism has subsumed caste divisions and been equally inclusive of upper as well as lower castes.[31] Malayali subnationalism has also been

[28] List of Memoranda relating to Tamil and Malayalam speaking Areas. National Archives of India. File no. 25/13/54-SRC, Volume III. From the report of the SRC it appears that these petitions were some of the most numerous, lengthiest and intensely worded of those received across Indian states, but the incomplete nature of the records available in the National Archives of India means that it is not possible to do a comparative analysis in terms of either numbers or content across Indian states.

[29] Onam: A Festival of Kerala; Census of India, 1961, Volume 1, Monograph Series, Monograph No. 2; Part VII-B; Office of the Registrar General, India; Ministry of Home Affairs, New Delhi, p. 11.

[30] "Rs. 15.75 crores for promotion of art and culture," Hindu, January 24, 2004; available online at http://www.hindu.com/2004/01/24/stories/2004012401720500.htm.

[31] It is interesting that *Neelakkuyil* (The Blue Cuckoo, 1954), considered to be the first 'authentic' Malayalam motion picture, was a sharp and poignant critique of the caste system (Gopalakrishnan 2004).

inclusive of the state's many religious communities, which participated actively in the *Aikya Kerala* movement and representatives of whom remain prominent in the public life of the state. Namboodiripad echoed a commonly expressed sentiment when he wrote that, "There is something *particularly Malayali* about the beliefs and practices of the Namboodiri, the Syrian Christian and the Moplah, though they claim to be true followers of Brahminism, Christianity and Islam respectively" (1952: 47, emphasis added). Ethnic discrimination and competition continues to be an important feature of sociopolitical life in Kerala.[32] The electoral arena in Kerala is characterized by an intense contest between the Izhava-led Communist party and Left Democratic Front, on the one hand, and the Congress party and the United Democratic Front backed by a Nair-Christian alliance, on the other hand. Yet, as Wilkinson points out, today both the LDF and UDF are "genuinely multi-ethnic" (2004: 182). It is also important to note that, unlike many other Indian states, Kerala has a record of "relative caste harmony" (Franke and Chasin 1991: 23) and very little Hindu–Muslim violence (Varshney and Wilkinson 2006).

UTTAR PRADESH

Muslim Dominance

In the mid-nineteenth century, Muslims constituted only 13 percent of the population of the Northwestern Provinces of Agra and Awadh, as UP was called at the time, but dominated the social, political, and economic life of the province. Muslims held sway over the two most important sources of power in the province – land and government service. In the late 1800s, Muslims controlled about one-fifth of the land and 66 percent of the land revenue demand in the province (Panigrahi 2004: 75; Robinson 1974: 17). The taluqdars were widely regarded to be "by far the most powerful group of landlords in the province" (Robinson 1974: 17); Muslims owned more than 64 percent of the total taluqdari assets (Panigrahi 2004: 75). Muslims were also preponderant in the colonial administration. Government servants were "the most powerful group in nineteenth century India" and the most influential of government servants was the tahsildar (Robinson 1974: 20).[33] In 1882, Muslims held nearly 35 percent of all government posts and 55 percent of all tahsildarships (Robinson 1974: 23). They also occupied positions far in excess of their share of the population in the army, the police, and the "all-important category of the village watchman" (Brass 1974: 151). In fact until the early twentieth century, Muslims were heavily over-represented not only in the critical domains

---

[32] For a powerful, albeit fictional account, see Arundhati Roy, *The God of Small Things*.

[33] Robinson notes that "so great an influence did the tahsildar have on the well-being of the community that in 1886 the Public Service Commission declared that it is impossible that such an officer can be too well-selected" (1974: 21).

of land and government service but also, according to Brass's estimates, "in every major category of employment both in the modern urban sectors of the economy and in elite sectors of the traditional rural economy" (1974: 151). In addition to their economic and political power, Muslims also prevailed over the social and cultural life of the province. Throughout the nineteenth century, Urdu had remained the "favored form of ... expression" (Robinson 1974: 76) in the regions that came to constitute UP and was the "pre-eminent symbol of the continued dominance of the Muslim elite in ... the cultural life of the province" (Brass 1974: 156). Life in the towns of the province was suffused with Persian-Urdu etiquette and was conducted in an overwhelmingly Muslim idiom.

Muslims had dominated the economic, political, and social life of the province since the rise of the Mughal Empire in the sixteenth century but their position had been further strengthened since the rebellion of 1857. The large-scale uprising by sepoys and native rulers in 1857 had caught the British government in India by surprise, and by the accounts of colonial administrators, shaken it to its very foundations (Crawford 1908: 1). The Northwestern provinces had been the epicenter of the rebellion and Muslims had played a pioneering role in it. In the wake of the rebellion, the wary and weakened provincial government sought the support of Muslims, who continued to be powerful and therefore also potentially dangerous (Robinson 1971: 313). Muslims – "watched with care and treated with caution" (315) – became the bulwark of British rule in the province.

Socioeconomic Changes Encourage Rise of Challenger Hindu Elites

Beginning in the mid- to late nineteenth century, the province witnessed a range of socioeconomic changes, notably the growth of means of transport and communication and, associatedly, trade and the beginnings of English education, which fostered the rise of a set of economically powerful, English-speaking Hindus.

The growth of means of transport and communication, especially the railways, triggered a massive expansion of trade in the province, which tended to benefit commercial middlemen, predominantly from the Hindu merchant castes. These increasingly wealthy Hindus – by the late 1800s, they paid more than half the total income tax of the province – began to aggressively buy land and thereby challenge the traditional dominance of the Muslim landlords (Robinson 1971: 319–21). The second half of the nineteenth century also witnessed the beginnings of the government system of education with a focus on higher education in English (Robinson 1974: 36). Hindu elites tended to make much better use of this new opportunity than their Muslim counterparts. According to the historian Francis Robinson, "For the supple Hindu service groups it presented little problem; they took to English and Western learning just as their ancestors had taken to Persian and later Urdu" (1974: 37).

Muslims, on the other hand, were relatively recalcitrant in seeking a Western education. As late as 1900 almost 40 percent of Muslim students attended private schools that taught the traditional Islamic syllabus.[34]

At around this time the colonial authorities in the province were also facing mounting pressure to reform what had come to be seen as an "increasingly unworkable" system (Robinson 1974: 41). The state "did not possess a common structure or history" (Kudaisya 2007: 5); instead it consisted of disparate regions that had been clubbed together by the British through a process of conquest and annexation that extended over three-quarters of a century (Robinson 1974: 10).[35] One of the by-products of such a "piecemeal" process of formation was that, in contrast to the presidencies of Bengal, Bombay, and Madras, the United Provinces lacked an integrated system of administration (Das Gupta 1970: 85). As more regions had been added to the province, the British merely took over as the principal revenue-collecting agency, but left most of the administrative tasks in the hands of local officials (Robinson 1971: 321). The weaknesses[36] of this system were the impetus for two main reforms – first, a modification of the rules of recruitment to government service and second, the introduction of the elective principle into local government.

Like in Tamil Nadu, the British in UP had become increasingly concerned with the dominance of members of a single community over the state administration. The prevention of the formation of "cliques of relatives in public service" became one of the primary objectives of the British (Robinson 1974: 42).

---

[34] Syed Ahmed Khan, the main leader of the Muslims at this time, traced their antipathy to Western education to "political traditions, social customs and religious beliefs and poverty" (cited in Robinson 1974: 38).

[35] These geographic-cultural-linguistic regions not only had little affinity with each other but merged into the physical, cultural, and linguistic environment of neighboring states (Weiner 1967: 64). The people of the northern hill districts of Uttarakhand, for example, spoke Garhwali and Kumaoni and had greater linguistic and cultural congruity with the people of the neighboring, mountainous state of Himachal Pradesh than with the residents of the plains of UP. The people of the southern hill and plateau districts spoke Bundeli and had historically thought of themselves as belonging to the region of Bundlekhand, the greater part of which lies in the adjacent state of Madhya Pradesh. The predominantly Jat and Gujar people of the western districts of UP spoke Braj-bhasha and viewed the Jats and Gujars of neighboring Haryana and Rajasthan, rather than other residents of UP, as their kinsmen (Narain 1976: 323). The Bhojpuri speaking region of Poorvanchal blended linguistically, culturally, and geographically into the plains of Bihar to the east.

[36] This decentralized system had two main weaknesses – first, it was inefficient and second, it vested political power in cliques of local men, leaving the colonial government distant from and consequently ignorant of its subjects. These shortcomings were brought into stark relief by two sets of developments in the mid- to late nineteenth century. For a start, the British government faced recurring financial crises due to rising prices and mounting imperial debts and urgently needed more revenue to pay for the administration of the province, especially in light of the expansion of the means of transport and communication. In addition, the rebellion of 1857 had brought security to the top of the British agenda. More than ever before, British administrators needed to keep a close check on the activities of their subjects (Robinson 1974: 41). As it stood, however, the administrative system thwarted both these critical objectives of the colonial rulers.

Toward the realization of this end, they had introduced caste and communal proportions in recruitment to government service.[37] By the late 1890s, these recruitment quotas were used to actively target Muslims. Unlike his predecessors who had treated Muslims as a primary prop of British rule, the new lieutenant governor, Sir Anthony MacDonnell, perceived Muslim power as a danger to security and sought to curtail their influence by decreeing that the ratio of Muslims to Hindus throughout the government services be reduced to three from five (Robinson 1971: 322). In their attempt to replace what had come to be seen as a closed, corrupt system with an open, meritocratic administration, the British also introduced educational qualifications for recruitment to government service. Competitive exams and not family connections were now to determine employment within the government. The second reform, made in response to the severe financial crisis of the late nineteenth century and the resultant need to generate local sources of revenue through the development of local government, was the introduction of local elections. These administrative reforms simultaneously opened up unprecedented opportunities for the political advancement of Hindu elites and severely threatened the centuries-long dominance of Muslim elites, setting the stage for an intense competition for positions of political power between the two.

Political Competition between Challenger Hindu versus Dominant Muslim Elites Triggers Elite Hindu and Muslim Identification

Until the late eighteenth century, the categories described as Hindu and Muslim were "malleable, not clearly defined and marked by immense internal differentiation" (Pai 2007). While the existence of some "fundamental" religious differences is undeniable (Robinson 1974: 13),[38] much scholarship suggests that in fact the differences *within* Hindu and Muslim communities were greater than the distinctions *between* the two. Hindus and Muslims had shared many symbols such as a common spoken tongue. Through most of the nineteenth century, Hindu and Muslim masses in UP conversed in the "standard, spoken, urban language of the North," whether called Hindustani or Hindi or Urdu (Brass 1974: 129), and Hindu and Muslim elites alike used Urdu written in the Persian-Arabic script (Brass 1979: 49). Yet, in their attempt to break Muslim dominance over positions of political power, challenger Hindi elites chose to emphasize the divisive symbols of Hindi and Urdu as the distinct, exclusive, and mutually opposed mother tongues of Hindus and Muslims respectively, over potentially unifying symbols, such as Hindustani as a shared

---

[37] The reasoning behind these quotas was summed up by a government statement of 1869: "there can be no doubt that where any single element prevails to the exclusion of all others it may be both necessary and advisable to introduce the admixture of castes" (Robinson 1971: 322).

[38] Robinson (1974: 13) summarizes these differences: "The Hindus worshipped idols, the Muslims abhorred them. The Hindus had many gods, the Muslims had one. The Hindus revered the cow, the Muslims ate it."

lingua franca for the province. This was because the symbols of Hindi written in the Devanagari script allowed the challenger Hindu elites or the "new men," as they were termed (Robinson 1974: 58), to bring together an inchoate Hindu community and separate it from and advance its interests vis-à-vis the dominant Urdu-speaking Muslims.[39] In contrast, subnational symbols, such as Hindustani, united Hindus *with* Muslims rather than *against* them, and were therefore not very useful tools for challenger Hindu elites in their political competition with the dominant Muslims. The need of the hour for challenger elites was for symbols that could be used to propagate Hindu interests over Muslim interests and not ones that underscored their joint cause with their competitors.

Anxious Muslims elites, who found their traditional dominance severely threatened by the Hindi movement, in turn attempted to retain their political and social authority by championing Urdu written in the Persian script as the exclusive, official vernacular of the province and berating Hindi as nothing more than an inferior form of Urdu. The counter campaign on behalf of Urdu by Muslim elites took the form, on the one hand, of the establishment of agitational associations such as the Urdu Defense Association and the Anjuman-i-Himayat-i-Urdu, which published pamphlets and organized meetings, and on the other hand, through activities carried on by Muslim leaders from within official institutions.[40] The most notable figure in this regard is Sir Syed Ahmed Khan, the preeminent leader of the Muslims in the United Provinces at the time who had "denounced the Hindi movement and characterized it as a deliberate plan to injure Muslim interest" (Dasgupta 1970: 104). He founded the Urdu Defense Association and when he was a member of the viceroy's Legislative Council, he worked actively in defense of Urdu against Hindi. As the Hindi movement gathered strength and Hindu elites began to make their mark in municipal elections, Muslims saw British patronage as the only way for them to preserve their privileges. To justify their demand, Muslim elites stressed a special history and destiny, distinct from and incompatible with that of the Hindus (Brass 1974). Sir Syed was again at the forefront of these demands for British concessions to Muslims. The cultural and economic status of the Muslims, which according to Sir Syed, was greatly threatened by the "anti-Urdu platform of the Hindi movements" could be effectively advanced only by, on the hand, the adoption of Western education[41] and, on

---

[39] The closing decades of the nineteenth century and early decades of the twentieth century witnessed the establishment of a number of local associations for the propagation of Hindi, notably the Nagari Pracharini Sabha and the Hindi Sahitya Sammelan.

[40] The efforts by the Muslim elites in support of Urdu could not, however, prevent the admission of Hindi in Devanagari to equal position with Urdu in Persian script as the official language of the province in 1900 (Brass 1974: 132).

[41] Sir Syed led the establishment of a series of associations notably the Mohammedan Anglo-Oriental College in 1875, which in 1921 became the Aligarh Muslim University, for the popularization of Western education among Muslims.

the other, through loyalty to and the reciprocal patronage of the British. The Mohammedan Anglo-Oriental Defense Association established by Sir Syed in 1893 was the first Muslim organization to put forth the demand for separate electorates for Muslims and weightage for Muslims in any representative system, which was to become the hallmark of Muslim separatism in India (Brass 1974: 169). This separate political arena for Muslims was justified more in terms of the distinctiveness of Muslims, their past historical and political importance and their "irreconcilable antagonism" with Hindus than in demographic terms (Dasgupta 1970: 93).

Growth of Popular Hindu and Muslim Identities

Until the early twentieth century mobilization around distinct and conflicting Hindu-Hindi and Muslim-Urdu identities had been limited, for the most part, to elites from the two communities. From the 1920s onwards, however, these competing identities began to take root among the people at large through the efforts of the Hindi and Urdu associations, which also came to be closely linked to explicitly Hindu and Muslim organizations respectively.

Gandhi was acutely aware of the danger that the growing rift between Hindi and Urdu in the United Provinces posed for Hindu–Muslim relations across North India, and attempted to bridge the divide by promoting Hindustani, written in either Devanagari or Persian script, as a shared tongue (Brass 1974: 136). He believed that the distinctions between a Sanskritized Hindi and Persianized Urdu would "dry up and fade away because its support was drawn from a small circle" (cited in Dasgupta 1970: 111). Gandhi's influence led many important nationalist leaders to support and seek to popularize Hindustani. Nehru wrote how Hindustani "will help in bringing national unity...it will bring Hindi and Urdu closer together." Rajendra Prasad believed that Hindi and Urdu represented a "common heritage of both Hindus and Musalmans" (cited in Dasgupta 1970: 113). Yet these efforts of Gandhi and other prominent nationalist leaders were outpaced, and eventually foiled, by the efforts of language associations with close links to religious associations who did not believe that Hindi and Urdu could or should be brought closer together.

The primary organization for the propagation of Hindi was the Hindi Sahitya Sammelan, which was led by Madan Mohan Malaviya and P.D. Tandon, who were both closely identified with Hindu revivalism. Just a few years before he founded the Hindi Sahitya Sammelan (in 1910) Malaviya had founded the Hindu Mahasabha (in 1906). This "ultra-Hindu organization" (Vohra 2012: 151) came into prominence in the 1920s when it joined the Arya Samaj in the highly controversial *shuddhi* (purification) movement, which sought to (re)convert non-Hindus, especially Muslims, to Hinduism, as well as the *sangathan* (unification) movement "to consolidate Hindu forces" (Das Gupta 1971: 117). Similarly, the Anjuman Taraqqi-i-Urdu, the vanguard of the Urdu movement, and its leader, Abdul Haq, maintained very close ties to the Muslim League. The Khilafat movement (1919–1924), organized by Muslims across India to defend the Caliphate in the wake of the attack on the Ottoman empire after the First World War, activated a large swathe of Muslims, especially in cities. The Khilafat Movement was initially in alliance with the Congress but the alliance had broken down by 1922 and it was the Muslim League which gained the "support of the bulk of the middle as well as the lower middle classes" (Brass 1974: 169).

The crystallization of distinct and antagonistic Hindu and Muslim identities and the spread of Muslim separatism among the people of the United Provinces was also greatly strengthened by the British acceding to the demands made by Muslims elites for special concessions. Clearly buying the idea of "Muslim separateness and specialness" (Robinson 1974: 162), in 1909 the British government had instituted separate electorates for Muslims, which guaranteed them representation in greater proportion to their population. Scholars seem to concur that these separate electorates, which were extended to municipalities and district boards in UP in 1916 and 1922 respectively, in turn served to further shore up public support for the cause of a separate Muslim nation (Chakravarty 2003).[42] By the 1940s Hindu and Muslim identities were firmly embedded in the popular consciousness of UP.

It is interesting to note that this depiction of UP as being characterized by competing Hindu–Muslim identities, and even nationalisms, might appear to be in tension with the status of UP as the epicenter of the Indian nationalist movement led by the Congress party. A number of historians, however, have pointed out that even though the Congress presented itself as a secular, national, modernizing political movement, it was influenced in important ways by Hindu communalism (Sarkar 1997). Seminal studies of the UP Congress have acknowledged the critical influence of Hindu revivalist leaders and its institutional overlaps with Hindu organizations such as the Hindu Mahasabha and the Arya Samaj (Freitag 1989; Hasan 1996; Pandey 2008,). Some scholars have gone so far as to say that the most significant forms of Hindu politics manifested themselves within the Congress movement in UP (Gould 2004: 1). Gould points out that on the one hand, the UP Congress was less a party with a single, coherent agenda and more a broad-based movement that allowed for a range of political voices and on the other hand, the terms Hindu and Hinduism too had fluid descriptive and representational meanings in this period. Thus Congressmen, whilst subscribing to a general stance of secular nationalism, found it possible and useful to draw on Hindu symbols to present and communicate the idea of the Indian nation, especially at the local level (Gould 2004: 8). Dasgupta writes that "in order to draw support from Hindu masses, the nation was to be identified with the religious

---

[42] For a more general argument about how state institutionalization of ethnic identities can deepen ethnic divisions and foster ethnic conflict see Lieberman and Singh (2009, 2012).

tradition of Hinduism...the myth of a glorious past, dominated by Hindu kings and philosophers, was evoked as a means to achieve solidarity and promote action" (1970: 106). As a result, by the 1930s and 1940s, Muslims found it difficult "to distinguish between Hindu leadership and Congress leadership, Hindu populism and Indian nationalism" (Robinson; cited in Gould 2004: 16). Gould points out that the Muslim League's fashioning of itself as the champion of the Muslim community against a Hindu Congress was only made possible by this image of the latter party (2004: 16).[43]

At the end of the colonial period UP therefore had clearly not witnessed the emergence of any kind of a subnational identity. Instead, the province had turned out to be the crucible for the creation of Pakistan as a homeland for the subcontinent's Muslims and the emergence of Hindu nationalism, which was to remain an important force in the politics of India after independence. In the postcolonial period, UP has continued to be characterized by the marked absence of a subnational identity. This is brought out perhaps most simply but starkly by the absence of a noun, such as Malayali, Tamil, Rajasthani, Punjabi, Bengali and so on, to describe the people of UP (Rao & Venkataraman 1976: 287). It is also exemplified by the controversy that broke out shortly after Indian independence over the naming of the state and the continued conflict over the boundaries of UP. Until the early twentieth century, the province was "known by the clumsy and inappropriate name of the North-Western provinces and Awadh" (Crooke 1897). In 1902, following the merger of the province with the state of Agra, it came to be known as the United Provinces of Agra and Awadh, which in 1937 was shortened to the United Provinces. There was a general dissatisfaction with this essentially administrative appellation, and only a few days after Indian independence, a debate on a new name began in the UP state legislature (Kudaisya 2006: 352). Subsequent events, however, bore out the astute prediction of British administrator W. H. Crooke that "it would be hard to find a really suitable name for this rather heterogeneous slice of the Empire" (1897: 2). Tamil Nadu, Kerala, and Rajasthan were adopted by consensus as the 'natural' names of these provinces; there were few alternative names floated and there was little debate on the question. In contrast, there was no such 'natural' name for UP. A committee appointed to look into the issue proposed more than twenty different names. The debates on these names were often acrimonious. Most of the suggestions ran aground because they were not seen to be equally reflective of all regions or religions of the state.[44] Aryavrat,

---

[43] As a representative of an important contrasting view, Pandey (1990) depicts communalism as the "other" of Indian nationalism, its opposite and chief adversary.

[44] 'Awadh', the name of an ancient kingdom that comprised a substantial part of the state, was not acceptable to the residents of the regions of Braj, Kashi, and Mathura; and the names with obvious Hindu connotations, such as Brahmavrat, Brahmadesh, Krishna Kushal Province, Nava Hindu, Ram Krishna Prant were resisted by Muslims (Kudaisya 2006: 353–54).

the name that met with the overwhelming support of the Cabinet of Ministers as well as the Provincial Congress Committee of up and was recommended to the Constituent Assembly, was shot down by national leaders as it was considered to be a name that signified the whole of India, rather than only UP. By now the drafting of the Constitution was in its last stages and it was imperative to include in it a name for the province. In a hastily convened meeting, Congress legislators from the state settled on "Uttar Pradesh" (Kudaisya 2007: 359), which rather than evoking some aspect of the state's history, language, or culture, like in the case of most other Indian states, simply means the "Northern Provinces."[45]

UP has also been characterized by dissension over its boundaries. As noted earlier, UP is "purely an administrative unit" (Srivastava in Narain 1976: 323); unlike in Tamil Nadu or Kerala, there has historically been no popular subnational movement in favor of the creation of the state. At various points in the twentieth century it has in fact been racked by powerful separatist movements for the division of the province. In the 1950s, for example, the States Reorganization Commission received scores of memoranda from political parties, associations, and individuals for the partition of the province on the grounds of the absence of cultural or linguistic links with other parts of UP and/or perceived neglect by the provincial government.[46] The SRC eventually ruled against the partition of UP, but the strength and number of the demands for the division of the state convinced one of its three members to record a dissenting note. It is also important to point out that those in favor of the retention of the boundaries of UP framed their claims less in terms of a shared history or culture, or of the residents' identification

---

[45] UP has also struggled historically to arrive at a unifying state symbol. The symbols for most Indian provinces illustrate some distinctive aspect of its culture (like the towering temple gopuram in Tamil Nadu) or geography (like the coconut tree of Kerala or Rajasthan's moniker as "the desert state"). The state symbol of UP, however, rather than representing a single, singular aspect of the state, is an amalgam of symbols that represent the two primary, historic units, which were conjoined to form the province in 1902 (a pair of fish for the ancient kingdom of Awadh, a confluence of two rivers for Agra) and a bow and arrow, which indicates the state's mythological association with the Hindu god, Rama. There was considerable criticism of this symbol when it was selected after much contention in the early 1900s. In 1923, the governor William Marris went as far as to refuse to use such a "hodgepodge" of symbols as the state seal (Pandey 2008: 762). UP's postcolonial leaders did not appear to be thrilled with the symbol either but justified its maintenance in terms of a lack of alternatives (Pandey 2008: 763).

[46] One of the most significant of these was a petition signed by 97 members of the UP legislative assembly asking that, because of the stronger cultural and linguistic links of the Western districts of UP to Delhi than the rest of UP, and the relative neglect of these districts by the UP government, they be merged with Delhi and the surrounding areas to form a new state (States Reorganization Commission 1955).

with or allegiance to the state, and more in terms of the furthering of the "national good."

The most important, and eventually successful, secessionist movement that UP faced has been the demand for a separate hill state of Uttarakhand/ Uttaranchal. This demand, which was first voiced as early as the 1920s and simmered through petitions, rallies, and protest marches in the 1950s–60s, was based on the claim that the northern hill districts of Kumaon and Tehri-Garhwal had historically been separate and were culturally and linguistically distinct from the plains of UP (Tiwari 1995). The protagonists of the movement argued that the region had been neglected by the UP government and that the full development potential of the hill people could only be realized in their own, separate state. After a vigorous and occasionally violent agitation in the mid- to late 1990s, the new state of Uttaranchal (subsequently renamed Uttarakhand) was inaugurated in 2001. In recent years, encouraged no doubt by the success of the Uttarakhand agitation, demands have (re)surfaced for the breakup of UP to form a range of new provinces: Harit Pradesh, Doab Pradesh, Bundelkhand, Purvanchal, and Awadh Pradesh, to name only a few.[47] In 2011, the then chief minister Mayawati proposed, and the UP state assembly passed, a resolution for the division of UP into four states – Purvanchal, Bundelkhand, Awadh Pradesh, and Paschim Pradesh.

In addition to the attachments to different regions within UP represented by these different separatist movements, the state has also been characterized by conflicting ethnic identifications. The Hindi-Hindu versus Urdu-Muslim divide has persisted into recent years and been a source of polarization in the state.[48] In the past couple of decades, the state has witnessed the resurgence of religious tensions associated with the espousal of Hindutva sentiments by the BJP. The most important ethnic fault line, however, has been that of caste, corresponding to the growing mobilization by lower castes since the 1980s and the rise of backward caste and *dalit* parties (Chandra 2000). The state has not experienced the emergence of a subnational party. The locus of popular identification in UP has tended to lie either above the subnational community, with the national realm, or with ethnic identities.

---

[47] The UP Reorganization Front, an umbrella organization, which included the Purvanchal Banao Manch, the Bundelkhand Mukti Morcha, and the Harit Pradesh Banao Manch, made its electoral debut in the 2002 Assembly elections (Kudaisya 2007: 26),

[48] Despite widespread protest from within the state as well as from national politicians such as Nehru, who hailed from UP, the Official Languages Act of 1951 stripped Urdu of its status as official language of the state, a status it had enjoyed for more than two centuries, and instituted Hindi as the sole official language. In response to the relentless campaigns for the reinstitution of Urdu by Muslim elites and associations through succeeding decades, in 1989 the UP legislature amended the Official Languages Act to include Urdu as a second language, but this has been met with popular opposition and legal challenges and remains "mired in controversy" (Pai 2002: 2707).

RAJASTHAN

Rajput Dominance

In the mid-nineteenth century Rajputs constituted less than 10 percent of the total population but monopolized positions of political power and controlled most of the land in almost all the princely states that came to constitute the state of Rajasthan. Members of the warrior caste had established their political dominance in the region as early as the fifth century. In the sixteenth century, the Mughals, and following them in the early nineteenth century, the British, established their sovereignty over these states. The British united them into a single province named after their Rajput rulers, "Rajputana." These princely states, however, remained virtually cut off from the changes emanating from the Mughal as well as British capitals and "maintained their political identity and politico-economic isolation from the rest of India" (Narain & Mathur 1990: 2). As a result, for more than a thousand years, Rajput political hegemony was preserved.

Socioeconomic Changes Encourage Rise of Challenger Brahmin, Mahajan, and Jat Elites

In the early twentieth century an unprecedented exposure to new ideas, through the increased mobility of people from and into Rajasthan, fostered the simultaneous but separate mobilization of a non-Rajput elite in both urban and rural areas, who came to increasingly challenge the political dominance of the Rajputs.

Traditionally the princely states of Rajasthan were characterized by a "de-Sanskritized" and inclusive culture (Narain and Mathur 1990: 36). The caste system was far less rigid not only as compared to the Southern states but also to the rest of North-Central India (Sharma 1998: 108). Rajputs were at the apex of Rajasthani polity, but other upper castes – the mercantile Mahajans and the priestly Brahmins – dominated the economic and religious/intellectual life of the region respectively (Narain and Mathur 1990: 38). In addition, while the peasants did not wield "much local power" they were also "not marked by indelible signs of social inferiority" (ibid.). Jats, the most numerous peasant caste in the region, were the rulers in the princely states of Bharatpur and Dholpur. In the early twentieth century, the improved means of transport and communication, notably the expansion of the railway network to the capital cities of most of the princely states, facilitated the travels of young Brahmin and Mahajan elites to other parts of British India. Members of the Brahmin caste had traditionally held important positions in the administrative services of many Rajputana princely states and young men from this caste were among the first to leave the state to acquire an English education in the early 1900s. As traders, Mahajans regularly traveled to other parts of the country. Their exposure to the world outside Rajputana infused Brahmin and Mahajan elites with "Western political ideas" and the spirit of social and political reform that was gripping other parts of India at the time (Sisson 1966: 606). Around the 1920s these high-caste elites returned to cities that had in turn become communication centers between the princely states and the British provinces to establish the "first movements of political protest in the Rajputana states" (Sisson 1972: 43). Initially these movements did not challenge the political hegemony of the Rajputs and were aimed at the redress of specific grievances within the framework of the traditional polity. By the 1930s, however, they had taken a more institutionalized form through the creation of *Praja Mandals* (People's Groups), which came to demand the introduction of representative government, and by doing so, voiced the first challenges to Rajput authority (Sisson 1966: 606). But the Praja Mandals were, for the most part, confined to a small, high-caste (Brahmin and Mahajan) urban elite; at no point did they constitute a popular movement.

At around the same time as the mobilization of a Brahmin and Mahajan elite in the cities, rural areas in Rajasthan experienced the growth of socio-political movements led by members of the dominant peasant caste, the Jats. As in urban areas, these movements were triggered by an exposure to ideas, especially of social reform, from the outside world. These were communicated in this case through Jats who had travelled out of the state, notably soldiers returning from military deployment to various parts of the world as part of the Jat regiment in the British army, and religious bards, especially from the Arya Samaj who toured Jat villages preaching about the existing inequities and the necessity for change (Sisson 1969: 948). Traditional religious fairs and festivals also brought Rajputana Jats into contact with their caste brethren from other states where reformist movements had taken hold from the early twentieth century and consequently served as key sites for the exchange of social and political ideas (Sisson 1972: 72, 78). *Kisan Sabhas*, literally peasant associations, but essentially organizations of Jats, were initially focused inward on the reform of caste rules, but by the late 1930s had begun to protest the social, economic, and political dominance of the Rajputs. Under the aegis of these associations Jats mobilized against the traditional caste deference they were obliged to show Rajputs; they demanded a renegotiated economic relationship with their Rajput landlords based on land reform, the abolition of forced labor, and a formal definition of tenancy rights; and agitated for representation in the state administrative services (Sisson 1966: 607).

Even though Brahmin and Mahajan elites in cities and Jat elites in villages began to mobilize at around the same time in response to a similar influx of new ideas and in support of analogous goals, these two sets of elites emerged autonomously and had little to no interaction until the late 1940s, when the *Praja Mandals* were merged to form the state Congress and the *Kisan Sabhas* were absorbed into the newly founded party (Sisson 1969: 955).

Political Competition between Challenger Brahmin, Mahajan, and Jat Elites versus Dominant Rajput Elites Trigger Elite Rajasthani Subnationalism

The watershed transition from the feudal princely states of Rajputana to the unified, democratic polity of Rajasthan in the late 1940s–early 1950s triggered a process of intense competition between, on the one hand, the challenger Brahmin, Mahajan, and Jat elites who sought to occupy the new ranks of political authority and, on the other hand, the Rajput elites who fought to maintain their traditional dominance. The challenger elites were now all members of the newly founded Congress party but unlike in other parts of India, especially those that were ruled by the British such as UP, the Congress had been established only a few years prior and did not have a strong popular base in the region. In the very first elections in the state in 1951, the challenger elites were caught by surprise by a powerful challenge from the Rajput aristocracy.[49] In an attempt to gain an upper hand in this competition for political power, the Brahmin, Mahajan, and Jat elites found it useful to evoke a superordinate subnational identity. Coming together as "Rajasthani" allowed the challenger elite to present themselves as the legitimate 'modern' leaders of a united, democratic Rajasthan, as opposed to the Rajputs, who were portrayed as embodying narrow, segmented princely state identities and regressive, traditional feudal values.

Subnational symbols clearly were an attractive strategy for the challenger elites to strengthen their position in their political competition with the Rajputs, but at the same time these elites sought to evoke them, they were much more distant from popular consciousness as compared to Tamil Nadu or Kerala. The challenger elites in Rajasthan therefore had to work harder than their counterparts in the Southern states to rediscover and invent subnational symbols. Through the 1950s and 1960s, these elites commissioned a series of

---

[49] Rajput notables contesting either as Independent candidates or under the newly formed Ram Rajya Party garnered about 40% of the popular vote, which was exactly equal to that of the Congress, and won 59 seats, as compared to the Congress's 82 seats. In a major embarrassment to the Congress, its leader and chief ministerial candidate Jai Narayan Vyas was defeated soundly by members of the Rajput nobility in both constituencies from which he contested. The death of the leader of the Rajput faction, Hanuwant Singh, the former prince of Jodhpur, in an air crash on his way to Jaipur after the announcement of the results, however, resulted in a dissipation of a unified Rajput challenge. The success of the Rajput princes in the assembly elections of 1951–52 spurred the Congress to co-opt these ex-rulers and give them tickets despite ideological differences (Jaffrelot and Robin 2009). Over the years, while a significant number of Rajputs did come to be incorporated into the Congress, the party has continued to be dominated by Brahmins, Mahajans, and Jats. These three groups together constituted 58.7%, while Rajputs formed only 11.6%, of all Congress MLAs between 1952 and 2003 (Jaffrelot and Robin 2009). Initially contesting as independents, through the 1960s and 1970s the Rajputs coalesced under the Swatantra Party and the Bharatiya Jana Sangh (BJS), representing more than 25% of the MLAs in both these parties. As will be discussed later, since the 1990s Rajputs have been an important presence in the BJP (ibid.).

histories of Rajasthan that glorified the state's past and culture, often in hyper-
bolic value (Sharma 1966: 16).[50] In addition, the challenger elites appropriated
and built on the classification of Rajasthani as a single and distinctive language
in the Linguistic Survey of India (1903–1922).[51] Monographs commissioned
by the state traced a long and illustrious history for the language to as far
back as the sixth century (Chib 1979: 92, 102).[52] The state government also
commissioned a number of Rajasthani grammars and dictionaries and supported the preservation of ancient manuscripts and the collation of folk songs
and folk tales. These elites also campaigned (unsuccessfully) for the recognition of Rajasthani as one of India's national languages.[53] During the 1950s, a
number of institutions devoted to the development of Rajasthani language and
literature were established in different parts of the state.[54] The movement for
Rajasthani received a boost with the recognition of the language by the Sahitya
Akademi, the National Academy of Letters in 1974. Beginning in the late
1960s, a cultural organization, the *Tarun Kalakar Parishad* (Rajasthan Young
Artists Society), organized a series of immensely popular festivals in Jaipur
which showcased the classical and folk music and dance forms of the state.
By the mid-1970s, the *Parishad* had collected sufficient private donations to

[50] Interestingly, even though the historical record and most scholarly accounts show that the formation of Rajasthan was the product of decisions by national politicians, notably Patel, and that
there was no popular subnational movement for the creation of the state, one of these volumes,
supporting Renan's assertion that sometimes "getting its history wrong is part of being a nation"
(1990: 12), describes the creation of Rajasthan in terms of an "urge for unity ... from below
(because of which) ... people in the different (princely) states felt impelled to form a Union"
(Sharma 1966: 15).

[51] In 1918, in the monumental Linguistic Survey of India, George Grierson classified the tongues
spoken in the various princely states of Rajputana not merely as dialects of Hindi, as they had
previously been identified (Kellogg 1875), but as constituting a single and distinctive Rajasthani
language. This is considered to be a key development in the scholarly recognition of Rajasthan
as a linguistic-cultural region (Lodrick 1994: 17) and paved the way for further work on
Rajasthani (Gusain 2005).

[52] The bardic tradition of poems commemorating the heroic deeds of kings was particularly
emphasized with Chand Bardai's "Prithviraj Raso," composed in the twelfth century, cited as a
"masterpiece" of Rajasthani (Chib 1979: 93; Gahlot 1981). A publication of the Rajasthan government in 1951 declared that "Our bards ... have given us more copious literature in this line
than their compeers in the other provinces of India ... many of our commemorative songs would
beat hollow the heroic ballads of any language, whether of the East or of the West" (Rajasthan
Government 1951).

[53] This failure is seen as a result of the combination of first, New Delhi's hostility to the proposal
owing to the fear that granting official language status to Rajasthani would further weaken the
position of Hindi, which had been accepted as the official language of India on the basis of a single vote, and whose status as such continued to be contested by the non-Hindi-speaking states;
and second, the more limited popular support for Rajasthani as compared with the mobilization
for other languages, such as Malayali or Tamil (Gusain 2005).

[54] The most important of these institutions were the Rajasthani Shodh Sansthan, the Rajasthani
Sahitya Peeth, the Sadul Rajasthani Research Institute, the Rajasthan Oriental Research
Institute, and the Rupayan Sansthan.

produce a traveling multimedia program, *Dharti Dhoran Ri* (Land of Shifting Sands) that toured the villages of Rajasthan with the aim of inculcating its viewers with "the idea of belonging to Rajasthan." Through a powerful combination of images, oratory, live music, and dance performances, *Dharti Dhoran Ri* attempted to invoke a sense of identification and pride with the heritage and traditions of the state and "to bring together attachments (to) generate a Rajasthani loyalty" (Erdman 1994: 52). Kaushal Bhargava, the president of the *Parishad* and creator of *Dharti Dhoran Ri* explained that the aim was to "develop a program which *all* Rajasthanis could feel was their own, and which would represent their social bonding in a sequence of images and statements" (Erdman 1994: 59).

In this way, through the decades following the creation of the state, challenger elites clearly "sought to develop cultural voices and historical significance for the future of their new state" (Erdman et al. 1994: 48). It is important to note that even though the challenger elites in the Congress were in competition with the erstwhile Rajput rulers in the political realm, the Rajasthani identity that they propagated was built around a Rajput "ethos" or "ethic" of valor, chivalry, and sacrifice.[55] This is not as contradictory as it initially appears inasmuch as a Rajput ethos is not exclusive to the Rajputs, but instead a cultural paradigm shared by all communities of the state (Babb 2004: 222).[56] This

---

[55] This emphasis on martial values, valor and honor has also tended to dominate representations of Rajasthan in the print and visual media. Government of India publications, for example, write of Rajasthan's "stirring story" full of the "bravery" and "heroic deeds" of Rajputs (Government of India 1959, 1962). *Dharti Dhoran Ri* began with the following "dramatic, booming announcement": "This land of heroes, Rajasthan! In each particle of this land is written a tale of bravery, courage, surrender and sacrifice" (Erdman et al. 1994: 68). Rajasthan's emergence as an important tourist destination in the 1990s has furthered the Rajput image of Rajasthan. Scholars such as Ramusack (1995), Babb (2004), and Henderson (2007) describe how an "idealized Rajput heritage" has been "relentlessly promoted" by the tourism industry (Babb 2004: 221).

[56] Rajasthan, unlike other parts of India, has historically been characterized by Rajput rather than Brahminical values and norms. Rajput polity and society have traditionally been extremely syncretic, incorporating people from different communities. Muslims, lower caste, and tribal groups, for example, enjoyed a much higher social status and occupied prominent positions of political power in Rajasthan compared to many other parts of India. The Rajputs' cultural behavior was in turn seen as an "ideal type," which was socially practiced by the elite as well as the non-elite (Narain and Mathur 1989: 18). The surname, Singh, for example, originally associated with Rajputs, was appropriated over a period of several centuries of acculturation by different Hindu castes, including lower castes as well as followers of Jainism (ibid. 17). Caste associations of various agricultural and pastoral castes included the appellation "Kshatriya" (warrior), previously exclusively associated with Rajputs, to their names. A range of Christian, Muslim, tribal, and lower caste groups in Rajasthan claim descent from Rajput clans (Jenkins 1998: 110–11). Rajput heroes and legends have been deified by members of all castes and communities (Blackburn 1989: 241). A sect of Muslims in Rajasthan, the Meo-Muslims, view some of their rituals, especially those associated with marriage, as distinctly Rajput (Jamous 1996).

Rajput ethos has helped frame a shared sociocultural heritage for the state, including common and distinctive myths[57] and heroes.[58]

Until the mid-1980s, however, subnationalism remained almost entirely an elite discourse. This was in large part due to the absence of a powerful, broad-based subnational movement or association. In Rajasthan, through the 1950s and 1960s, there was no popular sociopolitical movement or organization, such as the *Aikya Kerala* movement or the Communist and Dravidian parties, which could effectively communicate a Rajasthani identity to the population at large. The Congress party, as noted earlier, had not enjoyed a historical presence in the region. The Praja Mandals and the Kisan Sabhas had not been mass organizations (Jaffrelot and Robin 2009: 169). Through the early post-independence decades, the party operated through clientelistic "vote-bank" politics – it established relations with local notables in the villages and did not have a strong grassroots organization (ibid.). The spread of popular subnationalism was frustrated not only by the absence of a powerful, broad-based associational conduit but also because, as noted earlier, the subnational symbols of a shared Rajasthani history, culture, and language emphasized by the challenger elites had not enjoyed a prominent place in the popular consciousness. Historians of Rajasthan have pointed out that Rajasthan's demarcation as a single political space – whether by the Mughals, the British, or the post-Independence Indian elite in New Delhi – had occurred on the basis of "criteria that held far greater meaning for the outsider than for the area's inhabitants" (Lodrick 1994: 12). There was virtually no sense of a pan-Rajasthani solidarity across the different Rajput princely states, many of which had for centuries been hostile to, if not in active conflict with, each other (ibid.: 9). For centuries, princely states evoked powerful allegiances, but attachments to the native kingdoms were matched and occasionally trumped by loyalties to *jagirs* (fiefdoms) into which these states were further apportioned.[59] In

---

[57] The Rajput legend of origin from a fire pit on Mount Abu "functions as a unifying myth" of common origin for all of modern Rajasthan (Meister 1994: 145). The ancient ballad – "*Dhola-Maru ra Duha*," the tale of the love between a Rajput prince and princess, is accepted as "the love story of Rajasthan."

[58] Warrior heroes associated with a Rajput ethos of valor, such as Pabuji, Bhaironji, Tejaji, Ramdevji, Devji, are recognized as "Rajasthani folk deities" and worshipped by people from all castes in the state (Blackburn et al. 1989). Rajput kings such as Rana Pratap and Rana Sangha, famous for their prowess on the battlefield, and Rana Kumbha and Maharaja Jai Singh, well-known for their cultural accomplishments, have also been promoted, and are increasingly accepted as "Rajasthani heroes."

[59] The *jagirs/thikanas* were controlled by feudal lords (*jagirdars*) who not only were bound by kinship ties to the king but also had physically contributed to the establishment of the princely states (Narain and Mathur 1989: 20). These *jagirdars* were "all powerful" in their *jagirs* and did not stand for the king's direct interference in their affairs (Sharma 1993: 5). They collected taxes and maintained standing armies but were obliged to pay tributes to the king annually on certain occasions and to support him militarily if the need arose. It is estimated that at the end of the colonial period, more than 60% of the total territory of Rajputana was under *jagirs* and only 40% was under the direct control of the princely states.

addition, people also traditionally maintained strong caste, clan, and religious identities (Sisson 1966, 1969). The people, for the most part, therefore retained their "multi-layered and particularized" identities (Erdman et al. 1994: 46). The absence of a pan-Rajasthani solidarity is evidenced by the absence of popular support for both the creation of the province in the 1950s as well as for the movement for the constitutional recognition of the Rajasthani language through the 1960s and 1970s.[60] Anthropologists working in the region also found that "historic events, festivals and cultural performances, heroes and devotees, and even certain places in Rajasthan were perceived as belonging to certain local groups or regions, rather than representing a cultural entirety" (ibid.).

Beginnings of Popular Rajasthani Subnationalism

Beginning in the mid- to late 1980s, however, two key developments – generational change, which weakened people's loyalties to erstwhile territorial boundaries, and the growing strength of the Bharatiya Janata Party (BJP), which espoused and actively propagated Rajasthani subnationalism – facilitated the beginnings of an identification with Rajasthan on the part of the general population. A number of scholars have noted that "for the generations born during princely rule, their loyalties to their natal states ... persisted well into the post-independence period" (Erdman et al. 1994: 45). The boundaries of the erstwhile princely states, however, held less meaning for those who had grown to maturity in post-independence Rajasthan. By the 1990s, the post-princely state generations outnumbered people who had lived in, and consequently had retained at least some attachment to, the native kingdoms or *jagirs*. Narain and Mathur, two of the most prominent Rajasthani political scientists, believed that the "stable identities" of princely states "survived more than three decades of socio-economic changes and politico-constitutional transformations," but by the end of the 1980s, they identified "signs of a slow but stealthy emergence of an over-arching identity of Rajasthan which had tended to transcend earlier territorial loyalties" (1989: 23). This weakening of princely state attachments and the gradual emergence of a popular pan-Rajasthani identity was initiated

---

[60] Laxmi Kumari Chundawat, a prominent Rajasthani writer and folklorist who was a member of the Rajasthan Legislative Assembly from 1962 to 1971 and a member of the Upper House of the National Parliament from 1972 to 1978, has been one of the most prominent campaigners for the Rajasthani language. She recalled to me her "disastrous" attempt to introduce a bill for the designation of Rajasthani as the mother tongue of Rajasthan in the State Legislative Assembly in the 1960s. She said that in order to gauge the degree of popular support for their proposal, she and her collaborators released a public statement pertaining to the importance of recognizing Rajasthani as the mother tongue of their state in a leading daily, and invited people to write in to indicate their support for the cause. Only three people wrote in. Chundawat told me, "I was so embarrassed. How could I face the Assembly? I immediately dropped the proposal and did not speak of it again for a long time" (Interview at her residence in Jaipur, July 30, 2008).

by the process of generational change but greatly accelerated by the emergence of the Bharatiya Janata Party as a major player on the political stage from the 1980s onward.

Generally described as a "Hindu nationalist" political party, the BJP has functioned equally if not more like a regional, subnationalist party in Rajasthan (Jenkins 1998). The BJP, which governed Rajasthan from 1990 to 1998, first by itself and then as the core party in a coalition, played an important role in reinvigorating a Rajasthani identity. It did this primarily by adopting and broadcasting a Rajput ethos of ethic. This espousal of a Rajput ethos was a convenient strategy for the party because on the one hand, it represented a historically unifying set of symbols including all castes and religions of Rajasthan, which, as noted earlier, constituted the core of the preexisting elite Rajasthani identity. On the other hand, the uniquely valorous historical and sociocultural heritage for the state (Jenkins 1998: 103) associated with the Rajput ethos conformed closely to the assertive Hindutva that the BJP sought to project on a national scale. Rajasthan was depicted as a repository of Rajput valor, which represented "the assertive, self-confident, martial tradition of Hinduism" that had been subverted under the influence of foreign ideologies in other parts of India. Rajasthan was therefore "the preserver of the true faith, the sacred fire from which the rest of India can reignite its sense of lost strength and vitality" (Jenkins 1998: 105).[61]

The BJP drew heavily on this Rajputized Rajasthani identity[62] as a source of political mobilization in the state. Speeches by party leaders and manifestoes were replete with references to the traditions of Rajput chivalry and the greatness of Rajasthani civilization. In contrast to the Congress in the 1950s and 1960s, the BJP in the late 1980s and 1990s had a strong organization and a disciplined cadre

---

[61] It is important to note that while the BJP did use images of a "Rajput Hindutva," in general, it espoused a highly inclusive Rajasthani subnationalism. Rajput polity and society have long been marked by a "distinctive 'secular' orientation" (Narain and Mathur 1989: 31), with Rajput royal families being well known for entering into matrimonial alliances with and granting *sharan* (refuge), often at great risk to themselves, to Muslim rulers (ibid.: 32). The leaders as well as foot soldiers of the BJP repeatedly emphasized this historically equal place of Muslims in the Rajasthani political community. BJP leader Bhairon Singh Shekhawat reopened Jaipur's main mosque, the Jama Masjid, which had been locked by the British, and began the tradition of *iftar* parties at the chief minister's residence (Statesman 2002). He included some Muslim caste groups in the list of backward castes eligible for a range of benefits, including preferential admission to government educational institutions and employment, despite clear injunctions against this move by the heads of the national BJP (Interview with K. L. Kochar, retired IAS officer and press secretary of B. S. Shekhawat during his tenures as chief minister of Rajasthan during 1990–1992 and 1993–1998). The state has notably also not witnessed the outbreak of Hindu–Muslim violence of the sort that has been associated with the tenure of BJP governments in neighboring states such as Gujarat (Varshney and Wilkinson 2006).

[62] It is important to note here, following Babb (2004: 222), that this Rajputized Rajasthani identity is much more politically important in contemporary Rajasthan than the Rajputs themselves (2004: 222)!

of grassroots workers that played an important role in carrying the party's message to the masses. The people of Rajasthan, most of whom had been born or come of age in a united Rajasthan were also unprecedentedly receptive to a subnationalist appeal, especially one that drew on the familiar tropes of the Rajput ethic/ethos.

The mutually reinforcing forces of generational change and the emergence of the BJP as a subnationalist party were therefore critical in helping Rajasthani subnationalism develop a popular base. Writing in the early 1990s, Lodrick, for example, noted that a "Rajasthani regional identity appears to be emerging today that is based, at least in part, on an increasing awareness among the region's inhabitants of a common heritage originating in Rajasthan's broader cultural, historical and political traditions" (1994: 34). Similarly, Meister writes of the "sense of a distinct identity the region as a whole has come to share" (1994: 171). In the 1996 National Election Study in which more than 67 percent of all Rajasthani respondents agreed with the statement that "We should be loyal to our own region first and then to India," as compared with less than 50 percent of respondents in UP and 53 percent of all respondents nationally. Only 45 percent of Rajasthanis polled had agreed with this statement as compared with 67 percent of respondents across all of India in the 1971 National Election Study. The beginnings of some form of Rajasthani subnationalism among the people of the state is also demonstrated by the massive turnout at rallies in support of the demand for the constitutional recognition of the Rajasthani language. In stark contrast to the extremely limited popular backing for the cause in the 1960s, in the 1990s there was a surge of popular support for the inclusion of Rajasthani in the eighth schedule of the Indian constitution.[63]

While the past couple of decades has witnessed the beginnings of a sense of solidarity with Rajasthan on the part of the people of the state, it is important to note that the "great leap of conceptualization" that Erdman et al (1994: 46) had noted was called for in order for people to consider themselves as Rajasthani is far from complete. To what extent a Rajasthani subnational identity continues to become popularly rooted will depend to a large extent on

---

[63] During the 1990s and 2000s, there have been a number of rallies calling for the constitutional recognition of Rajasthani. A three-day rally in support of the cause at the Boat Club in New Delhi in 1995, for example, was attended by many "Rajasthani members of the national parliament and state legislative assembly, writers, journalists, the heads of the department and teachers of Departments of Rajasthani language in various universities of the state, office bearers of academies for the promotion of Rajasthani language, literature and culture *as well as people from different parts of Rajasthan*" (Saxena 07/22/95; emphasis added). The reporter who covered the event for the *Rajasthan Patrika* wrote that "From the crack of dawn overcrowded buses from various parts of Rajasthan began pulling in ... raising slogans such as "Long live Rajasthan and Rajasthani!" and "The language of eight crore people, that's our Rajasthani language!" In 2005 there was a twelve-day rally across different cities in Rajasthan, which ended in New Delhi with the submission of a memorandum demanding the national government's recognition of Rajasthani to the prime minister of India.

its continued espousal by a subnational party and/ or movement and its institutionalization in formal and informal institutions.[64]

It is also useful to point out here important limits to the inclusiveness of Rajasthani subnationalism. While the Rajput ethos that has formed the core of the Rajasthani subnational identity has been, as noted earlier, at least nominally encompassing across caste and religion, including within it *dalits*, tribals, and Muslims, it has been much less inclusive across gender lines. Gender-based inequalities, discrimination and violence have existed historically and persist across all states of India, as also across much of the world. Yet, as compared to other states, especially Southern states such as Tamil Nadu and Kerala, Rajasthan has had a particularly deep and long-lasting legacy of patriarchal feudalism. Critically, for our purposes, a number of gender-regressive practices, for the ostensible 'safeguarding' of the 'honor' of Rajput women and patriarchal households, have historically been at the center of the symbolic construction of the Rajput ethos (Harlan 1991). The most egregious of these practices include female infanticide, child marriage and the practice of sati, in which a recently widowed woman immolates herself, typically on her husband's funeral pyre.[65] These practices are said to have begun among Rajputs but in line with the emulative, unifying nature of the Rajput ethos discussed earlier, spread to other castes and communities in Rajasthan.[66] In 1987, the state gained international and national infamy as the site of the *sati* of eighteen-year-old Roop Kanwar. While feminist organizations condemned the act and urged police investigation into the act, the *sati* itself was witnessed by a "cheering" crowd of, by some estimates, 50,000, and subsequently glorified, through the construction of a commemorative temple and the organization of rallies attended by over a hundred thousand (Parihar 1999). The criticism of and measures

[64] In this regard the continued sponsorship by the Rajasthan Tourism Department, of celebrations across the state to mark the creation of Rajasthan, in the form of Rajasthan Diwas, as well as individual initiatives, such as the composition in 2014 of a hit Rajasthani anthem, Mharo Rajasthan (My Rajasthan), by folk singer, Swaroop Khan, and hip-hop duo, Rapperiya Baalam would appear to be signs for optimism. It is interesting that a disclaimer at the start of the music video for Mharo Rajasthan declares it "the anthem of young Rajasthan" that seeks to "show the world that who we are, and that we are proud of being born on the land of Rajasthan (sic). Jai Rajasthan" (https://www.youtube.com/watch?v=pINiLUrM65E). Yet the move of the BJP during the Chief Ministerial tenure of Vasundhara Raje Scindia away from an encompassing Rajasthani identity towards the mobilization of social divisions and appeal to particular identity groups under the ideology of Hindu nationalism would not be auspicious portents for the spread of Rajasthani subnationalism (Basu 2015).

[65] Sati is related to the Rajput practice of Jauhar, the collective immolation on the part of women of a community facing certain defeat in a battle – internicine battles with other Rajput kingdoms but especially battles against Muslims, to avoid "rape, torture and other ignominies" (Hawley 1994: 165).

[66] The Rajasthan bania or merchant castes have historically, and continue to, supply the capital for temples that valorize sati and while cases of Rajput women are the most prominent, there also well-known instances of sati among other castes, especially banias and Gujars (Hawley 1994: 166).

to restrict *satis* by the state were seen as "a threat to Rajput identity" and the Roop Kanwar incident "resulted in a massive rallying of support around a collective reinforcement of Rajput identity and tradition" (Unnithan-Kumar 1997: 71; Hawley 1994: 97).[67] This explicitly gendered nature of Rajasthani identity, as compared to subnational identities in Tamil Nadu or Kerala, has had, as will be discussed in Chapter 5, important implications for the nature of welfare outcomes in the state.

CONCLUSION

This chapter has sought to delineate the reasons why, and describe the ways in which, Tamil Nadu and Kerala have been characterized by a more cohesive subnational solidarity as compared to UP and Rajasthan. While it would be clearly inaccurate to suggest that this process of the emergence of subnational solidarity is entirely insulated from social policy and development outcomes, this chapter has sought to show that it is, for the most part, exogenous to them. Insofar as the remaining chapters in the book seek to show how subnational solidarity is an important driver of social policy and development outcomes, it is useful to conclude by returning briefly to the sequence of events in the emergence of subnationalism in Tamil Nadu, Kerala and Rajasthan with a specific eye towards the potential impact of social, in particular education, policy and outcomes at each stage.[68]

This chapter traced the origins of subnationalism to the evocation of a set of historical, sociocultural symbols by elites as a politically expedient strategy to strengthen their position in a competition for political power. Challenger elites sought to adopt subnationalism as a way to 'other' the established elites and present themselves as indigenes making a bid for their rightful share of political power. Sociopolitical movements and organizations played an important role in bringing this elite subnationalism to the popular consciousness. Could it be, however, that the rise of the challenger elites was itself a product of changes in policy and/ or gains in education? As will be discussed further in subsequent chapters, in neither of the four states discussed here does the historical record point to significant changes to social policy prior to the emergence of the challenger elites and their espousal of subnationalism. Census returns show that some caste groups such as the Vellalas in Tamil Nadu and Nairs in Kerala,

---

[67] Many Rajput political leaders, including future BJP Chief Minister, Vasundhara Raje Scindia, came out in support of the *sati*. A notable exception was Bhairon Singh Shekhawat who mentioned in subsequent interviews, including one with the author, that he was criticized for "going against his Rajput identity" and seen as "less of a Rajasthani" by condemning the *sati*. Interview with Bhairon Singh Shekhawat. New Delhi. 2008.

[68] I focus in particular on education policy and outcomes because they may arguably be seen, especially in light of the scholarship on the importance of mass schooling (Darden 2014; Weber 1976), as more important potential drivers of the emergence of subnational solidarity than health.

from which challenger elites were drawn, did witness important gains in literacy in the years around their emergence as challenger elites. At the same time, however, other groups from which challenger elites arose such as the Nairs and Chettis in Tamil Nadu and the Jats in Rajasthan, did not experience significant educational improvements. Moreover, there were other groups in these states that witnessed important improvements in their literacy rates and also had relatively higher absolute levels of education that did not throw up challenger elites.[69]

The emergence of the challenger elites had little to do with changes in social policy or outcomes and was instead critically a product of the change in socioeconomic status of particular groups associated with developments – changes in agriculture and patterns of land ownership, an expansion of trade, a weakening of the caste system, migration to cities, growth of means of transportation and communication – each of which were independent of welfare policy and social development. The one relevant development that it is important to note here is the role of English education. In order to be able to make a credible demand for their inclusion in the state services, it was very helpful for the challenger elite to have had at least some exposure to education in English. Access to education in English, however, can hardly be seen as indicative of, or a part of, social policy, or reflective of overall development outcomes. The emergence of opportunities for exposure to English were due to a set of historically specific factors – the efforts of Christian missionaries in Travancore and the initiative of individual colonial officers in Madras and UP – that were exogenous to state social policy. Moreover, English literacy remained confined to a miniscule proportion of both the general populations of these provinces as well as the groups from which challenger elites were drawn. As late as 1911, only 1.5 percent of the male population and 0.2 percent of the female population of Travancore possessed any knowledge of English. In Madras in 1911, all of the castes from whom the challenger elites were drawn had a rate of English literacy less than 0.1 percent.

Even though the rise of the challenger elites was not a product of social policy, could it be, however, that the espousal of subnational symbols by the challenger elites was related to a progressive social policy and/ or gains in education? Could

---

[69] In Tamil Nadu the gains in and absolute levels of Vellala literacy from 1901 to 1911 were comparable to those of the Tiyans and Nadars, the majority of whom, especially outside the "six towns of Ramand," remained distant from the Justice Party and the non-Brahmin movement (Hardgrave 1969). The overall literacy for these challenger elites in Madras was also very low – just over 2% for Vellalas, less than 1% for Chettis, less than 3% for Nairs and for Nadars, less than 0.3%. In Kerala the rise in the literacy rates of Nairs from 1875 to 1891 was comparable to groups such as the Konkanis and Talukkans (Muslims). The absolute levels of literacy of the Nairs in 1891 were comparable to those of the Konkanis and Vellalas and significantly lower than Malayali Brahmins. The Konkanis, Talukkans, Vellalas, and Malayali Brahmins were almost entirely disconnected from the emergence of a Malayali identity in the late nineteenth century.

it be that the reason that the challenger elites chose to espouse subnational symbols was less because this was a politically expedient strategy in their competition with the dominant elites, and more because of their experience of access to service provision? State service provision, especially schools, has historically been seen as an important tool for the inculcation of national ideologies (Weber 1976, Darden 2014). In the states discussed here, however, the limited access to education that was available at the time was primarily via schools run by Christian missionaries and/ or the colonial government. There is considerable evidence that the missionaries used their schools for proselytizing, for example, through compulsory catechism classes. But there is no indication either in the lengthy and numerous memoirs and personal correspondences of the missionaries or in scores of government reports that the missionary and government schools respectively imparted any form of Tamil or Malayali solidarity. Indeed, the missionaries or the British government would appear to have had no conceivable incentive to have done so. In Rajasthan most Brahmin and Mahajan elites acquired Western education outside Rajputana, so again there seems to be almost no possibility that they could have absorbed a sense of Rajasthani subnational solidarity in schools. Further, the very low overall level of provision of social services in these states at the time that the challenger elites espoused subnational symbols minimizes the possibility that a sense of satisfaction and pride with the health centers or schools prompted these challenger elites to adopt subnational symbols. A still further possibility to consider is whether the accessibility of subnational symbols to challenger elites might be related in some way to social policy and development outcomes. The possibility of this again seems to be minimal given that the subnational symbols that were recovered and "re-invented" by challenger elites, such as a belief in a shared past, a myth of common origin, a common culture characterized by shared heroes, customs, and festivals, can be traced back centuries, even millennia, in both Tamil Nadu and Kerala.[70]

Could it be that the opportunity for challenger elites to demand greater access to political power, thereby coming into competition with the established elite, was somehow related to developments in the realm of social policy? The reforms that created the opportunity for the challenger elite to gain access to political power were undertaken for diverse reasons – in Kerala as a response

---

[70] The legend of Kerala's creation by the Lord Parshuram, for example, is recorded in the *Brahmanda Purana*, which is believed to have been composed between 350–950 CE. The earliest record of celebrations of the festival of Onam, which celebrates the mythological King Mahabali's return to Kerala, dates back to around CE 800. The Malayalam language most likely originated from Tamil at least as early as the sixth century. The oldest literary work in Malayalam, distinct from the Tamil tradition, is dated from between the ninth and eleventh centuries. Variations of the word *Kerala* are recorded as far back as the third century BCE in a rock inscription left by the Maurya emperor Asoka (274–237 BCE). Similarly, as noted earlier, *Tamilakam*, a word signifying the home of Tamil language, culture, and the people, has been in use since at least the first century BCE (Pandian 1987). Tamil is one of the longest-surviving classical languages in India; the poems of the legendary *Sangam* academies were composed between 300 BCE to CE 600.

to increasingly severe pressures from the British administration in neighboring Madras Presidency; in Tamil Nadu and UP because of a growing realization of the dangers of vesting power in cliques, and in Rajasthan as a product of the adoption of democratic institutions in independent India. Each of these reasons was unrelated to, and independent of, social policy and development outcomes. Finally, the spread of popular subnationalism was also not related in any discernible systematic way to developmental gains. During the time that a subnational identity began to spread to the population at large in Tamil Nadu, Kerala and Rajasthan, education and health indicators in all three provinces remained very low.

In addition to discussing the potential influence of social development on the emergence of subnational solidarity, it is also useful to end by considering the possibility of whether subnational solidarity and social development might both in turn be influenced by another "hidden" factor.

Here I briefly discuss two such potential factors – ethnic diversity and mobilization against the caste system. It is certainly reasonable to conjecture that ethnic diversity might impede the emergence of a subnational solidarity. As discussed in Chapter 2, there is a large body of scholarship that suggests that ethnic diversity undermines public goods provision. Let the evidence presented throughout this book does not support either of these theses. Whether subnational solidarity emerges, or not, is independent of the ethnic demographics in Indian states. It is not the case that subnationalism emerges in more ethnically homogeneous states (see Table 1.1). Subnationalism is the deliberate construction of elites. In all four states discussed in this chapter, Challenger elites had the option of choosing symbols to construct an encompassing subnational solidarity or a narrower ethnic identity. Their choice was determined by which of a subnational or ethic identity was more useful in their attempt to wrest power from a dominant elite. In the late nineteenth and early twentieth centuries, both Kerala and UP were characterized by similar ethnic demographies. If anything, UP had lower levels of religious and caste fractionalization, and a higher proportion of the population of the province (98%) was reported as speaking Hindustani in the census of 1881 as compared to the 81% of malayalam speakers in Kerala.

Lower caste mobilization and the subsequent weakening of the caste hierarchy is a critical step in the emergence of subnationalism in both Tamil Nadu and Kerala. However, as the cases of Rajasthan and UP illustrate, challenges to the caste hierarchy are neither necessary nor sufficient for the emergence of a subnational solidarity. Rajasthani subnationalism emerged in the absence of any significant anti-caste mobilization. On the other hand, since the late 1980s, UP has witnessed powerful movements against upper-caste domination on the part of the backward and former untouchable castes, but this has not fostered the emergence of a subnational solidarity in the state. Anti-caste movements, rather than exerting an independent effect, seem to influence social development primarily *through* subnationalism. In both Tamil Nadu and Kerala, anti-Brahmin and anti-caste mobilizations were overlaid with a larger, more encompassing subnational solidarity, and it was this rather than the challenge to the caste hierarchy that was the critical condition for the initiation of a progressive social policy and developmental gains. Since the 1980s, UP has experienced powerful backward and lower caste movements but in contrast to the Southern states, these have occurred in the absence of any sense of subnational solidarity, and as will be discussed in detail in Chapter 5, have consequently not yielded developmental dividends.

4

How Subnationalism promotes Social Development

In this chapter I turn to an empirical substantiation of the subnationalism argument developed in Chapter 1, delineating the positive dynamic of how a cohesive subnational solidarity generates higher levels of social development through a historical analysis of two neighboring states in the deep south of India – Tamil Nadu, and Kerala. Kerala has come to be seen today as one of the most widely acclaimed cases of social development in the world (Franke and Chasin 1989; Sen 1991). The emphasis on the "Kerala model" (Franke and Chasin 1999; Kurien 1995; Rammohan 2000; Véron 2001) has, however, eclipsed the remarkable achievements in schooling and health made by other Indian provinces such as Tamil Nadu, which has, since the 1960s, maintained a substantial developmental lead over the all-India average. As noted in Chapter 1, however, Tamil Nadu and Kerala were virtually as underdeveloped as other parts of India in the late nineteenth and early twentieth centuries respectively. In addition, the educational and medical infrastructure and outcomes in Travancore at the time compared unfavorably with those in Madras Presidency (Bhattacharjee 1976; Singh 1944). This chapter traces how from roughly similar starting points, the Southern states gained a lead over other Indian provinces, especially those in North-Central India, such as UP and Rajasthan, due to their more cohesive sense of subnational solidarity. In addition, it shows how differences in the timing of the emergence and strength of Malayali subnationalism led Kerala to overtake Tamil Nadu in the early twentieth century and maintain its developmental lead over the state.

TAMIL NADU

This section compares four time periods – prior to the 1900s; from the 1900s to the 1940s; through the 1950s and '60s; and from the 1970s on – corresponding to the absence of subnationalism, the emergence of elite subnationalism, the strengthening of popular subnationalism, and the development of a cohesive subnational solidarity. The first subsection shows that until the 1900s, corresponding to the absence of any sense of a shared subnational solidarity, the Madras Presidency did not prioritize the social sector and the province remained mired in illiteracy and ill health. The second subsection highlights how the emergence of Tamil subnationalism among non-Brahmin elites in Madras city toward the beginning of the twentieth century led them to push for an increased prominence for social welfare onto the agenda of the British government in Madras presidency. The third subsection demonstrates how the spread of Tamil subnationalism among the people of the province at large during the 1950s and '60s was associated with an increase in popular political consciousness and involvement with social services, which fostered important improvements in education and health outcomes. The last subsection shows how, from the 1970s onward, a powerful Tamil subnationalism, firmly rooted in both the elite and popular consciousness, has continued to push forward Tamil Nadu's social development.

Absence of Subnationalism Impedes Social Development: Up to the 1900s

Until the early twentieth century, the symbols of a shared Tamil identity were not prominent in the sociopolitical life of the province. As noted in Chapter 3, virtually all the classics of Tamil literature lay forgotten in private collections. Tamil heroes, such as Tamilttay and Thiruvalluvar, had thus far not been recovered from the annals of history. The idea of an ancient, glorious Tamil/ Dravidian civilization had not yet been "invented." As a result, there was little sense of an overarching Tamil identity and the socioeconomic and political life of the region was structured primarily around the identity of caste. The absence of a sense of oneness among Tamils meant that there was little conception of or support for their collective welfare.

A review of the state of education among the "natives" in the province by the Board of Revenue in the 1820s reported that education had received "little encouragement" because there was "little demand" for it (Bradshaw 1894: 193). In 1822, the governor of Madras, Thomas Munro, who in his earlier appointment as the British Resident in Travancore had encouraged the kingdom to adopt a more progressive social policy, proposed the establishment of an extensive system of schools. These schools were established, but in large part due to the lack of popular demand or involvement, proved to be failures and were abolished. In 1858, Mill wrote that "The history of education at Madras, up to a recent period, presents little beyond a record of failures" (Mill, Robson, & Moir 1990: 144–45). Scholars concur that until the middle of the nineteenth century, Madras was mired in "educational backwardness" (Arooran 1980: 5).

In the later decades of the nineteenth century there was some expansion of the education sector in response to pressures from elites. However, in the

absence of a sense of subnational solidarity these elites were driven almost
entirely by their own narrowly defined self-interest, and as a result the focus
of their demands was on the type of education most likely to benefit their
children – higher and collegiate education and schooling in English. In 1853,
the government founded the first schools for instruction in English. Madras
University was established in 1857 and expanded in subsequent years. As late
as 1870–71, however, primary education, which was the main necessity for
the illiterate masses, remained "in its infancy" (Raghavaiyangar 1893: ccxiv).
Primary education received a fillip from the late 1870s onward through the
combined efforts of the provincial, municipal, and local governments, but in
1894 the "Memorandum on the progress of the Madras presidency during
the last forty years of British Administration" stated that "while there seems
to be an almost indefinite scope for the extension and the improvement in the
quality of village schools, the agencies who now mainly contribute towards
their upkeep are beginning to feel the pressure of cost, and complain that they
have gone far enough, in justice to other and more pressing demands upon
their resources" (Raghavaiyangar 1893: cccxiv). In 1872, slightly more than
6 percent of the population of the regions of Madras Presidency that went on
to constitute Tamil Nadu was literate, but this was still marginally higher than
Travancore and Cochin as well as the North-Central Indian provinces. This
had increased to 7.5 percent by 1901. Moreover, the Madras Census Report of
1891 stated that "The higher a caste or race stands in a social scale, the better
is its educational position." Essentially, this meant that most of those educated
were Brahmins, while the other castes, who constituted the overwhelming
majority of the population, remained illiterate.

A similar situation plagued the health sector. Arooran notes that there were
no initiatives in the field of health reform in the Madras Presidency until the
first decade of the twentieth century (1980: 5). At the close of the nineteenth
century, diseases such as smallpox, as well as famines, were endemic, causing
"terrible" mortality and suffering (Kumar et al. 1994: 381; Raghavaiyangar
1893: 27). The life expectancy of a native of Madras was a mere twenty-three
years (Raghavaiyangar 1893: 182). The best that could be said about the status
of public health in the Presidency was that it was likely no worse than in times
past (ibid.: 184).

Emergence of Elite Tamil Subnationalism Triggers Progressive Social Policy but Absence of Popular Subnationalism Limits Developmental Gains: 1900–1940s

The early years of the twentieth century witnessed the emergence of a Tamil
identity among a set of aspirational non-Brahmin elites. As discussed in detail
in Chapter 3, in their challenge to the Brahmin monopoly of government positions
in the early twentieth century, non-Brahmin elites drew on developments in the
cultural realm, notably the Tamil revival/renaissance, which portrayed a pristine,

ancient Tamil/ Dravidian civilization that had been sullied by corrupting Aryan influences, to construct a parallel narrative of how the indigenous inhabitants of the region had been reduced to a position of complete sociopolitical subservience by foreign Brahmins. The very emergence of Tamil subnationalism was therefore rooted in the idea of the restoration of Tamil welfare. Lifting the Tamil people out of the "downtrodden" status that they had been reduced to through Aryan hegemony and returning them to a position of glory was one of the leitmotifs of the early non-Brahmin/ Dravidian/ Tamil movement. The names of the earliest subnationalist organizations – for example, the South Indian *Welfare* Association, the *Justice* Party, and the *Self-Respect* movement – all indicate the close ties between the evolution of a Tamil identity and the themes of social justice and dignity. A growing affinity with the Tamil subnation motivated a large number of people to adopt Tamil names at this time. It is again indicative of the intimate connection between Tamil subnationalism and social justice that one of the most popular names adopted was Nedunchezhian, the name of an ancient Tamil king who died of shame when he learned that he had committed an act of injustice to a fellow Tamil (Spratt 1970: 37).

Non-Brahmin elites who were the first to espouse Tamil subnationalism thus came to emphasize social services almost as a corollary. In 1917 the Non-Brahmin Conference passed a resolution protesting against the utilization of Hindu religious and other charitable funds for founding Sanskrit schools, which only benefited members of the Brahmin community and urged the government and the trustees of such institutions to instead devote these funds to the establishment of primary schools, which can uplift the community at large (Arooran 1980: 146). In the elections of 1921 in which it was victorious, the Justice Party contested on the platform of "the improvement of the lot of the Dravidians." This included support for agriculture and crucially, the promotion of education and health (Rajayyan 1982: 315). Once in power, the Justice regime under Raja Panagal worked on its promise to uplift the Tamil people. The party's two most important policy planks in this regard were the enactment of affirmative action policies for members of non-Brahmin communities in state employment and the provision of social services, especially education and health, for all residents. In 1922, for example, the Justice Ministry passed a bill for the better administration of religious endowments, which recommended "the diversion of surplus funds of religious endowments for purposes of public utility" (Arooran 1980: 147).[1] The 1931 Census Report for Madras noted that

---

[1] This triggered a controversy about whether such a provision was in consonance with the intentions of the donors. The *Hindu*, a newspaper, widely seen as a sympathizer of the Brahmins, railed that it was in violation of the cy-près doctrine to use funds of *Hindu*, predominantly Brahmin, endowments for the establishment of schools and hospitals "of which other communities ... would be equal beneficiaries" (Arooran 1980: 148). In contrast, newspapers sympathetic to the Tamil subnationalist cause, such as the *Madras Mail*, lauded the "radical" impulse to direct the surplus monies toward works of public utilities, which would ameliorate the condition of all Tamils (Arooran 1980: 147).

the government had appointed an officer as the Commissioner of Labor among whose particular functions was attending to the needs of depressed classes, notably the provision of schools (1931: 343). In the 1930s, Periyar laid out a fourteen-point program for the Justice Party, which included the introduction of compulsory primary education (Arooran 1980: 181). In 1939, the Madras Presidency was the first province in British India to pass a Public Health Act, which put the responsibility for the provision of public health services, including maternal and child health, in the hands of the state. Through the 1940s the leaders of the subnationalist movement continued to stress their commitment to improving the welfare of Tamils.

From the 1900s to the 1940s, the Madras government allocated a relatively high proportion of its total budget to the social sector. As Table 4.1 shows, in 1910–11 Madras devoted 5.4 percent of its total expenditure to education, as compared with 5 percent in Mysore in 1911–12, 4.6 percent in Baroda in 1904–05, and 5.5 percent in Travancore in 1900–1901. By the early 1940s, spending on education had risen to 16 percent, which was equivalent to that of Baroda and Travancore, and higher than Mysore (10%). Expenditure on all social and developmental services constituted 38.24 percent of total expenditure in Madras, which was second only to Baroda and Travancore (see Table 4.2). Yet the level of social development in Madras was significantly below that of Baroda and Travancore and roughly equivalent to Mysore. This is because the absence of popular subnationalism and consequently the limited degree of sociopolitical awareness and participation circumscribed the benefits of a progressive social policy.

As noted in Chapter 3, during this period Tamil subnationalism was limited to an elite stratum. Non-elites, especially in rural areas, were not mobilized by either the Justice Party or the Self-Respect movement and for the most part remained politically apathetic. Consequently, while leaders of the subnationalist movement campaigned for and enacted social policies for the welfare of Tamils, most residents, especially in rural areas, were not very closely involved with the public services provided. The schools and hospitals established by the state were not well-utilized and/ or did not function effectively.

The lack of societal participation limited the potential development gains of substantial budgetary expenditures in Madras Presidency. Inspite of a fivefold expansion in hospital beds between 1880 and 1944, the health status of the population of Madras remained "deplorable" (MIDS). While the province did register important social gains – literacy, for example, increased from 6 percent in 1901 to approximately 11 percent in 1931 (Figure 1.4) – this improvement was limited as compared to other provinces, such as Travancore. As will be shown later in this chapter, Malayali subnationalism had taken root at both elite and popular levels, and consequently only marginally higher social spending, when supplemented by popular involvement with public services, led to a greater improvement in social indicators in Travancore.

TABLE 4.1. *Education Expenditure in Select Indian Provinces (1879–1901)*

	Cochin (1879–80)	Mysore (1911–12)	Hyderabad (1913–14)	Baroda (1904–05)	Madras (1910–11)	Travancore (1900–01)
Education Expenditure	Rs 28142	Rs 1075166	Rs 1164882	Rs 674011	Rs 3986092	Rs 531851
Total Expenditure	Rs 1364062	Rs 21814792	Rs 52310009	Rs 14586293	Rs 77200006	Rs 9584590
Education Expenditure as Percentage of Total Expenditure	2.1	4.9	2.2	4.6	5.4	5.5

Source: Bright Singh, "Financial Developments in Travancore (1800–1940)," Unpublished PhD thesis, Travancore University (1944), p. 406.

TABLE 4.2. *Expenditure on All Social and Developmental Services
in Indian Provinces as Proportion of Total Expenditure (1940s)*

Province	Percentage
Cochin	47.09
Travancore	39.5
Baroda	38.96
Madras	38.24
Hyderabad	35.68
Bengal	34.03
Bombay	33.1
Mysore	32.64
Bikaner	23.83
Indore	28.3
Kashmir	23.43

Source: Bright Singh, "Financial Developments in Travancore (1800–1940),"
Unpublished PhD thesis, Travancore University (1944), p. 654.

Strengthening of Popular Subnationalism Leads to Significant Improvements in Social Development: 1950s–1960s

As discussed in Chapter 3, Annadurai's rise to the helm of the Tamil nationalist movement, in particular his establishment of the DMK, played a critical
role in the expansion of the popular base of the Tamil nationalist movement. The 1950s and 1960s witnessed the mass internalization of Tamil
subnational solidarity, which was firmly foregrounded in the concept of
social justice and collective welfare through the speeches and writings of
leaders as well as via movies. In his writings Annadurai set out a vision of
a "good society" in the mold of the glorious, ancient Tamil civilization in
which all Tamilians had access to an equal and honorable life, as captured
by his famous dictum – "All are Kings in the Land" (Barnett 1976: 74). The
demand for an independent homeland of the Tamils, discussed in Chapter 3,
was, according to a prominent scholar of Tamil politics, made "(at least initially) to facilitate achievement of social reform" (ibid.). In support of this
argument, Barnett cites articles in *Murosoli*, the DMK spokespiece that echo
the theme that "all good things would come with Dravida Nadu." One article, for example, states that "In the Dravida Nadu that we are going to,
there will be absolute equality and it will be marked by social reformation"
(1976: 74–93). Similar themes were echoed in the memoranda submitted to
the States Reorganization Commission in support of the formation of Tamil
Nadu as a state in the Indian union in the mid-1950s. A petition submitted by the DMK, for example, stated, "States to be really happy, prosperous
and progressive need a cohesion which can be contributed by language, race,

history." Another petition presented the demand for the formation of the linguistic state of Tamil Nadu as "an urge in the hearts of millions of people concerned, to get their own homeland, and set it in order, sanctify it and ennoble it by their special contribution." Other memoranda spoke of "the awakening and progress" that would result from the uniting of people who spoke a common language into a single political unit.[2]

Cinema, one of the primary mediums for the spread of Tamil subnationalism, consistently and powerfully reflected the theme of Tamil welfare. MG Ramachandran, or MGR, as he was commonly known, was one of the most popular Tamil film stars and a prominent member of the DMK, who later formed a breakaway party, the Anna DMK, and served as Chief Minister from 1977 until his death a decade later. MGR played numerous "hero" roles that portrayed him as simultaneously upholding Tamil values and toiling for the welfare of the Tamilian masses. He is reported to have said that the main purpose of the runaway hit, *Nadodi Mannan* (1958), in which he had a double role and also wrote, directed, and produced, was to show that "the DMK party is serving the people of this country" (Dickey 1993: 356).[3] Another classic of Tamil cinema, *Parasakti* (1952), written by Karunanidhi, who succeeded Annadurai as the leader of the DMK and has served as Chief Minister of the state for five terms, for example, "opens with a long monologue bewailing the plight of Tamilians who had to leave their native country because of poverty" (Barnett 1976: 82). Barnett recalls that the scene that laments the "fate of the Tamilians who had to sleep in the streets because they had no homes" was still being cheered by the audience when she saw the movie in the late 1960s (83).

In the popular psyche Tamil subnationalism had therefore become closely tied to the concept of the collective uplifting of the Tamil people. After the 1957 elections, the Communist journal *Janasakthi* admitted that the DMK had been highly successful in creating the impression among Tamilians that as a Tamil subnationalist party it was "the only party really interested in their welfare" (Barnett 1976: 97). Barnett's interviews with a randomly selected sample of heads of households in a neighborhood in Madras city in 1968 show that Tamil subnationalism had penetrated widely, cutting across caste and class lines, and had served to inculcate both a positive conception of Tamilians, for example, "as generous to a fault" and "good and active people," as well as support for the welfare of all Tamilians (1976). This is brought out, for instance,

---

[2] Memorandum submitted by the Dravida Munnetra Kazhagam. National Archives of India. File no. 25/13/54-SRC, Volume III.

[3] As Forrester notes, "always, either explicitly or just below the surface, there was a political message in his films: the DMK was the party that does in real life what MGR does in the film, the party that loves and serves the poor, that does battle with evil, that delivers the oppressed" (1976: 288).

in the identification, even by wealthy and high-caste Brahmin interviewees, of the "elimination of inequality and injustice" and "better medical facilities" as the main problems facing the state (168–81).

It is interesting that the Congress party, which controlled the government until 1966, also tried to give itself a subnationalist image. Aware of the growing sense of subnational solidarity among the people of the Tamil country, the Congress Chief Minister Kamaraj Nadar appealed to Tamil patriotism and included no Brahmins in his cabinet (Fadia 1984: 221; Hardgrave 1964). The Congress also tacitly accepted the support of Periyar,[4] who hailed Kamaraj as a "*pachchai Tamizhan*" (pure Tamilian) (Subramanian 1999: 151). As Fadia writes, "The new government, while not abandoning the secular unity of the Indian constitution, took on a new regional image of Tamil nationalism" (Fadia 1984: 221). The party also made social development one of its primary policy platforms. Education and health were key topics for discussion in the state assembly during these decades. Only a few weeks into the first session of the inaugural democratically elected TN state legislature in independent India, education and health were the subjects of very lengthy and lively debates involving many participants and covering issues such as the challenges of providing basic education, school infrastructure, teachers' salaries, and the education of marginalized groups such as the former "untouchables," Muslims and girls, as well as primary health infrastructure; the number of doctors and nurses and their salaries; the means of tackling diseases such as TB and cancer; and the establishment of medical colleges to produce trained personnel (Tamil Nadu State Assembly 1952). The Congress government sharply increased budgetary outlays on the social sector – expenditure on health, for example, multiplied more than three times from 1956 to 1966 – and also implemented new policies, such as the introduction of Primary Health centers, of which nearly 200 had been established by 1970.

Senior journalists that I had an opportunity to interview were unequivocal that Congress's emphasis on the social sector through the 1950s and 1960s was indicative of the party's attempt to align itself with Tamil subnationalist sentiment.[5] Such an argument gains credence by the disjuncture between the policies of the Tamil Nadu Congress and that of the national Congress. The national policy agenda set by the Congress in New Delhi emphasized industrialization rather than social development. The policies of most state Congress governments, such as Uttar Pradesh, reflected these central priorities. While

---

[4] Periyar fell out with Annadurai when the latter broke away to form the DMK, ostensibly in objection to Periyar's marriage to a woman 40 years his junior.

[5] A senior journalist at the *Hindu* publication house told me that "Kamaraj picked up on the pulse of the people. He knew that the cry on the streets was Tamil nationalism so he adopted 'Tamilization' … he removed all Brahmins from his cabinet, promoted Tamil language … and introduced social welfare policies, which were the main programs of the Dravidians."

the Congress regime in Tamil Nadu did not entirely eschew industrialization, its adoption of a significant social program set it apart from Congress governments in New Delhi and the rest of India, with the exception of Kerala where, as will be discussed in the next section, a similar process of public support for Malayali welfare and competition with a subnationalist party served as an impetus for the Congress's expansion of the education and health sectors.

In the 1967 elections the DMK won a resounding victory and within a year of assuming power the party had enacted a number of significant social programs, such as the "one-rupee-per-measure-of-rice plan," the lowering of prices on a number of other food commodities, the provision of public houses for the most destitute sections of society, and the waiving of tuition fees for poor students of all castes in the pre-university and pre-technical courses (Subramanian 1999: 207). The DMK extended the numbers of schools and hospitals and paid special attention to the education of lower castes through the granting of scholarships and the opening of hostels (Spratt 1970: 52).

Progressive social policy from the top down was reinforced by bottom-up inputs from a citizenry that had been politicized by the subnational movement. Scholars concur that the emotional appeal of the ideology of Tamil subnationalism, together with the mass cultural means that were employed to disseminate the message, combined to mobilize large sections of the population in both urban and rural areas (Barnett 1976; Subramanian 1999). The vision of a Tamil society and polity articulated by the DMK drew heavily upon themes of a glorious Tamil past but also appeared "fresh and bravely innovational" to the people (Price 1996: 365). Scores of Tamilians were attracted to this "new cosmology" (ibid.) and politicized through the films, street theater, and public oratory of the DMK.

On the eve of the 1962 elections, the DMK leaders initiated a massive voter registration drive that resulted in the largest increase yet in voter participation in the state's electoral history, from 49.3 percent in 1957 to 70.7 percent in 1962. It is notable that this increase extended across gender and rural/urban divides. In the 1971 National Election Studies survey, respondents in Tamil Nadu reported a higher degree of political interest than in both UP and Rajasthan (see Table 4.3). The intense identification with the Tamil polity together with an associated rise in political awareness made people more likely to be involved with projects for the public good. Almost all districts of the state, for example, witnessed the emergence of the so-called Prosperity Brigades, usually led by young DMK activists and composed of local men and women who contributed an hour's labor for necessary public projects (Subramanian 1999: 207). Residents also tended to be more active in demanding and monitoring state social services. The Rudolphs report that during a field survey they conducted in 1957, villagers in Tamil Nadu pressured interviewers to communicate their demands, for example for the establishment or improvement of a clinic, laying of a tube well or road repairs, to the district collector (Rudolph & Rudolph

TABLE 4.3. *Political Consciousness in Case Study States (1971–2004)*

	Respondents with "Somewhat" or "Great Deal of Interest" in Election Campaign (%)			Respondents with "Somewhat" or "Great Deal of Interest" in Politics and Public Affairs (%)		
	1971	1996	2004	1971	1996	2004
Tamil Nadu	47.2	60.5	57.7	32.5	42.5	53
Kerala	49	73	53.4	53	50	49
Uttar Pradesh	21.6	47	34.2	22.8	47	37
Rajasthan	20.5	24	39.5	25.1	29	39
India	32	35	43	34	35	43

Source: National Election Studies, CSDS, New Delhi (1971, 1996, 2004).

1962). In her study of Tamil villages in the early 1960s, Joan Mencher notes the "surprising eagerness for schooling" especially among the lowest castes in rural Tamil Nadu and writes about how she was repeatedly requested to speak to the government authorities about arranging literacy classes (1980).[6]

Progressive social policy and popular involvement reinforced each other to generate substantial improvements in social development during this period. Literacy rates soared from 20 percent in 1951 to 45.4 percent in 1971 (see Figure 1.4), leading Tamil Nadu to overtake states such as West Bengal and Gujarat, which had a relative lead in 1951. The rate of increase in literacy in Tamil Nadu during this period was in fact marginally higher than in Kerala. The infant mortality rate of the state was halved from 123.1 in 1951 to 68 in 1966.

Tamil Subnationalism Fosters High Levels of Social Development: 1970s Onward

During this period, Tamil Nadu witnessed the consolidation of a powerful and widespread subnationalism. Writing in 1979 Brass noted that "a socially frag-mented society" had been transformed in to a "politically integrated region" (1979). In the early 1980s another scholar wrote that the Tamil subnationalist movement had brought "the people of Tamil Nadu to an awareness of itself as a community" (Fadia 1984: 219). From the late 1960s to the present date, the state government has been controlled by subnationalist parties, the DMK or its splinter party, the ADMK, which have competed to present themselves as greater champions of the Tamil people. Insofar as the promotion of the cause

---

[6] My interviews with elderly villagers in six villages across three districts in Tamil Nadu in 2005 also pointed to a high degree of involvement with the location and functioning of government schools and hospitals during the 1950s and 1960s.

of the Tamil people had by this time come to be firmly defined in terms of two, inextricably linked platforms – the protection and promotion of Tamil culture and the promotion of social services – the policy agenda through these years has been dominated by these twin concerns.

Upon assuming power in 1967, as discussed in Chapter 3, the DMK regime immediately adopted the policy of "Tamil everywhere and in everything." As part of this policy, a poem in praise of Tamilttay, the Goddess of Tamil, was institutionalized as the state "prayer song" in 1970. This glorification of Tamilttay is evocative of the relationship between Tamil subnationalism and Tamil welfare and in this respect, similar to the elevation of the symbol of Mahabali in Kerala. Parallel to the myth of Mahabali, described later in this chapter, Tamilttay was believed to have reigned in the "Tamil golden age of distant antiquity" in a time of "peace, prosperity and happiness." In Tamilttay's reign, "there had been no inequities based on caste, creed or gender. Learning, culture and civilization had flourished" (Ramaswamy 1993: 691). As in Kerala, the state's widespread evocation of the symbol of Tamilttay reinforced the association between Tamil subnationalism and the idea of an egalitarian and developed Tamil society. The ancient, resplendent Tamil civilization that the DMK presented as a model for contemporary Tamil society and polity was one where all Tamilians were equal, educated, and healthy.

In 1972 a personality clash between Karunanindhi and MGR led the latter to break away from the DMK to form the Anna DMK (ADMK), which maintained its continuity with Tamil subnationalism but emphasized its deeper commitment to questions of social justice. As exemplified by the name of the party and the introduction of his portrait into the flag, the party styled itself as the true successor of Annadurai, stressing that it would dedicate itself to implementing the great leader's vision of the welfare of the Tamil people, which they argued had been abandoned by the DMK. As a political leader MGR sought to reinforce his cinematic persona as the upholder of Tamil values and crusader for the development of the Tamil people. From the early 1970s, the DMK and the ADMK have competed fiercely in the electoral arena, moving in and out of power. Each party has attempted to outdo the other in terms of presenting itself as the authentic guardians of a splendid Tamil culture and as the "real friend of the poor" (Forrester 1976: 290).[7] It is interesting to note that the glorification

---

[7] What is especially interesting is the way in which the two parties have vied to celebrate the symbol of the ancient Tamil philosopher-poet, Thiruvalluvar, who, like Tamilttay, represents the close relationship between Tamil subnationalism and social welfare. Thiruvalluvar, the son of an untouchable mother, is the author of Thirukkural, a collection of more than a thousand rhyming couplets that is revered as a classic in Tamil literature. The couplets of Thirukkural reverberate with the theme of the importance of mutual obligations between, and the necessity of working for the welfare of, one's countrymen. In the early 1970s, the DMK government passed an order mandating the prominent display of sayings from Thirukkural in public places, such as buses and government offices, and also conceived of a project of installing a giant statue of the poet at the confluence of three seas at Cape Comorin, the southernmost point of the Indian peninsula.

of Tamil culture came to be closely tied to the idea of Tamil welfare not only in the elite but also equally in the popular imagination.[8]

The social programs of the DMK and ADMK regimes are commonly described/ derided both in the media and in scholarly literature as "populism" or "patronage." Such classifications, however, obscure more than they illuminate and have drawn attention away from the state's unwavering commitment to the social sector in general, and education and health in particular.[9] Both DMK and ADMK governments have allocated substantial budgetary outlays to the education and health sectors and have, between them, introduced a range of social programs that are distinguished by their autonomy, ingenuity, and scope. The issue of Tamil welfare has figured prominently in the dealings of the state government with New Delhi. Successive state governments have consistently petitioned the central government for financial support for their social schemes,[10] protested national directives perceived to be inimical to the social development of Tamilians,[11] rejected central programs that they do not

---

It was the ADMK regime that moved ahead with this idea, laying the foundation stone of the statue in 1975. The DMK allocated substantial funds for the construction of the statue when it returned to power in the 1990s. On January 1, 2000, Karunanidhi unveiled the colossal stone monument in a gala ceremony, which was preceded by a two-day literary festival that featured symposia on Thiruvalluvar and his work, the release of a compact disc and recitation of Thirukkural by children (Hindu 2000). Not to be left behind, when the ADMK assumed power in the early 2000s, it passed a unanimous resolution demanding that Thirukkural be given the status of national literature (Hindu 2005).

[8] Studies of Tamil villages in the 1970s (Harriss 1979) and in the 1990s (Price 1996) both discerned two main themes in the informants' responses about why they supported subnationalist parties – first, their emphasis on the "special nature of the Tamil people" and second, the stress on social justice (Price 1996: 366). Price notes that the DMK's focus "on the acquisition of knowledge and the widening of educational opportunities" should be seen in the context of these two "principles" (ibid.).

[9] Most scholars of Tamil Nadu recognize the close connection between "populism" and "patronage" and the institution of a progressive social policy. Subramanian for example writes that "the agenda of paternalist populism ... distributed ... forms of patronage, which addressed the basic needs of the lower strata ... the lunches which paternal populism dispensed ... improv(ed) the health and perhaps the life expectancy and educational attainments of many children from these strata" (1999: 309). He clarifies that "the patronage extended ... appeared to be aimed at social development, rather than to be a part of a political bargain, although such a bargain was implicit" (1999: 287). In a comparative analysis of the post-poll surveys of the state elections of 2011 and 2012 in Tamil Nadu and UP respectively, my co-author and I found that incumbent political parties were more likely to target welfare programs to supporters, and that recipients of welfare programs were in turn more likely to vote for the incumbent political party, in Tamil Nadu as compared to UP. (Singh and Shroff 2014). We take this as evidence for distinct subnational patterns of patronage-based on provision of social welfare (TN) or not (UP) – within the overall context of India as a "patronage democracy" (Chandra 2000).

[10] The Tamil Nadu state government for example, notably approached New Delhi for greater allotment of rice from the national pool in order to sustain their cheap rice scheme, which according to Subramanian, "signaled the regime's commitment to improving the lives of the lower strata" (1999: 205).

[11] In a speech at the meeting of the Central Advisory Board of Education (CABE) in 1970, the Tamil Nadu Education Minister complained that "The Centre should not distribute its resources

perceive to be relevant for Tamil needs,[12] and adopted social policies despite opposition from New Delhi. The flagship social scheme in Tamil Nadu, the free mid-day meal program was, for example, introduced under stiff opposition from the national government because of concerns of financial viability.[13] It is also important to note here the symbolic importance of this highly successful scheme. Insofar as sharing food is a key means through which social status is affirmed, the arrangement for members of all castes and religions to eat together sent a powerful message of their equal recognition as Tamil citizens (Subramanian 1999: 285). The program has been extended under successive DMK and ADMK governments, and in 1995 this scheme was used as a model by the national government to introduce a national mid-day meal program for all Indian states. In addition, the Tamil Nadu government has also initiated innovative policies to improve the state's educational infrastructure by encouraging local involvement[14] as well as providing free textbooks and uniforms to all children in government and government-aided primary schools.

During this period Tamil Nadu governments have also shown remarkable initiative in their interventions to improve the state's health indicators which, in the early 1970s were worse than or equivalent to the Indian average.[15] Two unique features of the state health sector are the institution of a specialized cadre of public health officials and the creation, in 1994, of an autonomous

in such a way that the so-called educationally backward States get grants from the Centre at the expense of the educationally forward States ... Every state should get its due share of the amount available with the Central Government and the educationally forward states should continue to develop further on right lines. As far as Tamil Nadu is concerned, there has been considerable taxation on the people during all the plan periods and the entire additional amount collected has been spent on the development of educational facilities. Even now there is considerable demand for opening more schools. I do not want that by increasing the amount available on educational development in the Central Sector and the Centrally-sponsored sector, the amount available to State Governments for education schemes is reduced" (http://education.nic .in/cd50years/g/12/1N/121No301.htm).

[12] In the 1990s, Tamil Nadu rejected the centrally sponsored *Navodaya Vidyalaya* scheme as not relevant to its situation. A senior bureaucrat in the Department of Education, Ministry of Human Resource Development in New Delhi told me, "You can call it courage or bull-headedness but Kerala, Tamil Nadu and West Bengal are the only states which have said no to central schemes, even when there has been substantial sums of money on offer." Interview on July 15, 2006, New Delhi.

[13] At the time of its initiation by the ADMK in 1982, the program provided a free lunch for approximately six million rural children in government schools between the ages of 2 and 9. In 1984 the program was extended to urban areas and to school children between the ages of 10 and 15. By 1986 it included more than twelve million children (a fifth of the state's population). About 200,000 people were employed to implement this scheme, with preference given to destitute widows and members of the Scheduled Castes. The scheme proved to be very popular, especially among the poor and women, and various independent studies confirm that is has boosted children's health and school enrollment figures.

[14] One innovative scheme in this regard was that the government would honor a private donor who contributed at least 50% of the expenditure for the building of a primary school or constructed two rooms for a school by naming the school after them (Mehrotra 2007: 18).

[15] From 1970 to 1975, life expectancy in Tamil Nadu was 49 years as compared with 50 years across all Indian states. In 1970, IMR in Tamil Nadu was 125 as compared with 129 in all Indian states.

medical services corporation (Tamil Nadu Medical Services Corporation), which serves as an apex body for the purchase, storage, and distribution of drugs and other medical supplies. In 1995 Tamil Nadu explicitly drafted a state policy on nutrition with technical support from the UNICEF. According to the Tamil Nadu Human Development Report, it is the first state to draft such a policy following the 1993 National Nutrition Policy. The policy was reformulated in 2002–03 as the Policy for Malnutrition Free Tamil Nadu (Tamil Nadu Human Development Report 2003).

Another distinctive feature of the state's social policy regime has been the introduction, since the 1990s, of a range of innovative social schemes based on a reward and incentive system that operates at both the individual and community levels. A female health worker who ensures that there is no infant death during a year in her area, is for example, rewarded with a gold sovereign. The medical officer of the primary health center (PHC) that registers the highest percentage reduction in infant mortality rate, and the collector of the district in which that PHC is located, are both awarded rolling shields. In order to reduce home deliveries by untrained personnel in rural areas, the village health nurse (VHN) is paid Rs. 50 for conducting a delivery at home. VHNs are also encouraged to refer complicated pregnancies to higher levels of care and are paid Rs. 25 for each timely referral. In order to facilitate their coverage of the area under their jurisdiction, the government also provides VHNs a monetary advance toward the purchase of a cycle or two-wheeler (Mehrotra 2007: 16). A similar incentive system has also been instituted in the education sector by which the three best-performing schools from each district are chosen for the Best School Award.

The creativity of the state government's social programs is especially evident in schemes that have the potential to improve health services and indicators at little or no extra cost to the exchequer. The Birth Companionship Scheme, introduced in 2003, which allows for the presence of a female relative in the labor room, has for example, decreased medical interventions during labor, reduced the number of instrumental vaginal births and caesarean sections, and increased satisfaction with the birthing process. This scheme along with others such as the Verbal Autopsy of maternal deaths, which adds to the traditional testimony by the doctors (who tend to blame the mother for coming to the health center too late), the testimony of the relatives of the deceased mother (who now have a chance to air their grievances), introduce critical elements of accountability into the provision of health services in the state, which are likely to improve their quality (Padmanaban et al. 2009).

Successive Tamil Nadu state governments have also initiated special schemes to tackle diseases such as malaria, leprosy, TB, and AIDS. Tamil Nadu has in fact been a pioneer in the institution of AIDS policies. It was the first state in India to form a state-level AIDS-control society to implement the program in a "fast-track mode" in partnership with NGOs, community-based organizations, the private sector, as well as national and international agencies (Tamil Nadu

Human Development Report 2003). The state's high rates of HIV infection certainly necessitated such an aggressive response, but as Lieberman's (2009) analysis convincingly demonstrates, this was only possible because the state government perceived AIDS as a potential risk for *all* Tamils. In contrast, other states, such as Maharashtra and Karnataka, which have comparable rates of HIV infection have not implemented such a proactive policy because ethnic boundaries are more salient, the subnational community is more fragmented, and the state government consequently perceives and portrays AIDS as a risk only for certain sections of the population rather than as an equal threat for all Maharashtrians and Kannadigas (Lieberman 2009).

The state has supplemented these education and health programs for the population at large with a number of targeted schemes to address the special needs of the underprivileged and historically oppressed communities. The Tamil Nadu government has, for example, maintained the system of special schools for the Scheduled Castes instituted by the British.[16] Students in these schools as well as SC/ST children in regular schools are entitled to tuition fee concessions, hostel accommodations, free textbooks, notebooks, slates, two sets of uniforms, free bicycles, and a range of merit-based awards and scholarships.

In addition to their creativity and the breadth of problems that they address, social schemes in Tamil Nadu are notable for the way in which they are integrated not only with each other but also with broader social initiatives. The TN Human Development Report describes how the state made "serious attempts" to combine the provision of the mid-day meal in schools with other services, such as healthcare, immunization, growth monitoring, pre- and post-natal care for women, and nutrition education through programs like the Integrated Child Development Scheme (ICDS) and the Tamil Nadu Integrated Nutrition Program (TINP) (2003: 55). Initiatives in related social sectors, for example, the establishment of women's self-help groups (SHGs) that seek to empower women financially and make them more responsible decision-makers vis-à-vis their family and children, are likely to reinforce maternal and child health schemes as well as increase female enrollment in schools.

The consistency of the Tamil Nadu state's emphasis on the education and health sectors reflects the shared social commitment of the Tamil subnationalist parties, the DMK and ADMK, which have alternated in controlling the government through this period.[17] The speeches and statements of both parties

---

[16] As of 2006, the state ran 1048 Adi Dravidar Welfare Schools with approximately 201386 students, and 283 Tribal Residential Schools with 36447 students.

[17] Bureaucrats who have worked in the education and health departments under both DMK and ADMK governments told me that these sectors have been equally prioritized under both regimes. Supriya Sahoo, a member of the Indian Administrative Service who has worked in the health sector in Tamil Nadu for many years, said that "At least in this respect there is not much difference between the two parties. For both, social schemes have been a central plank. Each party has its own pet policies, for example, the previous DMK government emphasized that the

highlight their policies for the promotion of Tamil culture and social development as their main achievements. The DMK manifesto for the assembly elections of 2006, which the party won, stated that "the DMK has been ceaselessly
working for the past 57 years for upholding the highest humanitarian values of
equality, social justice and egalitarianism, for protecting the ancient and living
Tamil race, language and cultural heritage."

In recent years, with the rise of coalitions at the national level and the concomitant importance of regional parties, the DMK and the ADMK have become
involved in politics in New Delhi. However, in contrast to UP where, as will be
discussed in the next chapter, an engagement of the state Congress and other parties with national politics led to a total eclipse of the subnational arena, the DMK
and ADMK have acted on the central stage as staunch representatives of Tamil
Nadu. Their participation in central coalitions has been framed firmly in terms of
the promotion of Tamil welfare. The DMK, for example, justified its decision to
join the UPA government in New Delhi in 2004 as the utilization of an opportunity "to continue to discharge its democratic duty for securing and implementing
various pioneering schemes for the development of Tamil Nadu."[18]

Tamil subnationalism not only motivated both the DMK and ADMK to
enact progressive social policies but also played an important role in politiciz-
ing the people of Tamil Nadu. In contrast to the Congress, which aggregated
already mobilized interests, the subnational parties have mobilized emergent
groups (Subramanian 1999: 319). The ADMK, which was formed in 1972,
reached out to the most marginalized communities, for example, women and
people from the lowest socioeconomic strata who had been at the margins of
DMK mobilization. Scholars of Tamil Nadu note that as popular mobilization
was crucial to the electoral success of the subnational parties, they "could not
afford to demobilize supporters too much even after they had attained power"
(Subramanian 1999: 319). Subnational mobilization therefore promoted a
high degree of political consciousness across a large cross-section of the Tamil

whole state should be cataract-free; while for the present Jayalalitha government the focus is on
the establishment of rural hospitals. But the social sector – health, education, women's empowerment, rural development – are very important for both the DMK and ADMK alike." Interview
with Supriya Sahoo, director, World Bank Project on Health, Government of Tamil Nadu, on
November 16, 2005, Chennai, Tamil Nadu. At the time of the interview, the ADMK controlled
the state legislature and Jayalalitha was Chief Minister.

[18] Incidentally, through the entire tenure of the UPA government (2004–2009), the DMK threatened to withdraw its support over only one issue – the perceived failure of New Delhi to demand
an end to atrocities against Tamils in Sri Lanka. In October 2008 fourteen DMK legislators,
including two ministers in the national government, tendered their resignations and all forty
legislators from Tamil Nadu threatened to resign if New Delhi did not act on the issue of the Sri
Lankan Tamils. On November 4, 2008 Tamil Nadu Chief Minister Karunanidhi defused the situation by issuing a statement that read, "we have a Centre, which realizes the plight of Tamils in
Sri Lanka, and the leaders there respect our sentiments." He claimed that New Delhi was doing
its best to mitigate the sufferings of the Tamils of Lanka but "We have to raise our demands to
increase their action" (Hindu 2008).

population. Table 4.3 indicates the high degree of political consciousness and interest among the residents of Tamil Nadu as measured by the National Election Survey of 2004, compared to other Indian states.

This high degree of politicization, in the context of subnational solidarity, has encouraged popular involvement with the social services provided by the state, which has contributed to their efficient utilization and functioning. My interviews with bureaucrats who had served as district collectors in different districts of the state from the 1970s onward revealed a high degree of local monitoring of schools and health centers. A comparative study of healthcare utilization among groups with similar socioeconomic status and roughly equivalent access to health services in UP and Tamil Nadu in the late 1980s reported a higher rate of use of healthcare facilities, for example, hospital deliveries, in Tamil Nadu (Basu 1990). Relative to the national average, Tamil Nadu shows a high degree of utilization of public sector facilities in both rural and urban areas in 1986–87 as well as in 1995–96 (Tamil Nadu Human Development Report 2003).

State commitment to the social sector supplemented by societal involvement with social services has yielded rich development dividends. According to both the 2001 and 2011 Censuses, Tamil Nadu now has the third position, behind Kerala and Maharashtra, among major Indian states both in terms of overall and female literacy. The state has also made striking gains in the health sector. As Figure 1.7 shows, in 1970 the IMR for Tamil Nadu and India were relatively close at 125 and 129 respectively. Since the 1970s however, Tamil Nadu's IMR has declined much more rapidly than the Indian average. By the end of the 1980s, IMR in Tamil Nadu had dipped to 68 while that of all Indian states was 91. By 2000, Tamil Nadu had an IMR of 51, which was one of the lowest of all Indian states (Tamil Nadu Human Development Report 2003: 47). Today, Tamil Nadu has one of the best records of immunization of all Indian states. According to the National Family and Health Survey, 84 percent of all births in Tamil Nadu in 1995 were attended by a trained health professional. This was double the Indian rate of 42 percent and second only to Kerala. This period also witnessed a significant improvement in life expectancy in Tamil Nadu, both in terms of overall levels as well as the equitability of its distribution. Life expectancy for the state as a whole increased by fourteen years, from forty-nine years in 1970–75 to sixty-six years in the early 2000s, and the lags in the rates for rural areas and women were virtually eliminated.

KERALA

This section compares three time periods – until the 1890s; from the 1890s to the 1950s, and from the 1950s on – corresponding to the absence, emergence, and strengthening of Malayali subnationalism, which in turn led to low, increasing, and high levels of education and health expenditures and development in Kerala respectively. In the first subsection I show that until the 1890s, in the absence of any sense of a shared identity, the government of the princely state of Travancore[19] paid minimal attention to the social sector and consequently the state was characterized by rates of illiteracy and mortality that were higher than or equivalent to those of many other Indian states. In the second subsection, which focuses on the period from the late nineteenth century to the end of British colonial rule, I highlight how the emergence of Malayali subnationalism, initially among elites and gradually among the population at large, triggered public support for collective welfare, which pushed the state to prioritize the social sector. A progressive social policy is shown to have been introduced, and an increase in education and health indicators occurred, only *after* and *as a consequence of* the emergence of a cohesive subnational community. In the third subsection I delineate how in the post-independence period a powerful Malayali subnationalism generated consistently high state social expenditures as well as active societal involvement with schools and clinics, which together led to the significant improvements in education and health that underlie Kerala's status as an exemplar of social development.

Absence of Subnationalism Impedes Social Development: Up to the 1890s

Until the late nineteenth century, the socioeconomic and political life of the regions that came to constitute Kerala were, like in Tamil Nadu, structured around the identities of caste and religion.[20] There was no conception yet of a broader Malayali solidarity. Around the middle of the nineteenth century, Travancore was in deep financial crisis and was "by all admissions … misgoverned" (Jeffrey 1976: 64). Until the late 1860s, the state made almost no systematic attempt to encourage the welfare of its people (Singh 1944: 15). It is certainly true, as scholars such as Sen (1991) have emphasized, that in 1817 the young queen of Travancore issued a Royal Proclamation recognizing the state's obligation to the education of its people, but this hardly heralded, as Sen (1991) suggests, a "public policy of enlightenment" on the part of the native

---

[19] As noted earlier, the modern state of Kerala was formed in 1956 by uniting the two princely states of Travancore and Cochin, which were ruled by native kings, who were under the suzerainty of the British, and the northern district of Malabar, which was a part of Madras Presidency that was ruled directly by the British. The discussion of the colonial period in the first two subsections focuses on the largest and most populous of these three units, the princely state of Travancore, but also includes references to the broadly similar trajectory of sociopolitical developments in the adjoining, relatively small princely state of Cochin.

[20] By almost all accounts, the caste system in Kerala was the most orthodox and oppressive of all Indian states. As noted in Chapter 3, a tiny minority of Brahmins were separated from the rest of the Sudra population by rigid and ruthless rules of pollution based not only on touch, like in the rest of India, but also on proximity. There were strictly enforced injunctions on the use of public facilities, such as roads, wells, temples by lower castes and elaborate specifications of the physical distance allowed between Brahmins and various Sudra castes. During his visit to the region in the late nineteenth century, the social reformer Swami Vivekananda famously termed Kerala "a madhouse of caste" (Desai 2005: 463; Franke & Chasin 1989: 75).

rulers that has driven Kerala's contemporary social achievements. As many historians of Kerala have pointed out, the proclamation itself was drafted by and adopted under pressure from the British resident Colonel Munro and remained a dead letter for nearly a century after (Krishnan 1995: 6; Ramachandran 1998; Tharakan 1984: 1918). At this time the Travancore government's expenditures were instead directed to the ideal categories laid out in the ancient Hindu books on polity – religious functions, the upkeep of the palace, army, and civil administration (Singh 1944: 9). In 1871, the British government in Madras claimed that maintenance of temples was "an unnecessarily heavy charge on the state" and advised Travancore rulers to cut down on such expenses to instead release money for more "useful" purposes like social services, but this advice went mostly unheeded (Kawashima 1998: 26). The limited social services that were available to the people were provided by indigenous schools and private physicians who practiced the traditional *ayurvedic* form of medicine, both of which were available, for the most part, only to members of upper castes (Jeffrey 1976: 81). These were supplemented by the activities of the Protestant missionaries who had arrived in the region in the early nineteenth century and considered education to be a necessary prerequisite for their religious work (Tharakan 1984: 1920). Missionary societies also opened the first allopathic dispensaries and hospitals toward the middle of the nineteenth century and provided instruction in hygiene and public health (Ramachandran 1998: 268).[21]

When the state did begin to pay some systematic attention to the social sector, this was in large part because of pressure from the British government.[22] Jeffrey points out that numerous complaints about maladministration through the 1850s led the Madras government to "favor some form of direct interference in Travancore's internal affairs" (1976: 64). Lord Dalhousie wrote the

[21] Christian missionaries are often described as pioneers in the field of social development (Gladstone 1984; Mathew 1999) but it is important to be precise about the exact nature of their pioneering contributions – the missionaries were the first to introduce "western" education and health and to make a systematic education available to lower castes and women. This model of service provision certainly boosted Kerala's social indicators, but insofar as the percentage of people educated in English, as well as literacy rates for lower castes and women, were very low in the early twentieth century, it is important not to overestimate the extent of that contribution. The truly pioneering role of Christian missionaries in Kerala, I believe, was less as providers of public services but, as discussed in Chapter 3, as the initiators of key social changes that fostered the rise of challenger elites from lower castes who in turn through their competition with the non-Malayali Brahmins came to espouse Malayali subnationalism (see also Singh 2011).

[22] Scholars such as Drèze and Sen have argued that Travancore could prioritize the social sector because by virtue of being "formally outside British India ... they were not subjected to the general lack of interest of Whitehall officialdom in Indian elementary education" (2002: 99). A closer reading of the historical evidence, however, suggests that at least until the late nineteenth century it was the consistent pressure from the British administration that pushed the princely state to expand state education and health services (Desai 2005: 460; Kawashima 1998: 100). Tharakan shows that the social policies of Travancore-Cochin in fact "broadly conformed to those prevailing in British India" (1984: 1919).

Maharaja of Travancore an ominous letter, which stated that "unless averted by timely and judicious reforms, annexation of Travancore is a distinct possibility" (Tharakan 1984: 1961). It was this very real threat of annexation by the British authorities on account of persistent charges of misrule that pushed the Travancore state under the new, reformist Dewan Madhav Rao to take some limited initiatives in the social sector beginning in the late 1860s. Through the 1870s, for example, the state supported the expansion of village vernacular schools but, as noted earlier, these were open only to students from the upper castes, which constituted a minority of the total population of Travancore. Despite increasing pressure, especially from the British government in Madras Presidency, the Travancore government remained reluctant to open government schools to students of all castes. Instead they arrived at a compromise – the institution of a large-scale grants-in-aid system for private institutions, targeted primarily toward Christian Missionary schools for lower castes. This, incidentally the Travancore government's first major initiative in the education sector, was less an enlightened princely initiative and more "the best possible option" for a state that was "not ready to deal with ... the education of the lower castes" but faced increasingly vociferous demands to do so (Kawashima 1998: 99–100). Similarly, while the state did open a handful of medical institutions including the General Hospital of Travancore in the 1860s ostensibly, in the words of the Maharajah, "to see that good medical aid is placed within the reach of all classes of (my) subjects" as the "obvious duty of the state" this does not seem to have been faithfully implemented (Aiya 1906: 199). In the 1890s the Durbar physician himself complained of the "total want of shelter" for the lower caste patients at the hospital and advised the building of a shed for them during the monsoon months. It was clear that even in the inaugural years of the twentieth century, lower caste, especially Pulaya, patients were systematically denied entry to state medical institutions (Kabir and Krishnan 1993: 15–16).

Unsurprisingly, the education and health sectors witnessed very limited gains during this period. According to the census of 1875, only 5.7 percent of the population of Travancore was literate (Ramachandran 1998: 257). In 1870–71, the chief medical officer the Durbar physician, Dr. Ross reported that Travancore was afflicted with a high rate of mortality arising from preventable disease. In relative terms, this compared unfavorably with the albeit also very low level of social development in Madras Presidency, and was not much higher than the North-Central Indian Provinces. Female literacy rates in the princely states of Travancore and Cochin in the 1870s were virtually as miniscule as those in the United Provinces (less than 0.5%).

Emergence of Malayali Subnationalism Triggers Progressive Social Policy and Social Development: 1890s–1950

As discussed in detail in Chapter 3, this period witnessed the first stirrings of Malayali subnationalism, albeit primarily at the elite level, brought out strikingly in the Malayali Memorial, a petition demanding greater native representation in public services submitted to the Travancore government in 1891, which had more than 10,000 signatories and "claimed to express the grievances of all Malayalis – Nambudris, Nairs, Syrians, other Christians and Izhavas" (Nair 1976: 168). This was the first "united protest" that "embodied not merely the grievance of a section of the people, but that of the community as a whole" (Koshy 1972: 31–32). A leading historian of Kerala writes that "by the beginning of the twentieth century caste-communal unification became … a reality" (Cherian 1999: 476).[23] By the early decades of the twentieth century, these subnational stirrings had mushroomed into a powerful demand for a united Malayali homeland. The *Aikya Kerala* movement, the campaign for the consolidation of all Malayalam-speaking regions into a single state of Kerala, which began around the 1920s, played a key role in transmitting Malayali subnationalism to the masses.[24] The tremendous popular response to signature campaigns as well as public rallies exemplified the emergence of a "Kerala-wide, consciousness of shared community" (Chiriyankandath 1993: 650).

The emergence of a cohesive subnational community encouraged the recognition of a "concept of equal rights for all" (Koshy 1972: 45). There developed an emergent societal consensus, espoused equally by members of lower as well as upper castes, on the need for the extension of educational and health facilities to all Malayalis irrespective of religion, class, or caste. A powerful sense of Malayali subnationalism fostered the understanding that the well-being of all sections of the population was necessary for the welfare of the Malayali subnation as a whole, and therefore the collective responsibility of all Malayalis. This appears to have enhanced the willingness of upper castes and classes to work for the good of other members of their subnational community, especially those from the most downtrodden groups such as the former slave castes

[23] This is not to deny the considerable sociopolitical conflict in the region during this period. The states of Travancore and Cochin were characterized by continued competition between different castes, notably the Izhavas and the Nairs, as also the Muslims. As noted in Chapter 3, each of these groups often organized around their own caste or religious identities, but this competitive mobilization happened within the context of an encompassing Malayali solidarity. During the 1930s and 1940s, sections of the Communist party, which as discussed in Chapter 3 and later in this chapter, had been an important part of the Malayali subnationalist movement, became more militant. This is represented by the Punnapra-Vayalar uprising, a struggle led by the Communist party against the Travancore government in which more than 150 people were killed. The conflicts in Travancore and Cochin, however, were relatively limited as compared to Malabar, which was at this time a part of Madras Presidency, and not part of the Malayali subnationalism emerging in the princely states to its south. In the 1920s Malabar witnessed the Moplah rebellion, an uprising by Muslim peasants against British rule and Hindu Nair landlords, which led by conservative accounts to over 2000 deaths.

[24] The development of the demand for a Malayali-speaking state was no doubt encouraged by the Indian National Congress's espousal, beginning in 1920 when the party itself was reorganized along linguistic lines, of the demarcation of provinces by language. From the Nagpur session in 1920 until 1946, the Congress passed regular resolutions in favor of the reconstitution of British provinces along linguistic lines.

of 'untouchables', the Pulayas and Parayas. While the representatives of lower castes were obviously key proponents of the eradication of caste disabilities and the equitable provision of social services to all communities, it is notable that members of the upper castes were equally involved in and committed to these movements. The Malayali press, controlled primarily by upper castes, espoused the "eradication of social disabilities of the downtrodden classes with unabated vigour" (Koshy 1972: 45). In the early 1890s the *Malayala Manorama* wrote an editorial urging the education of the Pulayas, a former slave caste (Nair 1986: 3). The Sri Mulam Popular assembly, a partially representative but predominantly upper-caste body established in the early 1900s, undertook "incessant and relentless efforts ... for securing more rights and opportunities for the backward sections of the population" (Nair 1976: 33); "Members of the Popular Assembly and other public men vociferously pleaded for social justice" (Koshy 1972: 46). The famous Vaikom Satyagraha of 1924 and other agitations, which were instrumental in securing lower castes the right of access to temples from which they had hitherto been prohibited, were spearheaded by Brahmins, Nairs and members of other upper castes. The emancipation of all, including the lowest sections of Malayali society, came to be seen as central for ensuring the welfare of the Malayali subnation as a whole.[25]

This support for collective welfare, particularly on the part of elites, brought out by the rapidly growing number of petitions to the government for the establishment of hospitals and schools, served as an important impetus for the introduction of a range of education and healthcare policies (Kabir 2002: 147). As Figure 4.1 shows, in the late nineteenth century the Travancore governments' expenditures on education and health increased sharply. Figure 4.2 shows the steady rise in the number of state educational institutions from the late nineteenth century onward. In contrast to the primarily elitist state education initiatives of the nineteenth century, mass education and health programs were introduced and executed in a systematic fashion in Travancore and Cochin beginning in the 1900s. In 1904 the government accepted in principle that the education of all children in the state, irrespective of caste, creed, or race, was its responsibility and declared that it would defray the entire cost of

[25] It is important to reiterate here that the support for the collective welfare of all Malayalis did not preclude caste and religious groups also launching initiatives for the welfare of their ethnic brethren, which they did with enthusiasm. However, unlike in the state of UP, discussed in the next chapter because of the presence of a broader shared subnational solidarity, elites did not view the development of their respective communities in exclusive or zero-sum terms but part of the broader cause of Malayali welfare. Sri Narayan Guru, the spiritual leader of the Izhava reform movement, for instance, while working for the welfare of the Izhavas also espoused the socioeconomic uplift of the untouchable Pulayas. Similarly, while the Nairs organized and provided social services for their caste Mr. Govind Pillai, a Nair, repeatedly raised the cause of the Pulayas in the Sri Mulam popular assembly, condemning, for instance, the practice of throwing medicines at Pulayas and demanding that they be treated in special wards in all the major hospitals of the state (Kabir & Krishnan 1993: 16–17).

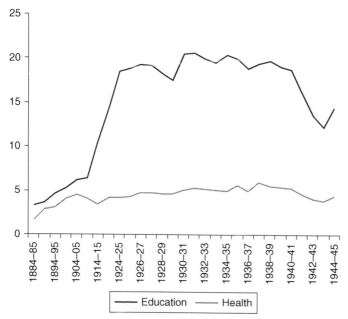

FIGURE 4.1. Expenditure on Education and Health as Proportion of Total Expenditure in Travancore (1884–1885 to 1944–1945).
Source: Based on data in Singh (1944)

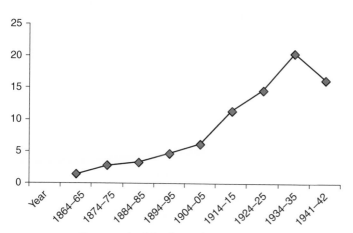

FIGURE 4.2. Increase in Number of State Educational Institutions in Travancore (1873–1930).
Source: Based on data in Singh (1944)

primary education in the state (Kabir 2002: 126). In 1911 the restrictions on the admission of untouchable children to departmental schools were removed and through the 1920s–30s the princely states introduced a range of affirmative action policies for lower castes such as fee concessions and scholarships. In the 1940s the Travancore government introduced the provision of midday meals to all students in government primary schools. This scheme constituted a significant, simultaneous intervention in the fields of education and health, continued uninterrupted in post-Independence Kerala and was significantly expanded in the 1990s. The expenditure on the provision of medical services, while lower than that on education, increased sixfold from 1900 to 1945.[26] Pressure from elites, through the press, memorials, letters, telegrams, resolutions before Town Improvement Committees and the Travancore Legislative Council, for checking the prevalence of and epidemics of diseases was an important factor in prompting the Travancore government to approach the Rockefeller foundation, which had spread its operations into India after the First World War to establish a "public health department on modern lines" in 1928 (Kabir 2003: 12). The Rockefeller foundation was driven by its own agenda of researching specific diseases, and rather than focusing on cholera and other waterborne diseases, which constituted the heaviest burden for Travancore, instead initiated programs directed towards filariasis and malaria. It's programs did, however, result in "remarkable success" with the control of these diseases (Kerala was to become the first Indian state to eradicate endemic malaria in 1965), and also laid the foundation for the institutionalization of public health in the state (Kabir 2003). The Travancore government, which had provided the funds, personnel and facilities for all the activities of the Rockefeller foundation, continued to initiate vaccination and sanitation campaigns. In 1941–42, 25 percent of the total expenditure on the medical department was allocated to measures designed to stem the outbreak of diseases such as cholera and smallpox, which had been one of the main causes of high mortality, particularly among the depressed castes, in the previous century (Singh 1944: 434). It is important to clarify that while pressure from the British had been a powerful motivation for the adoption of social reforms in Travancore in the previous period, welfare legislation in the 1900s was often passed in *opposition* to the Raj, which came to hold the view that the princely states were going too far in their commitment to welfare.[27] Incidentally, while social expenditures in Kerala had increased manifold, in relative terms they were not significantly above those of other provinces such as Madras and Baroda.

---

[26] By 1928 Travancore had 30 hospitals, 38 dispensaries, 18 grant-in-aid medical institutions and 14 mission hospitals that dispensed western medical care (Kabir 2003: 12).

[27] J. Andrew, the Resident of Travancore during 1903–04, for example, noted that "Travancoreans are willing to pay for the education of their children … and *I do not see why Primary Education should now be made free*" (cited in Nair 1981: 42; emphasis added).

It is also important to keep in mind the extent to which the progressive social policy of the Travancore state during this time continued to be motivated by elite and, increasingly, also popular pressure.[28]

What set Kerala apart was the active popular involvement with the public goods provided by the state. The new political consciousness initiated by the anti-caste movements and furthered by subnational mobilization, especially as it came to be led by the Communist party, encouraged people to monitor the growing range of social services. Complaints about the inaction of medical authorities in checking the spread of epidemics or about the quality of teaching in the local school became commonplace (Kabir 2002: 147). By the 1940s, as a consequence of the state's progressive policies supplemented by the growing popular involvement which ensured the effectiveness of government services, Travancore and Cochin had overtaken Madras Presidency as well as most other Indian provinces, establishing themselves as forerunners in the field of social development. They had gained a lead on most developmental indicators, including literacy rates (Figures 1.4–1.6) and infant mortality rates (Figure 1.7).

Yet it is important to note that despite its preeminent position among Indian provinces, the absolute levels of social development in Kerala in 1947 were quite low. More than half the population in both Travancore and Cochin was illiterate. In 1930, a man in Travancore was expected to live an average of 29.5 years, only a couple of years longer than a man in India (Ramachandran 1998: 225). Moreover, the social development gains in the state were not equally distributed across different demographic groups and geographic regions. Even though lower castes had made significant gains in education in the early twentieth century, according to the 1921 census only a very small proportion of the so-called depressed castes were literate. Illiteracy and infant mortality rates in Malabar, which had been under direct British control as part of the Madras Presidency, were significantly higher than the princely states of Travancore and Cochin. As will be explicated in the next subsection, the post-Independence years marked a critical period in Kerala's developmental history, characterized not only by unprecedented increases in education and health outcomes but also their marked equalization across gender, ethnic, rural-urban, and regional lines.

[28] In 1921 the Travancore sirkar decided to reduce its health budget on the grounds that it had "placed medical relief within fairly easy reach of all the people." It was only when this "tall claim" of the government was powerfully challenged by the people through petitions and representations that the government withdrew its decision two years later (Kabir 2002: 149). Similarly, Kabir (2003) discusses the close monitoring, and often criticism, of the Rockefeller foundation's priorities and programs by local elites through the 1920s and 1930s, which formed the backdrop for the Travancore state's increasing tension with, and the eventual withdrawal of, the Foundation from the state in the 1940s.

Malayali Subnationalism Fosters High Levels of Social Development: 1950s Onward

Subnationalism in Kerala reached a crescendo during the 1950s at the time of the linguistic agitations across India. An examination of petitions submitted by the *Aikya Kerala* campaign to the States Reorganization Commission (SRC), a body appointed by the Indian government to assess the demands for the creation of linguistic states, shows that subnationalism in Kerala was inextricably linked to the collective welfare of all Malayalis. In petition after petition, the creation of a "United Kerala State" was presented as an essential condition for "the development of the Malayalis" (Raja 1954). Many of the memoranda argued that the coming together of a people who had long yearned for unity would "unleash unharnessed energy, highly potential in its psychological impact" (Revolutionary Socialist Party 1954); "an attachment to the land and the people, which very often rises stronger and higher than reason and probably life itself" (Lauren & Bava 1954) would lead Malayalis to toil for Kerala's development. It is notable that the petitions submitted by organizations and individuals in Malabar were flush with the idea that the government of Kerala, composed of co-nationals, would be obligated to look after their welfare, which had been neglected by the "foreigners" in the Madras government. The Malayali districts were alleged to have been given "step-motherly treatment" by the Madras government, described as "a Government of the Andhra and the Tamil people" (Nair 1954). Another memorandum went on to say that "The feeling of the people of Malabar generally is that the district has suffered greatly being part of the Madras state ... *Malabar can come into her own only as a part of Kerala state*" (Pocker Sahib et al. 1954; emphasis added). Similarly, the Memorandum of the Wynad Taluk Aikya Kerala Committee argued that *"development can only materialize in an Aikya Kerala, as has been found by the people of Wynad who have had their plentiful share of wanton disregard of the current administration. If Wynad is left out of Kerala, the backwardness of this rich land would only be prolonged for decades"* (1954). The campaigners for a united Kerala from Travancore-Cochin, in turn, seemed more than willing to take up the responsibility of Malabar's development and vehemently refuted the not empirically unfounded argument that the region's relative backwardness would constitute a costly liability for an incipient state that was already in a precarious socioeconomic position, arguing instead that "Malabar has immense possibilities for development ... this is possible only in an *Aikya Kerala*" (CPI 1954: 3).

Malayali subnationalism remained strong and a key driver of social development through most of the post-independence decades. The primary mechanism by which Malayali identity fostered state emphasis on the social sector was through the activity of a subnationalist political party. The Communist party, defined by its leader EMS Namboodiripad as Kerala's "national party" (Harrison 1960: 195), had, as discussed in Chapter 3, from its very emergence been deeply embedded in, and continued in the post-independence period to embody, Malayali subnationalism. While there have clearly been other reasons, the embodiment and espousal of subnational solidarity has been an important factor in the success of the Communist party (Nossiter 1982).[29] Scholars such as Fic (1970) in fact emphasize the significance of subnationalism to the victories of the Communists, almost to the negation of Marxist ideology. Similarly, Harrison argues that the party's popular support and electoral victories, especially in the early years, can be explained, "above all, by its ability to manipulate the regional patriotism of all Kerala" (1960: 193). Nossiter describes a "distinctive 'Kerala Communism'" (1982: 367) that has remained independent of Soviet, British, or Chinese guidance and is best "seen more as being analogous to such regional parties as the DMK and its successors of TN and the Akali Dal of Punjab" (1982: 375).

The Kerala Communists' subnationalism was inextricably intertwined from the beginning with a focus on Malayali welfare, as is exemplified by their "Development-defined ideal vision of a unified Malayalee people" (Devika 2002: 53).[30] In the very first elections in the state, the Communist manifesto pushed voters to choose "a Government That Will Take Care of the Malayalee Nation" (Harrison 1960: 193). The close relationship between subnationalism and social welfare is also brought out strikingly by the Communist government's evocation, both as an overall goal and in key social schemes, of an important subnational hero, king Mahabali. The golden rule of the ancient king Mahabali (or Maveli), eulogized in the arts, literature, and festivals of the state, is believed to have been characterized by unity and solidarity among Malayalis and a concern for the well-being of his people on the part of the sovereign. This is captured nicely by the following song chanted even today during Onam festivities across Kerala[31]:

> When Maveli, our King, ruled the land,
> All the people were as One.
> There was neither anxiety nor sickness,
> Death of the children were never even heard of,
> When Maveli, our King, ruled the land,
> All the peoples formed one casteless race.

---

[29] The appeal of Communism has been attributed to socioeconomic factors such as the breakup of the joint family system, the intensity of caste discrimination, the agrarian situation, the scale and character of traditional industry (Nossiter 1982: 366). Herring (1983) traces the rise of the Communist party to the inability of the Congress party to address issues of exploitation along both class and caste lines.

[30] According to Devika (2010: 811), "The Communist vision of a linguistically united Kerala was driven not just by the desire to shape a more equitable society; underlying it was also the fear of 'backwardness' vis-à-vis the rest of South India, already evident in the writings of prominent intellectuals such as Kesari A. Balakrishna Pillai (1934)."

[31] Mahabali's reign ended when he was tricked into being sent to the underworld. The Malayali king was, however, granted the right to visit his beloved people once each year. As noted in Chapter 3, this occasion is celebrated as Onam, Kerala's "national festival" (Franke and Chasin 1989: 31).

Kerala's leaders had been self-conscious in their adoption of Mahabali's rule as a model for the newly unified state. Namboodiripad in fact explicitly characterized his vision for a developed Kerala as "the Mavelinadu of the future" (Devika 2002: 57). One of the most significant state initiatives in the public provision of food in the history of Kerala has been the opening of Maveli stores, which sell grains and other essential items such as sugar, palm oil, and kerosene at controlled prices. The decision to name stores established with the purpose of providing the most underprivileged segments of society access to affordable, good quality food after Mahabali exemplified the state's appreciation of, and desire to reinforce the historic association between Malayali oneness and Malayali welfare. Kerala was once again united and the people were bound together in a web of solidarity; this return to subnationalism necessitated state action directed towards Malayali welfare, reminiscent of Mahabali's mythical kingdom. Most other important social policies have also been couched in the language of the Communist government fulfilling its moral duty to the well-being of the Malayali people. In 2008, the Left government went as far as to undertake a "unique" initiative to "fulfill its obligation to non-resident Malayalis" by setting up a welfare fund that will provide pension, medical aid, and death assistance to Malayalis living outside Kerala and India and also to recent returnees. Social programs that are more difficult to implement such as the state's Family Planning Program have notably also been put forward as being necessary for "the national interest" (Devika 2002: 51). The Communists have justified their periodic demands for increased state autonomy as necessary for ensuring "Malayali welfare," which they claim is "neglected" by New Delhi (Nossiter 1982: 265). The link between the Communists' subnationalism and a progressive social policy would appear to be epitomized by the fact that today subnationalist occasions in Kerala are celebrated through the institution of new social policy. In 2006 Chief Minister Achutanandan, for example, announced that "The 50th anniversary of the formation of Kerala is intended for launching various developmental projects in the State … The fifty days of celebrations … would witness the unique and most comprehensive developmental programs in the history of the State."

It is important to point out that Communist party governments' activism in the social sector in Kerala is exceptional even compared to the experience of Communist governments in other Indian states. Communist party rule in West Bengal has been longer, more stable, and based on much larger popular mandates than in Kerala, which has been plagued by political instability.[32] Yet the Communist party in West Bengal has shown a much weaker commitment to the social sector. In Kerala the Communist party's prioritization of the education and health sectors has been part of a broader and deep commitment

---

[32] The first Communist government in Kerala, which was incidentally the first democratically elected Communist government in the world, was dismissed by the central government in New Delhi in 1959 and President's rule was established in the state. Successive regimes have had a hard time completing their term in power.

to redistribution brought out most starkly in the far-reaching land reforms instituted during the 1960s and 1970s, which were not only successful – Kerala is today characterized by one of the more egalitarian patterns of landholding found in most developing countries (Herring 1983, 1991) – but also relatively peaceful.[33] In contrast, the West Bengal Communists have been relatively ineffective at redistributing land to the poor.[34] Class mobilization in the state has also been much more divided and violent.[35] As explanation, scholars of Kerala such as Heller (1996, 2000) and Desai (2001) point to the fact that the Communist party, and labor mobilization more generally, have had stronger roots in civil society in Kerala. But this deeper popular embeddedness is in turn, a product, to a very significant extent, of the intimate historical connection between Communist mobilization and Malayali subnationalism.[36]

It is also important to further note that while the Communists have clearly played the pioneering role, the Congress, the other major political player in the state, has also displayed a strong commitment to the social sector in Kerala. Congress governments in Kerala have prioritized welfare to a much greater extent than at the center in New Delhi, or in other states. This can be explained by a combination of two main factors. Firstly, unlike in other states such as UP,

[33] The enactment and implementation of these land reforms was a lengthy and fraught process that generated considerable sociopolitical conflict including political instability, judicial challenges, as well as evictions by landlords and strikes, protests, and agitations, but these did not, for the most part, take on a violent form, unlike attempts at redistribution in many other parts of the world.

[34] The Communist party in West Bengal has instead been content with registering sharecroppers to protect the security of their tenure and ensuring just rents (Kohli 1987).

[35] There emerged in the 1960s in West Bengal a major schism between the parliamentary CPI (M) and the CPI (Marxist-Leninist) which advocated armed revolution and denounced participation in the electoral process. The CPI (M-L) spearheaded the insurrectionist Naxalite movement, which inspired by Maoist tactics, sought to foment a revolution against landlords and officials among the mostly tribal rural population of the district of Naxalabari in the north of West Bengal.

[36] As I have argued elsewhere (Singh 2010), the peculiar "solidaristic" and "encompassing" nature of class mobilization, which Heller (1996, 2000) takes as a starting point for his argument about state-society synergy in Kerala, can be attributed in large part to the fact that the left movement in Kerala took root in the context of an emerging Malayali identity and actively espoused and organized itself around this subnational solidarity. Desai (2001) emphasizes the Kerala Communist party's involvement with mass-based grass roots mobilizations that allowed it to develop greater organizational strength, political hegemony, and a broader social base than their Bengali counterparts. In particular, in line with the broader argument that the political ascendancy of leftist parties within an ongoing national conflict depends, in part, upon their espousal of the nationalist cause as was the case with the Chinese Communist Party, and the Vietnamese Communists (Johnson 1962; Kolko 1985), Desai (2001) singles out the Kerala Communists' involvement with the anti-colonial national struggle. However, the real 'national question' for the Kerala Communists, as is brought out clearly in the writings of Namboodiripad (1952), was subnational – the nation in question was the Malayali subnation. It was their active mobilization for the subnationalist cause, especially their leadership of the *Aikya Kerala* movement, that was much more important to the building of the Communists' strength and broadening of their support than their participation in the Indian independence struggle.

the Congress has retained a distinct subnational identity, functioning more like
a regional party than a wing of the central Congress – in the more than seventy
years since the institution of elections, all but one of Kerala's Congress chief
ministers have devoted their political careers entirely to state politics. Secondly,
almost since the first elections in the state, been locked in very tight electoral
contests with the Communists.[37] The need to build broad coalitions associated with close two-party competition, in this case the Communist-led Left
Democratic Front and Congress-led United Democratic Front has certainly
been an important motivation for the Congress, as also the Communists, to prioritize public goods, such as education and health (Chhibber and Nooruddin
2004). Their very close contests with the subnationalist Communists have,
however, been a particular trigger for Congress governments to give social welfare a prominent place on the policy agenda. Newspaper reports and interviews
with Congress and Communist leaders indicate that in addition to the general pressures of political competition, close competition with a subnationalist
party, which has put social development at the top of its agenda, has been especially important in driving Congress's social policies. As a result, social welfare
emerged as a key arena of competition between the Congress and Communists
in Kerala with each government attempting to outdo the other in the extension
of the social security net (Venugopal 2006).

From the 1950s onward, Kerala has been characterized by an extensive
social policy with a pronounced redistributive emphasis. Even though Kerala
has had a lower net state domestic product per capita than the national average
for most of the post-independence period, its per capita expenditure on education and health has consistently been higher than that of all Indian states.[38]
While the Communists in Kerala are best known for their initiation of land
reforms, the introduction of massive public health and education schemes to
benefit the relatively deprived sections of Malayali society – the poor, women,
scheduled castes, residents of rural areas and of socially backward Malabar –
have also been critical, if less emphasized, aspects of the state's redistribution
policies (Franke & Chasin 1989: 21). Successive state governments in Kerala,
both Communist and Congress, have focused their attention overwhelmingly
on the provision of primary education and basic healthcare, which catered
to the needs of the poorest Malayalis. This was in marked contrast to other
Indian states where education expenditures were targeted toward secondary or
higher education, which was of disproportionate benefit to the elite sections of
society who had already completed basic schooling. The state also initiated a

---

[37] The mean margin of victory for the victorious party in state assembly elections in Kerala has
been approximately 8%, as compared to an average of 18% across all Indian states.
[38] It is important to both acknowledge here that foreign remittances in the form of money sent by
Malayali workers in the Gulf have provided an important fillip for the economy of Kerala, but
also to clarify that these remittances became substantial in the mid-1980s and began to assume
a significant share of state income only in the 1990s, by which time Kerala's high levels of social
spending was an established pattern.

range of schemes for members of scheduled castes and women, whose social indicators had historically lagged behind those of the general population. There was a major redirection of funds toward the extension of social services in the rural areas, which remained less developed than urban areas and also toward the northern Malabar region, which as noted earlier had significantly lower levels of social development than other regions when it joined Kerala. The state's commitment to the social sector is brought out by the striking fact that despite endemic social unrest during the 1960s and 1970s; political turmoil and instability, periodically precarious financial situations through the 1980s; and New Delhi's liberalizing market reforms of the 1990s, no government, whether Communist or Congress, has *ever* reversed a major public service or redistributive program in Kerala (Heller 2005: 82).[39]

The dynamism of social policies during this period was matched by popular activism, which fostered an efficient and well-utilized network of public goods. In his analysis of Kerala, Ramachandran emphasized "political awareness and political action" as critical factors behind the better social conditions in the state. According to him, "people demanded more health facilities in Kerala than in the rest of India, and they utilized them better" (1998: 236). While left mobilization was also an important contributory factor, a strong identification with their state was critical in generating a high degree of political consciousness among the people of Kerala.[40] Table 4.3 shows that, as measured by NES surveys in 1971, 1996, and 2004, Malayalis report significantly higher political interest than the average Indian. Kathleen Gough's work (1965) on panchayats in the 1960s documented high levels of political participation and a well-developed civic sense. A recent study of village-level governance by the World Bank confirms the persistence of this pattern. A survey of villages on either side of the current borders of four Southern states (Kerala, Tamil Nadu, Andhra Pradesh, and Karnataka), which belonged to the same political entity (Madras) prior to the state's reorganization in 1956, showed that Kerala has the

---

[39] Heller (2012: 273) notes that while in the post-liberalization era social spending has begun to fall and some social programs have been adversely impacted by fiscal adjustments, "overall in no other major Indian state has the market been so successfully subordinated to social regulation," and yet this has not undermined economic growth, which has over the past two decades, in contrast to Kerala's previously laggard rates, been better than the national average. Higher consumption fueled by remittances has been an important motor for this growth but there is also some evidence of increased productivity with high rates of enterprise growth and a fall in the historically high unemployment rates in the state.

[40] The relatively lower level of electoral participation in West Bengal, which as noted earlier has a much longer record of Communist rule than Kerala, underscores the limits of an argument that attributes Malayalis' heightened political awareness purely to left mobilization. The average electoral turnout in state legislature elections through the 1990s in Kerala was 75% as compared with 69% in West Bengal. According to the 1971 NES, 72.5% of respondents in Kerala said that they cared very much who won in their constituency, as compared with 47% in West Bengal and 40% in India. Secondary studies, for example by Nag, also note the higher levels of political consciousness in Kerala as compared with West Bengal (1989).

highest voter turnout in all types of elections among the four states; households in Kerala were most likely to participate in political activities. Furthermore, Kerala's electorate is among the least likely to vote for candidates based on caste or religious lines. This leads the researchers to conclude that "Kerala has a more active civic culture with active participation in gram sabhas." In addition to the highest Gram Sabha attendance, those attending the Gram Sabha in Kerala are much more likely to speak during the meeting than those in other states (Ban et al. 2008).

Politically aware Malayali citizens bound by ties of solidarity have tended to act collectively on a range of issues, including the functioning of schools and health centers.[41] Social and political associations in Kerala frequently submitted written demands to higher officials for improved educational and healthcare facilities that were widely publicized in the vernacular press (Nag 1989: 418). Failure to meet these demands often resulted in public agitations – "in some cases, officials have been *gheraoed*, or surrounded by protesters who do not allow them to leave their office until demands have been met" (Franke & Chasin 1989: 46). The degree of popular involvement with social services is brought out by village-level studies of Kerala. Kathleen Gough recounts an incident in 1962 when angry neighbors dragged a physician from a cinema and forced him to go to the hospital to deliver the baby of a woman who was in great pain (cited in Franke & Chasin 1989: 45). Similarly, based on her fieldwork in the state in the 1960s and 1970s, anthropologist Joan Mencher notes that in Kerala, "if a PHC was unmanned for a few days, there would be a massive demonstration at the nearest collectorate [regional government office]"; the death of a child due to perceived physician neglect would prompt "an enormous procession and a big demonstration outside the PHC the next day. Articles would have appeared in the newspapers, and questions would have been raised in the state assembly" (1980: 1782). My field research showed that this popular monitoring of social services has continued.[42] Such public vigilance has been essential to ensuring the effective functioning of health centers and primary schools in Kerala (Drèze & Sen 2002: 92). Cherian, for example,

---

[41] A common identity has fostered collective mobilization among Malayali citizens on a range of other social issues. Franke and Chasin (1997) document many such instances. For example, in 1997, three hundred households in Chapparapadavu district contributed toward the building of a bridge in order to enable the village students to more easily access a government school on the other end of the river. In Methala, a village assembly organized monetary contributions of Rs 12,000 and several hours of volunteer labor to build a one-room house for a homeless, low-caste widow and her young daughter (Franke & Chasin 1997).

[42] In focus group interviews conducted in three different villages in Muvattupuzha municipality of Ernakulam district in 2006 residents told me that the openings of government schools and health centers were occasions of massive public involvement. The local elected representatives and party activists, government officials, local teachers, doctors and nurses, village elders as well as numerous people from the village, including many women, debated issues such as the location of the school or clinic or the logistics of the provision of the noon meal. I myself was witness to one such discussion on the timing and content of the midday meal provided in the local school.

notes that "The higher quality of life in Kerala is not merely the result of provisioning of services by the state in the form of physical facilities ... It is equally important to recognize the growth of awareness among the masses and collective action by them to ensure that these facilities are utilized fully and well" (1999: 73). A study of health centers in Kerala in the 1980s found that "all the staff were regularly at work" (Franke & Chasin 1989: 46). A UNICEF educational survey conducted in 1999 found that Kerala had one of the lowest rates of teacher absenteeism in the country (Mehrotra 2007: 264).

This combination of top-down state policies supplemented by bottom-up social activism has generated remarkable social gains in Kerala in the post-independence years. During the 1950s–1960s, despite considerable social upheaval including widespread rural protest and the highest incidence of strikes in the country, the state witnessed a "breakthrough" in education (Mehrotra 2000: 15) as indicated by a sharp rise in literacy rates. These have risen today to more than 90 percent, which is 25 percent higher than the literacy rate for India and equivalent to the average for all middle-income countries. The spread of education, especially among women, contributed to greater awareness of health problems and fuller utilization of health facilities, and has fostered striking improvements in Kerala's health indicators (Ramachandran 1998: 233). As Figure 1.7 shows, in the early 1950s Kerala's IMR was not substantially lower than India's, but in subsequent decades it declined far more steeply than for India. Today a child in Kerala is almost five times more likely to live beyond her first birthday as compared to the average for all other states in India. Kerala's IMR puts it among the top 33 percent of all countries of the world. In a global ranking it is placed roughly between Romania (11) and Barbados (13). Kerala's life expectancy of 74 years is eight years higher than the Indian average and puts it among the top 40 percent of the countries in the world, equivalent to Brazil and Jordan.

Such gains in social indicators are remarkable in themselves. In order to fully appreciate the "miracle" of Kerala's development (Mencher 1980: 1781), however, it is important to note the equity of improvements in education and health across class, gender, caste, religious, and regional lines. Through the post-independence period, education and health indicators for the poor, women, scheduled castes and tribes, religious minorities, and rural residents have been significantly higher in Kerala as compared with their counterparts in other Indian states. Moreover, while there do remain some differentials in levels of well-being across groups within Kerala (Devika 2010), these are minimal compared to the yawning gaps within these communities in other Indian states. Various surveys show that income has not been a major determinant of access to better health facilities in the state.[43] Similarly, the rural urban differential in

---

[43] Ramachandran (1996: 232) cites an all-Kerala study by the Kerala Shastra Sahitya Parishad (KSSP), which showed that the incidence of vaccine-preventable diseases was not significantly concentrated among low-income families.

development indicators in Kerala is lower than almost all other Indian states. For example, the average Indian rural female is expected to live eight years less than her urban counterpart (59 vs. 67 years) in Kerala; life expectancy for rural and urban females is almost equal at a high of 75 years. It is notable that Kerala bucks the national trend of relative backwardness of Muslims. With a 90 percent literacy rate, Malayali Muslims are as likely to be able to read and write as Malayali Hindus and about 30 percentage points more likely to be literate than the average Indian Muslim. A rural scheduled caste female in Kerala is more than twice as likely to be literate as compared to her average Indian counterpart. A member of the Scheduled Tribes is 20 percentage points more likely to be literate in Kerala as compared to the Indian average (Census of India 2001). Social indicators in the northern Malabari districts, which were at a distinct development disadvantage at the time of Kerala's formation, are now virtually equivalent to the rest of Kerala.

CONCLUSION

In the overall context of the book, the main purpose of this chapter has been to showcase the positive dynamic of the subnationalism argument laid out in Chapter 2, that is, how a strong sense of subnational solidarity generates a progressive social policy and popular involvement with public services, which combine to give rise to higher levels of social development. As noted earlier, the scholarship on social development has (rightly) celebrated Kerala's exceptional social achievements, but by tending to attribute its gains to peculiar socio-cultural, historical, and political factors, it has simultaneously prevented the development of a generalizable theory of the causes of social development and made the state's achievements seem less accessible to socially backward regions of the world that do not share Kerala's unique features. Rather than focusing on specific factors that explain the achievements of a single case, this chapter deliberately analyzes education and health policies and outcomes across two high-performing cases – Kerala as well as the neighboring state of TN – to put forward a unified explanation for social development that is generalizable across space and over time.

The juxtaposition of Tamil Nadu and Kerala also help brings out the nuances of the subnationalism argument. Within the overall context of a cohesive subnational solidarity, differences in the timing of the emergence of subnationalism and its scope (specifically, whether it was espoused only by elites or also by the people at large) are shown to explain why Kerala has achieved higher social indicators than Tamil Nadu. In the late 1800s, when both Tamil Nadu and Kerala had not yet witnessed the emergence of a subnational identity, the two provinces were characterized by similarly low levels of social development. In the 1880s, Tamil Nadu in fact had a slight edge over Kerala in both education and health. By the closing years of the nineteenth century, however, Malayali subnationalism had taken root among elites in Travancore, prompting an unprecedented state commitment to the social sector. Education and health expenditures in the states of Travancore and Cochin increased dramatically to equal and then gradually overtake those of Madras and other Indian provinces. Malayali subnationalism spread rapidly to the people at large and generated popular involvement with social services such that, by the early 1900s, Kerala had gained a significant lead over Tamil Nadu in literacy rates. The early decades of the twentieth century witnessed the emergence of a Tamil identity on the part of elites in Madras presidency who began to pressurize the state government to prioritize the social sector. In 1940 both Malayali and Tamil subnationalism were firmly entrenched among elites in Travancore and Madras respectively and, as a consequence, social spending in the two provinces was equivalent (see Table 4.2). However, because of the popular dimension of Malayali subnationalism, social expenditures translated into better outcomes in Travancore as compared to Madras Presidency. The confinement of Tamil subnationalism to the elite sphere led to less popular involvement with public goods and as a result developmental gains in Madras state were more limited. Social indicators in Tamil Nadu showed a marked improvement only during the 1950s–60s when Tamil subnationalism came to be internalized by the masses through the efforts of Dravidian parties. Since then, a cohesive subnational solidarity has continued to spur social improvements in Tamil Nadu. The discussion of these gains should by no means serve to obscure the serious outstanding developmental challenges that both Tamil Nadu and Kerala face.

5

How Absence of Subnationalism Impedes Social Development

The previous chapter focused on the positive dynamic of the theory developed in Chapter 2, that is, how a cohesive subnational solidarity fosters higher levels of social development. The chapter demonstrated how Tamil and Malayali subnationalism triggered a more progressive social policy and also greater societal monitoring of public services, which combined to generate higher levels of education and health outcomes in Tamil Nadu and Kerala respectively. It also showed how differences in the timing of the emergence as well as the strength of subnationalism resulted in higher levels of social development in Kerala as compared with Tamil Nadu. This chapter showcases the negative dynamic of the theory, that is, how a fractured subnational community can impede social welfare. Within this negative dynamic it also highlights the mechanism of change, that is how the move toward a more cohesive subnational solidarity, can trigger unprecedented state emphasis on the social sector and prompt developmental gains in a context of severe and long-standing backwardness. In the closing decades of the nineteenth century, social development outcomes and policies in UP and Rajasthan, as well as in Bihar, were, as noted in Chapter 1, roughly comparable to those in Tamil Nadu and Kerala. By the middle of the twentieth century, however, the chances of a resident of UP, Rajasthan, or Bihar growing up illiterate were more than twice those of Tamil Nadu or Kerala. In the 1990s, a woman in UP was expected to live an average of thirteen years less than her counterpart in Kerala. This chapter traces this dramatic falling behind of the North-Central Indian states vis-à-vis their Southern counterparts to their relatively weaker sense of subnational solidarity. It delineates how persistently weak subnational solidarity has discouraged the adoption of a progressive social policy and dampened public involvement with public services, which has contributed to low education and health outcomes in UP. Next, it showcases how the emergence of subnationalism among elites in the newly created state of Rajasthan in the post-Independence period reversed decades of almost complete neglect of social welfare by the predecessor princely states of

Rajputana; however, the limited percolation of this Rajasthani identity into the popular consciousness has limited developmental successes in the state. This dynamic of how a strengthening of subnational solidarity can prompt a change in social policy and even developmental outcomes is further illustrated through an analysis of the state of Bihar. Until only a few years ago, Bihar was globally known as a "byword for the worst of India" (Economist 2004) and a "global embarrassment" (Kirk 2011), but with the emergence of a strong Bihari identity among elites in the past decade, it has witnessed the allocation of substantial outlays to, and the institution of innovative schemes for, education and health, which are beginning to reap notable developmental gains.

FRAGMENTATION AND FAILURE

UTTAR PRADESH

This section shows how the persistent absence, from the turn of the twentieth century to the present day, of any sense of subnational solidarity on the part of the people of UP and the existence instead of powerful attachments below and above that of the subnation has impeded the overall social development of the state. I compare three time periods – from the 1900s to the 1940s, from the 1950s to the 1980s, and from the 1990s onward – corresponding to elite and popular allegiance to religious, national, and caste identities respectively. The first subsection shows that from 1900 to the 1940s, religious divisions led to social welfare being framed almost exclusively in terms of the advancement of particular communities impeding the development of a coherent social policy for the state as a whole and associatedly any significant developmental gains. The second subsection delineates how from the 1950s to the 1980s, the perception of the province as the "heartland" of India, fostered by UP's size, location, and historical and sociopolitical importance, encouraged elite and popular identification with the national rather than the subnational political community, giving rise to a situation in which the state government followed national priorities at the cost of the critical needs of the province, such as the provision of social services. From the 1990s onward, the locus of identification shifted down to caste-based identities. Elite discourse, popular demands, and consequently public policies have been framed in terms of the exclusive advancement of particular castes; targeted policies in the absence of a larger development agenda have resulted in very limited social gains. The low priority accorded to the overall social welfare of the state over virtually the entire last century has led to a situation in which residents of UP have access to some of the poorest public services and are characterized by the worst development indicators anywhere in the world.[1]

---

[1] In a global ranking, UP's levels of literacy are equivalent to nations such as Papua New Guinea, Rwanda and Djibouti and its infant mortality is equal to that of the Gambia.

Religious Nationalism Impedes Overall Social Development of the Province: 1900–1940s

Sociopolitical mobilization during the late colonial period in UP came to take place, as laid out in Chapter 3, not around potentially unifying subnational symbols, such as a shared lingua franca of Hindustani, but instead around the divisive symbols of Hindi and Urdu as the distinct, exclusive, and mutually opposed mother tongues of Hindus and Muslims respectively. As the political elites of the province came to adopt and organize around these counterposed linguistic-religious identities, an analysis of local newspapers in the province showed that they came also to mobilize for policies, and goods and services, including social services, for the exclusive benefit of their group.[2] Hindu and Muslim leaders demanded, for example, the opening of schools and colleges for the exclusive advancement of their "nation," "nationality," and "country-men," where these nouns were used to refer to their co-religionists, rather than, like in Tamil Nadu or Kerala, to the residents of the province as a whole.[3] Development was seen not only in religious but also in zero-sum terms. The promotion of the development of one religious community came to be perceived as occurring at the cost of the development of the other. Demands by Hindu and Muslim elites, therefore, came to be formulated not only *for* the sole development of one's own religious community but *against* the development of the other.[4] Even ostensibly secular developmental projects, such as Congress's Wardha scheme of education in the 1930s, came to be seen as serving the needs of a particular community (Gould 2004: 29).

Corresponding to the absence of any subnational solidarity, there was no conception of the collective welfare of the people of the state. The reports of British administrators during these years bring out the lack of popular support for the provision of public services for all residents of UP (Crooke 1897; Nevill 1904: 11). At the turn of the century, Crooke, for example, wrote of an "attitude of complacency" on the question of public education (1897: 151).

---

[2] This is based on editorials and articles in the following newspapers published from the United Provinces – *Ab-i-Hyat Hind, Agra Akhbar, Akhbar-i-Alam, Akhbar-i-Anjuman-i-Hind, Aligarh Institute Gazette, Anjuman-i-Hind, Azad, Benares Gazette, Bharat Bandhu, Hamdard, Hindustani, Jagat Samachar, Nagri Prakash, Oudh Punch,* and *Oudh Akbar.*

[3] The preeminent leader of the Muslims, Sir Syed Ahmed Khan, for instance, remained preoccupied with the cause of the "Muslim nation" (Dasgupta 1970) and sought British support during the late nineteenth century to found schools and also a college, the Mohammedan Anglo Oriental College, for Muslims. With backing from Muslim philanthropists, the college was expanded and became the Aligarh Muslim University in 1920. In a parallel process, Hindu leaders, notably Madan Mohan Malviya organized support and raised funds from Hindu businessmen and a large grant of land from the religious leader, the then Kashi Naresh, for the establishment in 1916 of the Banaras Hindu University.

[4] At the close of the nineteenth century, for example, the *Hind Pratap* (Allahabad), adverting to the memorial of the Muhammadan Association of Calcutta, wrote that "it would be as unwise to do anything to improve the condition of the Mussalmans as to feed a serpent. If they attain to power, they will only oppress the poor Hindus" (British Library 2005).

He elaborated that "It would hardly be just to assert that there is a demand among the people for a considerable extension of State schools, which the government has been unable or unwilling to meet" (Crooke 1897: 154). The lack of elite pressure or popular demand meant that social policy did not occupy a prominent place on the policy agenda.[5] The limited initiatives in education and health were mainly a result of the personal, progressive instincts of a few British administrators. For example, J. Thompson, the lieutenant governor of the North-Western Provinces from 1843 to 1853, was known to favor mass primary education and took some very preliminary steps toward inaugurating a regular system of vernacular village schools in the mid- to late nineteenth century (Nevill 1904: 111).[6] These schools were, however, "chiefly intended to educate the children of higher classes" (Imperial Gazetteer of India 1908: 131). Christian missionaries ran a handful of schools, some supported by grants from the government in select cities such as Meerut, Gorakhpur, and Allahabad (Varma 1994: 9). The British, again on their own initiative, also introduced Western medicine in the province (Crooke 1897: 159). Through the early 1900s there was a gradual but steady rise in hospitals and dispensaries (Imperial Gazetteer of India 1908: 139). There were also a few limited sanitary initiatives, especially as regards the adequacy and quality of public water, associated with the United Provinces Village Sanitation Act of 1892 (Imperial Gazetteer of India 1908: 139).

These few colonial and Christian initiatives for the collective welfare of all residents were, however, for the most part met with popular indifference. There was, for example, little support for the proposed increase in funding for primary education in the Education Report of 1904 and minimal societal involvement with the limited social services provided. W. H. Crooke, a British administrator who served as a magistrate and collector of various districts during his twenty-five-year tenure in the United Provinces from 1871 to 1895, noted that an absence of fellow-feeling among the residents of the state made them "destitute of regard for the public weal" and prevented them from acting "to secure what is of primary importance to their welfare" (Crooke 1897: 151).[7]

That colonial UP had very low levels of education and health outcomes should come as no surprise in light of the lack of state prioritization and absence

---

[5] Robinson notes that in the 1800s, "Police, law and justice accounted for just under one third of the UP government's ordinary provincial expenditure, a much greater sum than that spent on what might be termed the development departments – education, irrigation and public works" (1974: 317).

[6] Nevill traces the beginning of a regular system of village schools to 1845 when "instructions were issued for the collection of data as to the state of education in these provinces. The result of this inquiry was embodied in a report, and on this action was so far taken that a number of village schools were established in 1848" (1904: 111).

[7] Crooke (1897) argued that this prevented the imposition of checks on the public usage of water, but there is little reason to doubt that this was also important in dampening popular involvement with other public services, such as education and health.

of societal involvement with the public sector described previously. The British, however, who saw UP as a "model province" for other directly controlled areas of British India (Crooke 1897: 3; Kudaisya 2007: 8) were taken aback at its extent of underdevelopment. A report on UP at the turn of the century noted with some shock that "It has been regarded as an axiom that ... we were ... well ahead of other parts of the country in elementary instruction ... But the chill evidence of statistics proved that this feeling of satisfaction was ill-founded. We are now assured on the best authority that these Provinces enjoy the distinction of being the most illiterate tract in India, except the Central provinces, where educational facilities are few, and where the jungle-dweller had naturally no desire to learn" (Crooke 1897: 152). The impetus to the system of village schools did result in "a distinct, though small" (Nevill 1904: 112) growth of primary education in the late nineteenth-early twentieth centuries, but for the most part, the masses were mired in illiteracy (Crooke 1897: 157).[8] As Figure 1.3 illustrates, in the late nineteenth century the Southern states were at a roughly similar point as UP in terms of literacy rates, especially for females. Through the early decades of the twentieth century, however, corresponding to their burgeoning subnationalism, especially in Kerala, literacy in the Southern provinces increased rapidly while UP virtually stagnated. As a result, by the 1931 Census, literacy in UP was 5.5 percent, as compared with 11 percent in Madras and 30 percent in Travancore and Cochin. Even with such meager social indicators, however, UP was ahead of Rajasthan, which as an isolated region under the control of native rulers, had witnessed neither of the progressive influences of British administrators[9] and Christian missionaries that had been responsible for UP's very limited social gains.

Indian Nationalism Prompts Prioritization of National over Subnational Welfare: 1950s–1980s

In the post-independence decades, the politics of UP became closely intertwined with the politics of India. The province's historic importance as the birthplace

[8] The Imperial Gazetteer of India noted that "The proportion of the population of school-age children under instruction has increased from 3.4% in 1881 to 4.1% in 1891, 6.1% in 1901 and 7% in 1904 ... A considerable impetus was given by the revival of the system of aiding indigenous education" (1908: 136). It also noted that "The labors of the various missionary bodies have been especially valuable in the case of female education and the education of the lowest castes" (1908: 137). The juxtaposition of the "gross illiteracy of the masses" (Crooke 1897: 157) with the "rapid strides" in higher education (Nevill 1904: 112) prompted self-reflexivity by British administrators about their prioritization of the latter over the former. Crooke noted that the education policy has been "mistaken" – "the error lies in diverting the labors and expenditure of the Educational Department towards the provision of higher class teaching instead of instructing the mass of the people" (1897: 154).

[9] I am by no means suggesting that there were no progressive rulers among Rajputana's native princes – Maharaja Ram Singh of Jaipur (1833–1888) and Maharaja Ganga Singh of Bikaner (1880–1943) being notable examples of princes who displayed a strong commitment to the welfare of their people.

of Hinduism and the nerve center of some of the most influential ancient and medieval empires had been bolstered during the colonial period by both the significance that the British administrators bestowed on it as well as its leading role in the nationalist struggle, such that by 1947 the UP Congress "had succeeded in projecting their province as the 'heartland' of the new nation" (Pai 2007: 10).[10] By the 1950s, all the other important states of British India – the Presidencies of Bombay and Madras and the provinces of Punjab and Bengal – had been partitioned, leaving UP as the most populous province occupying a strategic, geographical location in the center of the Indo-Gangetic plains. The establishment of democratic, federal institutions sealed UP's premier position in independent India. On the basis of its demographic weight UP commanded the single largest number of seats by a large margin in the national legislature. People from the province came to occupy some of the highest echelons of political power in the country. For example, from 1947 to 1991, for all but two years, India was ruled by prime ministers who hailed from UP. "The future of India," Jairam Ramesh, a prominent politician from UP, has noted, "is inextricably linked to what happens or does not happen in UP" (1999: 2127). A familiar jibe in Delhi went – "India, that is Bharat, that is UP" (Sharma 1969: 181).

UP, in turn, did not take its defining role in Indian politics lightly. UP legislators' proposals, discussed in Chapter 3, to name the province Aryavrat, a name synonymous with India as a whole, and designate Allahabad rather than Delhi as the national capital, among other initiatives, suggest, as represented humorously in the cartoon in Figure 5.1, that political elites in the province essentially saw UP *as* India. Their close identification with the national sphere stymied the emergence of subnational solidarity. On the eve of Indian independence in 1946, Nehru who was himself from UP, had written that the state has "less provincialism … than in any other part of India. For long they have considered themselves, and been looked upon by others, as the heart of India. Indeed, in popular parlance, they are often referred to as Hindustan" (Kudaisya 2007: 10). During the debates over the reorganization of Indian states, legislators from UP presented the state's lack of subnationalism as an attribute. G. B. Pant, the First Chief Minister of the province for example, declared UP as "the only viable administrative unit that was unaffected by either linguism or provincialism" (Lok Sabha debates on the Report of the States Reorganization Commission 1956: 1504). The greatness of UP, he argued, lay "in its people's sense of oneness with other parts of India, overriding local and state considerations" (cited in Kudaisya 2007: 21).

Political elites and observers of UP politics have tended to celebrate the state's proximity to the national realm. This section however delineates how

---

[10] The idea of UP as the center of India was bolstered by the "towering presence of Nehru on the central stage" (Kudaisya 2007: 10). Kudaisya points out that "Nehru himself shared the view that the United Provinces lay at the core of India as a nation. In his *Discovery of India* published in 1946, he wrote that "The United Provinces are a curious amalgam, and in some ways *the epitome of India*" (2007: 10; emphasis added).

A GEOGRAPHICAL EXHIBITION
HAS OPENED IN U.P.
YOU KNOW NOW WHERE U.P. IS

Source: Shankar's Weekly, Vol VI, Nos. 1-26, 31 May 1953

FIGURE 5.1. Postcolonial UP: Political Elite's Self View.
Source: Kudaisya (2007)

a close identification with the nation has led to a preoccupation with the
"national good" over the development of U.P. It is notable that the very existence of the state of UP was justified in terms of the national rather than the
state good. During the states reorganization in the 1950s, debates over the
formation of most states, such as Tamil Nadu and Kerala, were framed in
terms of furthering the interests of the people of the state. However, as noted
in Chapter 3, political elites from UP argued for the maintenance of the state's
boundaries less in terms of how it would benefit the residents of UP and more
in terms of how it would benefit the nation.[11] Political leaders opposed the
division of UP, not on the grounds that it might adversely affect the development of the people but because they feared that it could unleash centrifugal,
destabilizing forces that might lead to the Balkanization of India (Kudaisya
2007: 18). Popular and scholarly work has tended to focus on how UP has
dominated national politics but it is critical not to ignore the ways in which UP
has in turn been dominated by New Delhi. Both UP and Rajasthan had been
characterized by one-party dominance of the Congress from the 1950s to the
late 1980s. There were, however, key differences in the nature of Congress rule

---

[11] The Report of the States Reorganization Commission noted that "One of the commonest arguments advanced before us by leaders in Uttar Pradesh was that the existence of a large, powerful
and well-organized state in the Gangetic Valley was a guarantee for India's unity; that such a
state would be able to correct the disruptive tendencies of other states, and to ensure the ordered
progress of India. The same idea has been put to us in many other forms such as that Uttar
Pradesh is the 'back bone of India'" (1956: 246).

in the two states. The Rajasthan Congress, in part due to its historical origins, had a largely autonomous existence from the center.[12] As will be discussed further in the next section, Rajasthan's first chief minister Sukhadia was a powerful, independent-minded leader who during his tenure of seventeen continuous years actively resisted central intervention in Rajasthani politics and did not at any point display an inclination to wield political power in New Delhi. This was both indicative of, and fostered, a distinct Rajasthani political arena dominated by elites who saw themselves primarily if not exclusively as leaders of Rajasthan pursuing distinct Rajasthani interests. In contrast, through this entire period, the UP Congress was essentially a "jagirdari" (fief) of the national Congress (Ramesh 1999: 2127) with the central "High Command" appointing and dismissing key political functionaries in the state at will.[13] This process became particularly intense under Indira Gandhi who was an insecure leader and anxious, because of UP's political significance in terms of seats in the national assembly, about the threat that a popular politician from the state might pose to her leadership. As a result, she deliberately appointed very weak leaders with no popular backing in the state to the post of chief minister[14] and kept them in very close check.[15] Most political leaders of UP in turn aspired for prominence in New Delhi. Political elites in UP, unlike in Rajasthan, did not envision their careers as being devoted to working in and for the state but instead saw their time in UP as waiting in the wings to play a role on the national stage. As Table 5.1 shows, from the time of Pant, one of the most prominent and experienced politicians of UP, who had been at the helm of the state since 1937 but relinquished the chief ministership to take up a post in

[12] The Congress Party in Rajasthan, as noted in Chapter 3, emerged from the State People's movements, which were strongly influenced by Gandhian ideas and had ties to the Congress but remained, for the most part, at the periphery of the nationalist movement.

[13] In the 1960s, for instance, CB Gupta was appointed as chief minister with the "concurrence" of Nehru (Manisha 2004: 196) and a few years later when Gupta resigned, Nehru "strangely enough" picked Sucheta Kriplani, a relatively low-profile leader over more senior and seasoned leaders in Gupta's cabinet for the post (https://www.scribd.com/doc/330287/women-scientist-of-india).

[14] V. P. Singh, for example, was "shunted off" to Lucknow to be chief minister, "knowing full well that the Government of UP would in effect be run from New Delhi by Indira Gandhi, Sanjay and their myriad minions and that he would be left with responsibility without power" (Sonntag 1996: 5). V. P. Singh was replaced with Sripati Misra whose selection, the news magazine India Today astutely observed, was "in keeping with Mrs. Gandhi's practice of choosing as Chief Minister a 'nobody' who will not be able to challenge her in any way" (cited in Stone 1988: 1018). Similarly, Zerinini-Brotel argues that N. D. Tiwari was such a "hot favorite" of the central leaders for the post of chief minister because he had no political base in UP and consequently was completely dependent on the patronage of New Delhi (1998: 79). UP politics was reduced to the "embarrassing and unedifying spectacle of a crop of chief ministers appearing or disappearing from the scene like quick change artists" (Pioneer, August 4, 1981; cited in Hasan in Ludden 1996: 89).

[15] Stone points out how UP chief ministers had to petition the center for even small decisions like a cabinet expansion (1988).

TABLE 5.1. *Chief Ministers' Involvement with National Politics in Tamil Nadu, Kerala, Rajasthan, and UP*

	Tamil Nadu	Kerala	Uttar Pradesh	Rajasthan	Bihar
1950s	Rajagopalachari Kamraj	A. J. John P. Thanupillai P. Govinda Menon Namboodiripad	G. B. Pant Sampurnanand	J. N. Vyas M. L. Sukhadia	Sri Krishna Singh DN Singh
1960s	M. Bhaktavatsalam C. N. Annadurai	P. Thanupillai R. Sankar Namboodiripad	C. B. Gupta *Sucheta Kriplani* C. B. Gupta *Charan Singh* C. B. Gupta		Binodanand Jha K.B. Sahay M. P. Sinha S. P. Singh B.P. Shastri
1970s	M. Karunanidhi M. G. Ramachandran	C. Achutha Menon K. Karunakaran A. K. Antony P. K. Vasudevan Nair C. H. Mohammed	*Charan Singh* T.N. Singh K. Tripathi H. N. Bahuguna N. D. Tiwari R. N. Yadav Banarsi Das	Barkatullah Khan Hari Dev Joshi B. S. Shekhawat	Harihar Singh D.P. Rai B.P. Shastri *Kedar Pandey* *Abdul Gafoor* *J. Mishra* K. Thakur
1980s	J. Ramachandran	E. K. Nayanar K. Karunakaran E. K. Nayanar	*V. P. Singh* *Sripati Misra* *N. D. Tiwari* *V. B. Singh* *N. D. Tiwari*	*J. N. Phadia* S. C. Mathur H. L. Devpura Hari Dev Joshi S. C. Mathur	R.S. Das *J. Mishra* *C. Singh* *B. Dubey* *B. J. Azad*

1990s	M. Karunanidhi J. Jayalalitha M. Karunanidhi	K. Karunakaran *A. K. Antony* E. K. Nayanar	*M. S. Yadav* Kalyan Singh *M. S. Yadav* Mayawati Kalyan Singh Kalyan Singh R.P. Gupta	Hari Dev Joshi B.S. Shekhawat	S. N. Sinha *J. Mishra* *Lalu Yadav*
2000s	J. Jayalalitha O. Pannerselvam J. Jayalalitha M. Karunanidhi	*AK Antony* Oomen Chandy VS Achutanandan	*Rajnath Singh* Mayawati *M. S. Yadav* Mayawati	*A. Gehlot* *V. Raje Scindia* *A. Gehlot*	R. Devi *N. Kumar* R. Devi *N. Kumar*

Names in italics indicate that the CM has also been a minister in the national government at some point in time.

the national cabinet in 1955 leaving the state's politics in disarray, Congress chief ministers in UP have tended to be more involved with national politics as compared with Congress chief ministers in Rajasthan, Tamil Nadu or Kerala. Moreover, in contrast to leaders from other states, such as Tamil Nadu or Kerala, who even in New Delhi acted as representatives of their regions, frequently raising problems facing their state, when UP's leaders moved to the national stage they shed any association with UP and conducted themselves as national leaders representing national interests (Kudaisya 2007: 24).

UP's propinquity to the national domain – both in terms of national leaders controlling state politics and state leaders pursuing power at the national level – completely crippled subnational politics in the state. There was no distinct subnational political arena; public life was marked by the absence of a "regional political culture." A preoccupation with national issues blocked the emergence of any sort of subnational developmental agenda in UP (Kudaisya 2007: 24). In the years immediately following the formation of a democratic UP, instead of focusing on the many key developmental issues facing the state, prominent UP politicians including Pant, Purushottam Das Tandon, and Sampuranand, dissatisfied with the central government's actions in this regard, devoted their energies to installing Hindi in Devanagari as the lingua franca of India (Kudaisya 2007: 378).[16] Political elites in UP took it upon themselves to work toward the removal of the primary impediments to the adoption of Hindi in national and state administrations, namely the non-availability of terms of administrative usage[17] and the standardization of the Devanagari script.[18] Through the next three decades, political life in the state continued to be driven more by national rather than state concerns. Through the 1960s, because of a lack of strong state-level leadership, the UP Congress was in a state of organizational disarray marked by "frequent instances of gross indiscipline" (Masaldan 1967: 278). An observer of UP politics during these years noted that the conflicts were only put aside for a year in the wake of the Chinese invasion "so that the best effort might be put forth to meet the aggression." He notes that this triggered "talk of a basic reorientation in the outlook of the ruling Congress party" and some

---

[16] In 1949 Pant announced that under his aegis the UP government had taken a crucial first step toward promoting Hindi as the national language by declaring it the exclusive state language of the province (Kudaisya 2007: 371). Within the next few years the UP government had mandated that the proceedings of the UP legislative assembly and the entire administration of the state would be conducted only in Hindi. In 1950 the UP government declared with pride that it was "leading the rest of India in the implementation of Hindi in official work" (Kudaisya 2007: 375).

[17] The UP government commissioned the development of Hindi equivalents of English terms used in administrative business. Two massive official lexicons containing more than 30,000 such words were released in the 1950s (Kudaisya 2007: 375).

[18] It is important to point out here that while the promotion of Hindi in Devanagari script had become, in the postcolonial context, a national issue, it also marked a continuation of the provincial politics of the clash of Hindu-Hindi and Muslim-Urdu interests of the late colonial period described in Chapter 3.

"drastic changes" in party organization, but such intentions dissipated as the threat to the integrity of the Indian nation subsided. In fact the following years witnessed a "distressing new low" in the political life of the province "with unrestrained and unabashed indulgence in factional strife" and "disgraceful scenes in the legislature." Such severe political fragmentation was clearly detrimental for the formulation of a cohesive policy agenda for the state. However, "it was only a grave national crisis again, which alone could make the warring Congress factions suspend their internecine quarrel. It required the invasion of the country by Pakistan in 1965 for political peace to be established in the state" (Masaldan 1967: 278).

Election campaigns in the state tended to be fought less on issues of relevance to the state, such as good governance, and more on national questions. During the 1960s the Jan Sangh, for example, contested and succeeded in UP elections because of its stance of protest against the ruling Congress's relations with Pakistan and its perceived failure to secure a just treatment for the Hindu minority in the country (Masaldan 1967: 282). Similarly, the election campaign of 1984 almost completely eschewed topics associated with UP's advancement to focus "nearly exclusively on the dangers to the country, posed by internal and external enemies and on the need for Indians to close ranks to save the country." The "only two themes" emphasized by the Congress elites in UP were *Desh Akhand* (The Country Indivisible) and the dangers to India from foreign forces (Brass 1986: 663).

In line with elite preoccupations with the national sphere, the people of UP also tended to associate more with the national rather than the state realm. The National Election Study of 1971 shows that respondents from UP express greater interest in national rather than state politics and greater concern with and faith in the actions of the government in New Delhi rather than the state government; the proportion of people identifying with the national realm was substantially higher in UP than other Indian states. In the National Election Study of 1971, for example, 42% of people from UP said that information about national politics interested them more than state politics, as compared with 19% of Rajasthanis and 24% of people nation-wide. When asked whether they had more faith in the central over the state government, 42% of the respondents in UP answered "Government in Delhi," compared to less than 20% of people from Rajasthan and 25% of people across India. As Table 5.2 shows, 36.4% of people in UP said they were more concerned with the actions of the national rather than the state government as compared with 21% across India and 19% in Rajasthan. In successive elections the UP electorate tended to vote on national rather than state issues. In his study of the 1984 parliamentary elections in UP, for example, Brass notes that "voters self-consciously rejected local considerations to cast a vote for the party, the Congress, which was perceived as the best party for the good of the country" (Brass 1986: 661).

From the 1950s through the 1980s, elite and mass preoccupation with questions of national significance therefore led to an almost complete eclipse of questions

TABLE 5.2. *Reported Concern with State and Central Governments in Case Study States*

Q: People are generally concerned about what governments do – some are more concerned about what the government in Delhi does, others are more concerned with what the state Government does. How about you? Are you more concerned about what the government in Delhi does or about what the (name the State Government) does?

	State Government (%)		Both (%)		Government in Delhi (%)	
	1971	1996	1971	1996	1971	1996
Tamil Nadu	17.5	30	25	41	14	3
Kerala	41	47.5	19	24	19	9
UP	13	18	12	24	36	16
Rajasthan	11	25.2	10	19	19	18
Bihar	6	22.5	16	19	28	15
India	19	23	14.5	21	21	11

Source: National Election Studies, CSDS, New Delhi (1971, 1996).

of state importance. A number of prominent scholars of UP have established a direct causal link between the close association of UP with national politics and the developmental failures of the state (Kudaisya 2007: 24; Zerinini-Brotel 1998: 79). An examination of the UP budget through these decades shows that the state, for the most part, followed the central agenda. It prioritized the sectors emphasized by New Delhi irrespective of whether or not they were the most urgent needs of the state. In light of the rampant illiteracy and high mortality rates, social development was clearly the need of the hour in UP. Yet, in line with central policies, state governments in UP prioritized economic services in the 1980s. For example, in 1985–86, UP was spending over 40 percent of its total investment (expenditure on the capital account) on economic services and just over 3 percent on social services. In comparison, Rajasthan invested only 27 percent in economic services and 16 percent on social services.

Until the late 1980s, both UP and Rajasthan had similarly low levels of economic development. The absence of subnational solidarity on the part of the political elites and their consequent lack of attention to subnational welfare, however, meant that the UP government allocated considerably smaller outlays to the education and health sectors. From 1975 to 1980, for instance, per capita expenditure on elementary education was Rs 29 in UP as compared with Rs 43 in Rajasthan (Srivastava 2007). In 1975, UP spent Rs 7 per capita on health as compared with Rs 16 in Rajasthan. From 1981 to 1991, new educational institutions in UP grew at a rate of 2.66 percent as compared with 6.11 percent in Rajasthan (Mehrotra 2006). UP was distinguished from Rajasthan not only by differences in *levels* but also the *nature* of its social spending. UP spent less on the social sector and what it did spend was characterized by a "distorted pattern" (Drèze & Gazdar 1998: 54). The most egregious example of this is the direction of large proportions of the outlays on health to family planning activities, a key central directive especially during Indira Gandhi's tenure. A number of scholars have pointed to the high toll that the focus on family planning has taken on the provision of essential health services in the state.[19]

The lack of identification with, or mobilization around, a subnational identity played an important role in the low levels of interest in, consciousness of, and proclivity to participate in, the public life of the state on the part of UP's citizens. As shown in Table 4.3, according to the National Election survey in 1971, an overwhelming proportion of respondents in UP said that they had no interest in the recently concluded electoral campaign or politics and public affairs in general. These figures compare unfavorably to respondents in Tamil Nadu, Kerala as well as across all Indian states. In the same survey, less than 14 percent of the residents of UP could correctly name their state chief minister, as compared to 48 percent in Kerala, 51 percent in Tamil Nadu, and more than 29 percent of all Indians.[20] Through the 1950s to the 1980s, electoral turnout in state assembly elections in UP remained substantially below that of Tamil Nadu and Kerala and lower than that of other Indian states. A number of field studies show that this low level of awareness of and proclivity to participate in the public life of the state resulted in minimal societal involvement with the limited public services provided by the state (Drèze & Gazdar 1998; Sinha 1995). Drèze and Gazdar document a long-standing pattern of popular indifference and inertia toward problems in the delivery of education and health services, notably teacher and doctor absenteeism. During my field research I conducted multiple semi-structured interviews with bureaucrats, all members of the nationally recruited IAS, who had been assigned to state cadres. All the bureaucrats I interviewed had served as state collectors, the government official in charge of the overall administration of the district across districts in the states of Tamil Nadu, Kerala, UP, Rajasthan, and Bihar from the 1950s to the 2000s. In contrast to their colleagues in other states, not even one of the bureaucrats who had served as a district collector in U.P. between the 1950s and the 1980s could recall a petition, demand or protest regarding the (mal) functioning of social services.[21] This lack of monitoring of government public services and of a more general challenge to the official neglect of the social

---

[19] Badakoti, for instance, wrote that "[the] preoccupation with attaining of given family planning targets has had devastating effects on the other health activities." In the early 1980s, Krishnamurty and Nadkarni note that "in [rural and tribal blocks] it was observed that the visits of medical staff were irregular as most of the time they were busy with family-planning and other campaigns." Similarly, a few years later Jeffrey describes how "during the main months of family planning campaigns ... virtually all energies of maternal and child health staff may be directed towards those ends" (all cited in Drèze & Gazdar 1996: 55).

[20] Incidentally, as further evidence of their greater identification with an interest in the national rather than state realm, 62% of the same set of UP residents could correctly name the prime minister and 50% could correctly name the political party to which she belonged (NES 1971)!

[21] Interviews conducted from 2005–2007.

sector resulted in abysmal levels of social development in UP. Even two decades after independence, in 1971, more than three-quarters of UP's total adult population could not read or write. During the 1960s, only three out of four children in UP survived to age two, as compared to nine of ten in Kerala (Bhat et al. 1984: 6). Until the mid-eighties, Uttar Pradesh had the highest levels of infant and child mortality among major Indian states, by a long margin, and also the lowest level of life expectancy (Drèze & Gazdar 1998: 39; fn 10). With 931 maternal deaths per 100,000 live births, the rate of maternal mortality in UP was lower than only five countries for which there was data at the time – Somalia, Bhutan, Ghana, Gambia, and Congo (Drèze & Gazdar 1998: 40).

Ethnic Divisions Prompt Prioritization of Sectional over Subnational Welfare: 1990s Onward

Since the early 1990s, the locus of elite and popular identification in UP has shifted from the nation down to ethnic groups. Scholars of UP concur that in the past couple of decades, religion and, to a greater extent, caste have come to dominate the political life of UP (Brass 1997: 1241; Zerinini-Brotel 1998: 74). Like in Rajasthan, UP witnessed the growth of the BJP in the late 1980s and early 1990s, but unlike in Rajasthan, the BJP mobilized around a Hindu rather than a subnational identity in UP. Lieten notes that the BJP fought the 1991 election, which catapulted it into power, "on the single issue of Hindutva sentiments" (1994: 779). Through the 1990s, the BJP consistently played the Hindu card, triggering an intensification of religious tensions (Ludden 1996: 81). The BJP, Hasan argues, successfully transformed public space in UP into a religious space (Ludden 1996: 97).

The rise of religious identities in UP was accompanied, and in recent years has arguably been overshadowed by, the growth of powerful caste allegiances. During the 1980s, UP witnessed the emergence of powerful lower caste movements. Ideologues such as Kanshi Ram "reconstructed and revived" a "forgotten" and stigmatized history of the *dalits* (Pai 2007: 261). By the early 1990s, the (then) militant *dalit* party, the Bahujan Samaj Party (BSP) headed by the charismatic Mayawati, was garnering a substantial proportion of the popular vote in state assembly elections. In the early 1990s, Mulayam Singh Yadav, a veteran politician of UP, established the Samajwadi Party (SP), which sought to represent the interests of backward castes, especially Yadavs and Muslims. The SP has been an important presence in UP's electoral arena, twice leading a coalition government from 1993–97 and 2003–07 and winning a clear majority in the 2012 legislative assembly elections. The BSP and SP are only the most prominent of the many new parties representing the interests of specific castes that have mushroomed in UP in the past decade.[22]

---

[22] The BSP and SP are believed to have served as "role models" for a range of new caste-based political formations such as the Apna Dal, which stands for the Kurmis; the Pragatisheel Manav

Unlike in Kerala and Tamil Nadu, lower caste movements in UP did not take place in the context of a unifying subnational ideology. The militancy of the *dalit* movement, as captured for instance by their election slogans, alienated the upper castes, which constituted a much higher proportion of the population of UP (more than 20% of the total Hindu population) as compared to the southern states, where their share was less than 3 percent.[23] Mayawati repeatedly told her supporters that they "should not trust upper castes," including those joining the BSP (Pai 2007: 265). Moreover, various lower castes have also tended to mobilize in antagonism rather than in alliance with each other. The BSP's initial claim to stand for social justice for the *bahujan samaj* (literally translated as the majority community), which was defined to include scheduled castes, scheduled tribes, other backward castes, and minorities who together constituted 85 percent of the total population, quickly narrowed to the claim of standing exclusively for the *dalits* (scheduled castes) and not the *bahujan samaj* as a whole (Pai 2002: 121). In fact, in the wake of the bitter breakup of the coalition between the BSP and the SP, the interests of the *dalits* and backward castes came to be seen not only as separate but also opposed to each other.

In the context of the widespread politicization of caste, by the early 2000s even the BJP began to seek support along caste lines. In the general elections of 2004, the BJP tried to reach out to individual castes by focusing on their "caste glory through references to their caste heroes; it sought to consolidate their caste identity by exhorting them to take pride in their caste-based professions" (Tiwari 2007: 138). Tiwari highlights a critical change in "the language of the political discourse" of the BJP from "one uniform language" to "different languages for different target groups" and attributes this to the "growing fragmentation of society [in UP] along caste lines" (155).

The salience of caste and religion in UP politics in the 1990s is evident in Table 5.3, which shows that according to the National Election Study, nearly half of the population of UP voted the same way as other members of their caste or religious group, as compared to only 5 percent in Kerala and an average of 26 percent across all other Indian states. In 1996, 26 percent of those polled in UP believed that there existed a political party that took special care of their caste or religious group's interests. This not only represented a marked increase from the 17 percent who had expressed the same sentiment in 1971, but was also much higher than the other case study states and the Indian average.[24] The NES also provides concomitant evidence of the UP masses' waning identification with

---

Samaj Party, which is backed by the Malhas; the Rashtriya Lok Dal, which represents Jats, and the Rashtriya Kranti Party, whose constituency are the Lodhi Rajputs (Gupta 2007: 121).

[23] A popular slogan went, "*Tilak, Tarazu, Kalam, Talwar; Inko maaro jute chaar*" (Forehead Mark, Scale, Pen and Sword, Thrash them with four shoes) (Pai 2007: 263). Symbolically, the *tilak* represents the Brahmin; the *tarazu*, the Vaishya; the *kalam*, the Kayasths; and the *talwar* represents the Kshatriyas.

[24] Brass's study of the 1996 parliamentary elections in UP (1997) also provides evidence of most members of a caste group voting along caste lines.

TABLE 5.3. *Caste-Politics Link across Case Study States*

	Tamil Nadu		Kerala		UP		Rajasthan		Bihar		India	
	1971	1996	1971	1996	1971	1996	1971	1996	1971	1996	1971	1996
Is there any political party that looks after the interests of your caste/religious group? Yes (%)	12.5	6	10	16	17	26	13	8	11.5	19	13.5	16
Generally speaking did most members of caste/ religious group vote for one or different parties? One party (%)	21.5	11	13	5	42	46	46	27	44	34	35.2	26

Source: National Election Studies (1971, 1996), Center for Study of Developing Societies (CSDS), New Delhi.

the national sphere. Table 5.2 shows that from 1971 to 1996 there was more than a 50 percent decline in the proportion of people in UP who claim to be most concerned with what the government in Delhi does, and a concomitant increase in the percentage of people who say they are either more concerned with the actions of the state government or both the center and state governments. These survey results taken together therefore suggest a shift in the locus of popular identification in UP away from the nation toward ethnic identities, notably caste and, to a lesser extent, religion.

Scholars of contemporary UP concur that the rise of caste and religious identities has had a very polarizing effect on the politics of UP (Zerinini-Brotel 1998: 92). The fragmentation of the polity has led to the conceptualization of welfare in narrow, sectional terms. Insofar as "no common notion of justice" could be built even across lower castes (Pai 2002:124), there was little idea of the collective welfare of all residents of UP. Drèze and Gazdar write, for example, of "the absence of a well-accepted consensus on the need to univer-salize primary education in Uttar Pradesh" (1998: 63). Social welfare came to be seen by different caste groups in exclusive and zero-sum terms. The *dalit* movement demanded goods for their exclusive benefit and spoke of "retribu-tive" social justice (Pai 2002: 126). This widespread framing of welfare in caste terms tilted the social agenda of UP heavily toward targeted policies aimed at the uplift of members of specific caste groups and away from universal poli-cies designed for the benefit of all residents of the state. While almost all the governments in power in UP since the 1990s have favored targeted over uni-versal social policies, the schemes of the BSP have been the most striking in this regard. The party has used its tenures to initiate programs for *dalits* that were unprecedented in both their scale and intensity of implementation.

The BSP introduced two main kinds of programs targeted toward *dalits*. The first were schemes designed to allow *dalits* to "reclaim their stigmatized past" by engendering pride about *dalit* history through the erection of (tens of thousands of) statues of, and renaming of districts, cities, universities and parks after, important *dalit* leaders, notably Ambedkar (Pai 2007: 261).[25] The

---

[25] Such "sociocultural" programs are widely dismissed as "mere symbolism" and criticized as "unproductive expenditure" (Pai 2007: 63). However, as I elaborate in the concluding chapter, spending on symbols is not necessarily wasteful. The key question is what is being symbolized. The Tamil Nadu government also devoted substantial expenditure to the installation of statues and the renaming of districts, cities, and parks, but the critical difference was that in contrast to UP, it glorified unifying Tamil figures that helped strengthen subnational identity and con-sequently served to shore up public support for social welfare. In UP, the problem was not so much the allocation of money toward symbolism (though given that UP was almost bankrupt at the time, it was more egregious than it would have been if UP had been in more sound finan-cial health, like Tamil Nadu) but that it was caste symbols that had come to be seen as divisive rather than unifying that were glorified. In UP, the jurist, social reformer, and chairman of the drafting commission of the Indian Constitution, B.R. Ambedkar, for instance, was deified as standing for dalit interests and *against* the interests of other castes. Interestingly, in Tamil Nadu the poet-philosopher Thiruvalluvar, who was the son of a *dalit* woman, came to be revered as

second were policies aimed at the social and economic development of *dalits*, the largest and most prominent of which was the Ambedkar Village Program (AVP), which located bundles of welfare schemes in villages with *dalit* majorities. While it is important not to undermine their importance in empowering *dalits*, on the whole these schemes have had only a limited effect on the welfare of their intended beneficiaries but have taken a grave toll on the social development of the state as a whole. Mayawati's "iconography spree" (Zerinini-Brotel 1998: 99) drained the already depleted coffers of the state, leaving precious little for investment in "key sectors such as education, infrastructure and health" which was especially harmful for "the poorest sections of the population, which includes a substantial section of *dalits*" (Pai 2007: 63). Similarly, the AVP involved the siphoning of funds away from developmental schemes meant for the entire state and concentrating them in small *dalit* enclaves. Pai points out that on assuming power in 1995, the Mayawati government issued orders to suspend all ongoing social welfare programs so that state moneys could be diverted to the Ambedkar villages (2002: 129). During her tenure in 1997, Mayawati directed that the Education Department must open all their sanctioned schools first in Ambedkar villages, and only after all such villages were covered should the opening of schools in other villages of the state be considered (Pai 2002: 130).

This targeting of social expenditures toward members of only one community has led to the neglect of other residents of UP, most egregiously the non-*dalit* rural poor who in some areas are poorer than *dalits* (Srivastava 2007: 348).[26] Moreover, many development experts have questioned the benefits of these targeted schemes even for their intended *dalit* beneficiaries. Mehrotra, for example, argues that the programs are so "narrowly focused as to be completely meaningless for the majority of the lower castes" (2007: 368). He points out that initiatives such as the opening of schools and establishment of hostels for *dalit* children are aimed at children who had at least completed primary school and overlook the substantial proportion of *dalit* children who remain out of school, not to mention ignoring the abysmal state of government schools in general, the main reason why so many children in UP, both *dalit* and non-*dalit*, do not complete primary school. In addition to their circumscribed focus, targeted social policies in UP have also been criticized for their tokenist and ad hoc nature. For example, while there are schemes to provide *dalit* families financial assistance during illness and other contingencies, there has been

a Tamil hero. In recent years, dalit mobilization in Tamil Nadu has been accompanied by the mushrooming of statues of Ambedkar, now an established all-India dalit icon. Yet unlike in UP, the statues of Ambedkar in Tamil Nadu are part of a representational space dominated by subnational icons.

[26] A recent UNICEF survey showed that while UP has devoted slightly higher per capita expenditures to the education of scheduled castes as compared with Rajasthan, it has spent substantially less on the education of scheduled tribes, who have tended to be more socioeconomically deprived than scheduled tribes (Mehrotra 2006: 337–38).

"no mention" of a systematic health- or nutrition-related intervention in the state (Mehrotra 2007: 394).

Scholars and policy analysts alike have also broached the broader and more critical issue of whether there can in fact be "sectional development in the larger context of underdevelopment in UP" (Pai 2007: 63). What is the value of targeted social schemes that are implemented in the absence of, and, to a large extent at the cost of universal education and health programs? Tamil Nadu and Kerala addressed the problem of underdevelopment, in the main, through the initiation of universal social welfare programs that sought to provide basic education and health to all residents of the states. Or, as Mehrotra aptly puts it, it was a case of "all boats rising with the level of the water" (2007: 393). Under conditions of abysmal levels of social development and barely functioning literacy and basic health programs, targeted schemes are unlikely to advance, and may even adversely affect, the welfare of the intended beneficiaries and the people of the state as a whole.

Quite apart from this dangerous skewing toward targeted policies, the social sector in UP has also been marked, more generally, by "resilient governmental inertia" (Drèze & Gazdar 1998: 53). This is reflected starkly in the public expenditures on education and health, particularly the sustained *decline* of almost 20 percent in the already meager per capita public expenditure on education in the state in the 1990s (ibid. 88). Srivastava notes that from 1990 to 2000, UP's annual growth rate of real expenditure on total education was only 2 percent, as compared with 5 percent in Rajasthan and a mere 4 percent on elementary education in contrast to 8 percent in Rajasthan (Mehrotra 2006: 152). Through the 1990s, per capita outlays on health in UP were substantially less than Rajasthan, and the lowest of all Indian states, except Bihar.

Insofar as UP, a hitherto revenue surplus state, witnessed economic stagnation and financial crisis in the 1990s, a generous reader might be tempted to attribute the state's poor record of social expenditures during this period to its fiscal problems rather than to government inertia. It is interesting to note, first of all, that the state's initiation of a plethora of targeted policies aimed at particular social groups have themselves been pointed to as an important cause for the fiscal crisis (Singh 2007). Moreover, UP state governments' lackadaisical implementation of externally sponsored social schemes in these years provides unequivocal evidence of the state's lack of political commitment to the social sector, independent of fiscal pressures. The adoption of the 1986 National Policy on Education set the stage for an unprecedentedly proactive role of the central government in the field of primary education. The involvement of New Delhi was further strengthened, and international actors began to play an increasingly important role in the 1990s. UP, however, is notorious for having massively under-utilized large grants earmarked for primary education from the central government and international agencies. The state government took "little interest" in the Total Literacy Campaign, despite the considerable potential of the campaign having been demonstrated in other Indian states

(Drèze & Gazdar 1998: 88). Similarly, the state has lagged behind in implementing the nationally sponsored Midday meal program, which had been shown to be strikingly successful in boosting school enrollment and raising nutritional standards in other states.[27] The UP government is also distinguished for not having introduced even a single noteworthy innovation in the social sector. Kerala is famous for its literacy drives, Tamil Nadu for its nutrition schemes, Maharashtra for employment guarantee, Gujarat for drought relief, Karnataka for panchayati raj, Himachal Pradesh for primary education, West Bengal for land reform (Drèze & Gazdar 1998: 93). Even poor, BIMARU states such as Rajasthan and Madhya Pradesh have launched important social initiatives such as the Shiksha Karmi program and the Education Guarantee Scheme respectively, which were subsequently adopted at an all-India level.[28] In UP, however, there are no examples of such initiatives. Jairam Ramesh, a prominent politician who hails from UP, presents this point powerfully: "In 50 years, is there anything that stands out in UP? Is there one big idea that is UP's contribution to the theory and practice of development? Is there one program that makes UP an example to the rest of the country? The answer, sadly, must be in the negative" (1999: 2127).

State apathy toward the social sector in UP has been matched by societal inertia. Not only have state governments in UP not been able to establish a progressive social agenda, but the limited social services that they have provided have functioned very ineffectively. This is to a large extent because of a lack of popular monitoring, reflective of the more general absence of political interest in, and awareness of, the public life of a state that most residents feel very little solidarity with. In 1996, only 40 percent of the people surveyed in UP could correctly name the state's chief minister. While this clearly reflects a much greater degree of political awareness as compared to the 1970s, it is still significantly below the proportion of people who could correctly identify the state CM in Tamil Nadu, Kerala, and Rajasthan as well as across all Indian states (NES 1996, 1971). The level of political participation in UP, as measured by turnout in the national as well as state assembly elections from the 1990s onward has also remained discernibly lower than the other case study states

[27] Describing the dismal record of UP in implementing national welfare schemes, Arundhati Dhuru, the Supreme Court-appointed adviser on the Right to Food, explained that "Poverty is a common problem in all states ... schemes being implemented here are the same as in other states. So how come states like Tamil Nadu, Karnataka, or for that matter even Rajasthan and Madhya Pradesh fare better in their implementation? Look at it this way: The centre has a scheme called the Midday Meal, where it gives Rs 2.50 per child from its side and the state has to contribute a somewhat equal amount. A state like Tamil Nadu contributes as high as Rs 5 per child, while UP contributes just Rs 1. So there is bound to be a difference. The Supreme Court says that as a part of the Midday Meal scheme, children should get a variety of food items, but then, what would you get for just Rs 3.50? Just *khichdi* (gruel) and poor quality of food" (South Asian 2007).

[28] BIMARU is an acronym for the North-Central states of Bihar, Madhya Pradesh, Rajasthan and Uttar Pradesh, that translates in Hindi into 'stick', prompting these states to be known as the 'sick states' of India.

TABLE 5.4. *Caste Harmony in Case Study States*

State	Percentage of Respondents Who Agreed with the Proposition that "Relationship between different castes has become more harmonious"	Percentage of Respondents Who Agreed with the Proposition that "Tension between different religious communities has decreased"
Tamil Nadu	54	40
Kerala	74	66
UP	52	28
Rajasthan	80	44
Bihar	50	41
India	62	43

Source: National Election Study (1996), Center for Study of Developing Societies (CSDS), New Delhi.

as well as the Indian average. The political fragmentation of UP along caste and religious lines has been mirrored in the social sphere. Table 5.4 shows that in the 1996 NES, a lower percentage of respondents agreed that there was greater harmony between caste and religious groups in UP, as compared to the other case study states and the Indian average. Scholars of development in UP have noted that the widespread implementation of policies meant exclusively for *dalits* has "neglected and alienated" large sections of the rural population, many of whom are at least as deprived as the *dalits* (Srivastava 2007: 348). Zerinini-Brotel speaks of the "rejection felt by upper caste members" (1998: 99). Based on extensive field research, Drèze and Gazdar argue that this "highly divided nature of the rural society" has "seriously constrained" collaborative public action to ensure the effective provision of social services in UP's villages (1998: 61). Residents with a low degree of political consciousness and interest, who are furthermore divided by caste and religion, are unlikely to mobilize collectively to protest the quality of teaching in the local school or doctor absenteeism in the PHC.

In this context, it is unsurprising that grave deficiencies in the functioning of education and health services have persisted in UP villages for years without any popular protest. The school in the village of Palanpur, for example, was found to be "virtually non-functional" for as long as ten years between 1983 and 1993 due to systematic absenteeism on the part of the local teacher without triggering any collective mobilization on the part of the residents (Drèze & Sen 1998: 88). This is symbolic of a more general "failure of village communities to discipline teachers" which has contributed to the "chaotic functioning of schools" (92) and the dismal state of social services more generally. Interestingly, the UP government itself highlights "public apathy" as one of the main causes for the "disarray" of social services in the state (http://upgov.nic .in/upinfo/up_eco.html).

Local government functionaries and political leaders report that when there is popular mobilization in the village, usually various castes organize on issues that they see as important for their advancement.[29] In fact, in no small part due to the symbolic nature of the BSP's policies, even the concept of advancement has come to be defined in identity-based rather than more substantive terms. Mayawati's transfer of hundreds of non-*dalit* government officials upon assuming power was representative of the idea that only officials who belong to the same caste can look after a group's interests. The idea that upper castes would/ could not adequately address *dalit* concerns gained ground, such that when *dalits*, who constitute the majority of the population in most UP villages, mobilize, they have tended to do so to demand the replacement of upper-caste functionaries, such as bureaucrats and school headmasters, with their *dalit* brethren, rather than protesting the quality of local schools or health centers.

The absence of a progressive social policy combined with a low degree of popular involvement with public services together have resulted in UP continuing to be plagued by some of the worst human development indicators of all Indian states. UP, for example, has the worst malnutrition rates in the country. Almost half of UP's children are underweight and more than half are stunted (Mehrotra 2007: 379). As of 2011, maternal mortality, infant mortality, and neonatal mortality rates in UP are the lowest of all Indian states. It is striking that the survival rates for baby girls in rural UP are worse than even Rajasthan, a state that is infamous for its male bias (Mathur and Rajagopal 2011).

Literacy rates in UP continue to be below the national average. The state has made important gains since the 1990s, particularly in the past decade, but development scholars have been quick to point out that this improvement occurred almost entirely because of the unprecedented and massive efforts of the central government and foreign donor agencies who initiated large-scale educational campaigns, including notably Operation Blackboard, the Education Guarantee Scheme, Sarva Shiksha Abhiyan, and the District Primary Education Program. External actors have pumped massive additional resources and provided logistical assistance as regards primary education in the state; even the limited schemes initiated by the state government have been at the impetus and often with the financial backing of New Delhi or international organizations such as the World Bank or UNICEF (Mehrotra 2007: 382). The targeted social policies, on which the UP government placed so much emphasis, have reaped some results in terms of an increase in the educational and health levels of *dalits*, but the comparisons with Rajasthan, which initiated no such policies, starkly reveal the limitations of such a policy bias. In 1991, the literacy rates of *dalits* were marginally higher in UP than Rajasthan, but by 2001, Rajasthan, which focused on broad-based literacy programs and introduced relatively few

---

[29] Interviews with district collectors, members of legislative assembly, block development officers (BDOs), sarpanches and panchayat officials conducted in 2006–07.

schemes targeted only at *dalits*, had attained a lead over UP. In the 2011 census *dalit* literacy rates in UP and Rajasthan were equivalent at just about 60 percent. Further, despite the plethora of targeted schemes, *dalits* in UP remain far more socially deprived than their counterparts in other states, most of which have introduced far fewer social policies targeted explicitly toward *dalits*. Across all Indian states, historically and even now, *dalits* have tended to have poorer social indicators than the rest of the population. The relative extent of UP's underdevelopment, however, is evidenced by the fact that even *dalit* women in Tamil Nadu have better social indicators than upper-caste women in UP (Mehrotra 2007: 377).

HOPE AMID BACKWARDNESS

RAJASTHAN

In this section I analyze how changes in the strength of subnational solidarity have led to variations in the progressiveness of social policy and the pace of social development in colonial and post-colonial Rajasthan. I begin by showing how, until the 1940s, the deeply fragmented subnational community in the British province of Rajputana led to an almost complete absence of state or societal action in the social sphere. At the end of the colonial period, Rajputana therefore had one of the lowest levels of social development of all provinces. I then discuss how the melding of the various princely states of Rajputana into a single, unified state of Rajasthan at the time of Indian independence and the ensuing political competition laid the foundation for the emergence of a subnational identity among elites, which triggered the introduction of a progressive social policy. From the 1950s to the 1980s, however, this subnational identification remained confined to an elite stratum and did not resonate with a majority of the residents of Rajasthan who retained strong loyalties to their former native kingdoms. The absence of any sense of attachment to the state led to a low degree of consciousness of and involvement with the sociopolitical life of the state, which manifested itself in popular apathy toward the functioning of public services, greatly limiting the potential gains of relatively generous government allocations to the social sector. In the third subsection I show that beginning in the 1980s the process of generational change and the espousal of Rajasthani subnationalism by the increasingly popular Bharatiya Janata Party (BJP) facilitated the entrenchment of a Rajasthani identity in the popular psyche. This fostered broader support for social welfare policies as well as increased political consciousness and participation, which triggered greater societal involvement with, and therefore more efficient, social services, resulting in important developmental gains in the state, especially in education. In both absolute terms as well as relative to other Indian states, however, Rajasthani subnationalism remains low and the state is correspondingly among the most socially backward of Indian states.

Absence of Subnationalism Impedes Social Development: 1900–1940s

As noted in Chapter 3, scholars concur that through much of the late nine-teenth and the first part of the twentieth century there was virtually no sense of a shared subnational identity in or across the various princely states of Rajputana (Grierson 1894: 46; Lodrick 1994: 9). Within the context of an entrenched feudal sociopolitical system, the absence of any sense of obligations towards the people that would arise from a subnational solidarity meant that, for the most part, the business of the state was seen in terms of the advancing the interests of the ruling class. Sharma notes that it was not considered "obligatory for (the *jagirdar*) to provide any public facilities to his *jagir* people. So much so that the *jagirdar* in the interior areas did not even give facilities for 'crude' drinking water or dispen-saries" (1993: 5). Until the last years of the colonial period, most princely states did not even distinguish their personal purse from state expenditure. When, under British pressure they did begin to publish budgets, it became evident that many princes' understanding of public works implied palace expenses. The peo-ple of the princely states of Rajputana "were politically irrelevant and thought that they should be" (Rudolph & Rudolph 1962: 142). Education and health spending barely even figured as categories in some of these rudimentary budgets (Rudolph & Rudolph 1962: 147). A Rajasthan Government Symposium in 1951 stated that during the colonial period, "The Education Department received min-imal attention" and consequently the state "has not made much progress during the last century or so" (Rajasthan 1951: 125–27). During the early decades of the twentieth century, Rajputana had one of the lowest levels of education and highest levels of mortality of all provinces in India. The colonial censuses show that from 1901 to 1921, when the princely states of Travancore and Cochin were making important strides in education, there was almost no improvement in literacy rates in the princely states of Rajputana. In 1931, 99.4 percent of the female and 93 percent of the male population of the province was illiterate (see Figures 1.3–1.5). According to the 1941 Census of India, the proportion of chil-dren dying before age two in Rajasthan (0.309) was significantly higher than in most regions of India (Bhat et al. 1984).

Emergence of Elite Rajasthani Subnationalism Triggers Progressive Social Policy: 1950s Onward

As discussed in Chapter 3, the last years of the colonial period and the early years after Indian independence witnessed the emergence of an idea of "Rajasthan" and of a sense of subnational solidarity on the part of a large cross-section of social, economic and political elites in the state. Notably, M. L. Sukhadia, who became chief minister in 1954 and held the post until 1971, was himself a leading espouser of Rajasthani subnationalism.[30] He had campaigned for the

---

[30] In an interview with Jamini Kaushik in 1968, Sukhadia declared that "Rajasthan is the only (Indian) state whose people have a certain courage".

formation of the state and took a series of steps during his tenure to encourage popular identification with Rajasthan.[31]

Their nascent subnationalist identification was an important motor for these elites to support the welfare of all Rajasthanis.[32] This translated into both private initiatives – as early as 1952–53, the finance minister in his budget speech acknowledged private charitable efforts in the fields of education and health[33] – and also pressure for state prioritization of the social sector. Education and health were also among the most important topics of debate in the Rajasthan state assembly from the 1950s to the 1980s.[34] In a legislative assembly debate in 1963, a Congress legislator went so far as to say:

> The greatest need of the state is that in order to fill the present vacancies of 400 doctors, two more medical colleges should be opened ... If the Rajasthan Canal project stalls, so be it. Let the construction of the Pong dam be delayed for a while but we cannot delay the alleviation of the problems of the people ... in a state that we call a social welfare state how can we even think of reducing the number of medical colleges![35]

It is notable that legislators not only from the majority party but also the opposition repeatedly underscored their commitment to public goods provision on the floor of the state assembly (Rudolph & Rudolph 1962).

Sukhadia himself repeatedly emphasized the importance of social development, and one of the clearest signals of the priority he accorded to it was his,

[31] As mentioned in chapter 3, Sukhadia's government commissioned a multi-volume history of Rajasthan. In his preface he evoked the idea of a single, glorious Rajasthani history and culture, writing, "We had heard and read the daring account of great warriors and patriots like Rana Sanga and Rana Pratap ... the touch of divine magic in the works of Rajasthan sculptors and painters has held us spell-bound. Behind all this, one can perceive the character and culture which has a unity of its own" (1966: 3).

[32] During 2005 and 2006 I conducted structured, open-ended interviews with seventeen individuals who had been prominent in the political, economic, and sociocultural life of the state during the 1950s and 1960s. In response to the question of what they had felt the topmost priorities of the newly created state of Rajasthan should be, all of them mentioned the advance of education and 88% (14 of 17) mentioned both education and health. In response to the question of why they thought it was important for the government to prioritize the social sector, while almost all the interviewees began by talking of the neglect of social policy by the princely states and the abysmal social infrastructure and low social indicators that the state inherited at the time of its formation, many of them also went on to discuss how essential it was for all residents of "our" state to have access to education and health services. One respondent spoke of "ending the shame associated with the backwardness of our ancient and glorious ... state." Another respondent told me that "of all the states in India we have one of the most valorous histories, richest cultures ... ours is a great civilization ... we needed to have an enlightened citizenry." All the individuals I interviewed believed that there was consensus among elites during this period that the state should focus on providing education and health services.

[33] Budget speech by Nathu Ram Mirdha, 1952–53. (Rajasthan Assembly Secretariat 2001: 26).

[34] For example, a transcription of debates in the Rajasthan State Assembly on education on May 21, 1956 was more than 77 pages long; a debate on public health on March 21, 1960 ran more than 130 pages, which were much longer than debates on other subjects.

[35] Speech by Jwala Prasad Sharma, Proceedings of Rajasthan Legislative Assembly, March 20, 1963, p. 3528.

relatively unusual, decision to retain the education portfolio even after becoming chief minister of the state.[36] The chief minister was known to frequently frame the introduction of welfare policies as necessary for the "greatness of Rajasthan."[37] The influence of subnationalism on social policy in Rajasthan more generally, is brought out, like in the case of Kerala, by the state government's attempts to couch social welfare initiatives in terms of an evocation of a glorious albeit mythical past. As noted in Chapter 4, state governments in Kerala attempted to establish a link between their social schemes and the "golden rule" of the ancient Malayali king, Mahabali, who is said to have been devoted to the well-being of his people. Similarly, the Rajasthan government portrayed its welfare initiatives as an effort to break out of its colonial backwardness and return to the high standards of development that had characterized the land during classical times. In his inaugural address at the meeting of the Central Advisory Board on Education in Jaipur in 1962, for example, Chief Minister Sukhadia declared:

The classical land of Rajasthan had once been a fountain head of learning and culture. Even when many of the independent Kingdoms of Rajasthan had fallen one by one before the onslaughts of invaders, the great tradition of learning was carried on by Rajasthanis ... Nor was the region backward in the production of literature in Rajasthani dialects ... Even during the ascendency of the Marathas when the Rajasthan States were hard-pressed, the rulers continued to encourage literature and poets ... But during the last two centuries or so education was confined to small sections of society ... The first problem on achievement of independence was therefore to push forward education programs.[38]

Another clear instance, this time in the 1990s, during the tenure of the BJP government under Bhairon Singh Shekhawat, of the influence of Rajasthani subnationalism on social welfare policies is the Bhamashah scheme. This scheme sought to encourage local involvement with educational institutions by honoring individuals who made financial contributions toward the upkeep of their village school with the appellation of 'Bhamashah', a historic figure who had financed the return of the great Rajasthani king, Maharana Pratap.[39] As the then education secretary recounted to me:

It was quickly decided that the most fitting way to recognize the contributions of these individuals was to designate them "Rajasthani heroes"... there was consensus on that.

[36] Through 2007–2009 I asked over forty IAS officers appointed across multiple ministries in the Government of India about the prestige associated with appointments to different ministeries. Over 90% mentioned the Ministry of Human Resource Development and 80% mentioned Health in their list of the three least prestigious ministeries. It is notable that this list included other ministries that are also broadly associated with social welfare, namely Women and Child Development, Minority Affairs and Tribal Affairs.

[37] Interview with Dr. Adarsh Kishore, Rajasthan cadre officer of the Indian Administrative Service (IAS), June 12, 2008, IMF offices, Washington, DC.

[38] http://education.nic.in/cd5oyears/g/12/1Z/121Z0101.htm.

[39] It is interesting to note here the continued evocation of the subnational figure of Bhamashah in one of the most important social initiatives, a women's financial empowerment, launched by the government of Rajasthan in 2014 (http://bhamashah.rajasthan.gov.in).

But how? Then the Education Minister (Gulab Chand Kataria of the BJP) came up with the idea of coining it the "Bhamashah Yojna" after the historical figure of Bhamashah. Bhamashah had been a prominent member of the business community who had given his entire wealth to Maharana Pratap to fight the Mughals. We thought it was perfect! The very name Bhamashah evoked the idea of love and sacrifice for your motherland. Individuals who made contributions for the schools in their village were the modern day Bhamashahs. We decided to organize felicitation ceremonies in schools where donors would be "crowned" Bhamashah. People really took to the idea and I think the scheme worked very well.[40]

It is important to note here that Rajasthan had entered the postcolonial period with a distinct economic and institutional disadvantage compared to UP. UP was widely hailed as a "model province" (Crooks 1897: 3); British adminis- trators marveled at the region's "soil of unrivalled fertility," the "magnificent" infrastructure of irrigation, roads, and railways. Rajasthan, on the other hand, was described as a bastion of deep backwardness (Markovits 2002: 406), and characterized by dysfunctional institutions and susceptible, due to its location in the most arid part of the subcontinent, to chronic food shortages and fre- quent famines (Stern 1988: 109). Moreover, the new state of Rajasthan faced the daunting task of integrating the distinct administrative apparatuses of twenty-two princely kingdoms,[41] while UP inherited a strong, well-integrated bureaucratic apparatus that had made it an example for other directly con- trolled areas of British India (Kudaisya 2007: 8). Despite this, the Rajasthan government displayed a stronger commitment to the social sector, steadily increasing its financial outlays on education and health, overtaking UP as well as all other North-Central Indian states. In 1951–52, for example, Rajasthan and UP committed a roughly equivalent proportion of their budgets (14%) to the education sector, but by the mid-1960s, while Rajasthan's allocation had risen to more than 20 percent, that of UP had stagnated at 14 percent. By 1969, Rajasthan's education spending as a proportion of total state domestic product (3.2%) was double that of UP (1.5%). Through most of the 1980s, 1990s, and 2000s, per capita expenditure on education in Rajasthan has remained higher than in UP. Similarly, in the health sector, both Rajasthan and UP spent next to nothing per resident in the early 1950s, but while Rajasthan's expenditure grew to Rs. 8.23 per capita in 1970–71, UP spent only Rs. 3.2. By 1985–86, Rajasthan was spending an average of Rs. 31 on the health of each resident, significantly higher than the average of Rs. 23 for the other BIMARU states and not much below the Rs. 36 in Tamil Nadu. This pattern of relatively higher

---

[40] Interview with Abhimanyu Singh, former education secretary, Rajasthan, August 30, 2008.
[41] As Chief Minister Jai Narayan Vyas explained "The budget year began on different dates in the different princely states that were integrated into Rajasthan. Therefore the first task was to establish 1 April to 31 March as the financial year. In addition, the budget classifications were also different ... the categories for sources of revenue were different" (Rajasthan Assembly Secretariat 2001: 35).

budgetary outlays on health in Rajasthan has continued through the 1990s and 2000s.

Additionally, the Rajasthan government worked hard to identify the most serious issues that plagued social services in the state and introduced a number of innovative schemes such as the *Shiksha Karmi* and the *Lok Jumbish* programs tailored specifically to address them.[42] These programs, which were initiated as partnerships with civil society organizations, met with international acclaim, inspired national policies, and are widely credited with having played a key role in Rajasthan's improvements in education in the 1990s.[43] In 1998, both *Shiksha Karmi* and *Lok Jumbish* were supplemented by, and gradually absorbed into, the District Primary Education Program (DPEP).[44] In 1998, the

[42] The *Shiksha Karmi* project sought to address the widespread problems of teacher absenteeism, poor enrollment, and high dropout rates by recruiting local youth with lesser educational qualifications than standard primary school teachers and training them to act as full-time para-teachers in their village schools (Ramachandran & Sethi 2000). A local teacher will be more likely to attend school regularly not only because of practical reasons, such as geographical proximity, an important issue for a state characterized by remote, inaccessible settlements like Rajasthan, but also because she is accountable to the community. Villagers can monitor the activities of the teacher who in turn is in a better position to motivate them to enroll and retain their children in school as opposed to a better qualified but non-local teacher. The success of *Shiksha Karmi* in Rajasthan prompted New Delhi to adopt the scheme at the national level. The distinctive feature of the *Lok Jumbish* program was its stress on community involvement with local educational facilities (Govinda n.d.). Toward this end it introduced a number of novel features such as school mapping and micro-planning, which were incorporated into the *Sarva Shiksha Abhiyan* (SSA), the national campaign for universal elementary education, launched by the central government in 2000.

[43] Some scholars attribute primary credit for Rajasthan's educational gains to the efforts of civil society (Chand 2006; Clarke and Jha 2006). While by no means inaccurate, an exclusive focus on the nongovernmental sector does however overlook the critical role of the government, both in terms of their recognition of the importance of NGOs as essential tools for promoting social welfare and their willingness to enter into close collaborations in which civil society organizations have a significant and autonomous role, as well as in terms of funding and logistical assistance that has been central to the functioning, and in some cases the very foundation, of civil society organizations in the state.

[44] This was a highly controversial decision, sharply criticized by educationists and social activists, who believed that insofar as the programs had been initiated by the BJP and dissolved under the Congress, they had become "hostage" to the "political warfare" between the two parties (Kishwar 1999). While the change in regime was certainly an important factor in the winding down of *Shiksha Karmi* and *Lok Jumbish*, it is important to view the Congress decision less as a "fracturing of the bipartisan consensus that had developed in education policy over the past two decades" (Clarke & Jha 2006: 25) and more as the adoption, in light of the changed politico-economic climate, of alternate (but similar) schemes toward the same end of universal primary education. India's decision to test nuclear devices in 1998 had prompted the Swedish International Development Cooperation Agency (SIDA), a primary donor for both *Shiksha Karmi* and *Lok Jumbish*, to withdraw its funding. Meanwhile, neoliberal reforms initiated by New Delhi in the early 1990s had paved the way for the growing influence of international organizations such as the World Bank, which in 1994 made in excess of $300 million available to the central government through the District Primary Education Program. In addition to the prospect of substantial central funding, DPEP also offered the Rajasthan government the prospect

state government initiated the *Rajiv Gandhi Swarana Jayanti Pathshala Yojana*, which sought to open schools in remote and inaccessible areas and incorporated many elements of Shiksha Karmi.[45] The Rajasthan government's continued commitment to collaboration with civil society organizations is reflected in the *Janshala* program, which was conceptualized and is supported by the *Bodha Shiksha Samiti* and works with a number of smaller NGOs on the ground.[46] *Janshala* is the first ever primary education initiative by any national or state government in India to focus exclusively on urban areas and was judged by the UN as one of the best practices in the world. In 2001–2002, New Delhi brought together DPEP as well as a number of state-specific programs for primary education under the umbrella of the Government of India's flagship program *Sarva Shiksha Abhiyan* (Universal Education Campaign).

It is also important to highlight how, reflecting the inclusiveness of Rajasthani subnationalism along these cleavages, social policy in the state has sought to be comprehensive across caste and religious lines. Successive governments have made special efforts to target the welfare of scheduled castes and tribes including the opening of special hostels for, provision of extra training in sciences and mathematics, and the granting of scholarships to, students from these groups. It is particularly instructive to contrast the Rajasthan governments' efforts to improve the conditions of Muslims with their relative neglect in other BIMARU states. In 2005, the Rajasthan government undertook a survey of Muslims to discover the reasons for their backwardness and drew up schemes to make them "self-reliant and economically strong" (Indo-Asian News Service 2005). In contrast, in 2006 some of the most notable Muslim leaders of UP spoke of the neglect of their community's interests

---

of greatly expanding the scope of its educational programs. Even critics of the Congress government's decision to move from *Shiksha Karmi* and *Lok Jumbish* to DPEP concede that "since *Shiksha Karmi* covered only remote areas and *Lok Jumbish* covered only a quarter of the state, the government felt a genuine need to pursue education reform across the state to ensure universal literacy" (Clarke & Jha 2006: 252).

[45] Like in *Shiksha Karmi*, the village committee was put in charge of the selection of teachers, who would ideally be a resident of the village. The minimum academic qualification was set at senior/ higher secondary pass, but could be relaxed to Class 8 pass in particularly remote areas. Teachers were trained using the *Shiksha Karmi* training module and infrastructure (Ray 2006: 162).

[46] The description of *Janshala* on the website of the NGO *Bodh Shiksha Samiti* reveals the truly horizontal and collaborative nature of the partnership between the state government and the NGO: "In 1998, United Nations Agencies (UNDP, UNESCO, UNICEF, TLO etc.) approached the Government of India to contribute funds for providing access to education to children of deprived social groups like Scheduled Castes, Scheduled Tribes, with a focus on the girl child. Some eight states in India, including Rajasthan, were selected. *Bodh* was commissioned by the Government of Rajasthan to conceptualize the program (which came to be known as *Janshala*) for the state. While in other states, *Janshala* focused on rural areas, in Rajasthan, *at the insistence of Bodh*, it was planned for urban poor children in cities where the situation was critical. *Janshala* was launched in Rajasthan in 1999 and *Bodh* was assigned the responsibility of providing Academic and Technical Support" (http://www.bodh.org/janshala.htm; emphasis added).

by the main political parties of the state.[47] Yet it is also important to take note of how the patriarchal nature of Rajasthani subnationalism has given rise to a much less proactive approach towards the welfare of women.[48]

A sense of solidarity with the newly formed state of Rajasthan and an associated set of obligations toward the welfare of all Rajasthanis on the part of elites in the state was an important motor for the institution of a progressive social policy; the impact of this progressive social policy, however, was greatly limited by the absence of a complementary subnationalism among the people at large. As discussed in Chapter 3, there was no popular subnational movement that transmitted elite ideas of Rajasthani subnationalism to the masses; sub-subnational boundaries such as those of *jagir* and clan continued to remain prominent in the public psyche. Insofar as most people did not harbor a sense of solidarity toward Rajasthan, they tended to remain relatively aloof from the political life of the state. Survey data from the NES 1971 indicate that residents of Rajasthan evinced a low degree of interest in, as well as awareness of, the political life of the state. Only 20 percent and 29 percent of Rajasthanis polled respectively expressed a "great deal" or "somewhat" of an interest in the recently concluded election campaign and in politics and public affairs more generally. Eighty percent of respondents could not correctly name the chief minister of the state. Relatively lower turnout rates in national and state assembly elections from the 1950s through the 1980s are indicative of a reduced proclivity to participate in public life. This is further supported by a report on the functioning of the local government institutions through the 1950s and early 1960s, which noted that meetings of the Village Assemblies (*Gram Sabhas*) were not well-attended because of a lack of "requisite interest and enthusiasm among the people" (Rajasthan Legislative Assembly 1950–2009). Similarly, a political participation study in a Rajasthani village in 1965 found a majority of respondents to be "non-participant" (Rudolph & Rudolph 1962). In addition, reflecting the continued importance of *jagir* identities, local villagers in the state appeared to be much more likely through this period to approach the local *thakurs* rather than the concerned state representative or official with problems, including those of public services. This was supported by a series of interviews with the *thakurs* of

---

[47] http://www.hindu.com/2006/07/06/stories/2006070609820500.htm.
[48] Through the post-independence period, of all Indian states Rajasthan had the largest gap between men and women on a range of developmental indicators. The practice of sati and its glorification are outlawed in the state and across India; yet the Rajasthan government continues to condone the practice, through the sponsorship of temples and festivals commemorating sati and naming projects, including a housing development project in the capital city of Jaipur after Sati mata. The state remains the "epicenter" of the practice of child marriage with millions of girls – by some estimates as many as 50% – being married before they are 15 years of age (Thomas 2012). Rajasthan also has the worst rates of female infanticide across India; according to unofficial estimates, nearly 2,500 cases of female feticide or female infanticide take place in the state on a daily basis. The 2011 census shows an "alarming" drop in sex ratio in the 0–6 age group from 909 in 2001 to 883 in 2011, this decline of 26 points being "indicative of a clear bias against the girl child" (Mathur and Rajagopal 2011).

these villages.[49] This low degree of interest in, awareness of, or involvement with, the public life of the state contributed to a lack of popular involvement with the schools and health centers established by the government.[50] In interviews with twelve bureaucrats who had served as district collectors from the 1950s to the 1960s and twenty-six bureaucrats who had served as district collectors interviewed in total during the 1970s and 1980s, virtually all of them spoke of the general political apathy of the people. Only three of the 38 former district collectors interviewed in total could recall an instance of popular mobilization as regards the provision of education and healthcare during their tenures. Social activists working in rural Rajasthan during these years also described the limited local involvement that they witnessed in welfare initiatives.[51] Similarly, in their speeches in the State Assembly, legislators regularly spoke of the people's lack of interest in and involvement with social services. During a debate on health on March 22, 1960, for example, a legislator spoke of public resistance to immunization campaigns (Rajasthan Legislative Assembly 1950–2009) while another described the non-utilization of the maternity wards (Rajasthan Legislative Assembly 1950–2009). In his budget speech in 1952–53, Chief Minister and Finance Minister Jai Narayan Vyas bemoaned the absence of "local interest" in the functioning of education and health services. He said that "for any scheme to improve education, medical and health services to be a success, it is necessary to have a strong local interest … local organizations, civil society should make their valuable and necessary contribution to education and health services … a democratic government can only succeed when citizens fully understand their responsibilities and take interest, and participate, in the functioning of local institutions" (Rajasthan Assembly Secretariat 2001: 24–26).

In the absence of societal involvement, these social services especially education services, tended, as Vyas feared, not to function very effectively. The lack of societal checks resulted in poor infrastructure and rampant teacher absenteeism, circumscribing the gains of a progressive social policy. In comparison to the all-India average, Rajasthan allocated greater budgetary resources to education but witnessed a slower rate of growth of literacy. As Figure 1.3 shows, literacy rates in Rajasthan increased from an abysmal 8.5 percent in 1951 to a more respectable 22.6 percent in 1971. But the state continued to hold the ignoble distinction of being home to the largest proportion of illiterates in the country.[52] The levels and rate of decline in infant death rates in

---

[49] Focus group meetings with elderly villagers, and interviews with former *Thakurs* across eighteen villages in the Udaipur, Pali and Jaipur districts of Rajasthan in 2005 and 2006.

[50] Interestingly, there was a relatively low association during the 1960s and 1970s between literacy and levels of education on the one hand, and political interest and participation on the other (NES 1971, Adams and Bumb 1973: 23).

[51] Interview with Charu Sharma of *Sankalp Sanstha* in October 2005 and with Sharda Jain of *Sandhan* in November 2005.

[52] In the 1991 census, Rajasthan finally managed to wiggle out of this dishonor by a mere 1% (Bihar's literacy rate was 37.5 as compared with 38.5 in Rajasthan).

Rajasthan contrasted unfavorably with India as a whole. During the 1960s, the first decade for which there appears to be data on infant/ child survival, the infant death rate in Rajasthan remained higher than all other BIMARU states (Vital Statistics of India). From the early 1970s to 1990, health indicators did show an improvement – infant mortality rates in Rajasthan declined from 123 per 1,000 to 84 per 1,000 and life expectancy rose from 48.4 to 55.2 years. These health indicators were better than the states of UP, MP, and Orissa and particularly creditable given the continued droughts and famines, which continued to plague Rajasthan during the period (Rathore 2005).[53] Their level as well as rate of improvement, however, compared unfavorably with the average for all Indian states and were modest when seen in light of nearly four decades of relatively generous budgetary outlays to the social sector.

Beginnings of Popular Subnationalism Foster (Limited) Gains in Social Development: 1990s Onward

From the early 1990s onward, the mutually reinforcing forces of generational change and the rise of the BJP, which, unlike in other states such as UP, espoused a subnational rather than a purely Hindu identity, combined as noted in Chapter 3 to give Rajasthani subnationalism a popular dimension. The spread, albeit limited, of subnationalism into the popular consciousness fostered greater political consciousness and participation on the part of the people of Rajasthan, which in turn gave a fillip to the utilization and efficacy of social services and buoyed education and health outcomes. The growing attachment to Rajasthan made people more likely to be interested in, aware of, and involve themselves in, the public life of the state. The proportion of respondents expressing an interest in politics and public affairs increased sharply from the 1970s to 2004 (Table 4.3). The number of respondents in Rajasthan who claimed to be "most concerned" with what the state government does more than doubled in 1996 as compared to 1971 (Table 5.2). The increased degree of political consciousness is evidenced by the fact that 60 percent of Rajasthani respondents could correctly name the chief minister of the state, which was not only a huge jump from 1971, but was also higher than the Indian average. The greater degree of political involvement is clear from the growth in electoral turnout from the 1990s onward. In 2003, a record 67 percent of all citizens cast their vote. In the state assembly elections in 2008, the figure was only marginally lower at 66.5 percent. Moreover, in the 1996 NES, 94 percent of respondents from Rajasthan trusted the state government a "great deal" or "somewhat" which was significantly higher than UP as well as the Indian average at the time. In contrast to their counterparts in previous decades, bureaucrats who had served as district collectors in the 1990s and

---

[53] From 1980 to 1983, virtually all regions of the state witnessed conditions of drought (Rathore 2005).

early 2000s were much more likely to report having witnessed mobilization, usually through the submission of a petition or, less frequently, through the organization of a protest, as regards the malfunctioning of public services.[54] My interviews with teachers, healthcare professionals, and local government representatives across eighteen villages in three districts of Rajasthan also clearly demonstrated a trend of increasing societal involvement with the functioning of state social services. The increased popular involvement with social services is reflected in the changed content of the speeches of legislators. By the late 1990s, legislators were announcing their motions and proposals in the legislative assembly as responses to pressures from their constituents. In a cut motion on April 11, 2000, for example, legislators drew attention to the "situation arising from" the absence or late arrival of teachers and the "unpleasant social atmosphere" and "widespread public discontent" because of the vacancy of teachers' posts (182–90). A comparative examination of debates from the 1950s to the 1970s indicates that during this earlier period legislators rarely referred to the demands of their constituents; their proposals were couched more in terms of their looking out for the welfare of their people. The increased public involvement with social services is also brought out by the stupendous response to the *Rajiv Gandhi Swarna Jayanti Pathshala Yojana*, mentioned earlier, under which the government was obliged to open schools in remote areas pursuant to the residents voicing such a demand. In 1999–2000, 12,355 schools were sanctioned, and as of 2006 around 11,847 of these schools were still functioning (Ray 2006: 163). The frequency and strength of popular monitoring of schools and health centers in Rajasthan, while greater than UP, remains considerably weaker than in Kerala or Tamil Nadu.[55] However, even this limited societal involvement has been critical in improving their functioning and has led to important improvements, especially in education.

During the 1990s, the state of Rajasthan achieved a "breakthrough" in the field of education (Ray 2006: 159). In the 2001 census, Rajasthan recorded the single largest increase in literacy rates of all Indian states in any decade since independence (Figure 1.3). What is even more notable is that Rajasthan's gains in education occurred primarily in rural areas, where political apathy had been most intense and where, consequently, the social indicators had been particularly laggard, and among those sections of society that had traditionally been the most educationally backward. The percentage of literate females increased

[54] Of twenty bureaucrats interviewed who had served as district collectors in the 1990s and 2000s, twelve mentioned having been personally approached regarding issues such as the absenteeism of teachers or doctors, lack of proper teaching in the village school, problems with school infrastructure, and the lack of drugs at the primary health center; another four mentioned having heard of mobilization for social services at least once during the course of their tenures.

[55] This is based on discussions with researchers in NGOs, notably Pratham, and developmental organizations including international organizations such as UNICEF and the World Bank, who have field experiences working in all four states.

from 20 percent in 1991 to 44 percent in 2001. During the same period the literacy rates for members of scheduled castes doubled from 26 percent to 52 percent. In 1991, the scheduled tribes of Rajasthan had the lowest literacy rate (19.4%) of all BIMARU states. By 2001, this had risen to 44.6 percent, which was higher than the literacy rate of scheduled tribes in Bihar, UP, MP, and Orissa. The proportion of literates among rural Scheduled Tribe women, historically one of the most marginalized groups in India, rose from a minuscule 3 percent in 1991 to 25 percent in 2001. Since the mid-2000s, however, there has been a slowing down of the pace of these educational gains, especially among women in the countryside.

Improvements in health indicators through the 1990s and early 2000s have been limited by the onslaught of "one of the worst droughts of the century" in the state during this period (United Nations Country Team in India 01/24/03).[56] Life expectancy in Rajasthan crept up at a snail's pace; and the decline in infant mortality rates was only a quarter of the national decline through the 1990s and 2000s.[57] Abetted no doubt by the reduction in the severity of the drought in the state, the rate of improvements in the health of the population has picked up in the last few years. When this book was going to press, a range of indicators including life expectancy, infant mortality, under-5 mortality, maternal mortality rates as well as a range of nutritional indicators in Rajasthan were better than in UP, and the marked improvement in the provision and utilization of government health services by the people that is evident in the third round of the National Family and Health Survey would seem to suggest that Rajasthan's health indicators are likely to decline even further in coming years.[58]

Social welfare in Rajasthan, however, clearly remains an "unfinished agenda" (Ray 2006: 160), characterized by serious challenges in provision, access, and quality of welfare services. The emancipation of women and removal of the gender gap in development indicators stands out as an especially urgent task confronting the state. Women in Rajasthan, and especially in the countryside, continue to face some of the most numerous and intense forms of deprivation

---

[56] From the late 1990s to the mid-2000s, Rajasthan faced a very severe drought, which became particularly intense in the early 2000s, affecting all 32 districts in the state and more than 10 million families. A number of studies have noted the association between droughts and a deterioration of health indicators, including increases in mortality rates (Sharma 1995). In 2001–2002, there were reports of drought-related starvation deaths in Baran district in south-eastern Rajasthan (http://articles.timesofindia.indiatimes.com/2002-10-24/india/27297653_1_starvation-wild-grass-seeds-rajasthan).

[57] IMR in Rajasthan decreased by only 6% from 1990 to 2003 as compared with a 20% decline for all Indian states.

[58] According to the NFHS, the proportion of births attended by trained medical personnel in the state, for example, increased from 19% in 1992–93 to 43% in 2005–06. The percentage of "fully immunized" children increased from 17% in 1998–99 to 26.5% in 2005–06. The proportion of women who had at least 3 antenatal visits for their last birth increased by 23% from 1992–93 to 2005–06.

of women anywhere in the world (Choudhry 2011; Goswami 2007; Mathur and Rajagopal 2011; Parihar 1999; Ray 2008; Thomas 2012).

BIHAR

In this section I will focus on the state of Bihar, which until recently was known pejoratively as the "armpit of India" (Economist 2004), but which has with the emergence of Bihari subnationalism attained a "breakthrough" in development (Chakrabarti 2013). I analyze three broad time periods. First, I review the colonial period, which did see the beginnings of a Bihari subnationalism among the region's elites but which also witnessed the development of a rival Jharkhandi identity among the people, especially the adivasis of the Chota Nagpur plateau region. The Bihari identity, limited as it was, led elites to push the British government of the province for the provision of social welfare, and the social schemes instituted by the colonial government did yield some gains – education and health outcomes in Bihar at the end of the colonial period were (albeit only by a small margin) the highest of all BIMARU states. Next I provide an overview of the period from the 1950s to the 2000s, during which ethnic caste-based polarization and the absence of any kind of subnational solidarity led to state policies being defined in entirely sectional caste-based terms. The almost complete neglect of the welfare of the state as a whole resulted in deep social backwardness. By the mid-2000s, Bihar placed at the very bottom of all Indian states in terms of the Human Development Index (HDI), had the highest proportion of people with "multi-dimensional poverty" (Sen 2013), and was "on the brink of disaster" (Chakrabarti 2013). Finally, I discuss the period since the mid-2000s when the emergence of a strong sense of Bihari pride has been an important trigger for a dramatic turnaround in the state. Bihari subnational pride among elites has been a powerful impetus for the state's unprecedented prioritization of social development and this is gradually resulting in important social gains and to the state shedding its pejorative associations with developmental dysfunction. While enormous challenges remain, it is clear that the growth of Bihari subnationalism has prompted "astounding" changes, such that the state is now being seen as providing lessons for other under-performing Indian states, a stark contrast to its established reputation of being "beyond redemption" (Chakrabarti 2013).

Regionally Circumscribed Elite Subnationalism Prevents Complete Neglect of Social Welfare: 1950s

Until 1912 the present-day region of Bihar was amalgamated into Bengal presidency; most positions of political power in this province were concentrated in the hands of Bengalis. During the early 1900s, in line with the formulation given in Chapter 3, a challenger native Bihari elite found it useful to evoke a Bihari identity to challenge the dominance of the Bengalis. Prominent professional

Bihari men espoused subnational symbols and used this as a basis to demand the separation of Bihar from Bengal (Gupta 1981).[59] This was an instrumental move on the part of the challenger Bihari elites insofar as the separation of the two states would limit the sphere of influence of the Bengalis to the administration of Bengal and create an entire new state bureaucracy, which they could control. It is notable that the Bihari elites, much like the Malayali and Tamil elites when they were petitioning the States Reorganization Commission for the creation of Kerala and Tamil Nadu respectively, framed the demand for a separate Bihar province as being necessary for the welfare of the Bihari people.[60] Unlike in Kerala and Tamil Nadu, however, this incipient Bihari subnationalism was confined to a regional subsection of elites. By the 1920s, there had emerged a strong Jharkhandi identity among the elites of Chota Nagpur plateau; in 1928, these same elites petitioned the visiting Simon Commission for the formation of the adivasi state of Jharkhand. Even the regionally circumscribed and incipient sense of Bihari subnationalism did generate some push for social welfare, especially education. Pandey, for example, writes that after the formation of the new province, "new hopes were entertained about the cause of education getting new dimensions and larger funds being arranged for its expansion. There was a strong desire among (the elite) to build up modern Bihar, and for the advancement of the new province, the educational progress was absolutely necessary" (1975: 104–05). Newspapers such as the *Beharee*, whose name itself is indicative of an emerging elite Bihari identity, campaigned for greater state attention to education, though the demands during this period were mostly focused on higher education. This pressure did foster some state support for education – in line with the nature of the demands, the emphasis was on the opening of a university and to a lesser extent on secondary education and then elementary education. In general, however, both the education and health sectors were characterized by state neglect. In the 1920s per capita expenditures on education and health in Bihar were the lowest of all British Indian provinces. Further, the welfare of the masses suffered "due to the indifference shown by the

[59] Sachidanand Sinha and Mahesh Narayan, who jointly wrote the book *The Partition of Bengal or the Separation of Bihar* in 1906, for example, wrote that "on cultural, historical, geographical, sociological and ethnological grounds," Bihar has been "separate and distinct" and should thus be constituted as a distinct political entity (cited in Pandey 1975: 101). The aptly named newspaper, *Beharee*, adopted the motto "we are Beharee first and Indian afterwards" (cited in Gupta 1981: 1499).

[60] In a memo to the Secretary of State, the Government of India noted "a strong belief" that "Bihar will never develop until it is disassociated from Bengal" (cited in Pandey 1975:104). An extraordinary session of the Bihar provincial conference presented the creation of the new state as an opportunity to return the state to its historical status as a center of learning – "In ancient times Nalanda was probably the most famous seat of learning in all India. It is needless to refer to the great fame of Mithila for learning. In more recent times, under Mohammedan rule, Patna was a famous centre to which students would come from distant quarters to learn the various branches of learning prevalent in those times. Why should not Patna then be once again the centre of learning that it used to be?" (cited in Pandey 1975: 104–06).

mass (sic) themselves" (the Report of the Indian Constitutional Reforms; cited in Pandey 1975: 68). At the end of the colonial period, literacy rates in Bihar were abysmal and mortality rates were very high, though marginally better than other North-Central Indian states, including UP and Rajasthan.

Absence of Subnationalism Impedes Social Development: 1950s–2000s

The years after Indian independence witnessed the dissipation rather than consolidation of even the incipient subnational solidarity that had emerged among the limited cross-section of Bihari elites in the early decades of the twentieth century. For a start, the state witnessed mobilization by its three main language groups – Magahi, Bhojpuri and especially Maithili.[61] More critically, however, it witnessed, on the one hand, the strengthening of the regional secessionist movement for the carving out of the state of Jharkhand, and on the other, the severe intensification of ethnic caste-based identities. Through the late 1940s and 1950s, the mobilization in favor of the creation of the state of Jharkhand became a "mass movement with overwhelming support" under the leadership of Jaipal Singh, former captain of the Indian Olympic Hockey team (Misra 1995). In 1949, in the first general elections in the state, Singh's Jharkhand Party swept the tribal districts; in the 1952 assembly elections it became the largest opposition party in the state. When the States Reorganisation Commission was formed, numerous memoranda were submitted demanding the creation of the state of Jharkhand, but the commission rejected the idea on the grounds that there was no single unifying language. This was a big blow to the movement. The Jharkhand Party declined through the 1960s with various splits and mergers, but the movement was revived with the formation of the Jharkhand Mukti Morcha in the early 1970s; during the 1980s the movement became violent.

In a parallel set of developments, the state also witnessed the emergence of radical and confrontational caste mobilization. Bihar was no stranger to caste mobilization. By the 1970s, however, according to a rough estimate, about six to eight major private caste armies emerged and operated as informal armed organizations of the upper castes and the landed backward castes (Kumar

---

[61] In his Linguistic Survey of India, Grierson designated Maithili, Magahi, and Bhojpuri as dialects of Bihari, though, as Brass points out, "there was no such thing as a Bihari spoken language" (1974: 62). The demand for the formation of a Mithila state was first formally made in 1940 at the meeting of Maithili Mahasabha in Darbhanga; the cause continued to be raised by elites, including the Maharaja of Darbhanga, at different public gatherings, in newspapers and pamphlets, and reached its "high point" in a series of meetings during 1954 that culminated in the submission of a memorandum laying out the case for the creation of Mithila state to the State Reorganization Commission. The demand, however, did not even find a mention in the report of the SRC and slowly died out (Brass 1974: 53, 54). However, the extensive reporting, in the 1961 elections, of Maithili, Magahi, and Bhojpuri as mother tongues – less than a majority (only 44%) claimed to be Hindi speakers – challenged the image of Bihar as a linguistically homogeneous Hindi-speaking state and provided a new fillip to language groups in Bihar demanding official recognition for their mother tongues (67).

2008: 4).[62] In retaliation for this upper caste mobilization, and against the domination of Brahminical culture and feudal power structures more generally, the 1990s saw unprecedented backward caste politicization under the leadership of Lalu Prasad Yadav. In a striking precursor to Mayawati's *dalit* politics in UP, Lalu declared open war on the so-called *Bhura Bhal* (Bhumihars, Rajputs, Brahmins, and Lalas-Kayasthas). He declared his regime as representing the ascendancy of the backward castes, which gradually came to be defined exclusively in terms of his numerically preponderant Yadav caste (Kumar 2008). In an escalating cycle of retribution, the 1990s also saw the formation and most intense activities of the Ranvir Sena, the private militia of Bhumihars, which was the most organized and ruthless of all caste armies.

Through almost all, and especially the later, decades of this post-Independence period, there was very little state emphasis on the social sector. A leading scholar and long-time observer of Bihari politics, Shaibal Gupta, has traced this explicitly to the absence of any kind of subnational solidarity on the part of the elites in the state (1981). Instead, corresponding to the dominant identity mobilizations, the limited developmental policies that were initiated were framed in either regional or caste terms. Elites from the Chota Nagpur Plateau region made repeated allegations, especially from the 1980s onward, of neglect, and even exploitation, from Patna and demanded greater resource allocation toward raising the region's poor development profile (Prakash 2001).[63] The issue of development "became inextricably linked to the Jharkhandi identity" (Prakash 2001: 300). It was, to a large extent, on the grounds of allowing the region control over its own development that the Bihar government conceded the formation of the Jharkhand Area Autonomous Council in the 1990s, and the state of Jharkhand itself was created in 2000.[64]

In the 1990s, during the Lalu regime, state politics and policies came to be defined entirely in caste terms. Lalu's exclusive focus on the backward castes was similar to, but arguably even more egregious than, Mayawati's emphasis, described earlier in this chapter, on *dalits* in UP a decade later. In moves that would be echoed by Mayawati, Lalu sought to portray himself as the savior of the oppressed and to provide the backward castes a new

---

[62] These caste armies include the Lorik Sena and the Bhoomi Sena, which protect the interests of the powerful backward caste Yadavs and Kurmis, the Sunlight Sena and Swarna Liberation Front correspond to the upper-caste Rajputs and Bhumihars respectively. While most of these armies have targeted the Maoist groups, composed mostly of adivasis, they have on occasion also clashed with each other.

[63] Through the 1950s, the relative development profile of the Chota Nagpur Plateau was better than that of the rest of Bihar, but from the 1960s on, the region deteriorated steadily such that by the 1980s, despite its industrial potential, it lagged behind the rest of Bihar.

[64] Irrespective of this framing in developmental terms, the creation of Jharkhand was a deeply political decision. The BJP government in New Delhi supported the demand for a separate Jharkhand as a way to gain the support of the tribal and nontribal populations of South Bihar, which was critical to displacing Lalu Prasad Yadav who was a staunch opponent of Jharkhandi statehood.

sense of *izzat* (respect) and *swar* (voice). He set the "annihilation" of the political power of the upper castes and the supremacy of backward castes, especially Yadavs, in the modern institutions of state power as his primary aim (Kumar 2008:77). Going even beyond Mayawati, whose limited social policies were targeted only toward dalits, as exemplified by the Ambedkar Village Yojna, Lalu questioned and jettisoned the concept of development itself.[65] Witsoe points out that "we might have expected the RJD government to pursue an agenda of redistributive policies ... but instead ... little in the way of pro-poor policy initiatives were even attempted" (2013: 300). As part of his agenda of lower-caste domination, Lalu centralized power in his own hands; replaced upper castes with Other Backward Classes (OBCs), SCs and Muslims in key positions of state power, and tolerated and even encouraged political interference in administration and policing at all levels. Public institutions were thought to be controlled by upper castes, and therefore simply allowed to collapse (Witsoe 2013: 302). There was a breakdown not just of governance but of even the very basic elements of everyday administration including law and order.[66] In 1990, Atul Kohli wrote, "If Bihar were an independent country, such conditions of breakdown would by now have precipitated a military coup or external intervention, or some combination of the two" (Kohli 1990: 225).

It is important to keep in mind that Bihar had begun its postcolonial journey with a number of disadvantages inherited from the colonial period, importantly a very low industrial base and pervasive rural indebtedness (Gupta & Singh 2013), but economic and social development had deteriorated so much during the postcolonial period that by the 2000s, Bihar was derided as the poster child even among the BIMARU states (Kirk 2011: 130).

Emergence of Bihari Subnationalism Triggers Beginnings of Social Development: 2005 Onward

The early 2000s witnessed a momentous change in Bihari politics. Following the pattern of emergence of subnationalism delineated in Chapter 3, a challenger elite found it politically advantageous to evoke subnational symbols as a way to counter the hegemony of an entrenched elite. In the elections of 2004, Nitish Kumar, who had broken away from Lalu's RJD, began to espouse an inclusive Bihari identity as a way to distinguish himself from, and

[65] A popular RJD slogan was "*vikaas nahiñ, samman chahiye*" (we need dignity, not development). Lalu famously commented, "*swarg nahin, swar diya*" (I may not have given them (the lower castes) heaven, but I have given them voice) (Witsoe 2013: 300).

[66] In 2000, the state of Bihar accounted for 26% of India's total murders with the use of firearms, and the relatively small city of Patna accounted for 40% of all murders with the use of firearms in Indian cities. Kidnapping for ransom became a booming industry; between 1992 and 2005, criminal groups with close links with politicians and the police, carried out a reported 30,000 kidnappings (Witsoe 2013: 303).

attack the more than decade-long caste-based hegemony of, his former ally
and now rival Lalu Yadav. There was nothing "natural" or "easy" about this
evocation of Bihari subnationalism. If anything, the demographic and sociocultural situation appeared to militate against the emergence of a subnational
solidarity. The adoption of Hindi as the state language of Bihar meant that
Bihar was not linguistically distinguishable from neighboring UP or MP, and
yet there was little "linguistic oneness" (Gupta 1981: 1497). "The politics of
language in Bihar," according to Brass (1974: 69), was further "complicated
by the fact that the official language of the state is not the mother-tongue of
any major population group." The state was instead home to speakers of three
very distinct dialects of Maithili, Magahi, and Bhojpuri, associated with distinct literary and cinematic cultures that crossed state lines into neighboring
UP and Madhya Pradesh. In addition to the linguistic divisions, the state was
also characterized by deeply ingrained and polarized caste identities.

The term "Bihari" has been a pejorative term associated with a country
bumpkin from a backward hinterland.[67] There was nothing inherently subnationalist about Nitish Kumar either. As Kumar (2013) points out, though
he portrayed Lalu Prasad Yadav as a politician preoccupied with caste, Nitish
Kumar himself was one of the first politicians in Bihar to organize a caste-based
Kurmi rally in early 1992. He had also "tried his luck" with the Communist
Party of India (Marxist Leninist) – Liberation during the Assembly elections
in 1995, and had been with the Bhartiya Janata Party (BJP) since the 1996
Parliamentary elections. Nitish Kumar's decision to espouse a Bihari identity was entirely strategic, aimed as an attack on, and an alternative to, Lalu
Yadav's caste politics. As summarized in an article that appeared in the Indian
weekly news journal, *Outlook*, during the campaigning for the assembly elections in Bihar in late 2005, "after a decade of fighting, and losing to, the RJD,"
Nitish had managed to transform himself "from being a mere *neta* [leader]
of the Kurmi caste" to "a pan-Bihar leader" (Naqvi 2005). In interviews and
campaign speeches, Nitish Kumar himself repeatedly presented "Bihari subnationalism," as an alternative to caste-based politics.[68]

Bihari subnationalism has, in a surprisingly short time, also entrenched itself
across a wide cross-section of social, cultural and economic elite across the state.

---

[67] Leading Indian artist Subodh Gupta's piece "Bihari" (1999) is a deliberate response to his experience moving to Delhi from his hometown Khagaul in Bihar and "seeing the word that defined
his identity used as a cuss word" (Adams 2014).

[68] An interview of Nitish Kumar on the campaign trail in 2010 with leading journalist Sagarika
Ghosh is particularly instructive. Ghosh asks Kumar, "You talk about Bihari *asmita;* you talk
about Bihari subnationalism; you talk about Bihari pride. What is the meaning of this?" to
which Kumar replies, "People should be inspired by their past. They should rise above caste, and
feel a sense of 'Bihari-ness', then Bihar will develop. I am happy about the fact that youth has
accepted this fact. If in this election, development wins, Bihar wins, 'Bihari-ness' wins. People
can try as hard as they want to create a caste divide but it won't happen. Caste and religious
beliefs have their own place, but everyone in Bihar is united for development. This sense of pride
is sometimes called subnationalism" (Kumar 2010).

While the most prominent and vociferous proponents of Bihari subnationalism have been the political elites associated with Nitish Kumar, powerful articulations of Bihari pride have also become commonplace among Bihari bureaucrats, scholars, artists, writers, and business elites.[69] This elite Bihari subnationalism has, in itself, been an important motor for the state's prioritization of the development sector. In an interview with the author, Kumar explicitly stated that "Bihari subnationalism impels us to do everything we can to promote the development of the state. As a Bihari, it is my responsibility to advance the cause of my people, as a whole ... this has been neglected for too long ... and what is so amazing is that this feeling of Bihari pride is rising among the people, especially the youth, and we are all joined together with a common aim of development. That is a powerful force."[70] A number of scholars have noted the strong political commitment of the Bihar government to social development.[71] The massive expenditures for, and inputs into, the social sector are the clearest evidence of this. The budget for, elementary education nearly doubled between 2006–07 and 2010–11 and there was a huge increase in the number of teachers, classrooms, and schools

---

[69] There is an emerging trend on the part of young Biharis who pass the highly competitive civil service examination system to request their home state as their cadre as a matter of Bihari pride (Jha 2005). Scholars, most prominently, Shaibal Gupta at the non-partisan Asian Development Research Institute in Patna, Bihar, who had bemoaned the "retarded subnationalism" of Bihar through the 1970s and 1980s, are now writing about the emergence of a powerful sense of Bihari subnationalism (1981, 2007). Incidentally, it is likely that it is Shaibal's (relatively unusual) usage of the term 'subnationalism' that has inspired Nitish Kumar's use of the central term of this book. Artist Subodh Gupta's famous "Bihari" (1999), referred to in an earlier footnote, a self-portrait with cow-dung smudged across the canvas and LED letters flashing the word "bi-ha-ri" in Devanagari script, "boasts of being a Bihari as his most important attribute"; Gupta says he deliberately chose this "as one of one of the first statements he wanted to make to the world" (Snehanshu 2014). Writer Amitava Kumar, whose latest book, *A Matter of Rats* (2014) is a biography of his hometown, Patna, the capital city of Bihar, has also repeatedly stressed the importance of his Bihari identity. In recent years Bihari business elites have also begun to organize formal networks of Bihari business people. Interestingly, an anecdote by Kaushik Basu seems to point to the presence of a sense of Bihari pride even among the 'criminal elite' in the state. Basu describes how, when during a drive in rural Bihar in the mid-1990s, the car that he was travelling in was held up by a local gang collecting an illegal "tax," his taxi driver's "appeal to regional pride" (that Basu was a "visitor from Delhi who had come to see rural Bihar, and it would create a very bad impression on me if I were forced to make a payment") "clicked" with the gang "boss" and they were allowed to drive away without making a payment (2001: 154–155).

[70] Interview with the author conducted at the Indian embassy to the People's Republic of China, Beijing in June 2011. Kumar and a contingent of deputies were on a tour of China in order to study agricultural practices that might be implemented in Bihar as well as to attend a scholarly conference and cultural events in Beijing associated with the history and spread of Buddhism that celebrated Bihar's status as the home of the Buddha.

[71] Banerjee (2013), for example, writes, "There is no doubt that compared to all other states in India, Bihar stands out as the state where top political leadership is continuously giving high priority to schools. The political desire is clear – that there should be education for all. Time and again in public meetings, the chief minister and his deputy state that the primary resource that Bihar has is its people and that development will happen when these people become educated and skilled and are able to have better life chances and to earn better livelihoods."

(Banerjee 2013).[72] There was a similar increase in the number of health facilities, with block primary health centers and additional primary health centers increasing by 34 percent and 23 percent respectively from 2006 to 2011, as compared with a one percent increase and no increase respectively in the preceding five-year period (Reddy and Dandona 2013).

Apart from the increased budgetary outlays, the Bihar government's commitment to the social sector is further illustrated by the institution of a host of innovative schemes that exemplify a careful and imaginative utilization of public funds. In the education sector, in addition to the launching of literacy campaigns, the most notable schemes are the provision of bicycles to female students upon completion of middle school, in order to make it easier for them to commute to a high school, which is usually located farther away, as well as the provision of free school uniforms.[73] In the health sector, the government has launched a number of programs including *Muskaan ek Abhiyaan* ('the Smile campaign'), which focuses on mass vaccinations, the provision of newborn as well as neonatal stabilization units, lifesaving ambulance services, and sanitation campaigns. Bihar is also the site of award-winning schemes that use mobile phones as a simple, high-impact solution for improving the survival chances of mothers and babies; these schemes are the product of the state's five-year partnership with the Bill and Melinda Gates Foundation.[74] The

[72] As compared to 2004–05, more than 100,000 additional classrooms have been built; 200,000 more teachers have been recruited; the number of primary schools has increased from about 38,000 to more than 41,000 and the number of upper primary schools has doubled from 11,000 to exceed 25,000 in 2010–11 (Banerjee 2013).

[73] About 4 million girls have benefited from these schemes and the sharp rise in girls' enrollment as well as in the number of girls passing the matriculation exam are clear signs of the success of the schemes. In my interview with him, Nitish Kumar explicitly cited these schemes as examples of his state's social initiatives, and it is notable that his description was couched in subnationalist language – "these schemes will ensure that the girls of Bihar are no less educated than girls in any other part of India. No one will be able to say that the children of Bihar are educationally backward."

[74] In Bihar, 83% of women have access to mobile phones, but, because of low literacy levels, only 9% have ever sent a text message. To get around this, BBC Media Action, the BBC's international charity, working under the umbrella of the Gates Foundation's Ananya program, instituted schemes that use Interactive Voice Response (IVR) to make audio content accessible from any mobile phone via a simple voice call. The schemes initiated include Mobile Academy, Mobile Kunji, and Kilkaari. Mobile Academy is an audio training course for community health workers, designed to refresh knowledge and enhance skills. The course costs health workers a fraction of what they would pay for face-to-face training, and can be completed at home, at a pace that suits them. In the fall of 2013, 14 months since Mobile Academy was launched, 31,995 unique users had started the course, accessing 4 million minutes of course content, and more than 13,100 health workers had completed it. Another health service is Mobile Kunji (which means "key" in Hindi), an on-demand mobile information service hosted on the same VR system as Mobile Academy, which supports the health workers on their family visits. The audio message, which is from a doctor character, adds credibility to the community health worker's interaction and helps to control for the variability of health workers' skills, by giving families the same quality of message every time. As a community health worker in Neerpur

government's reaching out to and forging such partnerships with international donors toward the acceleration of progress to attain its social goals is of course in itself further evidence of its commitment to social development.[75]

In line with the inclusive nature of Bihari subnationalism, the state government has chosen to adopt a broad-based welfare agenda that has been complemented by various schemes targeted toward the uplift of certain sections of the population, prominently the so-called *mahadalits*, the most socioeconomically backward among the scheduled castes; as well as Muslims.[76] It is important to note, however, that unlike in UP but like in Tamil Nadu and Kerala, these schemes have been a supplement to and not a substitute for mass programs such as literacy drives, vaccination, and sanitation campaigns that are directed toward the people of the state as a whole.

In addition to the adoption of an active social agenda, the Bihar government has also undertaken a number of initiatives in the cultural realm with the aim of spreading Bihari subnationalism into the popular consciousness, for instance through state-sponsored gala festivities on Bihar Day,[77] as well as initiatives to preserve and promote the arts, culture, and literary traditions of the state, through

village in Chautham block explained: "Ever since I started using Mobile Kunji during my visits with women and their families, the community's respect for me and what I do has grown. What's more, when I now walk into a village, people call me 'doctor didi' (sister) and ask me to give them information." Further, using mobile phones provides real-time data on which cards are being used by which health worker, when, and where. This provides valuable feedback on whether beneficiaries are receiving the advice they need. As of fall 2012, Mobile Kunji had 113,325 unique users who had accessed over 3.4 million minutes of content. A third service, Kilkaari, meaning "a child's gurgle" in Hindi, targets families with pregnant women and mothers of children under the age of 1 year, providing subscribers to the service with weekly phone calls about maternal and child health, linked to the stage of the woman's pregnancy or their child's age (MacPherson and Chamberlain 2013).

[75] In addition to its collaboration with the Gates Foundation, the Bihar government is also in partnership with the World Bank, which in late 2013 approved a $84 million credit for the "Bihar Integrated Social Protection Strengthening Project," which aims to deliver better quality, timely, and effective social protection (SP) programs for the poor and vulnerable people in the state.

[76] The Bihar government has instituted a special commission, the Mahadalit Vikas Commission, that is committed to formulating and implementing special schemes targeted toward this controversial newly constructed "most oppressed of the oppressed" category. The state government has also implemented policies to address long-standing Muslim grievances associated with the fencing of graveyards and justice for the victims of the 1989 Hindu-Muslim riots in Bhagalpur district, during which more than a thousand people, mostly Muslims, were killed (Mukherjee 2010).

[77] In 2010, the state government of Bihar initiated the celebration of the founding of the state as Bihar Day. The objective of this occasion, which was not previously marked, was very explicitly "to restore the pride of the state and to enthuse the feeling of Being Bihari in the citizens of the state." The celebrations, which have expanded every year, take place under the aegis of the Ministry of Human Resource Development within the state. The Bihar Foundation, an initiative of the Bihar government since 2009 that "aims to unite NRBs (Non-Resident Biharis)," organizes the festivities in hundreds of cities across the world (http://www.biharfoundation.in/events/bihar-divas/).

the establishment and revitalization of state institutions, including an institute to develop the state's famed Madhubani paintings, the inauguration of a Patna literary festival, plans to open a museum in the state capital, as well as the renovation of the Patna College of Arts and the Khuda Baksh museum. The state government is also planning to make Sonepur, presently the site of the world's largest annual cattle fair, the venue for the Bihar Folk Music and Handicrafts Festival, and market it as the world's biggest such event, combining a cattle fair, a folk music forum, and a handicrafts market (Varma 2013). That these and other initiatives to spread Bihari subnationalism among the masses have met with at least some success is evident from the establishment of various popular organizations and online communities affirming a Bihari identity, such as the Jai Bihar Facebook page and online newspaper, as well as the composition of songs such as "Jai Bihar" (https://www.youtube.com/watch?v=lA4hOezPvaE).

In at least some part because these were the first development initiatives in a state that had been starved of any meaningful social policy for decades, but also because of their growing consciousness ignited by this incipient subnationalism, these policies were enthusiastically embraced by the people of Bihar and have already begun to yield "impressive and unprecedented" gains (Singh and Stern 2013). Bihar has moved from, in 2005, being a state that had the highest percent of school-age children, especially girls, out of school to a state where, in 2011, the proportion of out-of-school children is below the national average and the gender gap has disappeared. There has also been a dramatic increase in the scope and utilization of government health services. The average number of patients visiting health centers per month increased nearly threefold (from 3,077 to 9,137) as did the bed occupancy rate (from 22.6% to 77.1%). The number of institutional deliveries jumped by a multiple of five from 2006 to 2011. Perhaps most notably, there has been a dramatic increase in routine immunization coverage from 18.6 percent in 2005 to around 70 percent in 2011, an achievement that won Nitish Kumar the first Gates Vaccine Innovation award in 2012. The rate of decline in infant mortality rates in the state has also seen a sharp drop. From 2001 to 2006, IMR in Bihar changed very slightly, from 62 to 60 deaths per 1,000 live births, but from 2006 to 2011, the IMR dropped by 27 percent, to 44 deaths. These gains clearly are only the first steps on what will be a long and arduous road for the state – the education sector, for example, continues to be plagued by low student attendance, substantial teacher absenteeism, shortage of trained teachers, and serious problems of quality. The per capita health expenditure in the state remains one-third that of Kerala. The state's development indicators remain some of the lowest in India and in the world. What is important, however, is that there has been a break from the stagnation of the past; the state that was backward "for as long as one could remember" (Chakrabarti 2013: 1960) has seen a decisive change. While there are obviously many factors at play, the espousal of Bihari subnationalism by a wide cross-section of elites, and the establishment of institutions toward embedding Bihari identity and pride among the people at large, generates cautious optimism for the future trajectory of Bihar's social development.

CONCLUSION

The primary purpose of this chapter was to showcase the negative dynamic of the subnationalism argument that was laid out theoretically in Chapter 2, that is, how a weak subnational solidarity can impede the adoption of a progressive social policy and also limit popular involvement with public services, contributing to low developmental indicators. It does this through an analysis of three neighboring North-Central Indian states – detailed case studies of UP and Rajasthan, combined with a briefer shadow study of Bihar – all of which have been characterized by a relatively fractured subnationalism compared to their Southern counterparts discussed in the previous chapter, and which are consequently some of the most socially backward regions not just in India but also worldwide. Within this overall negative dynamic, this chapter has also sought to delineate the mechanism of change, that is, of how changes in the strength of subnational solidarity can trigger changes in the nature of social policy and development outcomes. The analysis of the cases of Rajasthan and Bihar highlights how the emergence of a more cohesive sense of subnational identity among elites can prompt a reversal of state neglect of social welfare and also how the beginnings of popular subnationalism can provoke popular involvement with the social sector, which can help a progressive social policy yield developmental gains.

This chapter also extends the core insight of the book that the boundaries of identification and solidarity determine the contours of how welfare is conceptualized, demanded and provided. The previous chapter showed how Tamil and Malayali subnationalism fostered support for, and the institution of, social policies for the welfare of the people of Tamil Nadu and Kerala as a whole. This chapter shows how ethnic allegiances below the subnation – religious attachment in colonial UP; caste allegiances in post-independence Bihar and in UP since the 1990s – resulted in demands for welfare being framed, and social services being provided, along these respective ethnic lines; and how national identification above the subnation, during the immediate post-independence decades in UP, led to welfare being defined almost entirely in terms of New Delhi's priorities.

Looking ahead at the future provision of public services in UP, Rajasthan, and Bihar and the North-Central Indian belt more generally, it is important to note the growing and unprecedented role of actors other than the state government – on the one hand, the national government and international agencies, and on the other, the private sector – which might appear to affect the relevance of the argument for the cultural role of subnationalism advanced here. From the 1950s until the mid-1970s, provincial governments had exclusive jurisdiction over both education and health policies. In 1976, a constitutional amendment moved schooling from the state list to the concurrent list, giving the national government the power to formulate education policy, which it did a decade later with the landmark National Policy on Education (1986) followed by the Program of Action in 1992. The last few decades have witnessed exceptional international emphasis on social development, beginning with the World Declaration on Education for All in 1990 and then the adoption of the Millennium Development Goals in 2000. Moreover, the unfurling of the sails of its economy through the neoliberal reforms of the 1990s has meant that India can no longer steer its course indifferent to global winds. The growing international consensus on the urgency of providing education and healthcare has served as both a threat and an opportunity for the Indian government. It has become clear that, as home to more than half of the world's total illiterates and the site of more than a quarter of global infant deaths, India needs to see a more proactive role on the part of its national government and cannot afford, any longer, to leave social welfare entirely to its provinces. The availability of expertise and funding from international actors, including the various UN agencies and the World Bank means, however, that New Delhi now has access to an unprecedented amount of resources to confront this challenge. In the 1990s, a World Bank loan allowed the central government to initiate the ambitious District Primary Education Program (DPEP). This was incorporated in the early 2000s into the Sarva Shiksha Abhiyan (SSA), the national flagship program for the universalization of free elementary education, which since 2009 has been enshrined as a fundamental right in the country. In 2005, the central government launched the National Rural Health Mission, "the most ambitious rural health initiative ever" (Mahal, Debroy, & Bhandari 2010), which proposes a number of innovative mechanisms for healthcare delivery together with major improvements to hygiene and sanitation infrastructure.

It is important to note, however, that even though for the first time in post-Independence India major social schemes are being initiated by actors other than the state government, the *effectiveness* of these schemes is contingent on the state government, which is in charge of the implementation, and often at least partial funding, for these programs. Even the most innovative and technically sound national or international intervention cannot succeed unless it is supported by the political will and administrative apparatus of the state government. During the 1990s, for example, state governments in Rajasthan displayed a willingness to take on fiscal responsibilities in jointly funded social initiatives and an alacrity in utilizing funds made available by New Delhi for social programs.[78] In contrast, during the 1990s and early 2000s, both UP and

---

[78] The *Shiksha Karmi* program began with the Rajasthan government shouldering 10% of the financial responsibility to SIDA's 90%. However, the state government increased its fiscal responsibility to 50% in the second phase of the program. The state government also contributed approximately 15% of the funds in *Lok Jumbish*, the District Primary Education Program, and the *Sarva Shiksha Abhiyan* (SSA). For example, in 2007, Rajasthan chief minister

Bihar consistently failed to use funds for social welfare allocated by the central government. The national and international focus on education and health is, therefore, best seen as having provided an opportunity structure for state governments to utilize. While there are today more opportunities for funding and technical and logistical support, especially for BIMARU states, available from national and international actors than compared to any other time in the postcolonial period, states are distinguished by their responsiveness to these pressures and opportunities. These differences in proactiveness are in turn a product of the strength of their subnational solidarity. Rajasthan, for example, has not only been relatively efficient at implementing national schemes but has also through the 2000s taken the initiative in directly collaborating with international donors and agencies.[79] Similarly, under Nitish Kumar the Bihar government has worked to initiate major social welfare projects in association with New Delhi as well as international organizations such as the Gates Foundation and the World Bank.

   In addition to the growing role of the center and international actors, these North-Central Indian states have also, in large part because of the gap caused by the dismal state of government schools and health centers, seen a spurt of private education and health provision. It is important to clarify, first of all, that the umbrella category of private provision includes within it service delivery by a number of different agencies including missionary organizations, by

Vasundhara Raje called upon the Centre to release the outstanding amount of Rs.786 million for the implementation of the SSA and to approve the state government's new program for the universalization of secondary education. The national daily, the *Hindu*, reported that "In a letter addressed to Union Human Resource Development Minister Arjun Singh, Ms. Raje pointed out that the amount was due since the last financial year towards the Centre's 75 per cent liability for implementing SSA. She said the paucity of money was hampering the State Government's plan to upgrade schools and extend SSA's benefits to them … The Chief Minister said the HRD Ministry should immediately compensate for the shortfall … to enable the State Government to implement SSA effectively and achieve universalization of elementary education" (Hindu 2007).

[79] The Rajasthan government approached the European Commission-supported Sector Reform Investment Program in 2004 to support the *Sanjivani* Scheme, an initiative to provide specialist services to the rural poor suffering from acute and chronic illnesses. In the same year, the state, in collaboration with the World Bank, also launched a nearly $5 billion "ambitious health system development project" with the objective of "providing a high-quality healthcare delivery system" through institutional strengthening, improving service quality, and innovations to enhance access and equity to disadvantaged sections. In 2005, the state government arrived at an agreement with the World Economic Forum at Davos to launch the Rajasthan Education Initiative to improve education indicators in the state and introduce schemes for computer education. In 2006, the Rajasthan government launched an innovative joint initiative with UNICEF and selected civil society organizations, the *Janani Suraksha Yojana* Helpline, to reduce maternal and neonatal mortality rates in the state by promoting institutional deliveries. The Norway India Partnership Initiative (NIPI) seeks to provide support for the implementation of the National Rural Health Mission in five states that comprise 40% of India's total population and account for around 60% of child deaths: Uttar Pradesh, Bihar, Madhya Pradesh, Rajasthan, and Orissa. It is another indicator of the state government's initiative that as of 2008, Rajasthan was the only state to have implemented NIPI.

community initiative, NGOs, and for-profit organizations, which are reflective of the specific histories of the state. Further, private provision of social services has historically been more successful when undergirded by considerable state support. Liberal government aid, both in land and cash, was necessary for the Christian missionaries as well as Hindu caste associations to be able to establish their network of educational institutions in the late nineteenth and early twentieth centuries, and remains essential to their continued functioning in Kerala (Singh 2011). More generally, across India a large proportion of private schools today function with, and often only because of, massive financial support and under considerable regulation from the government. Tilak (1990) notes that 95 percent or more of the total expenses of aided private schools are borne by state governments.[80] Enrollment in "pure" private schools remains relatively small and, for the most part, confined to urban areas. This type of state engagement with private providers of social services, specifically education, is believed, across the board, to be associated with iniquitous consequences. Yet, some state governments have also chosen to enter into more innovative and progressive collaborations with the private sector, as represented by the Tamil Nadu government's collaborations with NGOs in their campaign against AIDS; the Rajasthan government's partnership with civil society organizations in the implementation of the *Shiksha Karmi, Lok Jumbish,* and *Janshala* programs; and Bihar's recent outsourcing and subsidizing of key medical services (Mukherjee 2010: 7). Like in the case of social schemes initiated and supported by the national government and international actors, the extent to which social service provision by private actors contributes to the overall social welfare of the state is dependent as much, if not arguably more, on the actions of state governments, as it is on their own.

---

[80] The primary subsidy that these privately aided schools receive is in the form of teacher salaries; teachers become part of the government civil service and receive salaries equivalent to that of regular government teachers. This leads to a highly iniquitous situation in which the state is essentially absorbing the schooling costs of those who can afford to pay. The inequity is further reinforced by the fact that the privately aided schools' share in enrollment tends to rise with the level of education, starting with relatively low levels at the primary level, and is the highest at the secondary level. UP, for example, has one of the highest shares of privately aided secondary schools in India, with 47% of secondary students enrolled in such schools in the late 1990s. These subventions to fee-paying secondary school students have greatly limited the ability of the state to allocate much-needed funds to the derelict government primary schools, which are the only option for a vast majority of the children of the state's poor citizens in the countryside (Mehrotra 2006: 31).

6

Subnationalism and Social Development across Indian States

Chapters 4 and 5 developed the subnationalism argument through a comparative historical analysis of the states of Tamil Nadu, Kerala, UP, and Rajasthan as well as a shadow case study of Bihar. Chapter 4 detailed how a cohesive subnational solidarity has generated relatively high levels of social development in Tamil Nadu and Kerala. Chapter 5 specified how weaker subnational solidarities have resulted in generally abysmal social indicators in UP, Rajasthan and Bihar but also how the strengthening of subnationalism in Rajasthan and Bihar prompted increased expenditures on education and health and important improvements in social indicators. Reading thus far, however, one might wonder if this relationship between subnationalism and social development is peculiar to the states of Tamil Nadu, Kerala, UP, Rajasthan and Bihar. This chapter explicitly addresses this question by testing the generalizability of the subnationalism argument across all Indian states.

In order to do so, the first part of this chapter develops a valid and reliable measure of subnationalism and then uses this index to score the strength of subnational solidarity across all major Indian states from 1960 to 2000. The second part of this chapter employs a combination of quantitative techniques, including descriptive statistics as well as cross-sectional and time-series cross-sectional regression analyses to assess whether the subnationalism model, which was generated inductively through the case studies presented in Chapters 4 and 5, is able to account for the variation in social development across the larger sample of all Indian states. The time-series cross-sectional analyses allow for an examination of the effect not only of the key explanatory variable – the strength of subnationalism – but also of a number of other factors discussed in Chapter 2, including economic development, the nature of the party system, the closeness of political competition, rule by a social democratic party, and ethnic fractionalization. Descriptive cross-tabulations indicate a generally positive relationship between the strength of subnationalism and education and health outcomes across Indian states. In cross-sectional regression analyses, controlling for levels of economic development, subnationalism is found to have a positive and statistically significant effect on social expenditures and development indicators. The time-series cross-sectional analyses show that subnationalism has a positive and statistically significant effect on social expenditures and indicators even after controlling for a range of socio-economic and political variables. This result is found to be robust to a number of different model specifications and estimation techniques and to alternative measures of both the outcome of interest as well as the explanatory variables.

MEASURING SUBNATIONALISM

The most common method within social science to measure the strength of an identity like nationalism has been through aggregations of responses to questions about closeness, belonging, pride, preference, and superiority in large-N representative surveys based on random samples. India, unfortunately, does not have a well-established tradition of survey research. Regular, systematic, nationally representative surveys with a province-level sample size (barely) large enough to permit statistically significant inferences about patterns of opinion across states began only in the mid-1990s, and these do not directly ask questions about the strength of subnational identification. It is also important to note that some of the foremost scholars of nationalism have expressed grave doubts about the reliability of such survey-based measures (Smith 1991), and even those who are sympathetic to the idea of capturing nationalism through attitudinal surveys have acknowledged severe weaknesses in the specific measures of identity that have been deployed in the major repeated, cross-national surveys of values and of social and political attitudes since the early 1980s (Sinnott 2006). Responses to "identity questions" in surveys in general have been shown to be highly sensitive to the wording of the question, response structure, and sequencing.[1] Primarily in light of the absence of appropriate data over time for Indian states, but also keeping in mind these concerns about their reliability, this study moves away from survey-based measures to instead develop a relatively novel but arguably more theoretically rigorous, valid, and

---

[1] There is, for example, a striking divergence in responses to differently worded nationality questions in leading cross-national surveys. In Hungary, 96% of respondents in the 1995 International Social Survey Program (ISSP) said they felt close to their nation, but in the 1990 European Values Survey (EVS) only 63% felt that they belonged to it. Differences exist even within the same survey. In the 1990 EVS, in the United States 98% of people said they were proud to be American, but only 58% said they felt a sense of belonging to the United States. The difference was even more conspicuous for a country such as Latvia where 92% of respondents indicated pride in their country, but only 15% felt that they belonged to it. Similarly, in India 91% of respondents claimed that they were proud of their nationality (World Values Survey 1995) but only 21% disagreed with the statement that they should be loyal to their own region first and then to the nation (National Election Study 1996).

reliable measure of subnationalism. In order to do so, I return to the conceptualization of subnationalism in Chapter 2 as the existence of a subnational consciousness in the form of an identification with, or aspiration for control over, a historic homeland on the part of people with a belief in a shared past and a common culture often but not necessarily based on language. As noted earlier in the book, such an understanding of subnationalism maps closely onto some of the core elements of the most influential theoretical formulations of nationalism identified by scholars such as Anderson (1991), Deutsch (1966), Gellner (1983), Hobsbawm (1990), and Renan (1882). Drawing on this conceptualization, I construct a measure of the strength of subnationalism across Indian states over time based around the core elements of language and subnational consciousness. The unit of analysis is province – year. I code the strength of subnational solidarity for major Indian states for each year from 1966 to 2006.

Language

The origins of the idea that language and national identity are inherently and inextricably linked can be traced to the German romanticism of the late eighteenth and early nineteenth centuries, most notably to Herder who famously wrote, "Has a nationality anything dearer than the speech of its fathers? In its speech resides its ... basis of life ... its heart and soul"; for Herder, a *Volk* without its own language was "an absurdity, a contradiction in terms" (cited in Fishman 1973: 48). Today scholars with diverse ideational and methodological leanings – historical (Connor 1994; Smith 1991), structural-functional (Gellner 1983), and rational-choice (Laitin 1992) – are united in their singling out of language as a core element of nationalism. Even if one questions the theoretical proposition that language constitutes the essence of a nation, it is impossible to deny its prominence in national and subnational movements across the globe (Fishman 1973). The most striking historic illustration of the close relationship between language and nation is found in Western Europe, where linguistic boundaries led to a redrawing of the national map of the region after the First World War. My analysis of all groups classified as "Ethnonationalist"[2] in the Minorities at Risk (MAR) project's "Minority Group Assessment of all Regions" shows that 71 percent are language groups. In comparison, less than 10 percent are religious groups and about 5 percent are racial groups. Language forms the backbone of some of the most prominent contemporary subnational movements including the Quebecois, Flemish, Walloon, Basque, and Catalan movements. Subnational movements, which have not organized around a common language such as Scotland or Wales, have nevertheless been

---

[2] Ethnonationalist groups are defined as "regionally concentrated peoples with a history of organized political autonomy with their own state, traditional ruler, or regional government, who have supported political movements for autonomy at some time since 1945" (Minorities at Risk Project 2014).

characterized by repeated attempts to bolster a common, and often forgotten, tongue such as Scots Gaelic or Welsh.

"Linguism," anthropologist Clifford Geertz noted, "is particularly intense in the Indian sub-continent" (Geertz 1990). The incidence and potency of linguistic subnationalist movements in the region support his claim. The successful secession of its Bengali-speaking province (now Bangladesh, literally translated as "the land of the Bengali-speakers") challenged the religious raison d'être of the Pakistani state, which continues to confront powerful subnationalist movements by the Baluchi, Sindhi, and Pashto language groups. Most scholars date the Tamil insurgency in Sri Lanka to Sinhala attempts to undermine the Tamil linguistic minority beginning with the Sinhala Only Act of 1956, which mandated Sinhala as the only official language of the state (Brown 2003; DeVotta 2004; Ginsburgh & Weber 2011). Language has been the basis for powerful subnationalist movements in India, which prompted the redrawing of the country's provincial boundaries along linguistic lines in the 1950s. The strength of linguistic subnationalism took India's national leaders by surprise, notably Nehru who recalled that "Some of the ablest men in the country came before us and confidently and emphatically stated that language in the country stood for and represented culture, race history, individuality, and finally a sub-nation" (cited in Harrison 1956).

Homogeneity of language within the political-administrative unit and differentiation from language speakers in other units are the key dimensions that have been hypothesized to link language to subnationalism.[3] The language indicator is therefore operationalized through data on the existence of a single, common language to capture internal homogeneity, and on whether or not this is a distinctive language to capture external differentiation (see Table 6.1).

Subnational Consciousness

I adopt a behavioral rather than an attitudinal approach to the measurement of subnational consciousness in Indian states. In the absence of survey data that might allow one to tap into individual attitudes, I rely on three observable manifestations of subnational sentiment – first, the existence of popular mobilization in support of the creation of the state; second, the absence of a

---

[3] This is brought out particularly nicely by Noah Webster's case for American spelling of English a decade after the American Revolution: "*A general uniformity through the United States* would be the event of such a reformation. All persons, of every rank, would speak with some degree of precision and uniformity. Such a uniformity in these States is very desirable; it would remove prejudice, and conciliate mutual affection and respect. But a capital advantage of this reform in these States would be, that *it would make a difference between the English orthography and the American.* Such an event is of vast political consequence. Besides this, a national language is a band of national union. Every engine should be employed to render the people of this country national; to call their attachments home to their own country; and to inspire them with the pride of national character." (Webster 1789, emphasis added).

TABLE 6.1. *Measuring Subnationalism: The Language Component of the Subnationalism Index*

Indicator	Measurement/Coding Rule	Data Sources
Single language	code as 1 if there is a single official language in the state in that year code as 0 if there is none or more than one official language in the state in that year	text of official language acts and relevant amendments passed by the respective state governments 41st Report of the National Commissioner for Linguistic Minorities (2001), available at http://nclm.nic.in/shared/linkimages/23.htm
Common language	proportion of people in the state who speak the official/dominant language (0–1) based on the last census difference between the proportion of people in the state who speak the official/dominant language and the second most commonly spoken language (0–1) based on the last census	calculated from language tables from the Census of India (1951, 1961, 1971, 1981, 1991, 2001) calculated from language tables from the Census of India (1951, 1961, 1971, 1981, 1991, 2001)
Distinctive language	code as 1 if the official/dominant language of the state is *not* the official/dominant language of any other state in the Indian union in that year code as 0 if the official/dominant language of the state is also the official/dominant language of another state in the Indian union in that year	text of official language acts and relevant amendments passed by the respective state governments 41st Report of the National Commissioner for Linguistic Minorities (2001), available at http://nclm.nic.in/shared/linkimages/23.htm

movement within the province for its division; and finally, the presence of a subnationalist political party (see Table 6.2).

Subnational Mobilization
The rationale behind this indicator is that those provinces whose boundaries reflect active mobilization on the part of its citizens may be seen to be characterized by a more powerful subnational identity than those states that were created by administrative diktat. Movements for the creation of new

TABLE 6.2. *Measuring Subnationalism: The Behavioral Component of the Subnationalism Index*

Indicator	Measurement/Coding Rule	Data Sources

Subnational Mobilization
Has there been mobilization in favor of creation of the state at any point of time since 1900?
	code as 1 if there is evidence of substantial mobilization in favor of creation of the state at any point in time from 1900 until that year.
	code as 0 if there is no evidence of mobilization in favor of creation of the state from 1900 until that year or secondary documents.
		1. primary document: SRC Report (1955)
		2. secondary documents:
		  (a) documents and books related to the integration of princely states
		  (b) histories of states
		  (c) books on language movements in India
		  (d) books on regionalism/federalism in India

Absence of Separatist Movement Has the state witnessed a separatist movement?	code as 0 if there is evidence of national or state government "recognition" of a separatist movement at any point in time from 1900 until that year and/or if a party based explicitly on the separatist cause gets more than 1% of the total vote in the last state assembly elections. code as 1 if there is no evidence of national or state government "recognition" of a separatist movement at any point until that year and if no party based explicitly on the separatist cause gets more than 1% of the total vote in the last state assembly elections.	1. SRC Report 2. national and regional newspaper reports 3. secondary literature 4. statistical reports of the state assembly elections issued by the Election Commission of India, New Delhi.
Subnationalist Parties Did a subnationalist party receive greater than 5% of the total vote share in the last state legislative assembly elections?	determine whether a party is subnationalist or not based on: (1) manifestoes of parties, speeches of leaders (2) newspaper descriptions of party/party platforms (3) secondary literature code as 1 if a subnationalist party gets over 5% of the vote; code as 0 if no subnationalist party gets over 5% of the vote	code based on statistical reports of the most recent elections to the legislative assembly of the state issued by the Election Commission of India, New Delhi.

boundaries and/or the redrawing of provincial boundaries in India go back to the colonial period. The British administration faced frequent demands for the redrawing of state boundaries along linguistic lines in the early years of the twentieth century.[4] The Congress party, which was at the helm of the nationalist movement, supported such demands from 1905 onward, and at its annual session in 1920 adopted a new constitution that organized the party along twenty-one linguistically defined units. After gaining independence, however, the Congress government decided that despite popular demand, because of the "formative state" of the nation, it was not "an opportune time" for the creation of linguistic provinces. They feared that such an undertaking might unleash "forces of disruption and disintegration" (Windmiller 1954). But by the early 1950s, the mobilizations by language groups reached a crescendo and began to take a violent turn. In 1953, the central government was forced to appoint the States Reorganization Commission (SRC), which conceded the principle of the linguistic reorganization of Indian states and also recommended the specific boundaries of the provinces. The 1950s and, to a lesser extent, the early 1960s were the most intense period of subnational mobilization in India in terms of the volume, frequency, and intensity of demands for linguistic states. Many states owe their present boundaries to this time. The report of the SRC published in 1955, and secondary accounts of these decades therefore form the primary basis for the coding of this indicator but these are supplemented by a review of the history of demands for the formation of the state in question beginning from 1900 until the year of coding.[5]

Absence of Separatist Movement within a State

Insofar as popular mobilization in favor of the formation of a state may be seen as indicative of a stronger subnationalism, the existence of a separatist movement *within* a province for its division by carving out a separate, breakaway state can be seen as a sign of a more fragmented subnational identity in the "mother state." A state that faces a separatist movement within its territory is likely to be characterized by a less cohesive subnational solidarity than a state

---

[4] The Simon Commission, a visiting commission of British parliamentarians in 1930, for example, stated that "There is a considerable body of opinion in India, which calls for some readjustment of boundaries and redistribution of areas, and we entirely share the views of those who think that the present arrangement is not altogether satisfactory. The existing provincial boundaries in more than one case embrace areas and peoples of no national affinity, and sometimes separate those who might under a different scheme be more naturally united" (cited in Windmiller 1954).

[5] My research assistants and I closely examined the SRC report as well as a comprehensive bibliography of secondary material on the histories of individual states, integration of princely states, linguistic reorganization of states, language/ subnational movements, and Indian federalism for any mention of the existence of popular mobilization in favor of the creation of each state beginning in 1900. There was a very high degree of correlation between our codings (0.96). In case of divergence, we resolved the issue through discussion based on our collective reading of the documents.

that does not. Movements for the carving out of new provinces from within the territorial boundaries of an existing province have developed and subsided through virtually all of India's post-Independence years. I focus on separatist movements within a province that are "recognized" in one of two ways. First, they can be recognized by the state, either the national government or the government of the province in question, for example, through negotiation with or explicit refusal to negotiate with key actors of the separatist movement and/or armed action against the separatist movement or the granting of the separatist demand. Second, they can be recognized in the electoral arena, that is, if a party that espouses the separatist cause contests a past state assembly elections and garners at least 5 percent of the total vote. The existence of a separatist movement within a state that is recognized in one of these ways is coded based on an examination of a range of sources, including the SRC report;[6] state government documents, especially the reports of the state Home Ministry; newspaper reports, as well as the reports of the Assembly elections in that state.[7] It is important to note that the indicators for the presence of subnational mobilization and separatist movements are potentially closely related. If/when a separatist movement succeeds in obtaining a new state, its separatist agitation against the mother state will now be counted as subnational mobilization in favor of the creation of the new progeny state. Accordingly, the mother state will no longer be coded as characterized by that separatist movement.

Subnationalist Parties

The existence of a subnational party, conceptualized as a party that is founded on the basis of a subnationalist ideology and/or that espouses subnationalist causes, may be seen both as a consequence of subnational consciousness as well as, often, a means toward its further strengthening. The coding of this indicator proceeds in three stages. First, for each state for each year a list of political parties that contested in the most recently concluded assembly election is drawn up using the Reports of the National Election Commission. Second, each of these parties is coded as either subnationalist or not. A party is counted as a subnationalist party in a particular period of time if it meets *any one* of the following three criteria:

1. If at the time of the most recently concluded state assembly election it has a subnationalist name, that is, if some aspect of state identity figures

---

[6] As noted earlier, the mandate of the SRC report was to assess the demands by various groups for separate states. This meant that the Report discusses, often in great detail, the mobilization in support of states whose creation it recommended against, and which were consequently amalgamated into larger provinces. My research assistants and I examined the SRC Report to draw up a list of movements for "failed" provinces and located them within the boundaries of present Indian states.

[7] The degree of correlation between the coding by members of our research team of the existence of a separatist movement based on our respective readings of these documents was 0.92. In cases of divergence, we resolved the issue through discussion.

in the name of the party, such as the Parti Quebecois in Quebec, Canada or the Scottish National party in Scotland, UK. In India, parties coded as subnationalist parties include the DMK (Dravida Munnetra Kazhagam translated as the Dravidian Progress Foundation) in Tamil Nadu; Telugu Desam Party (Party of the Telugu Nation) in Andhra Pradesh; and Asom Gano Parishad (Assam People's Party) in Assam.

2. If it was founded explicitly on the basis of a subnationalist ideology, that is, if either the founder or founding documents of the party explicitly state that it is a subnational party. For example, as noted earlier, E. M. S. Namboodiripad, one of the founders of the Kerala Communist Party, clearly stated that the party was the "national party of Kerala" (Harrison 1960).

3. If it prominently used subnationalist rhetoric or espoused subnationalist causes in election manifestoes and/or the speeches of the leaders of the party during the last state assembly elections. The definition of subnationalist rhetoric and causes is necessarily unspecified because it varies over time and across Indian states. However, it is important to note that general statements about promoting the overall or some specific aspect of the welfare of the people *do not* count as either subnationalist rhetoric or the espousal of subnational causes. References to a single, glorified past; historical subnational figures; a myth of common origin; a common culture and heritage; the "greatness" of or "pride" in the subnation do count as subnationalist rhetoric. "Sons of the Soil" policies, which seek to grant special privileges to those perceived as members of the subnation, and schemes that are explicitly directed towards promotion of a single common language, a common culture, and heritage would be counted as subnational causes.[8]

In order to ensure that only subnationalist parties that have some popular support are included in the dataset, the analysis is limited to those parties that have secured at least 5 percent of the total popular vote in a province in the last state assembly elections.[9] It is important to note that the coding of the same party as subnationalist or not varies over time and across states. A party could be counted as subnationalist at a particular point in time in one state but not at a prior or later point of time in that very state or at the same point of time in another state. The coding rules and data sources for all three indicators that comprise the subnational consciousness component of the subnationalism index are detailed in Table 6.2.

---

[8] Because of the difficulties faced in gaining access to election manifestos, we relied on scholarly and print media analyses of political parties in the to code this aspect of the indicator.

[9] This is admittedly an arbitrarily set cutoff, but it is important to note that in constructing the subnationalism index I have varied the threshold (1%, 10%, 20%) for the share of popular vote necessary for a party to be coded as subnationalist, and the positive association between subnationalism and social development indicators is maintained in the cross-tabulations as well as regression analyses.

TABLE 6.3. *Confirmatory Factor Analysis of the Indicators of Subnationalism*

Factor analysis/correlation	Number of obs = 122
Method: principal-component factors	Retained factors = 1
Rotation: (unrotated)	Number of params = 4

Factor	Eigenvalue	Difference	Proportion	Cumulative
Factor1	2.04236	1.27113	0.5106	0.5106
Factor2	0.77123	0.13928	0.1928	0.7034
Factor3	0.63195	0.07749	0.1580	0.8614
Factor4	0.55446		0.1386	1.0000

Method: principal-component factors, N = 122
LR test: independent vs. saturated, $\chi^2(6)$ = 71.22; Prob $>\chi^2$ = 0.0000

Factor loadings (pattern matrix) and unique variances

Variable	Factor1	Uniqueness
Language 2	0.7476	0.4412
Absence of separatist movement	0.6477	0.5805
Subnational mobilization	0.7469	0.4422
Subnationalist parties	0.7115	0.4938

These four components of the subnationalism measure are best seen as cues, which signal the cohesion or fragmentation of subnational solidarity in a state.[10] In Table 6.3, I use confirmatory factor analysis to examine the empirical relationships between these different indicators and find, based on the widely used Kaiser criterion, that there is indeed a single common factor underlying the indicators of language, subnational mobilization, the absence of a separatist movement, and the presence of a subnational party.

The four indicators that constitute the subnationalism index are characterized by a "family resemblance structure," which according to Goertz (2006) is best seen as "a rule about sufficiency with no necessary condition requirements." No single indicator is necessary, but all four indicators together are sufficient for solidarity. In line with this structure I use the "substitutability relationship" (or the theory of "functional equivalence") as the central organizing tool for the subnationalism index (Goertz 2006). The relationship of substitutability is tied to the logical operator OR, which is union in set theory (ibid.). Mathematically, this means that indicators such as those of subnationalism, which are bound together by the substitutability relationship, should be

[10] The inclusion of indicators, some of which are building blocks and others that are manifestations of subnational consciousness, in a single index of subnationalism is not problematic. As Coppedge puts it, "if theory tells us that X causes Y, it makes little difference whether we treat Y's thin indicators Y1 and Y2 as observable implications of Y or as component dimensions of Y; either way we end up testing for associations between X, on the one hand, and Y1 and Y2 on the other" (Coppedge 1999).

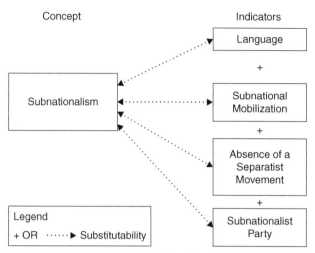

FIGURE 6.1. The Concept of Subnationalism.

combined using arithmetic addition.[11] For comparability I first undertook a linear transformation of the aggregate scores for the language indicator. This meant that each of the four indicators now range from 0 to 1. As indicated in Figure 6.1, the scores for each of the four indicators are then summed to arrive at a subnationalism index, which ranges from a theoretical minimum of 0, indicating a deeply fragmented subnational solidarity, to a maximum of 4, indicating a very powerful subnationalism.[12] Figure 6.2 provides an overview of the strength of subnationalism across major Indian states from 1960 to 1990. Having specified the operationalization of the concept of subnationalism, I will now use this subnationalism index to test the relationship between subnationalism and social development across all major Indian states.

TESTING THE SUBNATIONALISM ARGUMENT

This book has argued that the strength of subnationalism is a critical determinant of the level of social development in a province. In this section I present

---

[11] Necessary conditions do not permit substitutes, but in the absence of the stipulation of a necessary condition, the absence of one characteristic can be substituted for by the presence of others (Goertz 2006). The necessary condition structure is mathematically modeled by AND or intersection in set theory. Indices with necessary condition structures should be multiplied to arrive at a final score.

[12] It is important to note that in line with the substitutability relationship, dropping individual components of the index does not alter the positive and statistically significant influence of subnationalism on social development outcomes or expenditures. Further, tables A6.4–A6.7 in the data appendix show that across Indian states over a 30 year period from 1971 to 2001, each of the individual components has the same positive effect on social development outcomes and expenditures as the subnationalism index as a whole, and that these relationships approximate conventional levels of significance.

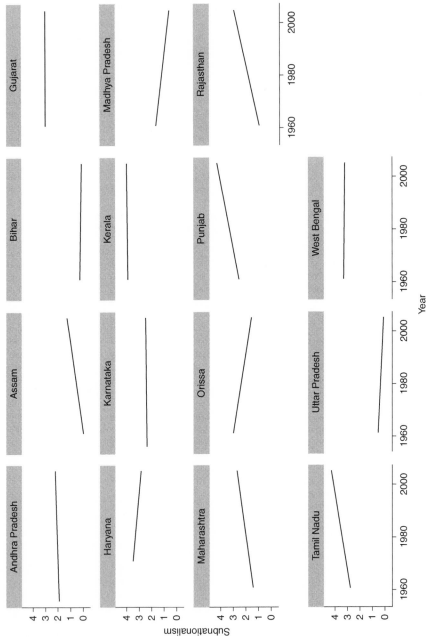

FIGURE 6.2. Subnationalism in Major Indian States (1960–2000).

both cross-sectional and temporal evidence in support of this claim. I present two types of cross-sectional evidence. First, I present descriptive statistics that show that from 1966 on, Indian states with a stronger subnationalism have also been characterized by higher social development indicators. Second, I present cross-sectional regressions that show that controlling for the most prominent explanation for social development, that is, levels of economic development, subnationalism has a positive and statistically significant effect on social development across Indian states from 1971 to 2006. In addition, I also present evidence on the relationship between subnationalism and social development over time. In Chapters 4 and 5, I delineated the way in which the strength of subnational solidarity influenced social policy and development outcomes across Tamil Nadu, Kerala, UP, and Rajasthan as well as Bihar beginning in the mid to late nineteenth century until the present day. Ideally, I would have liked to examine the effect of subnationalism on social development outcomes in all Indian states across this same time period but due to the lack of availability of data on key control variables, the most demanding temporal test of my theory that I can undertake begins in the 1970s. From 1971 to 2001, subnationalism is shown to have a consistently positive and statistically significant influence on social development expenditures and outcomes in Indian states across a range of different models, controlling for factors such as economic development, the presence of a left party, the nature of the party system, the intensity of political competition and ethnic (religious) diversity, all of which have been, as discussed in Chapter 2, hypothesized to be associated with social development.

The Data

I test the subnationalism model through data on Indian states for each year from 1966 to 2006. As noted at the outset in Chapter 1, Indian states are the appropriate unit of analysis for a study of social development because of the nature of Indian federalism. The Indian constitution vests considerable economic power as well as jurisdiction over social services, including education and health, with state governments. The state is the unit at which key developmental policy decisions are taken. More than 90 percent of expenses on education and health are incurred by state governments (Mehrotra 2006). Despite recent moves toward decentralization, especially through the revival of traditional *panchayats* or village councils, virtually no power rests at the local level of government. Neither village councils nor district governments possess much financial or administrative autonomy. The state is therefore the "natural" unit of analysis for studies of public goods provision in India (Chhibber & Nooruddin 2004; Drèze & Sen 2002; Kohli 1987; Lieberman 2009; Saez & Sinha 2010).[13] I restrict my

---

[13] As noted in chapter 1, some analyses of public goods provision in India by economists including Banerjee & Somanathan 2004; Banerjee, Somanathan, & Iyer 2005 and Betancourt & Gleason 2000, have focused on districts as the units of analysis. While this has the distinct

analysis to the major states of India that include more than 95 percent of the total national population from 1966 to 2006.[14] The primary outcome variable of social development is measured through two indicators – literacy and infant mortality rates (IMR). These are the most prominent and widely used summary measures of the educational and health status of populations globally.[15] Crucially, they are also widely acknowledged to be reliable statistics for India.[16]

Descriptive Statistics

Before proceeding to the regression analysis, it is useful to present some descriptive statistics that help clarify the relationship between subnationalism and social development that is observed in the data. Tables 6.4 and 6.5 present the relationship between subnationalism and literacy and infant mortality rates respectively across Indian states from 1966 to 2006. Table 6.4 shows that all provinces that have a weaker subnationalism than the all India mean are also characterized by literacy rates below the mean for all Indian states. Similarly, Table 6.5 shows that, with the exception of Gujarat and Haryana, in

---

methodological advantage of providing access to a much larger and concomitantly greater degrees of freedom – as of 2014, there were over 600 districts as compared to 29 states in India – insofar as districts are purely administrative divisions with no political power, including over social policy, they are not meaningful units of analysis for studies interested in the determinants of social policy. It is also useful to note that all studies of public goods provision across Indian districts find state fixed effects to have a substantive and statistically significant impact, indicating that unobserved characteristics of states, such as subnationalism, that vary across states, but not across districts within a state explain a large part of the variation in social welfare.

[14] The following states are included in the sample – Andhra Pradesh, Assam, Bihar, Gujarat, Haryana, Karnataka, Kerala, Madhya Pradesh, Maharashtra, Orissa, Punjab, Rajasthan, Tamil Nadu, Uttar Pradesh, and West Bengal. In the case of the creation of new states, like Uttarakhand, Jharkhand and Chattisgarh, the rump states, in this case, U.P., Bihar and M.P. are retained in the analysis.

[15] The widely used UN Human Development Index (HDI) conceptualizes its social dimension in terms of education and health, which are in turn measured through indicators including prominently literacy and IMR. In addition to the UN Human Development Report virtually all of the reports by the UN's development agencies, such as the, UNICEF's State of the World's Children, WHO's World Health Report, and UNESCO's Education for All Global Monitoring Report focus on literacy and/or IMR. Literacy and IMR are regarded in development circles as highly sensitive proxies for a number of other indicators of education and well-being.

[16] Other official statistics, gross enrollment ratios, for instance, have been questioned by a number of economists, notably Amartya Sen and Jean Drèze, who have refused to use official data on enrollment ratios, stating that these figures are known to be grossly inflated, partly due to the incentive that government employees at different levels have to report exaggerated figures. They point out that although official statistics portray a gross enrollment ratio of 98–99% at the primary level, data from the census and a national sample survey in fact show that only 40–42% of girls in rural areas, between the ages of 5 and 14 attend school (Task Force on Higher Education and Society 2002).

TABLE 6.4. *Relationship between Subnationalism and Literacy across Major Indian States from 1966–2006*

	Literacy Below or Equal to Indian *Mean*	Literacy Above or Equal to Indian *Mean*
Subnationalism below or equal to mean	Andhra Pradesh Assam Bihar Madhya Pradesh Orissa Rajasthan Uttar Pradesh	
Subnationalism above or equal to mean		Gujarat Haryana Himachal Pradesh Karnataka Kerala Punjab Tamil Nadu West Bengal Maharashtra

TABLE 6.5. *Relationship between Subnationalism and Infant Mortality across Major Indian States from 1966–2006*

	Infant Mortality Above or Equal to Indian *Mean*	Infant Mortality Below *or Equal to* Indian *Mean*
Subnationalism below or equal to mean	Andhra Pradesh Assam Bihar Madhya Pradesh Orissa Rajasthan Uttar Pradesh	
Subnationalism above or equal to mean	Gujarat Haryana	Himachal Pradesh Karnataka Kerala Maharashtra Punjab Tamil Nadu West Bengal

states where subnationalism is above the mean, infant mortality rates are lower than the mean for India. Further, the clear positive relationship between subnationalism and education and health expenditures, all averaged for the period 1960–2000, is shown in Figures 6.3 and 6.4 respectively.

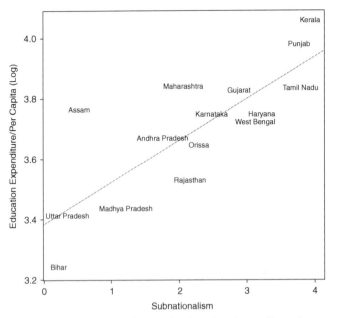

FIGURE 6.3. Subnationalism and Education Expenditure (1970–2000).

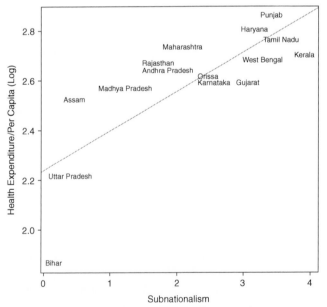

FIGURE 6.4. Subnationalism and Health Expenditure (1960–2000).

Statistical Analyses

Subnationalism and Social Development across Indian States

The basic empirical strategy followed in this chapter, in line with the scholarship on public goods provision in India (Banerjee, Iyer, & Somanathan 2005; Banerjee & Somanathan 2001; Chhibber & Nooruddin 2004; Saez and Sinha 2010) as well as more generally (Alesina, Baqir, & Easterly 1999), is to regress different measures of social development on the subnationalism index.[17] Regression analysis has been a fecund topic of research and there is considerable debate among political methodologists on the applicability and trade-offs associated with the use of different estimation techniques. There does, however, appear to be consensus on the desideratum that regression analyses should be underpinned and guided by a clearly specified theory. It is useful, therefore, to briefly recap here the subnationalism theory and specify its testable hypotheses. Longitudinal and comparative historical analyses of my five case study states revealed that elites in states characterized by a stronger subnationalism are more likely to support the collective welfare of the subnational community and allocate state resources toward the provision of collective goods, such as education and health, as compared with their counterparts in states with a more fragmented subnational solidarity. States with a stronger subnationalism are therefore more likely to be characterized by higher levels of social development than states with a relatively weak subnational solidarity. This model gives rise to the following testable hypothesis – states with a more powerful subnational solidarity are likely to be characterized by better social development outcomes than states with a weaker subnational identity, all other things being equal. Further, corresponding to the top-down mechanism, one would expect states with a more powerful subnational identity to institute more progressive social policies than states with a weaker subnational identity, all other things being equal. It is important to note here that Chapter 2 also specified a secondary bottom-up mechanism, that citizens in states with a stronger subnational solidarity are more likely to be more sociopolitically involved in the life of the province, and with the provision of public services, more generally. The lack of availability of systematic data across states over time on citizen levels of sociopolitical consciousness and activism and involvement with schools or health centers, however, makes it impossible to directly test this latter mechanism.

In testing the subnational model across Indian states, it is useful to start by looking at the relationship between subnationalism and social development controlling for the most prominent alternative explanation of economic development.

Figures 6.5 and 6.6 plot the coefficients on the subnationalism variable along with the 95% confidence interval (+ or − 1.96*standard error), for a cross-sectional regression of literacy and infant mortality rates, respectively, on subnationalism while controlling for economic development, measured in

---

[17] Insofar as the relationship between social development and subnationalism as well as the other independent variables is linear, least squares regression analysis will be used.

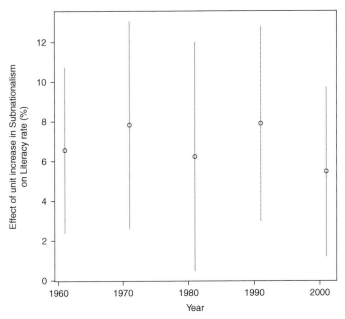

FIGURE 6.5. Effect of Subnationalism on Literacy (1960–2000).

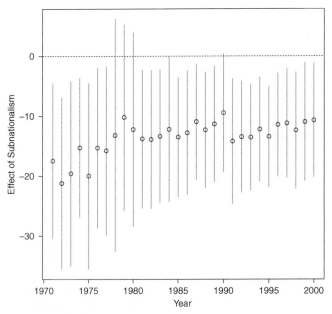

FIGURE 6.6. Effect of Subnationalism on IMR (1960–2000).

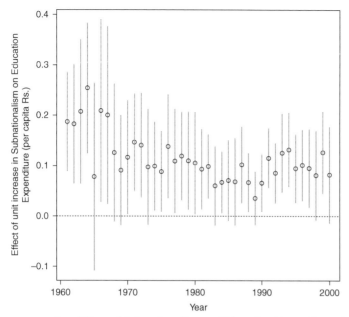

FIGURE 6.7. Effect of Subnationalism on Education Expenditure (1960–2000).

terms of per capita income, for each individual year between 1960 and 2000. Figures 6.7 and 6.8 plot the coeffecients on the subnationalism variable along with the 95% confidence interval (+ or − 1.96*standard error), for a cross-sectional regression of education and health expenditures respectively on subnationalism while controlling for economic development between 1960 and 2000.

In addition, in Table 6.6 I estimate the effect of subnationalism on social development outcomes and expenditures across Indian states using the following seemingly unrelated regression (SUR) models:[18]

$$SD_{it}^k = \alpha^k + \beta^k X_{it-1} + \tau^k SN_{it-1}^k + \mu_{it}^k \tag{Model 1}$$

$$SE_{it}^k = \alpha^k + \beta^k X_{it-1} + \tau^k SN_{it-1}^k + \mu_{it}^k \tag{Model 2}$$

---

[18] Seemingly unrelated regression (SUR) is more efficient than equation-by-equation OLS in estimating a model (such as the subnationalism model), which consists of a set of linear equations, using the same set of explanatory variables to estimate related outcome variables where one would expect that the equation errors are almost certainly correlated. The small N in our dataset makes SUR particularly attractive because one of the main advantages of estimating a SUR system is that fewer observations are required to obtain reliable function estimates than if each of the regression equations is estimated separately and the correlation ignored (Smith & Kohn 1998). This technique has been used in recent works of comparative politics by Tsai (2007) and Lieberman (2009) among others.

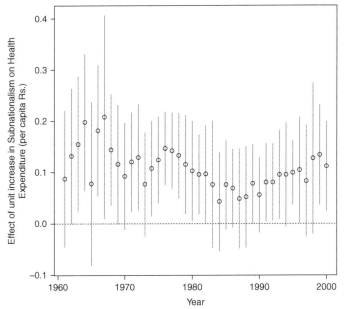

FIGURE 6.8. Effect of Subnationalism on Health Expenditure (1960–2000).

In model 1, *SD* is the social development outcome measure, where *k* may denote literacy or infant mortality rates. In model 2, *SE* is the social expenditure measure, where *k* may denote state spending on education or health. In both models, *i* denotes a particular Indian state, and t refers to a period in time. X_{it-1} refers to economic development in state *i*. *SN* refers to the subnationalism measure. In order to show that the findings are not unique to a single moment in time, I present results across Indian states over five-year periods from 1971 to 2001. To run this model, I collapse the explanatory variables to their means for each of the states over every five-year period between 1971 and 2001. This counters the influence of "odd" years and random events and therefore provides a more reliable analysis. The explanatory variables are lagged by one time period. Therefore, *t* – 1 denotes a lagged variable whose value is within the average for the states during the previous five-year period.

Holding levels of economic development constant, subnationalism is found to have a positive influence on literacy rates and a negative impact on infant mortality rates. Both of these effects reached conventional levels of significance. The magnitude of these effects is also substantial. Keeping per capita state domestic product constant at its mean, a standard deviation increase in the strength of subnationalism generates an increase of between 9.45% (during 1971–76) and 9.46% (during 1996–2001) in literacy rates and a reduction of between 24.13 (in 1971–76) and 14.90 (in 1996–2001) infant deaths per 1,000 live births. Table 6.6 also provides support for the hypothesis that the stronger the subnationalism, the greater the social spending in a state. A one standard deviation increase in subnationalism increases the log per capita spending on education and health by an average of Rs. 0.126 and Rs. 0.117, respectively. These represent an increase of approximately 4% over the mean education and health expenditure. Therefore, cross-sectional regression analyses bear out the predictions of the subnationalism model. Subnationalism is shown to have a positive effect on levels of social development as well as spending across all major Indian states from 1971 to 2001.

Subnationalism and Social Development Across Indian States over Time

As is clear from Chapters 4 and 5, the relationship between subnationalism and social development is one that develops over time. I therefore supplement this cross-sectional perspective with results from a range of time-series, cross-sectional models. The additional degrees of freedom provided by the presence of data points for each state over a range of time periods allows for the examination of the strength, in addition to economic development, of some of the other alternative explanations for social development discussed in Chapter 2 – the presence of a left party, the nature of the party system, the intensity of political competition, ethnic specifically religious diversity. These explanatory variables are summarized in Table 6.7 and the outcome variables are summarized in Table 6.8.[19]

I estimate the effect of subnationalism on social development outcomes and expenditures across Indian states over a 30-year period from 1971 to 2001 using the following models. Model 1 corresponds to the central theoretical claim that subnationalism fosters social development, while models 2 and 3 correspond to the top-down mechanism, that subnationalism influences state

[19] A further note is in order as regards the ethnic diversity variable. Ethnic diversity is measured through the widely used ethnolinguistic fractionalization (ELF) index, which reflects the likelihood that two people chosen at random will be from different ethnic groups. Following the classic work by Easterly and Levine (1997), the ELF is generally calculated for ethnolinguistic groups. I, however, calculate ethnic diversity based on the number and size of religious groups. As discussed in the section on Alternative Explanations in Chapter 2, the causal logic in most studies of the relationship between ethnic fractionalization and public goods provision is that polarization and conflict between ethnic groups leads to a breakdown of consensus in favor of, and creates difficulties in collectively working towards the provision of public services. Based on a dataset on collective mobilization from 1950 to 1995 collected from newspaper reports, Wilkinson (2008) found that among all the different ethnic cleavages in India – language, tribe, caste and religion, religion has been most strongly associated with conflict and violence. Seeking to stay faithful to the mechanism linking ethnic diversity and social services in most studies in the political economy scholarship, I use data on Hindu, Muslim, Christian, Sikh, Buddhist, and Jain groups to calculate the ELF index. It is also important to note that I avoid including a linguistic fractionalization variable for methodological reasons, insofar as the inclusion of the proportion of speakers of the dominant/ official language as a component of the subnationalism measure could potentially lead to a problem of multicollinearity.

TABLE 6.6. *Seemingly Unrelated Regressions of Social Development Outcomes and Expenditures on Subnationalism in Indian States, 1971–2001*

	1971–76	1976–81	1981–86	1986–91	1991–96	1996–01
(Mean) Literacy						
Subnationalism	7.855***	7.034***	7.085***	6.417**	6.452***	7.816***
	(3.021)	(2.660)	(2.741)	(2.552)	(2.190)	(2.310)
Income per capita	−0.007	−0.023#	−0.006	−0.005	0.000	−0.003
	(0.018)	(0.015)	(0.011)	(0.010)	(0.008)	(0.006)
Constant	26.055*	38.043***	32.104***	34.649***	39.778***	40.305***
	(14.759)	(12.063)	(9.874)	(10.606)	(9.480)	(7.661)
(Mean) Infant Mortality						
Subnationalism	−20.055***	−14.787**	−14.714**	−12.754***	−9.410**	−12.386***
	(6.841)	(6.530)	(6.237)	(4.918)	(4.201)	(3.699)
Income per capita	−0.012	0.022	−0.003	−0.002	0.000	0.006
	(0.041)	(0.038)	(0.025)	(0.019)	(0.015)	(0.009)
Constant	169.794***	127.018***	133.793***	115.211***	91.468***	83.678***
	(33.417)	(29.613)	(22.464)	(20.440)	(18.187)	(12.266)
(Mean) Education Expenditure						
Subnationalism	0.109**	0.122***	0.114***	0.096***	0.075**	0.114***
	(0.048)	(0.044)	(0.030)	(0.024)	(0.032)	(0.030)
Income per captita	0.000	0.000	0.000**	0.000***	0.000	0.000#
	(0.000)	(0.000)	(0.000)	(0.000)	(0.000)	(0.000)

	(1)	(2)	(3)	(4)	(5)	(6)
Constant	2.587***	3.059***	3.096***	3.424***	3.686***	3.903***
	(0.233)	(0.200)	(0.109)	(0.098)	(0.140)	(0.099)
(Mean) Health Expenditure						
Subnationalism	0.079**	0.097***	0.092*	0.087**	0.094***	0.134***
	(0.036)	(0.018)	(0.052)	(0.036)	(0.029)	(0.038)
Income per capita	0.001***	0.000*	0.000**	0.000*	0.000	0.000
	(0.000)	(0.000)	(0.000)	(0.000)	(0.000)	(0.000)
Constant	1.582***	2.211***	2.215***	2.595***	2.839***	2.829***
	(0.177)	(0.083)	(0.186)	(0.150)	(0.124)	(0.126)
N	12	13	14	14	15	15
R-squared	0.364	0.351	0.357	0.338	0.443	0.527

Figures in cells are seemingly unrelated regression coefficients. Standard errors are in parentheses. # $p < 0.15$, * $p < 0.10$, ** $p < 0.05$, *** $p < 0.01$.

TABLE 6.7. *Descriptive Statistics: Independent Variables in Regression Analysis*

Name	Measure	Mean	Standard Deviation	Range
Subnationalism	Subnationalism index	2.17	1.20	0–4
Economic Development				
Income	Net state domestic product deflated by the consumer price index for agricultural workers (Rs. per capita)	1220.27	569.72	390.56–3546.92
Poverty	Poverty headcount index for rural India (%)	50.03	14.34	11.05–81.13
Inequality	Gini coefficient for rural India	3.34	0.37	0.46–4.56
Left Party Rule	Coded as 0 or 1 depending on whether or not a Communist party controls the state government	0.06	0.24	0–1
Nature of the Party System	Coded as 1 (two-party competition) on the basis of the effective number of parties holding seats in the state assembly (ENPV) $$ENPV = \frac{1}{\sum p_i^2}$$ p_i is the proportion of seats received by each party in the state assembly elections.	0.11	0.32	0–1
Political Competition	Margin of victory (Seat share of victorious party − Seat share of runner-up party) in the last elections to the state legislature.	41.69	22.09	85.27
Ethnic (religious) Diversity	Ethnolinguistic fractionalization index (ELF) $$ELF = 1 - \sum_{i=1}^{I}\left(\frac{n_i}{N}\right)^2$$ N is the population, I is the number of religious groups, and n is the population in the ith group.	0.40	0.28	0.05–1

TABLE 6.8. *Descriptive Statistics: Dependent Variables in Regression Analysis*

Name	Measure	Mean	Standard Deviation	Range
Literacy	Percentage of people who have the ability to both read and write in any language	42.748	18.962	7.13–90.86
Infant Mortality	Number of deaths of infants under the age of 1 year for every 1,000 live births	82.560	34.923	6.8–202
Education Expenditure	Logarithm of per capita education spending on the revenue account (Rs. per capita)	3.464	0.64242	1.674–4.980
	Education spending on the revenue account as a proportion of total state spending	21.251	4.371	8.545–37.921
Health Expenditure	Logarithm of per capita health spending on the revenue account (Rs. per capita)	2.5658	0.64543	0.655–3.787
	Health spending on the revenue account as a proportion of total spending	7.483	2.292	2.246–13.869
Social Expenditure	Social spending on the revenue account as a proportion of total spending	38.858	5.441	18.620–55.304
Non-Development Expenditure	Non-development spending on the revenue account as a proportion of total spending	35.228	7.572	17.953–62.924

social expenditures (model 2) and that these social expenditures in turn promote social development outcomes (model 3).

$$SD_{it}^k = a^k + \beta^k X_{it-1} + \tau^k SN_{it-1}^k + \gamma^k D_t + \mu_{it}^k \qquad \text{(Model 1)}$$

$$SE_{it}^k = a^k + \beta^k X_{it-1} + \tau^k SN_{it-1}^k + \gamma^k D_t + \mu_{it}^k \qquad \text{(Model 2)}$$

$$SD_{it}^k = a^k + \beta^k X_{it-1} + \tau^k SN_{it-1}^k + \gamma^k D_t + \mu_{it}^k \qquad \text{(Model 3)}$$

The unit of analysis in all models is the state-year.

In models 1 and 3, SD is the social development outcome measure, where k may denote literacy or infant mortality rates. In models 2 and 3, SE is the social expenditure measure, where k may denote state spending on education or health measured in terms of the log of state's per capita spending on education and health. X_{it-1} refers to a vector of economic, political, and ethnic diversity controls, all lagged by one year. SN refers to the subnationalism measure, where i denotes the province; again this is lagged by one year. The independent variables are lagged because their effects on social indicators and spending are expected to occur gradually, and because this goes some way toward addressing the concern of reverse causality that higher literacy and lower IMR are fostering stronger subnationalism. D_t is a vector of decade dummies. These are included in light of the deterministic time trend in the data and because they allow one to take into account effects, notably developments at the national level, such as a war or other emergency, that may influence all states in a given decade to the same amount, thereby eliminating a possible source of spuriousness due to common trends in observed variables.

It is well known that the errors in time-series, cross-sectional models cannot be assumed to be independent and identically distributed and that this violates the assumption of spherical errors required for OLS to be the optimal estimation strategy (Beck & Katz 1995: 636). In addition, the diagnostic tests run on my data indicated that the errors display serial correlation as well as heteroskedasticity. Following Beck and Katz (1995, 1996, 2001, 2004), Table 6.9 therefore presents the results of OLS regressions with panel corrected standard errors with a first-order auto-regressive correction.[20] As a robustness check, in

[20] Beck and Katz (1995, 1996, 2001, 2004) popularized the use of panel corrected standard errors for time-series, cross-sectional analysis as a low-cost, flexible method to improve on OLS standard errors with respect to panel heteroskedasticity and contemporaneous correlation of the errors. Since the publication of Beck and Katz's original article in 1995, this has become one of the most popular estimation techniques in time-series, cross-sectional analyses. Wilson and Butler (2007) found nearly 200 published articles in political science which used this method. There has recently been criticism of the blind applicability of this method (ibid.). This is not the case here, however, as panel corrected standard errors were adopted after a number of sensitivity analyses and a careful consideration of the nature of the data. It is also important to note that other prominent studies that have used similar data on Indian states, notably Chhibber and Nooruddin (2004) and Saez and Sinha (2009), also employ this estimation technique.

TABLE 6.9. *Time-Series Cross-Sectional OLS Estimates of Determinants of Social Development Outcomes and Expenditures across Indian States (1971–2001)*

	1.1 Lit	1.2 IMR	2.1 Education expenditure	2.2 Health expenditure	2.3 Non-development expenditure	3.1 Lit	3.2 IMR
Subnationalism	3.861***	−6.766***	0.085***	0.104***	−1.998***		
	(0.399)	(1.382)	(0.018)	(0.018)	(0.340)		
Income per capita	0.005***	−0.010***	0.000***	0.000***	0.003***	0.004***	−0.010***
	(0.001)	(0.003)	(0.000)	(0.000)	(0.001)	(0.001)	(0.004)
Left party rule	1.107	−3.712	0.018	0.016	0.041	1.689	−5.538*
	(1.627)	(3.137)	(0.045)	(0.046)	(1.100)	(1.558)	(3.267)
Two-party competition	−0.695	1.568	0.052**	0.031	−0.768*	−0.723	1.235
	(0.641)	(1.974)	(0.026)	(0.027)	(0.614)	(0.637)	(2.026)
Closeness of political competition	−0.029*	0.128***	−0.001**	−0.001*	−0.003	−0.010	0.109**
	(0.015)	(0.045)	(0.001)	(0.001)	(0.014)	(0.014)	(0.046)
Ethnic diversity	45.267***	−104.828***	0.377**	−0.465***	13.959***	49.723***	−123.221***
	(5.082)	(11.409)	(0.153)	(0.160)	(3.419)	(5.350)	(11.096)
Poverty	0.103***	−0.289***	0.000	−0.001	0.000	0.053#	−0.229**
	(0.033)	(0.103)	(0.001)	(0.001)	(0.029)	(0.033)	(0.105)
Inequality	−1.540	1.001	0.083	0.228**	−3.369***	−0.616	−1.138
	(1.637)	(4.630)	(0.092)	(0.097)	(1.518)	(1.618)	(4.704)

(continued)

TABLE 6.9 *(continued)*

	1.1 Lit	1.2 IMR	2.1 Education expenditure	2.2 Health expenditure	2.3 Non-development expenditure	3.1 Lit	3.2 IMR
Education expenditure						9.755***	
						(1.433)	
Health expenditure							−13.704***
							(4.518)
1970s	2.864***	170.357***	0.157***	0.277***	−3.901***	−1.697#	196.546***
	(0.950)	(16.538)	(0.039)	(0.040)	(0.870)	(1.173)	(20.792)
1980s	9.546***	153.409***	0.529***	0.649***	−7.141***	1.846	185.766***
	(1.160)	(16.146)	(0.047)	(0.049)	(1.036)	(1.503)	(21.074)
1990s	15.349***	136.769***	0.723***	0.787***	−4.925***	3.904**	172.778***
	(1.394)	(15.716)	(0.057)	(0.059)	(1.244)	(1.841)	(20.820)
2000s	27.669***	133.653***			0.734	12.044***	173.977***
	(2.498)	(15.238)			(2.252)	(2.868)	(20.166)
Constant	8.113		2.138***	0.978***	47.232***	−11.848*	
	(6.018)		(0.333)	(0.350)	(5.476)	(7.101)	
N	491	370	482	482	496	492	371
R²	0.823	0.654	0.856	0.785	0.684	0.814	0.629

# $p < 0.15$, * $p < 0.10$, ** $p < 0.05$, *** $p < 0.01$.
Figures in cells are Prais-Winsten regression coefficients.
Figures in parentheses are panel corrected standard errors with first-order auto-regressive correction.
Time dummies included.

Tables A6.1–A6.2 in the Data Appendix, I estimate the relationship between subnationalism and social expenditures and development across Indian states from the 1970s to the 2000s, using different estimation techniques including the inclusion of lagged dependent variables and different error structures including clustered standard errors.[21] I also include estimations with alternate measures of the outcome variables (Table A6.3), and with each of the individual components of the subnationalism index (Tables A6.4–A6.7).

Discussion of Regression Results
The time-series, cross-sectional analyses presented here as well as in the data appendix support the results of the cross-sectional regressions and provide further support for the central claim of this book that the stronger the subnationalism, the better the social development outcomes in a state. Table 6.9 shows that taking into account economic development, conceptualized in terms of per capita income, poverty and inequality, the presence of a social democratic party, the nature of the party system, political competition, and religious fractionalization, subnationalism has a positive and statistically significant impact on literacy and a negative and statistically significant impact on infant mortality. Holding all other variables constant at their mean, a standard deviation increase in subnationalism leads to a nearly 5% increase in literacy rates and a decrease of around 8 deaths per 1,000 live births in the following year.

The pooled analysis also supports the top-down mechanism of the subnationalism model, that is, subnationalism fosters greater state commitment to the

---

[21] While I recognize the general arguments in support of doing so (see, for example, Butler & Wilson 2007; Green et al. 2001; Kristensen & Wawro 2003), I have chosen to not include a state fixed effects estimation for a combination of theoretical and methodological reasons. For a start, a fixed effects within-group estimator soaks up all the across-state variation in the outcome variables, which is the primary variation that I set out to explain. I began this book by posing the puzzle of why some states in India have attained far higher levels of social development than other states. The inclusion of state dummies would make it impossible to study this central animating question. Also, because fixed effects are perfectly collinear with time invariant variables and highly collinear with variables that exhibit low variation, it is very hard to precisely estimate the effects of these stationary or sluggish variables, which will generally need to be dropped from the analysis. Insofar as the key explanatory variable in my model, the strength of subnationalism, as well as a number of other variables such as religious fractionalization exhibit low variation over time, the use of fixed effects would make it extremely difficult to test my theory. It is useful to note here, however, that my results are consistent with the use of Plümper and Troeger's (2007) technique to estimate the effect of time-invariant and sluggish variables in panel data models with unit effects; I chose not to present these estimates because of the controversy around this method (see, for example, Breusch et al. 2011; Greene 2010). Moreover, the inclusion of state dummies is highly inefficient in that it would eat up multiple degrees of freedom, which has a direct effect on the precision of the parameter estimates especially in analyses over relatively limited periods of time such as this (Adolph, Butler, & Wilson 2005: 23). In addition, the primary concern with not running a fixed effects model, that of omitted variable bias, is much less of a problem in analyses such as this that are undergirded by in-depth comparative case analyses.

social sector, which is in turn an important determinant of social development outcomes. Models 2.1 and 2.2 in Table 6.9 show that controlling for all other variables, subnationalism has a positive and statistically significant influence on both education and health expenditures. Holding all other variables constant at their mean, a standard deviation increase in subnationalism increases per capita spending on education and health by roughly Rs. 0.10 and 0.13 respectively.[22] This is a roughly 3% increase over mean education expenditure and about 5% increase over mean health expenditure. Subnationalism continues to have a positive and statistically significant effect on literacy and social expenditures, and negative and statistically significant effect on IMR in the alternative estimations in the Data Appendix. These findings are also robust to different measures of social spending. Data appendix table A6.3 shows that subnationalism has a positive and statistically significant effect when education and health expenditures are operationalized not as per capita expenditures but as shares of total state expenditure, and also when the dependent variable is the expenditure on the social sector as a whole. As a further robustness test, column 2.3 in Table 6.9 presents a model that tests the corollary that states with a more fragmented subnational identity tend to focus on "non-development" issues. Holding all other variables constant at their mean, a one-standard deviation increase in the fragmentation of subnationalism (moving from a more cohesive subnational community to a more fragmented one) is shown to lead to an approximately 2.5% increase in non-development expenditure, measured as a proportion of total state expenditure. This is an approximately 6% increase over the mean nondevelopment expenditure.[23] Models 3.1 and 3.2 in Table 6.9 also confirm that, in line with the top-down mechanism, education expenditures have a positive and statistically significant impact on literacy (model 3.1), and health expenditures dampen IMR and this effect is statistically significant (model 3.2). All of the findings reported here are also consistent with alternative measures of the explanatory variables, including each of the individual components of the subnationalism index (see tables A6.4–A6.7), different constructions of the key explanatory variable of subnationalism, the inclusion of additional control variables, different lag specifications, different units of analysis, and the dropping of particular states.[24]

[22] Expenditures on education and health in India are predominantly on the revenue account (Shariff & Ghosh 2000), and therefore this is what I focus on here, but the results remain mostly unchanged if we operationalize social expenditures in terms of expenditures on the capital account.
[23] Government expenditure in India is classified into development and non-development expenditure. Development expenditure is broadly defined to include all spending designed "directly to promote economic development and social welfare." Nondevelopment expenditure includes "expenditure pertaining to the general services rendered by the Government such as preservation of law and order, defense of the country, and the maintenance of the general organs of the Government" (www.rbi.org.in).
[24] The results remain unaltered, for example, if left party rule is measured not as a dummy variable based on whether or not a social democratic party is in power but as the total number of

Alternative Explanations

I noted earlier that one of my motivations for undertaking a time-series, cross-sectional analysis was to be able to examine the strength of the other factors that have been hypothesized to affect social development and spending. In the regressions in table 6.9 in this chapter and the alternative estimates in tables A6.1–A6.7 in the Data Appendix, I included variables corresponding to a number of the alternative hypotheses discussed in Chapter 2 – economic development, conceptualized in terms of per capita income, poverty and inequality; rule by a left party; nature of the party system; political competition; and ethnic fractionalization.

Economic Development

The most prominent explanation proposed for social development, as noted earlier in this book, is economic development. In line with the "universally acknowledged" impact of wealth on welfare (Filmer & Pritchett 1999: 1310), the analysis here confirms that per capita income is a consistently statistically significant predictor of social development outcomes and spending. In almost all the different models, the per capita income of a state has a statistically significant positive effect on literacy and social expenditures and negative effect on IMR but the size of these effects is relatively small. While certainly an important determinant of social development, a state's per capita income is by no means a sufficient explanation. Further evidence for the limited explanatory power of economic development as an explanation for social welfare is provided by the positive and statistically significant impact of rural poverty on literacy rates and a negative and statistically significant impact on IMR. This result, which seems surprising at first blush, is reflective of literacy rates being higher and infant mortality rates lower in the poorer states of India through much of the initial post-Independence decades (Datt and Ravallion 1997). This is brought out most strikingly by the juxtaposition of UP and Kerala. In the mid-1990s, the poverty head count ratios were similar and close to the Indian average in both states – yet infant mortality in UP was more than six times higher than in Kerala. Many other studies have found similar results for the limited predictive power of poverty for developmental outcomes across

years that a state has been ruled by a Communist party; if political competition is measured not as the winning differential but as the number of political parties contesting in the last elections; if instead of the proportion of seats, I use the proportion of votes to calculate the effective number of political parties used to measure the nature of party competition; and if poverty is measured by the poverty gap rather than the headcount index. The results remain unchanged when additional control variables such as the level of and rate of growth of the population, the level of urbanization, the level of electoral volatility, whether or not a coalition government is in power, percentage of landless households, and the amount of monsoon rainfall are included in the analysis. The results are also robust to different time lags of the independent variables and if the unit of analysis is state-decade or state-quinquennium rather than state-year, as well as to the dropping of individual states, including Kerala.

Indian states (see, for example, Murthi, Guio and Dreze 1995). Within the discussion of economic factors, it is also important to note the findings of the lack of any clear association between inequality and social welfare. In line with the general consensus among scholars and policy makers that "inequality is socially costly" (Acemoglu 2001: 5), in Table 6.9, the gini coefficient for rural areas is negatively associated with literacy and positively associated with IMR across Indian states, but this is not a statistically significant relationship.

The overall finding of the statistical analysis presented here, as regards the inadequacy of economic development as an explanation for social expenditures and outcomes, is in line with "recent research (that) suggests that the 'income effect' can be quite slow and weak"; the point is not that economic factors are unimportant; indeed there is clear evidence of their significance. Instead, to echo Murthi et al the "the point is that many other factors, not all of which are themselves strongly correlated with income, also have a strong influence on demographic outcomes." (1995: 746).

Rule by Social Democratic Party
There is an important body of work that emphasizes party ideology as an explanation for the differing policies enacted by governments. One strand of this argument, also equally a variant of class-based arguments, emphasizes, in particular, the presence of social democratic parties.

Scholars of the welfare state in Western Europe have argued that when social democratic parties are in power, states are more likely to focus on the social sector and consequently experience higher levels of social development (Hibbs 1977; Korpi 1983; Shalev 1983). In the statistical analysis presented here, in line with other work on Indian states, notably Kohli (1987), Herring (1988) and Heller (2000), rule by a Communist party is found to have a generally positive effect on literacy and social expenditures and a negative effect on infant mortality. This effect, however, only rarely achieves statistical significance. This finding of the relative weakness of rule by a left party as a determinant of social expenditures and development outcomes is in line with our analysis of Kerala in Chapter 4, which shows that the Communist party's pioneering role in the state's welfare outcomes is a product less of its Communist ideology and more its embeddedness in and espousal of Malayali subnationalism. The same Communist party has been able to achieve far more limited social gains in West Bengal (Desai 2007).

Nature of the Party System
A number of scholars, notably Chhibber and Nooruddin (2004), argue against viewing the role of a particular party or its ideology in disconnect from the electoral arena in which it competes. They argue that the nature of the party system – specifically, whether there is competition between two or multiple political parties – affects the provision of public goods. The necessity of reaching

out to multiple groups to secure the majority needed to win in two-party competition encourages the making of broad appeals and the provision of public goods. In contrast, because the proportion of seats and votes needed to win is less in a situation of multiparty competition, politicians are more likely to seek to reach out to specific groups by making particularistic appeals and providing clientelistic goods. Our statistical analysis provides some support for this hypothesis. The move from either a single party or a multiparty to a two-party system, where the nature of the party system is a dichotomous variable coded on the basis of the effective number of electoral parties in the last state assembly elections (Chhibber & Nooruddin 2004: 165), leads to a statistically significant increase in education expenditure. Insofar as the determinant of electoral victory in a first-past-the-post system such as India is the share of seats rather than votes, as noted in Table 6.7, in all the models in this book, the effective number of political parties is calculated on the basis of seats won by different parties. The results remain unchanged if we instead make a calculation on the basis of votes.

Political Competition
The intuitive hypothesis, rooted in democratic theory and especially the work of V. O. Key (1949), is that political parties in a more competitive electoral environment will be more keyed up to provide social services as compared to political parties in a less competitive political system who do not face, in Key's (1949: 307) words, a similar "anxiety over the next election." The statistical analysis here lends support for this hypothesis. While there is no unanimity, the most common way of measuring political competition is through the margin of victory (Cleary 2007; Kauneckis and Andersson 2006; Moreno 2005). As Table 6.9 shows, a less competitive environment, measured by the margin of legislative seats by which the winning party was victorious in the last state assembly election, lowers literacy and raises IMR (models 1.1 and 1.2), and dampens education and health spending (models 2.1 and 2.2), and these effects are significant at conventional levels. The results are also robust to the measurement of political competition in terms of the margin of victory in votes rather than seats.

Ethnic Diversity
As discussed in Chapter 2, there is a large body of research, mostly by economists, that posits a negative relationship between ethnic heterogeneity and the provision of public goods, with Banerjee, Iyer, and Somanathan (2005: 639) going so far as to term this "one of the most powerful hypotheses in political economy". The statistical analysis in this chapter, however, does not support this diversity-development deficit thesis. Instead, across a range of different models, ethnic diversity, which, following the causal logic of the scholarship on the topic (Posner 2004, Singh 2011), is measured in terms of what has been found to be the most divisive cleavage in India, that is, religion

(Wilkinson 2009), has a positive, statistically significant and often large effect on literacy and social expenditures and a negative effect on IMR. The size of this effect reflects, to a great extent, the state of Kerala, which is the most religiously diverse of all Indian states but which also has the highest levels of social spending and outcomes. It is important to emphasize, however, that religious diversity continues to have a statistically significant, positive effect on social development outcomes and spending even after Kerala is dropped from the regression analysis, though the size of the effect is much smaller.

This finding is not as surprising as it may initially appear. In other work, I have highlighted serious conceptual reasons to question the assertion that diversity necessarily impedes public goods provision (see Singh and & vom Hau 2014). Further, there is a growing body of scholarship that does not find empirical support for the diversity-development deficit thesis (see, for example, Bouston et al. 2010; Hopkins 2011; Rugh & Trounstine 2011; Trounstine 2013; Miguel 2004; Glennerster et al. 2013; Foa 2014; Wimmer 2015; Gao 2015), especially when analyzing on the one hand, subnational units of analysis and, on the other hand, the religious cleavage.

Even among the most seminal contributions that form the very foundation of the political economy scholarship on the topic, religious diversity is found to not dampen, and even to be *positively* associated with lower public goods provision (Alesina et al. 2003; see also Jackson 2007; Balasubramanian et al. 2009). More recently, experimental studies, which overcome the problem of the potential endogeneity of ethnic diversity that plagues the political economy scholarship and therefore elicit greater confidence in their findings, also find that religious diversity is not negatively associated with (McQuoid 2012), and even encourages, public goods provision (Mirza 2014).[25]

This supports the general point that ethnic demographics need not map directly on to ethnic politics or conflict (Posner 2005; Singh 2011; Singh and vom Hau 2014; Posner 2005). Ethnic conflict might certainly dampen public goods provision but ethnic diversity does not necessarily translate into ethnic divisions or conflict. In this book I have argued that one of the conditions under which the presence of more people of different ethnic affiliations need

---

[25] Most of the political economy scholarship is based on correlations between public goods provision and measures of ethnic diversity but the robustness of these associations is endangered by the potential endogeneity of the measure of ethnic heterogeneity and relatedly the possibility of reverse causality (Banerjee, Iyer, & Somanathan 2008: 20). In a review of the scholarship on which the diversity-development deficit thesis is based, Banerjee et al. (2008) explicitly discuss this issue of potential endogenecity and point to problems in the way that it has been tackled by influential studies. For instance, Alesina et al. (1999) try to address the endogeneity issue by using community fixed effects, but once they include fixed effects, the effect of heterogeneity becomes insignificant or even positive. Banerjee et al. (2008) also express doubts about whether the use of region-level heterogeneity to measure school-level heterogeneity solves all the identification problems in the study by Miguel and Gugerty (2005). Wimmer (2015) shows that contemporary levels of ethnic diversity are endogenous to historical levels of state capacity.

not dampen the provision of social services is when there is a subjective sense of a superordinate identity, such as nationalism or subnationalism. In Kerala, an overarching Malayali solidarity brought together Hindus, Muslims, and Christians, and generated support across religious affiliations for the provision of public goods (Singh 2011). Such an argument about how a unifying overarching identity can mitigate the potentially negative influence of ethnicity on public goods provision is in line with work by Glennerster et al. (2010) and Miguel (2004), as also Charnysh, Lucas, and Singh (2015); Gibson & Gouws (2005); Robinson (2011); Sachs (2009) and Transue (2007) that use experimental set ups to provide evidence for the underlying micro foundations of how a shared national identification fosters prosocial attitudes and cooperative behavior between members of different religious groups. In the most directly relevant study for this book (Charnysh, Lucas, and Singh 2015), my coauthors and I found that the increased salience of a shared Indian identity encouraged prosocial behavior on the part of Indian Hindus towards Indian Muslims.

Other studies have pointed to potential mechanisms through which religious diversity might encourage the provision of social services, including that religious pluralism prompts competing religious entities to provide more social services (Chaves and Gorski 2001);[26] that mixed religious gatherings generate social capital, which encourages interreligious cooperation; that the occupational structure of religious minorities might generate greater demand for the provision of public goods (Mirza 2014);[27] or that religiously diverse places are more likely to elect minority leaders who are in turn more likely to prioritize social services (Bhalotra et al. 2014).[28]

---

[26] Chaves and Gorski (2001: 272) point out that the increase in religious diversity associated with the Protestant Reformation – when the Catholic monopoly gave way to three large multi-nationals (the Catholic, Lutheran and Reformed Churches) and a host of smaller "religious suppliers" such as the Baptists and Unitarians – meant that these were all "forced to battle for territory and people" which led to "improvements in the quantity, quality, and availability of religious products," including essential social services.

[27] Exploiting a natural experiment associated with the expulsion of religious minorities in the partition of India, Mirza (2014) finds that those districts that had a higher proportion of minorities, and therefore higher religious fragmentation during the pre-partition period experienced a slower growth in the number of schools per capita post-partition relative to more homogeneous districts that had a lower proportion of minorities in the pre-partition period. He interprets this finding in terms of the occupational structure of minorities during pre-partition but more importantly, that more religiously diverse places were characterized by social capital created through mixed religious gatherings and that this higher social capital in turn facilitated better collective action, which was a key condition for public school provision.

[28] In a study, also incidentally based on India, Bhalotra et al. (2014: 15) suggest that representation by minorities can improve overall education and health outcomes because minority politicians have stronger preferences for publicly provided services because minority voters are, on average, poorer and so more reliant upon them, but that minorities are not sufficiently residentially segregated for targeting to be feasible; or perhaps there are political incentives for minority politicians to avoid showing favor for members of their own group, and therefore, they prioritize the social welfare of all their constituents. Alternatively, minority leaders may act to

CONCLUSION

This chapter tests the generalizability of the subnationalism argument, which was laid out theoretically in Chapter 2 and developed through the comparative historical analyses of Tamil Nadu and Kerala in Chapter 4, and Uttar Pradesh and Rajasthan, and the shadow case study of Bihar, in Chapter 5. In order to do so, I constructed a valid and reliable indicator of subnationalism and used it to score the strength of subnational solidarity across major Indian states during the post-Independence period. I showed a positive bivariate relationship between subnationalism and literacy as well as education and health expenditures, and a negative relationship between subnationalism and infant mortality rate. Further, in both cross-sectional and time-series cross-sectional regression analyses, the subnationalism index is found to have a positive, statistically significant, and sizable influence on social development outcomes and expenditures across Indian states. In addition, the temporal analysis of Indian states finds that, as we would expect, social expenditures strongly boost development outcomes and that this effect is statistically significant.

In light of the recommendation that "the bar for confirming theories with regression analysis should be very high" (Wilson & Butler 2007: 19), a battery of robustness tests were undertaken. Using different estimation techniques, operationalizing welfare expenditures and outcomes and subnationalism and other explanatory variables in alternate ways, adding more control variables, specifying different lag structures, and slicing time periods differently did not challenge any of the central findings. The time-series, cross-sectional analysis also allowed for the assessment of the validity of a range of prominent alternative explanations for social development and expenditures, namely economic development including income, poverty and inequality; rule by a social-democratic party; the nature of the party system; political competition; and ethnic, specifically religious, fractionalization. The key finding from the point of view of this book is that even after controlling for all or some combination of these variables across various models, subnationalism remained a consistently important and statistically significant predictor of social development across Indian states over time.

Like virtually all statistical analyses, however, this study suffers from its share of limitations, the primary of which is the relatively small sample size. Data on more Indian states over a longer period of time would not only allow for more precise estimates but would also let me specify a more complete model with a larger number of controls. I could also control for time fixed effects through dummies for each year rather than for each decade, as I do presently. Another concern is that by its very nature the key explanatory variable,

provide public goods strategically to attract votes from the majority community. Finally, another possibility, consistent with minority leaders representing minority interests, that Bhalotra et al. (2014: 15) propose is that minority leaders prioritize reducing interreligious conflict, and greater and more equitable provision of public goods is a means towards this end.

subnationalism, is relatively slow-moving. There is substantial variation in the strength of subnationalism across Indian states, but because the strengthening or weakening of subnational solidarity is a gradual process, the cohesiveness of the subnational community varies little over time within a single state. This could, in certain situations, raise the fear of a bias in estimates. However, insofar as the statistical analysis in this chapter is undergirded by historical case analyses, these shortcomings are less troubling than they might be for a purely statistical analysis.

DATA APPENDIX

TABLE A6.1. *Alternative Estimate: Time-Series Cross-Sectional OLS Estimates of Determinants of Social Development and Expenditures across Indian States (1971–2001)*

	1.1 Lit	1.2 IMR	2.1 Education expenditure	2.2 Health expenditure	2.3 Non-development expenditure	3.1 Lit	3.2 IMR
Subnationalism	0.716*** (0.139)	-2.348*** (0.703)	0.014*** (0.007)	0.028*** (0.006)	-0.526*** (0.153)		
Income per capita	-0.000 (0.000)	-0.002 (0.002)	0.000*** (0.000)	0.000*** (0.000)	0.001# (0.001)	-0.000 (0.000)	-0.001 (0.002)
Left party rule	0.013 (0.505)	-0.304 (1.300)	-0.018 (0.020)	-0.011 (0.023)	0.390 (0.630)	0.325 (0.503)	-1.256 (1.287)
Two-party competition	-0.090 (0.277)	0.227 (1,184)	0.026* (0.046)	0.015 (0.014)	-0.471 (0.338)	-0.116 (0.286)	0.316 (1.197)
Closeness of political competition	0.001 (0.006)	0.009 (0.029)	-0.000 (0.013)	-0.000 (0.000)	-0.001 (0.008)	0.001 (0.007)	0.013 (0.029)
Ethnic diversity	5.174*** (1.472)	-28.127*** (5.733)	0.026 (0.053)	-0.099* (0.058)	2.980** (1.424)	3.846*** (1.463)	-30.030*** (5.980)
Poverty	0.043*** (0.014)	-0.167*** (0.054)	0.002*** (0.001)	0.001* (0.001)	0.004 (0.015)	0.026* (0.014)	-0.134*** (0.051)
Inequality	-0.095 (0.738)	-1.489 (3.245)	0.004 (0.046)	0.066 (0.051)	-1.535* (0.915)	0.003 (0.753)	-1.547 (3.233)
Literacy rate	0.889*** (0.018)					0.920*** (0.018)	

	(1)	(2)	(3)	(4)	(5)	(6)	(7)
Education expenditure	0.905*** (0.032)	0.892** (0.361)					−7.907*** (2.957)
Health expenditure			0.834*** (0.030)	1.056* (0.618)			
Non-dev expenditure					0.748*** (0.31)		
IMR						0.777*** (0.035)	0.800*** (0.072)
1970s	−0.020 (0.021)		0.075*** (0.022)	0.458** (0.443)	−2.513*** (0.474)	0.000 (0.0)	0.000 (0.0)
1980s	0.076# (0.031)	2.858*** (0.464)	0.177*** (0.035)	1.342** (0.590)	−2.422*** (0.628)	−8.440*** (1.902)	−2.876# (1.822)
1990s	0.066# (0.042)	4.715*** (0.630)	0.186*** (0.042)	2.276*** (0.744)	−1.259* (0.690)	−13.572*** (2.859)	−5.611** (2.217)
2000s	0.000 (0.0)	16.455*** (1.097)	0.000 (0.0)	13.242*** (1.222)	1.226 (1.339)	−14.550*** (5.337)	−4.278 (4.498)
Constant	0.147 (0.169)	−1.626 (2.677)	−0.024 (0.173)	−3.090 (3.089)	14.659*** (3.599)	54.080*** (12.319)	61.842*** (14.836)
N	482	490	482	490	496	357	357
R^2	0.950	0.973	0.945	0.972	0.793	0.913	0.912

# $p < 0.15$, * $p < 0.10$, ** $p < 0.05$, *** $p < 0.01$.

Figures in cells are Prais-Winsten regression coefficients.

Figures in parentheses are panel corrected standard errors with lagged dependent variables and standard errors corrected for panel heteroskedasticity.

Time dummies included.

TABLE A6.2. *Alternative Estimate: Time-Series Cross-Sectional OLS Estimates of Determinants of Social Development and Expenditures across Indian States (1971–2001)*

	1.1 Lit	1.2 IMR	2.1 Education expenditure	2.2 Health expenditure	2.3 Non-development expenditure	3.1 Lit	3.2 IMR
Subnationalism	0.716***	−2.348***	0.014***	0.028***	−0.526***	−0.000	−0.001
	(0.166)	(0.736)	(0.005)	(0.006)	(0.150)	(0.008)	(0.027)
Income per capita	−0.000	−0.002	0.000***	0.000***	0.001#	−0.000	−0.001
	(0.000)	(0.002)	(0.000)	(0.000)	(0.000)	(0.000)	(0.002)
Left party rule	0.013	−0.304	−0.018**	−0.011*	0.390#	0.325	−1.256
	(0.333)	(1.544)	(0.008)	(0.006)	(0.256)	(0.336)	(1.473)
Two-party competition	−0.090	0.227	0.026***	0.015	−0.471#	−0.116	0.316
	(0.308)	(0.788)	(0.009)	(0.013)	(0.319)	(0.352)	(0.897)
Closeness of political competition	0.001	0.009	−0.000	−0.000	−0.001	0.001	0.013
	(0.009)	(0.025)	(0.000)	(0.000)	(0.007)	(0.008)	(0.027)
Ethnic diversity	5.174***	−28.127***	0.026	−0.099**	2.980*	3.846*	−30.030***
	(2.001)	(10.159)	(0.027)	(0.044)	(1.701)	(2.095)	(9.574)
Poverty	0.043**	−0.167**	0.002***	0.001**	0.004	0.026#	−0.134**
	(0.017)	(0.067)	(0.001)	(0.001)	(0.013)	(0.016)	(0.061)
Inequality	−0.095	−1.489	0.004	0.066#	−1.535	0.003	1.547
	(1.013)	(2.695)	(0.037)	(0.044)	(1.068)	(1.022)	(2.725)
Literacy rate	0.889***					0.920***	
	(0.019)					(0.019)	
Education expenditure			0.905***			1.056**	
			(0.025)			(0.433)	

236

	(1)	(2)	(3)	(4)	(5)	(6)	(7)
Health expenditure							−7.907** (3.705)
Non-dev expenditure					0.748*** (0.039)		
IMR	0.892*** (0.320)	0.777*** (0.071)		0.834*** (0.025)			0.800*** (0.072)
1970s	2.858*** (0.688)	14.550*** (3.411)	−0.020 (0.017)	0.075*** (0.019)	−2.513*** (0.520)	0.458** (0.215)	4.278 (3.994)
1980s	4.715*** (1.199)	6.110*** (2.290)	0.076*** (0.026)	0.177*** (0.027)	−2.422*** (0.617)	1.342*** (0.502)	1.401 (2.2664)
1990s	16.455*** (1.293)	0.978 (1.267)	0.066** (0.026)	0.186*** (0.031)	−1.259** (0.557)	2.276*** (0.842)	−1.333 (1.921)
2000s		0.000	0.000	0.000	1.226 (0.991)	13.242*** (1.614)	0.000
Constant	−1.626 (3.054)	39.530** (15.888)	0.147 (0.139)	−0.024 (0.152)	14.659*** (4.782)	−3.090 (3.993)	57.564*** (20.972)
N	490	357	482	482	496	490	357

# p < 0.15, * p < 0.10, ** p < 0.05, *** p < 0.01.

Figures in cells are random effects generalized least squares regression coefficients with lagged dependent variables and robust standard errors clustered by state name. Time dummies included in all models.

TABLE A6.3. *Time-Series Cross-Sectional OLS Estimates of Determinants of Social Development and Expenditures across Indian States with Alternative Measures of Social Expenditures (1971–2001)*

	Education expenditure (%)	Health expenditure (%)	Social expenditure (%)	Social expenditure (per capita)	Development expenditure (per capita)
Subnationalism	0.502**	0.413***	1.009***	0.073***	0.105***
	(0.203)	(0.099)	(0.307)	(0.018)	(0.015)
Income per capita	−0.002***	−0.001***	−0.003***	0.000***	0.000***
	(0.001)	(0.000)	(0.001)	(0.000)	(0.000)
Left party rule	0.326	0.159	3.033***	0.164***	−0.003
	(0.643)	(0.300)	(0.915)	(0.053)	(0.047)
Two-party competition	0.429	0.029	0.213	0.036	0.033
	(0.328)	(0.174)	(0.536)	(0.031)	(0.026)
Closeness of political competition	−0.015**	0.005	−0.000	−0.001	−0.001
	(0.007)	(0.004)	(0.012)	(0.001)	(0.001)
Ethnic diversity	16.439***	0.984	2.338	−0.261#	−0.543***
	(1.914)	(0.882)	(3.315)	(0.165)	(0.134)
Poverty	0.084***	0.023***	0.063**	−0.003*	−0.002*
	(0.016)	(0.008)	(0.027)	(0.002)	(0.001)
Inequality	0.041	0.542	1.291	0.444***	0.286***
	(0.784)	(0.457)	(1.465)	(0.130)	(0.070)
1970s	−0.517	0.621**	0.000	0.000	0.274***
	(0.482)	(0.248)	(0.000)	(0.000)	(0.037)
1980s	−0.069	−0.054	0.613	0.316***	0.710***
	(0.571)	(0.301)	(0.921)	(0.050)	(0.053)
1990s	0.202	−2.087***	−1.136	0.000	0.000
	(1.186)	(0.649)	(1.723)	(0.000)	(0.000)
2000s	0.202	−2.087***	35.314***		0.971***
	(1.186)	(0.649)	(1.723)	(0.000)	(0.000)
Constant	14.156***	4.881***	33.036***	2.161***	2.759***
	(2.896)	(1.640)	(5.021)	(0.469)	(0.315)
N	490	490	378	294	482
R^2	0.582	0.392	0.715	0.814	0.901

# $p < 0.15$, * $p < 0.10$, ** $p < 0.05$, *** $p < 0.01$.
Figures in cells are Prais-Winsten regression coefficients.
Figures in parentheses are panel corrected standard errors with first-order auto-regressive correction.
Time dummies included.

TABLE A6.4. *Time-Series Cross-Sectional OLS Estimates of Determinants of Social Development and Expenditures across Indian States Using Language Component of Subnationalism Index (1971–2001)*

	1.1 Lit	1.2 IMR	2.1 Education expenditure	2.2 Health expenditure	2.3 Non-development expenditure
Language	17.246***	−8.011#	0.318***	0.252***	−7.572***
	(1.453)	(5.143)	(0.067)	(0.072)	(1.280)
Income per capita	0.005**	−0.014***	0.000***	0.000***	0.003***
	(0.001)	(0.003)	(0.000)	(0.000)	(0.001)
Left party rule	2.782*	−6.344**	0.049	0.049	−0.841
	(1.437)	(3.233)	(0.041)	(0.048)	(1.077)
Two-party competition	−0.688	1.691	0.053**	0.030	−0.834
	(0.629)	(2.001)	(0.027)	(0.028)	(0.614)
Closeness of political competition	−0.031*	0.114**	−0.001**	−0.001*	−0.002
	(0.014)	(0.045)	(0.001)	(0.001)	(0.014)
Ethnic diversity	49.573***	−116.289***	0.497***	−0.277*	11.643***
	(4.683)	(11.939)	(0.139)	(0.162)	(3.431)
Poverty	0.068**	−0.174*	−0.001	−0.002*	0.027
	(0.031)	(0.105)	(0.001)	(0.001)	(0.030)
Inequality	0.465	−0.579	0.102	0.244**	−4.313***
	(1.526)	(4.750)	(0.092)	(0.099)	(1.509)
1970s	2.199***	164.683***	0.142***	0.249***	−3.202***
	(0.913)	(17.550)	(0.039)	(0.042)	(0.877)
1980s	8.831***	150.589***	0.504***	0.584***	−6.059***
	(1.101)	(17.130)	(0.047)	(0.052)	(1.045)
1990s	14.954***	136.265***	0.691***	0.704***	−3.951***
	(1.320)	(16.672)	(0.057)	(0.062)	(1.244)
2000s	27.456***	135.909***			1.823
	(2.377)	(16.084)			(2.255)
Constant	1.066		2.101***	1.012***	49.291***
	(5.615)		(0.332)	(0.359)	(5.58)
N	491	370	482	482	496
R^2	0.839	0.623	0.857	0.771	0.688

# $p < 0.15$, * $p < 0.10$, ** $p < 0.05$, *** $p < 0.01$.
Figures in cells are Prais-Winsten regression coefficients.
Figures in parentheses are panel corrected standard errors with first-order auto-regressive correction.
Time dummies included.

TABLE A6.5. *Time-Series Cross-Sectional OLS Estimates of Determinants of Social Development and Expenditures across Indian States Using Subnational Mobilization Component of Subnationalism Index (1971–2001)*

	1.1 Lit	1.2 IMR	2.1 Education expenditure	2.2 Health expenditure	2.3 Non-development expenditure
Subnational Mobilization	11.807***	−33.002***	0.179***	0.117*	−5.391***
	(1.169)	(6.070)	(0.061)	(0.066)	(1.141)
Income per capita	0.004**	−0.005#	0.000***	0.000***	0.003***
	(0.001)	(0.003)	(0.000)	(0.000)	(0.001)
Left party rule	2.135	−3.108	0.039	0.048	−0.404
	(1.724)	(3.055)	(0.046)	(0.049)	(1.121)
Two-party competition	−1.466**	2.027	0.044**	0.020	−0.357
	(0.680)	(1.868)	(0.027)	(0.028)	(0.613)
Closeness of political competition	−0.042***	0.151***	−0.001**	−0.001*	0.003
	(0.015)	(0.046)	(0.001)	(0.001)	(0.015)
Ethnic diversity	45.525***	−97.792***	0.432***	−0.301*	13.104***
	(5.162)	(10.488)	(0.153)	(0.168)	(3.437)
Poverty	0.066**	−0.152#	−0.000	−0.002	0.023
	(0.034)	(0.095)	(0.001)	(0.001)	(0.030)
Inequality	−0.628	−0.943	0.102	0.248**	−3.765**
	(1.633)	(4.657)	(0.093)	(0.101)	(1.502)
1970s	3.431***	0.000***	0.163***	0.279***	−4.740***
	(1.008)		(0.038)	(0.041)	(0.866)
1980s	10.449***	−17.005***	0.530***	0.635***	−8.176***
	(1.201)	(2.803)	(0.047)	(0.051)	(1.024)
1990s	16.833***	−35.331***	0.717***	0.753***	−5.646***
	(1.459)	(3.575)	(0.058)	(0.062)	(1.250)
2000s	28.954***	−41.436***			0.152
	(2.580)	(6.804)			(2.291)
Constant	7.847	162.524***	2.157***	1.000***	47.286***
	(5.993)	(16.198)	(0.335)	(0.359)	(5.480)
N	492	371	486	486	500
R^2	0.814	0.674	0.8571	0.764	0.671

# $p < 0.15$, * $p < 0.10$, ** $p < 0.05$, *** $p < 0.01$.
Figures in cells are Prais-Winsten regression coefficients.
Figures in parentheses are panel corrected standard errors with first-order auto-regressive correction.
Time dummies included.

TABLE A6.6. *Time-Series Cross-Sectional OLS Estimates of Determinants of Social Development and Expenditures across Indian States Using Absence of Separatist Movement Component of Subnationalism Index (1971–2001)*

	1.1 Lit	1.2 IMR	2.1 Education expenditure	2.2 Health expenditure	2.3 Non-development expenditure
Absence of Separatist movement	6.135*** (0.901)	−6.336** (2.913)	0.316*** (0.039)	0.169* (0.040)	−1.363* (0.814)
Income per capita	0.007*** (0.001)	−0.015*** (0.003)	0.000*** (0.000)	0.000*** (0.000)	0.001 (0.000)
Left party rule	2.093 (1.708)	−5.056# (3.328)	0.038 (0.046)	0.039 (0.048)	−0.831 (1.135)
Two-party competition	−0.881 (0.665)	1.560 (1.985)	0.051* (0.027)	0.027 (0.028)	−0.482 (0.633)
Closeness of political competition	−0.026* (0.015)	0.109** (0.046)	−0.001* (0.001)	−0.001# (0.001)	−0.004 (0.015)
Ethnic diversity	56.297*** (5.408)	−119.321*** (12.362)	0.631*** (0.142)	−0.136 (0.156)	8.936*** (3.463)
Poverty	0.100*** (0.034)	−0.181* (0.108)	0.000 (0.001)	−0.001 (0.001)	0.002 (0.031)
Inequality	−0.671 (1.653)	0.354 (4.948)	0.099 (0.092)	0.240** (0.098)	−3.784** (1.535)
1970s	3.356*** (1.004)	161.954*** (18.212)	0.156*** (0.038)	0.282*** (0.040)	−3.941*** (0.897)
1980s	9.984*** (1.221)	148.744*** (17.792)	0.522*** (0.047)	0.647*** (0.050)	−6.930*** (1.078)
1990s	15.081*** (1.456)	135.129*** (17.323)	0.697*** (0.057)	0.765*** (0.060)	−4.263*** (1.288)
2000s	25.455*** (2.547)	135.196*** (16.681)			2.787 (2.321)
Constant	3.556 (6.125)	0.000 (0.000)	2.062*** (0.334)	0.876*** (0.354)	48.239*** (5.610)
N	492	371	486	486	500
R^2	0.809	0.609	0.852	0.771	0.668

# p < 0.15, * p < 0.10, ** p < 0.05, *** p < 0.01.
Figures in cells are Prais-Winsten regression coefficients.
Figures in parentheses are panel corrected standard errors with first-order auto-regressive correction.
Time dummies included.

TABLE A6.7. *Time-Series Cross-Sectional OLS Estimates of Determinants of Social Development and Expenditures across Indian States Using Subnationalist Party Component of Subnationalism Index (1971–2001)*

	1.1 Lit	1.2 IMR	2.1 Education expenditure	2.2 Health expenditure	2.3 Non-development expenditure
Subnationalist Party	3.024***	−6.479**	0.059	0.129***	−1.617*
	(1.035)	(3.898)	(0.039)	(0.039)	(0.876)
Income per capita	0.007***	−0.014***	0.000***	0.000***	0.001
	(0.001)	(0.003)	(0.000)	(0.000)	(0.001)
Left party rule	0.920	−4.542	0.042	0.036	−0.719
	(1.678)	(3.457)	(0.046)	(0.049)	(1.141)
Two-party competition	−0.097	1.851	0.046*	0.016	−0.390
	(0.610)	(1.951)	(0.027)	(0.028)	(0.625)
Closeness of political competition	−0.014	0.112**	−0.001*	−0.001#	−0.004
	(0.014)	(0.046)	(0.001)	(0.001)	(0.015)
Ethnic diversity	50.537***	−109.016***	0.488***	−0.393**	11.763***
	(6.329)	(13.730)	(0.168)	(0.171)	(3.625)
Poverty	0.017	−0.166#	0.000	−0.001	0.003
	(0.032)	(0.108)	(0.001)	(0.001)	(0.030)
Inequality	−2.028	2.324	0.097	0.231**	−3.384**
	(1.681)	(5.046)	(0.093)	(0.099)	(1.556)
Education expenditure					
Health expenditure					
1970s	2.160**	0.000	0.137***	0.282***	−3.729***
	(0.971)		(0.039)	(0.040)	(0.899)
1980s	6.729***	−12.700***	0.484***	0.641***	−6.554***
	(1.221)	(3.040)	(0.048)	(0.050)	(1.079)
1990s	10.089***	−25.832***	0.647***	0.746***	−3.879***
	(1.434)	(3.855)	(0.058)	(0.060)	(1.288)
2000s	20.662***	−24.486***			3.458#
	(2.562)	(7.501)			(2.319)
Constant	19.143***	148.839***	2.221	1.065***	45.375***
	(6.165)	(18.504)	(0.337)	(0.357)	(5.630)
N	492	371	486	486	500
R^2	0.799	0.608	0.849	0.769	0.671

# $p < 0.15$, * $p < 0.10$, ** $p < 0.05$, *** $p < 0.01$.
Figures in cells are Prais-Winsten regression coefficients.
Figures in parentheses are panel corrected standard errors with first-order auto-regressive correction.
Time dummies included.

7

Conclusion

This book is an attempt to answer a question that first struck me many years ago, living in and visiting different parts of India, and for which I had yet to find a convincing explanation – Why are Indian states with identical democratic institutions characterized by such dramatically different levels of social development? My research has led me in directions that I would not have been able to predict at the outset. In the preceding chapters I have sought to delineate the unexpected relationship that I found between the politics of a shared solidarity on the one hand, and social policy and development outcomes on the other. Based on a combination of comparative historical case studies and regression analyses, I have sought to delineate the ways in which the strength of subnational solidarity has influenced the provision of public goods and social policy outcomes across Indian states over time.

It is important to clarify here that I am not suggesting that the levels of social development in a province are a product only and/or entirely of its strength of subnationalism. As I discuss in Chapter 2, there are a number of factors that have been hypothesized to influence public goods provision. In Chapter 6, I show that a number of these factors, such as the level of economic development, the nature of electoral competition, and ethnic diversity, have a statistically significant effect on education and healthcare expenditures and outcomes across Indian states. This book, however, puts the spotlight on a novel and hitherto understudied variable – a sense of solidarity with a political community, in this case, subnationalism – that even after controlling for a range of alternative explanations, has an additional significant and substantial effect on social expenditures and development. An argument about the causes of social welfare that does not take into account the strength of solidarity with the political-administrative unit that is in charge of social policy is therefore, I suggest, an impoverished one.

This chapter begins by exploring the theoretical and empirical generalizability of the subnationalism argument, and then highlights the primary contributions including the policy implications of the book as a whole.

EXTENDING THE ARGUMENT: HOW SOLIDARITY WORKS FOR WELFARE BEYOND INDIAN STATES

The central theoretical insight of this book, as stated in the introduction, is how a shared solidarity can generate a politics of the common good, and relatedly how political-administrative units that are the locus of collective identification and engender a sense of solidarity are more likely to initiate a progressive social policy and witness developmental gains. The analysis so far has focused on a shared identity at the subnational level, but the argument is not limited to subnationalism and is generalizable to a sense of "we-ness" at different units of analysis above and below – at the national level and to municipalities, cities, villages, or localities. Also, this book has focused in particular on education and health expenditures and outcomes, but theoretically a shared identity should be conducive to public goods and services more broadly defined. While it is beyond the scope of this book to systematically test it, in this section I will bring together an influential, if diverse, set of scholarly works that point to the plausibility of this more general argument. I will begin with exploring the extension of the theory to the national level. Connecting to classic writings that point to the constructive role of national solidarity for the success of collective projects, I then specifically discuss an important body of works that points to the critical role of national identification in the institution of welfare policies. I move onto examining the most immediate empirical extension of the argument, that is, whether subnationalism also generates a progressive social policy and encourages social development in other subnational units across the world through a brief analysis of two of the most prominent contemporary cases of subnationalism in the world – Quebec and Scotland. I conclude by briefly bringing together studies, including one that I conducted, that showcase the micro logic of the theory presented in this book, that is, that the increased salience of a shared superordinate identity encourages pro-social behavior toward fellow members even if they belong to different subgroups. The overall attempt in discussing these otherwise very distinct pieces of scholarship is to weave together a diverse but rich tapestry of evidence in support of a robust and general relationship between a shared identity, and public goods provision and social development.

National Solidarity and Social Welfare

It is useful to begin a discussion of the theoretical reach of the argument presented herein by connecting it to a classic set of writings that point to the constructive potential of a collective and specifically national, identity. Scholars at

least as far back as Saint-Simon, Friedrich List, and John Stuart Mill, for example, emphasized a sense of national solidarity as an important determinant
in pushing people to think of, and work toward, a common national project,
whether it be, in Saint-Simon and List's case, a country's economic development, or, in Mill's case, the working of representative institutions.

In his classic work on "Economic Backwardness in Historical Perspective,"
Gershenkron (1962) describes how in early nineteenth-century France,
Saint-Simon had come to a realization about the power of "faith," a "New
Christianity," but also, critically, national identification as an important, even
necessary impetus "to break through the barriers of stagnation in a backward
country, to ignite the imaginations of men, and to place their energies in the
service of economic development." This, according to Gershenkron, was "a
stronger medicine ... than the promise of better allocation of resources or
even of the lower price of bread," "a more powerful stimulus than the prospect of high profits" (1962: 24). The key role that Saint-Simon believed that
national identification might play in mobilizing the French for the tasks of
economic development is exemplified by his (successful) urging, shortly before
his death, of Rouget de Lisle, the by-then aged author of the French national
anthem "Marseillaise," to compose a new national anthem, an "Industrial
Marseillaise" that called upon the "enfants de la patrie" to become "enfants de
l'industrie" (Gershenkron 1962: 24). Writing a few decades after Saint-Simon,
List outlined a critical role for the national economy, which was the outcome
of national ideas, national institutions, and people's desire to belong to a
nation, in a country's industrial and economic development. Specifically, for
List, national solidarity was a key factor in an individual's long-term investment decisions, which were critical for economic growth. An individual was
more likely to be willing to invest in the future if she thought of herself not
just as a producer or a consumer but also as a member of a national community (Levi-Faur 1997: 170). Individuals who were not bound by this sense of
national solidarity and community were likely to have much narrower time
horizons since, as List wrote, "mere individuals do not concern themselves for
the prosperity of future generations – they deem it foolish ... to make certain
and present sacrifices in order to endeavor to obtain a benefit which is as yet
uncertain and lying in the vast field of the future (if events possess any value at
all); they care but little for the continuance of the nation" (List 1841: 173; cited
in Levi-Faur 199: 170). A similar logic is proposed by Mill, who argued that a
common national culture and the attendant "common sympathies" were necessary for the working of representative institutions. He wrote, "It is in general
a necessary condition of free institutions that the boundaries of government
should coincide in the main with those of nationalities ... Among a people
without fellow-feeling, especially if they read and speak different languages,
the united public opinion, necessary to the working of representative government, cannot exist" (Mill 1875: 298). As noted in Chapter 1, contemporary
political philosophers in the liberal nationalist mold, including Miller (1995)

and Tamir (1993), have continued this line of thinking by stressing a shared identity as a precondition for widespread support for institutions and policies that promote social justice (Mason 2000: 118).

Focusing on the narrower outcome of interest for this book, there is a substantial and long-standing body of scholarship that points to the central role of national solidarities in the institution of social welfare policies. The so-called 'Progressive theorists', which include scholars of varying ideational leanings, have all drawn a link between the strengthening of national identities in the wake of the Second World War, and the establishment of modern welfare states in Europe (Burke 1985). Instrumental reasons including ensuring the physical health of a population such that it could effectively wage wars, or during and after the war, rewarding civil support for the war effort were obviously important. However, it is clear that the war brought the idea of a national collective to the forefront and that this fostered what was variously described as an "aura and practice of solidarity" (Furniss & Tilton 1977), a "societal cohesion" (Wilensky 1975), an "enlargement of obligations" (Titmuss 1958), and a "new universalism" (Sleeman 1973), which were key drivers for the institution of radical and unprecedented "cradle to the grave" social policies including education, health, and housing that were made freely available to all citizens irrespective of their ability to pay for them (Burke 1985). McEwen and Parry summarize such positions, writing that "During the Second World War, explicit associations were made between the solidarity and national consciousness engendered by the war, and the task of constructing a post-war welfare state" (2005: 45).

Following the influential work of Tilly (1985), wars are recognized as arguably the most important drivers of state-building. Yet, it is worth noting here that despite the substantial body of evidence showing the critical role that it has played in the institution of social policies, war is not an explanatory variable that figures prominently in the contemporary scholarship on welfare states (see, for example, Mares and Carnes 2009, for a review). The studies analyzed previously might then together be seen, on the one hand, to provoke an addendum to classic theories of how war not only makes states but also welfare states, while also on the other hand injecting a new, or rather bringing back, a "forgotten" set of arguments about the role of national solidarity in the establishment of welfare states, especially in Europe.

Interestingly, even discussions about the recent retrenchment of the welfare state in Europe are characterized by an underlying assumption about the role of national solidarity in supporting social policies. In the UK, rollbacks to the National Health Service, an institution whose establishment is especially strongly associated with the nationalism arising from the Second World War, have prompted opposition movements that have deliberately invoked the national cohesion associated with the war. The "UK uncut" campaign, for instance, urged supporters to hold 1940s-style "street parties" in opposition to the cuts, as a reminder that just like at the time of the war, when people "partied in the streets and dreamt of what we could achieve as a people and a country," we were "all in this together" (Noakes & Pattinson 2013: 12). Further, the main mechanism by which increased ethnic and racial diversity has been hypothesized to strain the welfare state is through its corroding of the national solidarity and trust required to sustain support for redistributive policies. Wolfe and Klausen, for example, argue "if the ties that bind you to increasingly diverse fellow citizens are loosened, you are less likely to share your resources with them" (2000: 8). Summarizing the argument that policies that recognize and accommodate ethnic diversity weaken the welfare state, Banting and Kymlicka write that "citizens have historically supported the welfare state, and been willing to make sacrifices to support their disadvantaged co-citizens because they viewed these citizens as 'one of us', bound together by a common identity and common sense of belonging ... Multi-cultural policies are said to corrode this overarching common identity. MCPs (multi-cultural policies) tell citizens that what divides them into separate ethno-cultural groups is more important than what they have in common, and that co-citizens from other groups are therefore not really 'one of us' " (2006: 11). Even those who argue against this position, such as Banting and Kymlicka (2006), do not deny the importance of bonds of solidarity and trust, but instead contest the claim that multicultural policies necessarily reduce a sense of national "oneness."

The importance of a sense of a shared national identity and community for the institution of social welfare policies also features strongly in analyses of the historic difficulties that the United States has faced in instituting comprehensive social programs on a national scale. Scholars such as Skocpol have pointed out that the end of the Civil War did not lead to reconciliation between the North and South but instead to a "regionally bifurcated federal polity" (1995: 31). The conflict and its aftermath had reinforced solidarity on opposing sides and led to the solidification of the view that "We are two people" (Marx 1998: 125). There was little sense of an overarching 'American identity'; instead two distinct and opposed political communities, the Union North and Confederate South, continued to command popular loyalties. This resulted in a situation, as scholars such as Skocpol (1992), Carruthers (1993), and Quadagno (1996) have shown, in which (fairly generous) social welfare policies were instituted in the North and South for fellow members, especially those who had put their lives on the line for their "nation."[1] The absence of any sense of a shared American identity, however, meant that for more than five decades after the end of the civil war and the reestablishment of a United States of America, there were no national social programs. It does appear, however, that when it is successfully invoked,

---

[1] In the federal government's pension program, a sharp distinction was made between "deserving veterans of the Civil War (former Union soldiers)" and the "undeserving (veterans of the Confederate Army) (Carruthers 1993: 675). Such a distinction cut across class and race lines (ibid.) such that black Union veterans had about as good a chance of getting a pension as similarly situated white veterans (Skocpol 1992: 138). Most Southern states also allocated pensions to Confederate soldiers (Quadagno 1996: 244).

a shared American identity encourages support for social programs, such as public schools (Transue 2007).

Across the border in Canada, which has historically instituted a much wider social welfare program than the United States, a recent study has shown that Canadians who have higher national identity scores, calculated based on their response to survey questions, are more likely to support redistribution, including support for public healthcare and state pensions (Johnston, Banting, Kymlicka, & Soroka 2010).

Among African countries, where in general, the absence of a sense of national cohesion that can bring together diverse ethnic groups is seen as one of the major causes of backwardness, it is notable that the countries that have worked to create a more cohesive national identity are also the ones that have seen relatively more promising development trajectories. Persson (2012), for example, points out that Botswana was characterized by broadly similar levels of ethnic diversity and substantially lower state capacity than other African states such as Zambia and Uganda at the time of their independence from colonial rule. Yet, through the postcolonial period, Botswana has been seen as the African development "success story," doing a much better job not just at economic development but also at providing essential social services and, consequently, ensuring the welfare of its people, than almost all its African counterparts. This, Persson (2012) argues, is to a large extent because Botswana has worked to successfully create a cohesive national solidarity.[2]

The way in which national identification has promoted public goods provision in Africa is powerfully illustrated by Miguel (2004), who uses a colonial-era national boundary placement as a natural experiment to compare the provision of primary schools, as well as the maintenance of water wells, in neighboring districts across the border in western Kenya and western Tanzania. Miguel finds that, unlike their Tanzanian counterparts, ethnically diverse Kenyan communities have lower public goods provision than ethnically homogeneous ones, and he traces these differences in regions that were otherwise similar on many key geographical, historical, and institutional dimensions in the 1960s to the more serious and consistent nation-building strategies undertaken by Tanzania. An overarching sense of national solidarity has allowed Tanzanians of different ethnic groups to act collectively to raise money for primary schools and maintain school infrastructure and common wells, while diverse communities in adjoining Kenya typically fail. Looking at the national level for further evidence, Miguel (2004) suggests that the broad patterns of faster economic growth, better governance, institutional quality, and regime stability in Tanzania also reflect its nation-building project, which stands out in sub-Saharan Africa as a whole.

---

[2] In their analysis of Botswana, Acemoglu, Johnson, and Robinson (2002) point to a different but not necessarily contradictory explanation, the "good institutions" of private property and the rule of law.

Subnational Solidarity and Social Welfare

Moving down from the national to the more familiar subnational unit of analysis, in this section I will review some scholarship that suggests how subnational solidarity influences social policy beyond Indian states. I will be drawing, in particular, on the important work by Beland and Lecours (2008), to briefly analyze two prominent cases – Quebec in Canada and Scotland in the UK, which have significant control over social policy and where subnationalism has been an important driver of relatively generous welfare regimes.

Subnationalism and Social Welfare in Quebec

Nationalism among French Canadians who had inhabited the region of Quebec since the early 1600s emerged in opposition to British rule in the region in the mid-eighteenth century. The Quebec Act of 1774 allowed French Canadians to retain their distinctive language (French), faith (Catholicism), and way of life. Pressure from French Canadian elites played a critical role in Canada being founded as a federal rather than as a unitary state in 1867. In the division of powers, the Catholic Church, the central institution for French Canadians, continued its traditional role as the primary provider of social services in Quebec. The Quiet Revolution (late 1950s to the late 1960s) marked the secular transformation and territorial rooting of French-Canadian nationalism. Beland and Lecours argue that as the definition of Quebecois subnationalism shifted away from religion to territory and language, and Quebec came to be seen as the homeland of the French-speaking political community, the Quebec state rather than the church came to be seen as bearing the exclusive responsibility for promoting the well-being of Quebeckers. Toward this promotion of Quebecois welfare, the provincial government rapidly intervened in various sectors of the economy, taking control notably, of the provision of key social services. Beland and Lecours write that "these changes brought a new configuration to the nationalism-social policy nexus: social policy expansion was a direct consequence of the Quiet Revolution's new nationalism" (2008: 54).

Quebec governments began to resist federal social policies on the grounds that these could not adequately address the "special" needs of Quebeckers. Beland and Lecours argue that only the Quebec government came to be seen as bearing "the unique responsibility of overseeing a Francophone majority" (2008: 57). Through the 1960s, politicians from the Union Nationale and the Parti libéral du Québec (PLQ) demanded greater autonomy to be able to preserve the two pillars of Quebecois distinctiveness – its language and distinctive, egalitarian ethos. The Parti Quebecois (PQ), founded in 1968, articulated its demand for political independence for Quebec in very similar terms. Beland and Lecours point out that for Rene Levesque, the founder of PQ, the emphasis placed on the French language when making a case for independence was inseparable from the ideal of forging a more just and equal Quebecois society (2008: 59). So long as it remained a province of Canada, PQ leaders argued, the Quebec government would be unable to institute radically progressive social policies and create a more equal and socially developed Quebecois society (Beland & Lecours 2008: 59).

By the end of the 1970s, according to Beland and Lecours, "the PQ could credibly depict itself as both a 'sovereignist' and a social-democratic party. It had connected nationalism to left-leaning positions on social policy" (2008: 60). It campaigned on the commitment to the protection and further-ing of the French language and social issues of universal and publicly funded healthcare, education, and social assistance regimes, support for progressive taxation and substantial redistribution. During its first term in power, the PQ enacted key legislation on both language and social policy. The Charter of the French Language (Bill 101) declared French as the only official language of Quebec. Some of the important social policies that were instituted included raising the minimum wage to make it the highest in North America, introduc-ing income-maintenance programs, and adjusting the taxation rates to benefit the lowest-income strata (Beland & Lecours 2008: 60).

Both the referendums for sovereignty in 1980 and 1995, especially the former, brought out the connection between subnationalism and social wel-fare quite starkly. In advance of the 1980 referendum, Quebeckers were por-trayed as "more just, solidaristic and egalitarian than 'elsewhere in Canada'"; the referendum was framed as "paving the way for a more egalitarian society grounded in a strong vision of national-Quebec-solidarity" (Beland & Lecours 2008: 62). The PQ responded to the narrow defeat of the 1995 referendum by enacting a series of seminal social policies such as the $5 per day daycare and the universal prescription drug insurance plan. Quebec governments continued to maintain university tuition rates at the lowest levels in North America. PQ leaders framed these policies as a reflection of the "different cultural and politi-cal ethos" in Quebec as compared to the rest of Canada, "meaning that it is more egalitarian and solidaristic." Another 'proof' of the distinctive nature of Quebec's values and ideology was said to be the adoption by the PQ in 2002 of an "anti-poverty law" that formally committed the government to guarantee income support for low-income residents of the province (Beland & Lecours 2008: 69). The 2000 platform of the Parti Québecois stated, "Unitary Canada is developing following a vision different than ours, and its decisions stand in the way of our social projects." Similarly, in 2005 the Bloc Quebecois (BQ) argued that when it comes to social matters, "Quebec is a creative society with high levels of solidarity" but warned that "the measures that have allowed Québec to become the society in North America where wealth is most exten-sively redistributed are threatened by the structures of Canadian federalism" (69–70).

Beland and Lecours write that today support for social policy has become such an essential component of Quebecois identity that references to the retrenchment of welfare policies in Quebec have become tantamount to an attack on Quebecois subnationhood (72). Consequently, almost all political parties in Quebec support, although to varying extents, the maintenance of a proactive social policy.[3]

In fact, Quebec's social policies have had an agenda-setting effect on Canadian welfare legislation. The province's generous and innovative social policies are regularly cited as models to emulate by left-leaning elites in other provinces and at the national level. Quebec's child care program, in particular, has been presented as a template for the adoption of a similar Canadian national policy (Beland & Lecours 2008: 87). In sum, Beland and Lecours argue that "Quebecois nationalism has formulated claims about the existence of a national and territorial unit of solidarity according to which Quebeckers have an obligation to each other's welfare ... the PQ [states] that 'solidarity and sharing are a key component of Quebec society's values' ... Such claims about the Quebecois identity legitimize the quest for further policy decentralization and the related creation of social programs unique to the state" (2008: 89).

Subnationalism and Social Welfare in Scotland

Scottish subnationalism, which is widely believed to predate the "artificial" union with England (Hanham 1969: 10), has, from its inception, been closely tied to a fraternal, communitarian spirit and rooted in a progressive philosophy (McCrone & Paterson 2002: 119). The "powerful" Scottish myth was that "Scottish society was a more collectivist, egalitarian, and solidaristic society than England" (Beland & Lecours 2008: 123).[4] Being Scottish came

[3] Beland and Lecours note that while the PQ has obviously been the most vociferous in this regard, even non-sovereigntist parties of different ideological hues such as the center-left PLQ and the more neoliberal Action Democratique du Quebec (ADQ) have supported welfare policies. To the surprise of many political observers, both these parties backed the PQ's anti-poverty legislation in the early 2000s because endorsing such a resolution was "perceived as being 'in sync' with Quebec's identity" (2008: 69). Beland and Lecours describe how both the PLQ and the ADQ have witnessed the political cost of turning away from social welfare policies. In the 1998 provincial elections, the PLQ leader Jean Charest's proclamation of the end of the Quiet Revolution and the beginning of a new era in Quebec politics came to be widely perceived as a neoliberal attack on the Quebec social welfare model. The PQ responded by portraying Bouchard as someone who "did not love Quebec" and who was voicing ideas that were in violation of cherished Quebecois solidaristic ideals. The PQ defeated the PLQ in these elections (Beland & Lecours 2008: 72). Similarly, the ADQ's espousing of neoliberal policies, such as school vouchers and a flat tax during the 2003 provincial elections, sparked sharp criticisms from the PQ, and to a lesser extent the PLQ, that the ADQ's platform would "destroy the building blocks of the Quebec nation" (Beland & Lecours 2008: 73). The ADQ quickly backtracked on these policies and emphasized its commitment to keeping Quebec's signature day care and drug insurance plans, but this could not prevent it from registering dismal election results.

[4] On this "Scottish myth," Beland and Lecours cite David McCrone, who argues that allusions to Scots' commitment to equality and fairness can be seen in particular forms of Scottish vernacular, for example in "we're a' Jock Tamson's bairns" and in Robert Burns's song "A Man's A Man for A' That" (1992: 90).

to be seen as reflective of a belief in social justice (Henderson & McEwen 2005). This close association of Scottish subnational solidarity with progressive policy preferences has been maintained and strengthened in recent years. Interestingly, survey evidence from the late 1990s and early 2000s shows that even after controlling for sociocultural factors Scots are more likely than the English to support redistribution and collectivist policies and values (Beland & Lecours 2008: 127; McEwen 2002: 77; Paterson 2000: 200). In 1998, Donald Dewar, then Secretary of State for Scotland, for example, described Scotland as "a country where equality of opportunity and social justice are central to our sense of self" (cited in McEwen 2003: 12).

The union with England allowed Scotland to preserve, even foster, a sense of distinctiveness. The autonomous institutions of Scots law, the Kirk (the Church of Scotland), and the education system were the key historic symbols around which the Scottish nation was built (Beland & Lecours 2008: 103). In its broadest form, Scottish subnationalism has promoted some kind of institutionalized political autonomy within the United Kingdom (109). Bills on Scottish home rule were presented to parliament by liberal MPs in the 1920s. Home rule claims surfaced sporadically throughout the late nineteenth century and early twentieth century – 1886 saw the formation of the Scottish Home Rule Association, which demanded devolution within the existing structure of the United Kingdom. Through the 1930s and 1940s, a number of subnationalist parties – the Scottish Party (SP), the National Party of Scotland (NPS), and the Scottish National Party (SNP), which was formed as a result of the amalgamation of the SP and NPS – continued to demand political self-determination, conceptualized either as devolution within the union or separation, in turn understood either as complete separation or dominion status for Scotland.

Scottish home rule became popular in the 1950s, and there was a widespread belief at this time that home rule was required because Scots' more progressive preferences for welfare legislation were being held back by English conservatism (Beland & Lecours 2008: 110). The connection between the subnationalist demands for home rule and a progressive social policy was strengthened in the wake of the Thatcherite reforms rolling back the welfare state. Beland and Lecours write that "Scottish political and intellectual leaders reacted to Thatcher's ideas by arguing that Scotland was a more collectivist, egalitarian and decent society than was England ... Scotland needed political autonomy to be in a position to develop more progressive social policies than those enacted in Westminster" (117–20). As Mooney and Williams put it, "In the case of Scotland social policy was central to the demand for devolution itself." The establishment of the Scottish Parliament came to be portrayed as a prerequisite for the pursuit of a progressive social policy and the collective welfare of all Scots.

The Scottish Constitutional Convention in 1995 formally proposed the creation of a parliament for Scotland as necessary for public policy "which accords more closely with its (Scotland's) collective and community traditions" (Scottish Constitutional Convention 1995: 2–3; cited in McEwen 2006: 543). Similarly, one of the arguments proposed by the Scotland Forward campaign was that representatives of the Scottish people could enact "social policies more in line with the solidaristic preferences of Scots on redistribution and the specific needs of Scotland" (Beland & Lecours 2008: 120). Organizations such as Doctors for Devolution, repeatedly emphasized that devolution held the potential to improve Scotland's poor health indicators, which have long lagged behind those of England. Survey evidence suggests popular support for this idea. In a 1996 poll, 80 percent of Scots agreed with the statement, "Money for Scotland's public services such as schools and hospitals would be spent more wisely if the decisions about it were made by the Scottish Parliament." Sixty-four percent of respondents believed that under an autonomous Scottish Executive, public services such as health and education would get better (as compared to only 55% and 43% who felt that governance and the economy respectively would improve) (Beland & Lecours 2008: 121).[5] Incidentally, there is also some survey evidence in support of the idea that being a Scottish subnationalist makes you more likely to support collective welfare. Data from the 2001 and 2003 Scottish Social Attitudes surveys show that Scots who see themselves as solely or mostly Scottish, and Scots who favor devolution, are typically more supportive of redistribution (128).

   The subnationalism-social welfare link has been rhetorically and symbolically strengthened since the devolution of power to the national, unicameral legislature of Scotland in 1999. It was no coincidence that the inauguration of the Scottish parliament featured the singing of Robert Burns's "A Man's A Man for A' That," a song that, as mentioned earlier, showcases the distinctly egalitarian national values of Scotland. The subnationalism-social welfare link has also critically been borne out in terms of the social policies instituted in post-devolution Scotland. In her study of "Welfare Solidarity in a Devolved Scotland," Nicola McEwen writes that "In the early period of devolution, the Executive has been keen to promote its social justice ambitions. All three of Scotland's First Ministers have felt the need to stress that social justice is at the heart of their programs for government, and the objective against which all other policies will be measured. On his election as First Minister, Jack McConnell insisted he would ensure that 'everything we do, every policy we initiate and every spending decision that we make is measured against the standard of social justice' (Scottish Parliament Official Report, 22 November, 2001, col. 4155; see Scottish Parliament Official Report, 9 September, for a similar sentiment expressed by his predecessor, Henry McLeish)" (McEwen 2003: 12). Despite considerable institutional and fiscal constraints, Scotland has instituted

---

[5] It is notable that Scots voted in favor of the creation of a Scottish Parliament, even though an overwhelming number (76%) expected that this would lead to higher taxation (Surridge & McCrone 1999: 45).

seminal social policies that made it seem the "happening place" for social policy in the UK (Beland & Lecours 2008: 129). Notable among these policies is the Scottish Parliament's decision to abolish the up-front tuition fees in higher education (131) as well as to ensure Scottish teachers substantially higher salaries than their English counterparts. The "most distinct and far-reaching social measure adopted in the aftermath of devolution," however, is the enactment of a universal personal long-term care program for the elderly. This free personal care for the elderly "is grounded in the universalistic logic of social citizenship"; "the implementation of this program involves a significant reterritorialization of social policy grounded in the idea of sub-state national solidarity. In England, the Blair government decided to enact means-tested benefits even though it could afford citizenship-based provisions like the ones now provided in Scotland" (Beland & Lecours 2008: 134–35).

Based on Beland and Lecour's analysis, the Scottish executive's commitment to welfare seems likely to be maintained and even strengthened, as virtually all political parties in Scotland espouse a more progressive social agenda than their counterparts in the UK. The manifestoes of all of Scotland's primary political parties – the Scottish Labor Party, the SNP, the Scottish Liberal Democrats as well as the smaller Scottish Green party and the Scottish Socialist party – all emphasize that the Scottish government has the responsibility to act in the "national interest," providing efficient, inclusive, and affordable social services to all residents of Scotland.

The prospect of establishing a more generous welfare state is also at the heart of the SNP's continued demand for independence. The party argues that while devolution was good for Scotland insofar as it allowed for the enactment of important social legislation, independence would be even better because the Scottish Parliament, which at present is constrained both financially and in terms of the issues over which it has constitutional jurisdiction, could cast a wider and stronger net of social policies. Much like the Parti Québecois, the SNP has argued that an independent Scotland would be able to offer more generous social benefits than it can from within the UK and create a "fairer Scotland" and a "healthier Scotland" (Beland & Lecours 2008: 128–29). Strikingly, one of the main platforms in the campaign for the 'yes' vote in the (eventually unsuccessful) 2014 referendum, was called the 'Common Weal' and sought a more socially egalitarian and progressive Scotland through a move from a politics of "me first" to "all-of-us first." In addition to its emphasis on cultural policy and the promotion of Scottish music and the arts, through the organization for instance of a series of festivals, the policy agenda of the Common Weal emphasized a range of social policies including, in an interesting parallel with Quebec, subsidized childcare (see http://www.allofusfirst .org). It is also notable that, like in Quebec, Scotland has begun to emerge as a source of policy innovation in the social domain and as a consequence has put pressure on Westminster to implement similar policies in England. There has, for example, been growing pressure in the UK to implement free, long-term care for the elderly of the kind introduced in Scotland (Beland & Lecours 2008: 137).

In summary, Beland and Lecours argue that historically, but especially since the Thatcher era, "Scottish politics has featured claims about the existence of a national unit of solidarity where Scots have a special obligation to each other's welfare … the drive towards home rule was often framed in terms of Scotland's need to be able to develop progressive social policy." Post-devolution Scotland has initiated a number of distinctive social policies, which have been "framed as a necessary consequence of Scottish values" (Beland & Lecours 2008: 141). Demands for greater institutional autonomy, including sovereignty, continue to be powerfully framed as essential for furthering the collective welfare of the Scottish nation.

Solidarity and Welfare: The Micro-logic at the Individual Level

Traveling with the core insight of this book all the way down to the individual, in this section I will briefly review a batch of recent studies whose findings support a key micro logic of the argument presented in the book, that is, that a shared superordinate identification can prompt individuals to adopt more positive attitudes and behavior, even toward those from a different subgroup. As I have already noted, there is evidence from a number of different surveys that individuals who hold a strong sense of superordinate – national or subnational – identification, are also more likely to support redistributive policies (see, for example, Johnston et al. 2010; Beland and Lecours 2008: 128). Further, and more convincingly, there are a number of studies, best seen as real-world extensions of the common in-group identity model discussed in Chapter 2, that use survey experiments to show that the increased salience of politically relevant superordinate identities, such as national identities, trigger more positive opinions of, and also cooperative actions toward, members of different ethnic groups.

Transue (2007) for example, finds that when self-identified whites in America perceive a shared American identity, they are more likely to support a tax increase that benefits public schools (perceived as benefiting both whites and African Americans) as well as a tax increase to specifically fund educational programs that only benefit minorities. Based on an analysis of original survey data collected in a border region of Malawi and Zambia, Robinson (2011) argues that the degree of national identification extends trust in co-nationals, even across ethnic lines. Gibson and Gouws (2002) find that for white South Africans, a superordinate South African national identity reduces intergroup antipathy (cited in Transue 2007:79). The positive effect of national identification is also found to extend to individual behavior. Sachs (2009), for example, finds that priming an Indonesian national identity appears to strongly and significantly raise generosity by the Javanese toward the non-Javanese.

Additionally and critically, in an online survey experiment, my co-authors and I found that the increased prominence of an Indian national identity promoted generous behavior across even a historically competitive ethnic boundary. Recategorization within a shared Indian identity made members of a majority high-status ethnic group (Hindus) less likely to discriminate in altruistic giving toward a rival, relatively low-status ethnic minority (Muslims). We found that when the salience of the national identity is primed, Hindu respondents contribute roughly the same amount to members of the out-group (Muslims) as to fellow members of the in-group (Hindus). Moreover, increasing the salience of a common national identity has a strong, positive, and statistically significant effect on contributions from Hindus to Muslims (Charnysh, Lucas, & Singh 2015).

These studies together, provide evidence for the working of the micrologic of the argument of this book in India as well as different empirical contexts by showing how a superordinate national identification can encourage pro-social attitudes and behavior toward fellow nationals even if they are from a rival ethnic group.

IMPLICATIONS FOR SCHOLARLY DEBATES

This book pushes us away from the dominant scholarly view of the destructive implications of collective identities. If, following Huntington (1996: 20–21), "we know who we are only when we know who we are not and often only when we know whom we are against," all identities are based on some exclusion and even animosity. Nationalism, in particular, has come to be strongly associated with such odious tendencies as intolerance, xenophobia, and chauvinism (Cederman et al. 2011; Hroch 1985; Kedourie 1966; Pavković 2000; Saideman & Ayres 2008; Schrock-Jacobson 2012; Snyder 2001), with a distinguished political theorist going so far as to call it "the starkest political shame of the twentieth century" (Dunn 1979: 55). This book marks a radical departure from these pejorative understandings by showcasing the relatively underemphasized constructive potential of collective identities such as nationalism and subnationalism.

Relatedly and importantly, this book complicates the conventional wisdom around the negative relationship between ethnic diversity and public goods provision. That ethnic diversity has a detrimental impact on public goods provision, as noted elsewhere in this book, is seen to be a virtually settled matter (Banerjee, Iyer, & Somanthan 2005: 639). So much so that scholars working in this research tradition have sought to move beyond this "consensus" to the "next step" of analyzing the micrologic of how ethnic diversity dampens the provision of essential social services (Habyarimana et al. 2009: 5). Yet as I have discussed at length in other works (see Singh and vom Hau 2014; also Singh 2011; Lieberman and Singh 2012), serious conceptual problems with the political economy scholarship might instead suggest a need to pause and take a step back. This book represents an addition to a bulging quiver of studies taking empirical aim at the diversity-development-deficit thesis, showing how in varying contexts around the world and at different points in time, ethnic, and in this case, specifically religious, diversity might not be an impediment to the provision of social services (see Singh & vom Hau 2014 for a review). Further, this book presents a theoretical framework, resting on the distinction between the objective and subjective aspects of identity, to explain these contrary findings. Demographic diversity does not necessarily imply a divisive ethnic politics (Posner 2004; Singh 2011). The analysis presented here highlights the importance of one potential set of conditions, the increased salience of a shared superordinate identity, under which ethnic diversity might not dampen the provision of social services (see also Glennerster et al. 2010; Miguel 2004,).

This book also seeks to contribute to the scholarship on the determinants of social welfare policies and outcomes social welfare. Not only does it push forward this literature by putting the spotlight on a relatively underexplored factor, the power of a collective solidarity, but it also offers a fresh analytical window in to long-established perspectives, notably traditional class-based arguments, about welfare. Class formation, especially in the tradition of E. P. Thompson, is seen as a process of forging new solidaristic identities (Thompson 1963). Class mobilization has been argued to be most successful in pushing for universalistic welfare policies when it is based on an encompassing solidarity (Esping-Andersen and Korpi 1987: 81–83; Fantasia 1989). In India, class-based mobilization in Kerala has succeeded in pushing a far-reaching and successful set of land reforms – Kerala is today characterized by one of the more egalitarian patterns of landholding found in most developing countries (Herring 1983) as well as a progressive social policy. Conversely, in West Bengal, where incidentally the Left has enjoyed longer, more stable tenures than in Kerala, class mobilization has been relatively ineffective at redistributing land to the poor and has not prioritized the social sector to nearly the same extent. Moreover, class mobilization in West Bengal been much more divided and violent. This has been explained in terms of the peculiar "solidaristic" nature of class mobilization in Kerala, which has led it to be, on the whole, peaceful and also supportive of "cooperative and inclusionary social policies" (Heller 2000: 1060, 1066, 515, 519). So the question then is under what conditions is class mobilization likely to be more solidaristic? My historical analysis traces the "encompassing" and "universalistic" nature of class politics in Kerala (Heller 2000: 494) to its embeddedness in a broader Malayali subnationalism. Seen in this light, the solidarity associated with a unifying superordinate identity such as subnationalism might be seen as the missing element in overly deterministic accounts of class mobilization.

This book may also be seen as an addition to the rich body of scholarship that looks beyond strictly defined rational actor models of human behavior (see for example Sen 1977; Collard 1978; Etzioni 1988). In India, as in many other parts of the developing world, elites can and often do secede from state provision of welfare; government schools and health centers cater predominantly to the poor. Why then do elites prioritize social welfare? Contrary to explanations that point to the strategic reasons for elites to do so, notably to maximize their chances of winning elections, this book showcases the powerful motivational consequences of an affective subnational solidarity. A shared subnational solidarity pushes elites to prioritize the collective welfare of the subnational community as a whole and consequently to back social policies, such as those for primary schooling and basic healthcare, which have a strong redistributive component. Such "solidary" behavior (Wilson and Clark 1961) on the part of elites is in fact much more common than the emphasis on the self-interest axiom by studies within the rational choice or public choice framework would predict. Interestingly, Downs himself wrote that "in reality, men are not always selfish, even in politics. They frequently do what appears to be individually irrational because they believe it is socially rational – that is, it benefits others even though it harms them personally. For example, politicians in the real world sometimes act as they think best for society as a whole even when they know their actions will lose votes" (Downs 1957: 29). Indeed, there is considerable evidence that political elites, far from being driven only or even primarily by considerations of reelection, are motivated by altruism, commitment to a cause and a desire to 'do good'. In his classic study of Congressional committees, Richard Fenno (1973) pointed to the motivations of legislators to make good public policy. James Kau and Paul Rubin (1982) argue that beliefs about the structure of the world and ways of improving it are better predictors of congressional votes on regulatory legislation than the economic interests of constituents or campaign contributors. Kalt and Zupan (1984) point to the pervasiveness of legislators prioritizing collective, publicly interested goals over reelection concerns.

Pro-social behavior on the part of elites is part of the broader phenomenon of the everyday transgression of self-interest on the part of people across the world when they, for instance, make the effort to assist a stranger in need; donate money, material possessions, and blood; volunteer their time; pay their taxes or vote. There is considerable evidence that human beings do not behave in an entirely self-interested fashion even in their economic interactions (Collard 1978). In a variety of situations, individuals "do not invest in something that is unproductive for others but that would increase there own income" (cited in Meier 2006). Scores of laboratory experiments have found evidence for pro-social behavior. Mansbridge notes "hundreds" of experiments with a range of ultimatum games that reward self-interested behavior, which demonstrate "a stubborn refusal on the part of a significant fraction (usually 25 to 30 percent) to take rational self-interested action, even under conditions of complete anonymity and no possibility of group punishment" (1990: 17). In a path breaking study based on experimental ultimatum games in 15 small-scale societies around the world, Henrich et al. (2001: 77) report that "the canonical model of the self-interested, material-payoff-maximizing actor is systematically violated."

A range of different explanations have been put forward to explain why everyday people across the world act beyond their self-interest, accepting costs to themselves to behave in a pro-social way. These include the power of additional, often dominating motives such as empathy, sympathy, commitment to a principle, ideology, fairness and justice. The argument presented in this book may be seen as closest to scholars who have stressed the importance of "solidary" (Wilson and Clark 1961) and normative and affective incentives for action (Etzioni 1988).[6] Social solidarity is a foundational concept for sociologists since Durkheim. The subnationalism argument is closest to affective conceptions of solidarity and theories of cohesiveness that emphasize the importance of a sense of "we-ness" (Doreian and Fararo 1998). It has important resonances with the communitarian paradigm, especially as articulated by Etzioni (1988), which sees emotional attachment to a community – an affective "we" – as an enabling condition for individual action. It can also usefully be seen as presenting an important source of motivation for "public spirit-edness" (Mansbridge 1990). The idea that subnationalism serves as an affective basis for action is also in line with a move in the field of judgment and decision-making away from the traditional focus on "cold" deliberative and reason-based decision-making toward the relatively neglected influence of "hot processes" related to affect (Peters et al. 2006). Affective processes, including emotion and even subconscious intuition, are now at the center of some of the most important theories of decision-making (Gigerenzer 2007). This should not be surprising given that neurologists are confident that pure reason is in itself insufficient for an individual to arrive at a decision; the ability to "feel" is an essential component of decision-making[7] (Damasio et al. 1994).

Insofar as the solidarity generated by subnational identification is an affective process and generates a set of ideas about the importance of the welfare of the subnational community as a whole, the argument presented here is also in line with the so-called ideational turn in political science, which argues for ideas as an important, even "primary source of political behaviour" (Beland & Cox 2011). Jacobs (2011) writes that "an ideational theory is a causal proposition in which the independent variable is a cognitive structure and the dependent

---

[6] Drawing together evidence from across a range of disciplines, Etzioni argues that the "most important bases of choices" are "affective and normative" rather than rational and self-interested (1988: 4, 90, 151; cited in Mansbridge 1990: 18).

[7] This is demonstrated most famously in the case of Phineas Gage, a nineteenth-century U.S. railway construction worker who had an iron tamping rod accidentally driven through his head, as well as in the case of other patients who suffered damage, either through an accident or illness, to their ventromedial prefrontal cortex, Neurologists found that even if all of the instruments of rationality and cognition typically viewed as important for decision-making such as logical and reasoning skills, a working memory, ability to process factual knowledge, possession of social knowledge, were intact, as was the case with Phineas, the impairment of an ability for emotion and feeling somehow caused him, and others like him, to become unable to engage in decision-making activities.

variable is a response to a choice situation by actors who possess that cognitive structure." He goes on to specify that cognitive structures are generalized mental representations of some feature of the social or natural world and that such representations may have either normative or descriptive content. The subnationalism argument very much aligns with such a specification, the emphasis on the collective welfare of all members of the subnational community being seen as a cognitive structure with a normative content.

The perception and prioritization of the common good that a sense of subnational identity is hypothesized to generate is also very much in line with broader conceptions of rationality beyond the widely criticized lens of neoclassical economics. Max Weber, for example, famously set out a conceptualization of different forms of rationality, in particular the distinction between "formal rationality" and "substantive rationality." According to Weber, "formal rationality" refers to a simple means-ends rational calculation – you have a goal and you take rational steps, that is, steps that are based on past experience, observation, logic, or science – to attain that goal, while the concept of "substantive rationality," on the other hand, refers to goal-oriented rational action within the context of ultimate ends or values, which in this case would be the promotion of the welfare of the subnational community as a whole (Elwell 2013). In a different but analogous way, one might think of working for the collective welfare in self-interested terms, except that there is a recasting of interests beyond the individual to include the interests of the – in this case subnational – group as a whole (De Cremer & Van Gugt 1999: 887; Brewer 1979: 322). This is akin to the move away from the long-standing debate between idealist and materialist theories to recognize the interplay between ideas and interests, specifically that the ideas held by individuals affect how they define their interests in the first place (Blyth 2002; Campbell 2002).

POLICY IMPLICATIONS

The primary and relatively novel policy recommendation that emerges from this book is that, as far as possible, there should be an overlap between the locus of social policy-making and social solidarity. This gives rise to two sets of suggestions. First, the jurisdiction over social policy should be vested with the political-administrative unit with which citizens most strongly identify. Second, policies should be initiated to increase the extent of popular identification with the administrative unit which has primary authority over social policy.

The scholarship on social welfare is characterized by arguments both for and against decentralization. My research suggests that a judgment about which is better for social development cannot be reached in isolation from the question of which political-administrative unit commands the primary allegiance of the people. On the one hand, scholars such as Immergut (1992), and Huber, Ragin, and Stephens (1993), argue that constitutional structures, such as federalism, that disperse political power and offer multiple points of influence on the making and implementation of policy are inimical to the working and expansion of the welfare state. This book, however, suggests that if the primary locus of citizens' identification is subnational, devolution of power might in fact boost the provision of social welfare. Decentralization of state welfare need not lead to a "race to the bottom," as scholars of Europe fear, but might instead allow substate regions to tap territorial solidarity and identity, strengthening and bringing social policy and distributional questions back into the consideration of development policy (McEwen & Moreno 2005: 34). My discussion of how innovative social policies instituted in Indian states, such as the midday meal program in Kerala and Tamil Nadu, and the *Shiksha Karmi* program in Rajasthan, were later adopted by the central government, shows that federal state structures might stimulate social policy innovation by serving as an arena for policy experimentation and a vehicle for change at the national level.

On the other hand, there is also a large body of scholarship that argues that decentralized governments are more effective than centralized governments at the provision of public services. It has almost become conventional wisdom that decentralized governments are closer to the needs of the people and more agile and innovative, while centralized governments are distant and rigid (Taylor 2008). In the words of Pranab Bardhan, decentralization is the "rage" and has been at the center stage of policy experiments in the last couple of decades, for instance in terms of devolution in the European Union, states' rights in the United States, as well as across a large number of developing countries in Latin America, Africa, and Asia, with the World Bank embracing it as one of the major governance reforms on its agenda (Bardhan 2002: 185).

This study cautions against such a doctrinaire commitment to a policy of decentralization. It suggests that decentralization is likely to be more successful if the political-administrative unit to which power is being devolved is a locus of elite and popular solidarity. If the political-administrative unit to which power is devolved has no affective meaning for the people and their popular representatives, if they feel no sense of belonging to it, decentralization might not lead to significant gains in social development.[8]

In addition to ensuring congruence between the unit of social policy making and popular identification, a second recommendation of this book toward improving social development is the initiation of policies to encourage popular solidarity with the unit of social policy-making. It suggests that in addition to direct interventions in the social sector, such as literacy campaigns or vaccination drives, policies aimed toward fostering a shared identity and solidarity among residents of a state could also promote public goods provision. This

---

[8] In a distinct but analogous argument, Mansuri and Rao (2013) argue that participatory development projects designed to improve service delivery and access to local public goods are far more likely to be successful when they are based on 'organic' participation by the community; as compared to when the participation is induced, either by donor agencies or by national governments.

opens up a novel and entirely distinct realm of possible policy interventions for improving education and health outcomes. The promotion of a state language, arts and cultural forms; designation and celebration of 'state days' and festivals; and glorification of state heroes are likely to foster subnationalism and in doing so, can further social policy and development. By highlighting the potential inter-linkages between different policy arenas, such as initiatives in arts and culture and social policies, this book encourages policy-makers not to approach social policy in isolation. It also shows the potentially constructive aspects of expenditure often seen as "wasteful," such as the state sponsorship of festivals; renaming of roads and cities; and the erection of statues.[9]

CONCLUSION

In this book I have attempted to put forward a new theoretical explanation for social welfare. In contrast to studies that stress economic development, the ideology of the political party in power, the nature of the party system, ethnic diversity, and the strength of civil society, I hypothesize that variations in levels of social expenditures and development can be traced to differences in the cohesiveness of the political community. Through a comparative historical analysis of five Indian provinces and a statistical examination of all Indian states from the 1960s to 2000, I have sought to show how the strength of subnationalism influences state social policy and social development. In this chapter I have pointed to the ways in which this study might push forward the influential bodies of scholarship on identity politics and on social welfare, and put forward a clear and new policy recommendation that has important implications for contemporary debates about decentralization.

Most studies of social welfare in developing countries such as India portray a very bleak scenario. These analyses are by no means inaccurate. The story of social development in India has, on the whole, been one of state neglect and societal inertia. Within this generally dismal picture, however, this study may be seen as representing a ray of optimism. The analysis here suggests that even under conditions of relatively limited economic resources, a multitude of ethnic groups, and the weakness or absence of left parties, a political unit might be able to register social gains if it is a locus of elite popular solidarity. Most studies seek to showcase ways to overcome the adverse effects of collective

---

[9] The erection of statues has become a particularly controversial issue in light of BSP chief Mayawati's installation of thousands of statues of herself and other *dalit* leaders such as Ambedkar and Kanshi Ram during her tenure as UP Chief Minister. While the scale and the expenses associated with Mayawati's so-called statue spree are certainly excessive, it is not so much her decision to install statues but that she has chosen to erect statues of figures that have come to be seen as polarizing that is problematic. This study suggests that if she had instead decided to install (far fewer) statues of a figure viewed and/or portrayed as a unifying UP state hero, it would have been less egregious insofar as it could have served to increase the cohesiveness of subnational solidarity in UP.

identities. In contrast, this study highlights their creative potential – how collective identities can be a force for the common good. It suggests that societal solidarity and cohesion are not only ends desirable in themselves, but can also serve as a basis for better social services. Whether or not a state is characterized by a shared solidarity can have profound implications for the welfare and well-being of its residents.

Bibliography

(1956). *Lok Sabha debates on the Report of the States Reorganisation Commission, 14th December to 23rd December, 1955.* New Delhi, Lok Sabha Secretariat.

(2000). CM unveils Thiruvalluvar statue. *Hindu.*

(2001). Speech by Jai Narayan Vyas. 1952–53. Budget Speeches by finance ministers in the Rajasthan Legislative Assembly (1952–1980). *Rajasthan Assembly Secretariat.*

(2001) "French Parliament Approves Limited Autonomy for Corsicans." *The New York Times*, December 19, sec. World.

(2002) "Rajasthan Starvation Deaths." *The Times of India*, October 24, 2002. http://timesofindia.indiatimes.com/india/Rajasthan-starvation-deaths/article-show/26101220.cms.

(2003) "Tamil Nadu Human Development Report." The Government of Tamil Nadu.

(2004–2005). Rajasthan Planning Commission Report. Rajasthan.

(2004). An area of darkness. *Economist.*

(2005) {14 April} Tamil Nadu Seeks National Status for 'Thirukkural'. *Hindu.*

(2006). Another Muslim political front launched in U.P. *Hindu.*

(2007). Raje seeks outstanding fund for Sarva Shiksha Abhiyan. *Hindu.*

(2007). UP lags in implementing welfare schemes. *South Asian.*

(2007) "WOMEN SCIENTIST OF INDIA." *Scribd*, September 26. https://www.scribd.com/doc/330287/WOMEN-SCIENTIST-OF-INDIA.

(2007) "Another Muslim Political Front Launched in U.P." *Hindu*, July 6. http://www.thehindu.com/todays-paper/tp-national/tp-otherstates/article3100930.ece.

(2008). Karunanidhi 'satisfied' with measures taken by Centre. *Hindu.*

Abizadeh, A. (2002). "Does Liberal Democracy Presuppose a Cultural Nation? Four Arguments." *American Political Science Review* 96(3): 495–502.

Acemoglu, D. (2001). "Good Jobs versus Bad Jobs." *Journal of Labor Economics* 19: 1–22.

Acemoglu, D., S. Johnson, and J. A. Robinson (2001). "The Colonial Origins of Comparative Development: An Empirical Investigation." *American Economic Review* 91 (December): 1369–401.

(2002). *An African Success Story: Botswana* (No. 3219). CEPR Discussion Papers.

Achen, C. (2000). "Why Lagged Dependent Variables Can Suppress the Explanatory Power of Other Variables." *Annual Meeting of the Political Methodology Section of the American Political Science Association Meeting*, Los Angeles.

   (2002). "Toward a New Political Methodology: Microfoundations and ART." *Annual Review of Political Sciences* 5: 423–50.

Achutanandan, V. S. (2006). "Kerala Initiatives." *Kerala Calling* 4–7.

Adams, G. (2014). Subodh Gupta – Everything Is Inside, National Gallery of Modern Art, New Delhi – Review. *Financial Times*. http://www.ft.com/cms/s/2/3d6279b6-93d0-11e3-a0e1-00144feab7de.html

Adams, J. and B. Bumb (1973). "The Economic, Political and Social Dimensions of an Indian State: A Factor Analysis of District Data for Rajasthan." *Journal of Asian Studies* 33(1): 5–23.

Adolph, C., D. M. Butler, et al. (2005). "Like Shoes and Shirt, One Size Does Not Fit All: Evidence on Time Series Cross-Section Estimators and Specifications from Monte Carlo Experiments." 101st annual conference of the American Political Science Association, Washington, DC.

Ahmed, B. (1970). "Elections and Party Politics in India: A Symposium." *Asian Survey* 10, no. 11 (November): 979–92.

Aiya, V. N. (1906). *Travancore State Manual*. Trivandrum: Government Press.

Alesina, A., R. Baqir, et al. (1999). "Public Goods and Ethnic Divisions." *Quarterly Journal of Economics* 114(4): 1243–84.

Alesina, A., E. Glaeser, et al. (2001). "Why Doesn't the US Have a European-Style Welfare State?" *Harvard Institute of Economics Research Discussion Paper No. 1933*.

Alesina, A., A. Devleeschauwer, et al. (2003). "Fractionalization." Working Paper. National Bureau of Economic Research.

Algan, Y., C. Hémet, and D. Laitin (2011). "Diversity and Public Goods: A Natural Experiment with Exogenous Residential Allocation" (No. 6053). *Discussion Paper series, Forschungsinstitut zur Zukunft der Arbeit*.

Allport, G. (1954). *The Nature of Prejudice*. Cambridge, MA: Addison-Wesley Pub. Co

Anderson, B. (1991). *Imagined Communities: Reflections on the Origin and Spread of Nationalism*. London; New York: Verso.

Anderson, L., Mellor, J., and Milyo, J. (2003). "Inequality, Group Cohesion, and Public Good Provision: An Experimental Analysis." Working Papers 0308, Harris School of Public Policy Studies, University of Chicago.

Annamalai, S. and J. V. Kumar (2000). "CM Announces Award for Proficiency in Thirukural." *Hindu*, January 1.

Armstrong, J. (1982). *Nations before Nationalism*. Chapel Hill: University of North Carolina Press.

Arooran, K. N. (1980). *Tamil Renaissance and Dravidian Nationalism, 1905–1944*. Madurai: Koodal.

Arunima, G. (2006). "Imagining Communities Differently: Print, Language and the (Public Sphere) in Colonial Kerala." *Indian Economic Social History Review* 43(1): 63–76.

Babb, L. A. (2004). *Alchemies of Violence: Myths of Identity and the Life of Trade in Western India*. New Delhi; Thousand Oaks, CA: Sage Publications.

Balasubramaniam, D., S. Chatterjee and D. B. Mustard (2014). "Got Water? Social Divisions and Access to Public Goods in Rural India." *Economica* 81(321): 140–60.

Baldwin, K. and J. Huber (2010). "Economic versus Cultural Differences: Forms of Ethnic Diversity and Public Goods Provision." *American Political Science Review* 104, no. 4 (November): 644–62.

Ban, R., M. Das Gupta, and V. Rao (2008). "The Political Economy of Village Sanitation in South India – Capture or Poor Information?" The World Bank Development Research Group, Human Development and Public Services Team & Poverty Team.

Banerjee, R. (2013). "Elementary Education: Learning the Hard Way." In N. K. Singh and N. Stern, eds., *The New Bihar*. India: HarperCollins.

Banerjee, A. and R. Somanathan (2001). "Caste, Community and Collective Action: The Political Economy of Public Good Provision in India." Working Paper, Department of Economics, MIT.

(2004). "The Political Economy of Public Goods: Some Evidence from India." *Journal of Development Economics* 82(2): 287–314.

Banerjee, A, A. Deaton and E. Duflo (2004). "Health Care Delivery in Rural Rajasthan." *Economic and Political Weekly* 39(9): 944–49.

Banerjee, A., L. Iyer, and R. Somanathan (2005). "History, Social Divisions and Public Goods in Rural India." *Journal of the European Economic Association* 3: 639–47.

Banerjee, A., L. Iyer, and R. Somanathan. (2006). Public Action for Public Goods NBER Working Paper No. 12911.

(2008). "Public Action for Public Goods." *Handbook of Development Economics* 4: 3118–54.

Banerjee, A., R. Banerji, et al. (2008). "Pitfalls of Participatory Programs: Evidence from a Randomized Evaluation in Education in India," NBER Working paper No. 14311.

Banerjee, A. and E. Duflo (2010). "Giving Credit Where It Is Due." *Journal of Economic Perspectives* 24(3): 61–80.

Banerjee, D. and E. Duflo (2004). "Wealth, Health, and Health Services in Rural Rajasthan." *American Economic Review* 92(2): 326–30.

Banting, K. (2000). "Looking in Three Directions: Migration and the European Welfare State in Comparative Perspective." In M. Bommes and A. Geddes, eds., *Immigration and Welfare: Challenging the Borders of the Welfare State*. London: Routledge.

Banting, K. and W. Kymlicka. (2006). *Multiculturalism and the Welfare State: Recognition and Redistribution in Contemporary Democracies*. Oxford University Press.

Bardhan, P. (2000). *Readings in Empirical Microeconomics*. Massachusetts Institute of Technology.

(2002). "Decentralization of Governance and Development." *Journal of Economic Perspectives* 16(4): 185–205.

Barnett, M. R. (1976). *The Politics of Cultural Nationalism in South India*. Princeton: Princeton University Press.

Barrilleaux, C. (1997). "A Test of the Independent Influences of Electoral Competition and Party Strength in a Model of State Policy-Making." *American Journal of Political Science* 41, no. 4 (October): 1462–66.

Basu, K. (1990). *Agrarian Structure and Economic Underdevelopment*. Chur, Switzerland; New York: Harwood Academic Publishers.

(2001). "The Role of Norms and Law in Economics: An Essay on Political Economy." In *Schools of Thought: Twenty-Five Years of Interpretive Social Science*, by Debra Keates and Joan Wallach Scott. Princeton University Press.

Basu, S. (1995). "Intermediate Goods and Business Cycles: Implications for Productivity and Welfare." *American Economic Review* 85(3): 512–31.

Baumeister, R. and E. Finkel (2010). *Advanced Social Psychology: The State of the Science*. New York: Oxford University Press.

Baumgartner, F. and B. Jones (1993). *Agendas and Instability in American Politics*. Chicago: University of Chicago Press.

Bayly, S. (1984). "Hindu Kingship and the Origin of Community: Religion, State and Society in Kerala, 1750–1850." *Modern Asian Studies* 18(2): 177–213.

Beall, J. (1997). "Social Capital in Waste – A Solid Investment?" *Journal of International Development* 9(7): 951–61.

Beck, N. and J. N. Katz (1995). "What to Do (and Not to Do) with Time-Series – Cross-Section Data." *American Political Science Review* 89: 634–47.

(1996). "Nuisance vs. Substance: Specifying and Estimating Time-Series – Cross-Section Models." *Political Analysis* 6(1): 1–36.

(2001). "Throwing Out the Baby with the Bath Water: A Comment on Green, Kim, and Yoon." *International Organization* 55(2): 487–95.

(2004). "Random Coefficient Models for Time-Series-Cross-Section Data." *California Institute of Technology, Division of the Humanities and Social Sciences* Working Papers (1205).

Beland, D. and A. Lecours (2008). *Nationalism and Social Policy: The Politics of Territorial Solidarity*. New York: Oxford University Press.

Béland, D. and R. H. Cox. (2011). "Ideas and Politics," in D. Béland and R.H. Cox (eds), *Ideas and Politics in Social Science Research*, pp. 3–20. Oxford: Oxford University Press.

Berman, S. (1997). Civil Society and the Collapse of the Weimar Republic. *World Politics* 49(03): 401–29.

Besley, T. and M. Kudamatsu (2006). "Health and Democracy." *American Economic Review* 96(2): 313–18.

Besley, T., R. Pande, et al. (2004). "The Politics of Public Goods Provision: Evidence from Indian Local Governments." *Journal of the European Economic Association* 2(2–3): 416–26.

Betancourt, R. and S. Gleason (2000). "The Allocation of Publicly Provided Goods to Rural Households in India: On Some Consequences of Caste, Religion and Democracy." *World Development* 28(12): 2169–82.

Bhat, M., Preston S. and Dyson T. (1984). *Vital rates in India 1961–1981*. Washington DC: National Academy Press.

Bhattacharjee, P. J. (1976). *Population in India: A Study of Inter-State Variations*. New Delhi: Vikas Publishing House.

Birdsall, N. (1999). *Globalization and the Developing Countries: The Inequality Risk*. Remarks at Overseas Development Council Conference, Making Globalization Work, International Trade Center, Washington, D.C.

Björkman, M. and J. Svensson (2007). *Power to the People: Evidence from a Randomized Field Experiment of a Community-Based Monitoring Project in Uganda* (Vol. 6344). World Bank Publications.

(2009). "Power to the People: Evidence from a Randomized Field Experiment on Community-Based Monitoring in Uganda," *Quarterly Journal of Economics* 124(2): 735–69.

Blackburn, S. H. (1989). *Oral Epics in India*. Berkeley: University of California Press.

Blyth, M. (2002). *Great Transformations: Economic Ideas and Institutional Change in the Twentieth Century*. Cambridge: Cambridge University Press.

(2003). "Structures Do Not Come with an Instruction Sheet: Interests, Ideas, and Progress in Political Science." *Perspectives on Politics* 1(4): 695–706.

Boix, C. (2001). "Democracy, Development, and the Public Sector." *American Journal of Political Science* 45:1–17.

Boustan, L. P. (2010). "Was Postwar Suburbanization White Flight? Evidence from the Black Migration." *The Quarterly Journal of Economics* 125(1): 417–43.

Bradshaw, J. (1894). *Sir Thomas Munro and the British Settlement of the Madras Presidency*. Oxford: Clarendon Press.

Brass, P. (1964). *The Congress Party Organization in Uttar Pradesh: The Transformation from Movement to Party in an Indian State*. University of Chicago, Department of Political Science.

(1979). "Elite Groups, Symbol Manipulation and Ethnic Identity Among the Muslims of South Asia." In M. Yapp and D. D. Taylor, eds., *Political Identity in South Asia*, London: Curzon Press.

(1997). *Theft of an Idol: Text and Context in the Representation of Collective Violence*. Princeton: Princeton University Press.

Brass, P. R. (1974). *Language, Religion and Politics in North India*. London; New York: Cambridge University Press.

(1986). "The 1984 Parliamentary Elections in Uttar Pradesh." *Asian Survey* 26(6): 653–69.

Breuilly, J. (1994). *Nationalism and the State*. Chicago: University of Chicago Press.

Breusch, T., M. B. Ward, H. T. M. Nguyen, and T. Kompas (2011). "On the Fixed-Effects Vector Decomposition." *Political Analysis* 19(2): 123–34.

Brewer, M. B. (1979). "In-Group Bias in the Minimal Intergroup Situation: A Cognitive-Motivational Analysis." *Psychological Bulletin* 86(2): 307.

British Library. (2005). *Indian Newspaper Reports, c1868–1942, from the British Library, London*. Marlborough: Adam Matthew Publications.

Brown, D. and W. Hunter (1999). "Democracy and Social Spending in Latin America, 1980–92." *American Political Science Review* 93(4): 779–90.

(2004). "Democracy and Human Capital Formation: Education Spending in Latin America 1980–1997." *Comparative Political Studies* 37(10): 1283–89.

Brown, D. S. and A. M. Mobarak (2009). "The Transforming Power of Democracy: Regime Type and the Distribution of Electricity." *American Political Science Review* 103(02): 193–213.

Brown, M. E. and S. Ganguly (2003). "Introduction." In M.E. Brown and S. Ganguly, eds., *Fighting Words: Language Policy and Ethnic Relations in Asia*. Cambridge; Massachusetts: MIT Press.

Burke, V. (1985). *Guns or Butter?: War and the Making of the Welfare State*. Ann Arbor: University of Michigan Press.

Burstein, P. (2006). "Why Estimates of the Impact of Public Opinion on Public Policy Are too High: Empirical and Theoretical Implications." *Social Forces* 84(4): 2273–89.

Cammett, M. C. and L. M. MacLean (2011). "Introduction: The Political Consequences of Non-state Social Welfare in the Global South." *Studies in Comparative International Development* 46:1, 1–21.

Campbell, J. (2002). "Ideas, Politics, and Public Policy." *Annual Review of Sociology* 28: 21–38.

Carmines, E. G. (1974). "The Mediating Influence of State Legislatures on the Linkage Between Interparty Competition and Welfare Policies." *American Political Science Review* 68(3): 1118–24.

Carruthers, B. G. (1993). "Gender, States, and Social Policies: Skocpol's View." *Law & Social Inquiry* 18(4): 671–88.

Castels, S. (1979). *The Education of the Future: An Introduction to the Theory and Practice of Socialist Education*. London: Pluto Press.

Catt, H. and M. Murphy (2003). *Sub-State Nationalism: A Comparative Analysis of Institutional Design*. London; New York: Routledge.

Cederman, L. E., N. B. Weidmann and K. S. Gleditsch (2011). "Horizontal Inequalities and Ethnonationalist Civil War: A Global Comparison." *American Political Science Review* 105(03): 478–95.

Census Commissioner (1931). *Report on the Census of British India*. New Delhi: Government of India Press.

Chakrabarti, R. (2013). *Bihar Breakthrough: The Turnaround of a Beleaguered State*. New Delhi: Rupa Publications.

Chakravarty, D. (2003). *Muslim Separatism and the Partition of India*. New Delhi: Atlantic Publishers and Distributors.

Chand, V. K. (2006). *Reinventing Public Service Delivery in India: Selected Case Studies*. New Delhi: Sage Publications.

Chandra, K. (2000). *Why Ethnic Parties Succeed: A Comparative Study of the Bahujan Samaj Party Across Indian States*. New York: Cambridge University Press.

Chandra, K. and S. Wilkinson (2008). "Measuring the Effect of 'Ethnicity'." *Comparative Political Studies* 41(4–5): 515–63.

Charnysh, Volha, Christopher Lucas, and Prerna Singh. (2015). "The Ties that Bind: National Identity Salience and Pro-Social Behavior toward the Ethnic Other." *Comparative Political Studies* 48, no. 3 (March 1): 267–300.

Chasin, B. H. and R. W. Franke (1991). "The Kerala Difference." *New York Review of Books* 38.

Chaves, M. and Philip S. Gorski (2001). "Religious Pluralism and Religious Participation." *Annual Review of Sociology* 27: 261–81.

Cherian, P. J. (1999). *Perspectives on Kerala History: The Second Millennium, Kerala State Gazetteers*. Thiruvananthapuram: Government of Kerala.

Chhibber, P. K. (1999). *Democracy without Associations: Transformation of the Party System and Social Cleavages in India*. Ann Arbor: University of Michigan Press.

Chhibber, P. K. and I. Nooruddin (2004). "Do Party Systems Count? The Number of Parties and Government Performance in the Indian States." *Comparative Political Studies* 37(2): 152–87.

Chib, S. S. (1979). *Rajasthan*. New Delhi: Light & Life Publishers.

Chiriyankandath, J. (1993). "Communities at the Polls: Electoral Politics and the Mobilization of Communal Groups in Travancore." *Modern Asian Studies* 27(3): 643–65.

Choudhry, P. (2011). "In Rajasthan's Jaisalmer, Daughters Are Born to Die." *India Today*, 20.

Chowdhary, S. (1999). *Education for All in Rajasthan: A Case-study with Focus on Innovative Strategies*. New Delhi: National Institute of Educational Planning and Administration.

Clark, Peter B. and James Q. Wilson (1961). "Incentive Systems: A Theory of Organizations." *Administrative Science Quarterly* 6(2): 129–66.

Clarke, P. and J. Jha (2006). "Rajasthan's Experience in Improving Service Delivery in Education." In V. K. Chand, ed., *Reinventing Public Service Delivery in India: Selected Case Studies*. New Delhi: Sage Publications.

Cleary, M. (2007). "Electoral Competition, Participation, and Government Responsiveness in Mexico." *American Journal of Political Science* 51(2): 283–99.

Cohn, B. (1998). "Regions Subjective and Objective: Their Relation to the Study of Modern Indian History and Society." In *An Anthropologist among Historians and Other Essays*. Delhi: Oxford University Press.

Collard, D. (1978). *Altruism and Economy: A Study in Non-selfish Economics*. Oxford: Martin Robertson.

Colley, L. (2005). *Britons: Forging the Nation 1707–1837*. New Haven: Yale University Press.

Collier, D. and R. E. Messick (1975). "Prerequisites versus Diffusion: Testing Alternative Explanations of Social Security Adoption." *American Political Science Review* 69(4): 1299–315.

Communist Party of India (CPI), T.-C. C. (1954). "Memorandum Submitted to the States Reorganization Commission, File no. 25/13/54-SRC. 2." *National Archives of India. New Delhi*.

Connor, W. (1978). "A Nation Is a Nation, Is a State, Is an Ethnic Group." *Ethnic and Racial Studies* 1(4): 377–400.

  (1994). *Ethnonationalism: The Quest for Understanding*. Princeton: Princeton University Press.

Controller of Publications (2001). *Census of India*. New Delhi: Government of India Press.

Cook, F. L., with J. Manza. (2002). "A Democratic Polity? Three Views of Policy Responsiveness to Public Opinion in the United States." *American Politics Research* 30(6): 630–67.

Coppedge, M. (1999). "Thickening Thin Concepts and Theories: Combining Large N and Small in Comparative Politics." *Comparative Politics* 31(4): 465–76.

Crawford, D. G. (1908). *A History of the Indian Medical Service: 1800–1915 by Lieutenant-Colonel D.G. Crawford, Bengal Medical Service*. London: W. Thackeray and Co. 1914. In two volumes.

Crooke, W. (1897). *The North-Western Provinces of India: Their History, Ethnology, and Administration*. New Delhi: Asian Educational Services.

Damasio, H., T. Grabowski, R. Frank, A. M. Galaburda, and A. R. Damasio (1994). "The Return of Phineas Gage: Clues about the Brain from the Skull of a Famous Patient." *Science* 264: 1102–05.

Darden, Keith. (2014). *Resisting Occupation: Mass Literacy and the Creation of Durable National Loyalties*. New York: Cambridge University Press.

Darden, K. and A. Grzymala-Busse. (2006). "The Great Divide: Literacy, Nationalism, and the Communist Collapse." *World Politics* 59: 83–115.

Darden, Keith and Harris Mylonas (2015). "Threats to Territorial Integrity, National Mass Schooling, and Linguistic Homogeneity." In Prerna Singh and Mathias vom Hau (eds.), *Ethnicity in Time: Politics, History, and Whether Diversity Undermines Public Goods Provision?* Forthcoming as a Special Issue of *Comparative Political Studies*.

Dasgupta, J. (1970). *Language Conflict and National Development: Group Politics and National Language Policy in India*. Berkeley: University of California Press.

Datt, G. and M. Ravallion (2002). "Is India's Economic Growth Leaving the Poor Behind?" *Journal of Economic Perspectives* 16(3): 89–108.

Davis, T. and A. Kalu-Nwiwu (2001). "Education, Ethnicity and National Integration in the History of Nigeria: Continuing Problems of Africa's Colonial Legacy." *The Journal of Negro History* 86(10): 1–11.

Dawson, Andy. (2012). "Boyle Command Performance Is Hampered by Not-so-Clever Trevor." *The Mirror*, July 28, sec. Opinion.

Dawson, M. (1994). *Behind the Mule: Race and Class in African American Politics*. Princeton, NJ: Princeton University Press.

Dawson, R. E. and J. A. Robinson (1963). "Inter-Party Competition, Economic Variables, and Welfare Policies in the American States." *Journal of Politics* 25(02): 265–89.

Deacon, R. T. (2005). Dictatorship, Democracy and the Provision of Public Goods. Paper provided by Department of Economics, UC Santa Barbara in its series University of California at Santa Barbara, Economics Working Paper Series with number qt9h54w76c.

Deaton, A. and J. Dreze (2002). "Poverty and Inequality in India: A Reexamination." *Economic and Political Weekly*, 3729–48.

De Cremer, D. and M. Van Vugt (1999). "Social Identification Effects in Social Dilemmas." *European Journal of Social Psychology* 29(7): 871–93.

Deepu Sam. (2012, January 11). Manoj Tiwari – Jai Bihar Full Song.mp4. Retrieved from https://www.youtube.com/watch?v=lA4hOezPvaE.

Deliege, R. (1997). *The World of the "Untouchables": Paraiyars of Tamil Nadu*. New Delhi: Oxford University Press.

Desai, M. (2005). "Indirect British Rule, State Formation, and Welfarism in Kerala, India, 1860–1957." *Social Science History* 29(3): 457–88.

  (2007). *State Formation and Radical Democracy in India*. London; New York: Routledge.

Desmet, K., S. Weber, and I. Ortuño-Ortín (2009). "Linguistic Diversity and Redistribution." *Journal of the European Economic Association* 7(6): 1291–318.

Deutsch, K. W. (1966). *Nationalism and Social Communication: An Inquiry into the Foundations of Nationality*. Cambridge, MA: MIT Press.

Devika, J. (2002). Domesticating Malayalees: Family Planning, the Nation and Home-centered Anxieties in Mid-20th Century Kerala. *Open Seminar*. Center for Development Studies. Working Paper 340.

  (2010). "Egalitarian Developmentalism, Communist Mobilization, and the Question of Caste in Kerala State, India." *The Journal of Asian Studies* 6(3): 801.

DeVotta, N. (2004). *Blowback: Linguistic Nationalism, Institutional Decay, and Ethnic Conflict in Sri Lanka*. Stanford: Stanford University Press.

Dharma Kumar, T. R. and Meghnad Desai (1983). *The Cambridge Economic History of India*. Cambridge; New York: Cambridge University Press.

Dickey, S. (1993). *Cinema and the Urban Poor in South India*. Cambridge: Cambridge University Press.

Directorate of Public Relations, Rajasthan India. (1951). *Rajasthan: A Symposium*. Jaipur.

Doreian, P. and T. Fararo (1998). *The problem of solidarity: Theories and models*. Amsterdam: Gordon and Breach Publishers.

Dovidio, J. and S. Gaertner (1999). "Reducing Prejudice: Combating Intergroup Biases." *American Psychological Society* 8(4): 101–05.

Dowley, K. M. and B. D. Silver (2000). "Subnational and National Loyalty: Cross-National Comparisons." *International Journal of Public Opinion* 12(4): 357–71.

Downs, A. (1957). *An Economic Theory of Democracy*. New York: Harper and Row.

Drèze, J. and H. Gazdar (1998). "Uttar Pradesh: The Burden of Inertia." In J. Dreze and A. Sen, eds., *Indian Development: Selected Regional Perspectives*, pp. xx, 420. Delhi; New York: Oxford University Press.

Drèze, J. and A. K. Sen (1998). *Indian Development: Selected Regional Perspectives*. Delhi; New York: Oxford University Press.

(2002). *India: Development and Participation*. Oxford; New York: Oxford University Press.

Duflo, E., P. Dupas, and M. Kremer (2007). *Peer Effects, Pupil-Teacher Ratios, and Teacher Incentives: Evidence from a Randomized Evaluation in Kenya*. Unpublished manuscript.

Dunn, J. (1979). *Western Political Theory in the Face of the Future*. Cambridge; New York: Cambridge University Press.

Dye, T. (1966). *Politics, Economics, and the Public; Policy Outcomes in the American States*. Chicago: Rand McNally.

D'Souza, D. (2002). *Two Cheers for Colonialism*. Oxford University Press.

Easterly, W. and R. Levine (1997). "Africa's Growth Tragedy: Policies and Ethnic Divisions." *Quarterly Journal of Economics* 112(4): 1203–50.

Easterly, W., J. Ritzen, et al. (2006). "Social Cohesion, Institutions, and Growth." *Economics and Politics* 18(2): 103–20.

Elkins, D. J. and R. E. B. Simeon (1979). "A Cause in Search of Its Effect, or What Does Political Culture Explain?" *Comparative Politics* 11(2): 127–45.

Elwell, F. W. (2013). *Sociocultural Systems: Principles of Structure and Change*. Alberta: Athabasca University Press.

Erdman, J. L., K. Schomer, et al. (1994). *The Idea of Rajasthan: Explorations in Regional Identity*. New Delhi: Manohar Publishers & Distributors: American Institute of Indian Studies.

Erikson, R. S., M. B. MacKuen, and J. A. Stimson (2002). *The Macro Polity*. New York: Cambridge University Press.

Erikson, R. S., G. C. Wright, et al. (1993). *Statehouse Democracy: Public Opinion and Democracy in American States*. New York: Cambridge University Press.

Erk, J. (2005). "Sub-State Nationalism and the Left–Right Divide: Critical Junctures in the Formation of Nationalist Labour Movements in Belgium." *Nations and Nationalism* 11(4): 551–70.

Esping-Andersen, G. (1990). *The Three Worlds of Welfare Capitalism*. Cambridge: Polity Press.

Esping-Andersen, G. and Walter Korpi. (1987). "From Poor Relief to Institutional Welfare States: The Development of Scandinavian Social Policy." *International Journal of Sociology* 16(3/4): 39–74. Published by Taylor & Francis, Ltd.

Etzioni, A. (1987). "How Rational Are We?" *Sociological Forum* 2(1): 1–20.

(1988). *The Moral Dimension: Toward a New Economics*. London: Collier Macmillan.

(2003). "Communitarianism." In Karen Christensen and David Levinson (eds.), *Encyclopedia of Community: From the Village to the Virtual World*, Vol 1, A-D, Sage Publications. pp. 224–228.

Evans, P. (1997). *State-Society Synergy: Government and Social Capital in Development.* Berkeley: Univ. of California Press.

Fadia, B. (1984). *State Politics in India.* New Delhi: Radiant Publishers.

Fantasia, R. (1989). *Cultures of Solidarity: Consciousness, Action, and Contemporary American Workers.* Berkeley: University of California Press.

Fearon, J. D. and D. D. Laitin (1996). "Explaining Interethnic Cooperation." *American Political Science Review* 90(4): 715–35.

Fenno, R. (1973). *Congressmen in Committees.* Boston: Little, Brown and Co.

Ferguson, N. (2004). *Empire: The Rise and Demise of the British World Order and the Lessons for Global Power.* Reprint edition. New York: Basic Books.

Fic, Victor M. 1970. *Kerala: Yenan of India.* Bombay: Nachiketa Publications.

Filmer, D. (2003). *The Incidence of Public Expenditure on Health and Education.* Washington, DC: World Bank.

Filmer, D. and L. Pritchett (1999). "The Impact of Public Spending on Health: Does Money Matter?" *Social Science & Medicine* 49(10): 1309–23.

Filmer, D., L. Pritchett, et al. (1997). "Child Mortality and Public Spending on Health: How Much Does Money Matter?," *World Bank Policy Research Working Paper No. 1864,* Washington, DC.

Fishman, J. A. (1973). *Language and Nationalism: Two Integrative Essays.* Rowley, MA: Newbury House Publishers.

(2006). *Language Loyalty, Language Planning, and Language Revitalization: Recent Writings and Reflections.* Clevedon, UK; Buffalo, NY: Multilingual Matters.

Flora, P. and J. Alber (1981). "Modernization, Democratization and the Development of the Welfare States in Western Europe." In P. Flora and A. J. Heidenheimer, eds., *The Development of Welfare States in Europe and America.* New Brunswick, NJ: Transaction Publishers.

Forrest, J. (2004). *Subnationalism in Africa: Ethnicity, Alliances, and Politics.* Boulder, CO: Lynne Rienner Publishers.

Forrester, D. (1976). "Factions and Filmstars: Tamil Nadu Politics since 1971." *Asian Survey* 16(3): 283–96.

Franke, R. W. and B. H. Chasin (1989). *Kerala: Radical Reform as Development in an Indian State.* San Francisco: Institute for Food & Development Policy.

(1989, 1991). *Kerala Radical Reform as Development in an Indian State.* 2 edition. Oakland, CA: Food First Books.

(1997). "Power to the (Malayalee) People: Kerala's 9th Plan – People's Plan Campaign for Local Democracy." *Economic and Political Weekly* 32(48): 3061–68.

Franke, Richard W. and B. H. Chasin (1999). "Is the Kerala Model Sustainable?" *Rethinking Development: Kerala's Development Experience* 1: 118.

Freitag, S. (1989). *Culture and Power in Banaras: Community, Performance, and Environment, 1800–1980.* Berkeley: University of California Press.

Furniss, N. and T. Tilton (1977). *The Case for the Welfare State: From Social Security to Social Equality.* Bloomington: Indiana University Press.

Gaertner, S. L., J. F. Dovidio, et al. (2000). "Reducing Intergroup Conflict: From Superordinate Goals to Decategorization, Recategorization, and Mutual Differentiation." *Group Dynamics: Theory, Research, and Practice* 4(1): 98–114.

Gahlot, J. (1981). *Rajasthan: A Socio-Economic Study.* Jodhpur, Rajasthan: Hindi Sahitya Mandir.

Gahlot, S. S. (1982). *Rural Life in Rajasthan*. Jodhpur, Rajasthan: Hindi Sahitya Mandir.

Ganguly, S., L. J. Diamond, et al. (2007). *The State of India's Democracy*. Baltimore: Johns Hopkins University Press.

Gao, Eleanor (2015). "Tribal Mobilization, Fragmented Groups, and Public Goods Provision in Jordan." In Prerna Singh and Mathias vom Hau (eds.), *Ethnicity in Time: Politics, History, and Whether Diversity Undermines Public Goods Provision?* Forthcoming as a Special Issue of *Comparative Political Studies*.

Geertz, C. (1963). *Agricultural Involution: The Processes of Ecological Change in Indonesia*. Berkeley: University of California Press.

 (1990). *Works and Lives*. Stanford: Stanford University Press.

Gellner, E. (1983). *Nations and Nationalism*. Oxford, UK: Blackwell.

George, A. and A. Bennett (2005). *Case Studies and Theory Development in the Social Sciences*. Cambridge, MA: MIT Press.

Gerring, J. (2001). *Social Science Methodology: A Criterial Framework*. Cambridge; New York: Cambridge University Press.

Gerring, J. and S. C. Thacker (2008). *A Centripetal Theory of Democratic Governance*. Cambridge; New York: Cambridge University Press.

Gerring, J., S. C. Thacker, Y. Lu and W. Huang (2015). "Does Diversity Impair Human Development? A Multi-Level Test of the Diversity Debit Hypothesis." *World Development* 66:166–88.

Gershenkron A. (1962). *Economic Backwardness in Historical Perspective*. Cambridge, MA: Harvard University Press.

Gibson, J. and A. Gouws (2002). *Overcoming Intolerance in South Africa*. Cambridge; New York: Cambridge University Press.

Gigerenzer, G. (2007). *Gut Feelings: The Intelligence of the Unconscious*. Penguin Books.

Ginsburgh, V. and S. Weber (2011). *How Many Languages Do We Need? The Economics of Linguistic Diversity*. Princeton: Princeton University Press.

Giraudy, A., Eduardo Moncada and Richard Snyder (2014). "Subnational Research in Comparative Politics." Paper presented at the Annual Meeting of the American Political Science Association, Washington D. C.

Gladstone, J. W. (1984). *Protestant Christianity and People's Movements in Kerala: A Study of Christian Mass Movements in Relation to Neo-Hindu Socio-religious Movements in Kerala, 1850–1936*. Trivandrum: Seminary Publications

Glennerster, Rachel, Edward Miguel and Alexander Rothenberg (2010). Collective Action in Diverse Sierra Leone Communities. Working Paper.

Gnanagurunathan, A. D. (2015). "BJP's Last Frontier." *DNA India*, 15 April.

Goertz, G. (2006). *Social Science Concepts: A User's Guide*. Princeton: Princeton University Press.

Gopalakrishnan, K. K. (2004). "Blazing New Trails." *Hindu*. Chennai.

Goswami, S. (2007). *Female Infanticide and Child Marriage*. Jaipur: Rawat Publications.

Gough, K. (1965). "Village Politics in Kerala." *Economic Weekly* 17(8 and 9): 363–72, 413–20.

Gould, W. (2004). *Hindu Nationalism and the Language of Politics in Late Colonial India*. Cambridge; New York: Cambridge University Press.

Government of Bihar (2011). Bihar Day Celebrations around the Globe. Retrieved from http://www.biharfoundation.in/events/bihar-divas/.

Government of Rajasthan (2014). Bhamashah Yojana. Retrieved from http://bhamashah
   .rajasthan.gov.in
Government of Tamil Nadu (2005). Tamil Nadu Human Development Report.
   Chennai: Government of Tamil Nadu in association with Social Science Press, Delhi.
Govinda, R. "Lok Jumbish: An Innovation in Grassroots Level Management of Primary
   Education." India: UNICEF/UNESCO.
Green, D. P., S. Y. Kim, et al. (2001). "Dirty Pool." *International Organization* 55: 441–68.
Greene, W. (2010). "Fixed Effects Vector Decomposition: A Magical Solution to the
   Problem of Time Invariant Variables in Fixed Effects Models?" Working Paper,
   New York University.
Greenfeld, L. (1992). *Nationalism: Five Roads to Modernity*. Cambridge, MA: Harvard
   University Press.
Grierson, G. A. (1894). *Linguistic Survey of India*. Calcutta: Office of the Superintendent
   of Government Printing.
Grindle, M. (2007). *Going Local: Decentralization, Democratization, and the Promise
   of Good Governance*. Princeton: Princeton University Press.
Guibernau, M. (1999). *Nations without States: Political Communities in the Global
   Age*. Cambridge: Polity Press.
Guibernau, Montserrat (2008). *The Identity of Nations*. Cambridge, UK: Polity.
Gupta, S. (1981). "Non-Development of Bihar: A Case of Retarded Sub-Nationalism."
   Economic and Political Weekly, 1496–1502.
   (2007). "The Rise and Fall of Hindutva in UP, 1989–2004." In S. Pai (ed.), *Political
   Process in Uttar Pradesh: Identity, Economic Reforms, and Governance*. New
   Delhi: Pearson Education India.
Gupta, S. and N. K. Singh (2013). "'Bihar' an Idea Whose Time Has Come." *Paper pre-
   sented at Fourteenth Annual Conference on Indian Economic Policy Reform, May
   30–31, 2013*. Stanford Center for International Development, Stanford University.
Gusain, L. (2005). *Reference Grammar of Rajasthani*. Berlin: Mouton De Gruyter.
Habyarimana, J., M. Humphreys, et al. (2007). "Why Does Ethnic Diversity Undermine
   Public Goods Provision?" *American Political Science Review* 101(4): 709–25.
   (2009). *Coethnicity: Diversity and the Dilemmas of Collective Action*. New York:
   Russell Sage Foundation.
Hall, P. and M. Lamont (2009). *Successful Societies: How Institutions and Culture
   Affect Health*. Cambridge; New York: Cambridge University Press.
Hanham, H. J. (1969). *Scottish Nationalism*. Cambridge, MA: Harvard University Press.
Hansen, R. and D. King (2001). "Eugenic Ideas, Political Interests, and Policy
   Variance: Immigration and Sterilization Policy in Britain and the U.S." *World
   Politics* 53(2): 237–63.
Hardgrave, R. (1964). "The DMK and the Politics of Tamil Nationalism." *Pacific Affairs*
   37(4): 396–411.
Hardgrave, R. L. (1965). *The Dravidian Movement*. Bombay: Popular Prakashan.
Hardgrave, R. (1969). *The Nadars of Tamilnad: The Political Culture of a Community
   in Change*. Berkeley: University of California Press.
Harlan, Lindsey (1991). *Religion and Rajput Women: The Ethic of Protection in
   Contemporary Narratives*. Berkeley: University of California Press.
Harrison, S. S. (1956). "Jawaharlal Nehru." *Foreign Affairs* 34(2): 620–36.
   (1960). *India: The Most Dangerous Decades*. Princeton: Princeton University Press.

Harriss, B. (1979). *Paddy and Rice Marketing In Northern Tamil Nadu.* Sangam Publishers for Madras Institute of Development Studies.

Harty, S. (2001). "The Institutional Foundations of Sub-State National Movements." *Comparative Politics* 33: 191–210.

Hasan, Z. (1996). "Communal Mobilization and Changing Majority in Uttar Pradesh." In D. E. Ludden (ed.), *Contesting the Nation: Religion, Community, and the Politics of Democracy in India*, p. ix. Philadelphia: University of Pennsylvania Press.

Hastings, A. (1997). *The Construction of Nationhood: Ethnicity, Religion, and Nationalism.* Cambridge; New York: Cambridge University Press.

Hayek, F. A. (1960). *The Constitution of Liberty.* Chicago: University of Chicago Press.

Hechter, M. (2000). *Containing Nationalism.* New Delhi: Oxford University Press.

Heclo, H. (1972). "Review Article: Policy Analysis." *British Journal of Political Science* 2(01): 83–108.

Henrich, Joseph, R. Boyd, S. Bowles, C. Camerer, E. Fehr, H. Gintis and R. McElreath (2001). "In Search of Homo Economicus: Behavioral Experiments in 15 Small-Scale Societies." *AEA Papers and Proceedings* 91, no. 2 (May 2001): 73–78.

Heller, P. (1996). "Social Capital as a Product of Class Mobilization and State Intervention: Industrial Workers in Kerala, India." *World Development* 24(6): 1055–71.

(1999). *The Labor of Development: Workers and the Transformation of Capitalism in Kerala, India.* Ithaca: Cornell University Press.

(2000). "Degrees of Democracy: Some Comparative Lessons from India." *World Politics* 52(July): 484–519.

(2005). "Reinventing Public Power in the Age of Globalization: the Transformation of Movement Politics in Kerala." In R. Ray and M. F. Katzenstein (eds.), *Social Movements in India: Poverty, Power, and Politics.* Lanham, MD: Rowman & Littlefield.

(2013). "Movements, Politics and Democracy: Kerala in Comparative Perspective." In Atul Kohli and Prerna Singh (eds.), *Handbook of Indian Politics.* London: Routledge.

Henderson, A. and N. McEwen (2005). "Do Shared Values Underpin National Identity? Examining the Role of Values in National Identity in Canada and the United Kingdom." *National Identities* 7(2): 173–91.

Henderson, C. (2007). "Virtual Rajasthan: Making Heritage, Marketing Cyberorientalism?" In C. Henderson and M. Weisgrau (eds.), *Raj Rhapsodies.* Aldershot, Hampshire, UK: Ashgate Publishing.

Herder, J. G. (1795). *Briefe Zu Beforderung Der Humanitat.* Riga: Hartknoch.

Herring, R. J. (1988). *Stealing Congress Thunder: The Rise to power of a Communist Movement in South India.* In Peter Merkl and Kay Lawson (eds.), *When Parties Fail.* Princeton: Princeton University Press.

(1983). *Land to the Tiller: The Political Economy of Agrarian Reform in South Asia.* New Haven: Yale University Press.

Hibbs, D. A. (1977). "Political Parties and Macroeconomic Policy." *American Political Science Review* 100(04): 670–71.

Hickey, S., B. Bukenya et al. (eds.) (Forthcoming). *The Politics of Inclusive Development: Interrogating the Evidence.*

His Majesty's Secretary of State for India in Council (1908). *Imperial Gazetteer of India.* Oxford: Clarendon Press.

Hiskey, J. T. (2003). "Demand-Based Development and Local Electoral Environments in Mexico." *Comparative Politics* 36(1): 41–59.

Hobsbawm, E. (1990). *Nations and Nationalism since 1780: Programme, Myth, Reality.* Cambridge; New York: Cambridge University Press.

Hopkins, D. (2009). "The Diversity Discount: When Increasing Ethnic and Racial Diversity Prevents Tax Increases." *Journal of Politics* 71(1): 160–77.

(2010). "The Limited Local Impacts of Ethnic and Racial Diversity." *American Politics Research* 39(2): 344–79.

Horowitz, D. L. (1985). *Ethnic Groups in Conflict.* Berkeley: University of California Press.

Hroch, M. (1985). *Social Preconditions of National Revival in Europe: A Comparative Analysis of the Social Composition of Patriotic Groups among the Smaller European Nations.* New York: Columbia University Press.

Huber, E., C. Ragin, et al. (1993). "Social Democracy, Christian Democracy, Constitutional Structure, and the Welfare State." *American Journal of Sociology* 99: 711.

Huber, E. and J. D. Stephens (2001). *Development and Crisis of the Welfare State: Parties and Policies in Global Markets.* Chicago: University of Chicago Press.

Huddy, L. and N. Khatib (2007). "American Patriotism, National Identity, and Political Involvement." *American Journal of Political Science* 51(1): 63–77.

Huntington, S. P. (1996). *The Clash of Civilizations and the Remaking of World Order.* New York: Simon & Schuster.

Huo, Y. J., H. H. Smith, et al. (1996). "Superordinate Identification, Subgroup Identification, and Justice Concerns: Is Separatism the Problem? Is Assimilation the Answer?" *Psychological Science* 7: 40–45.

Hutchinson, J. and A. D. Smith (1996). *Ethnicity.* Oxford; New York: Oxford University Press.

Immergut, E. M. (1990). "Institutions, Veto Points, and Policy Results: A Comparative Analysis of Health Care." *Journal of Public Policy* 10, no. 4 (October–December): 391–416.

(1992). *Health Politics: Interests and Institutions in Western Europe.* Cambridge, UK; New York: Cambridge University Press.

India. Parliament. Lok, S. (1956). *Lok Sabha Debates on the Report of the States Reorganisation Commission, 14th December to 23rd December, 1955.* New Delhi: Lok Sabha Secretariat.

Irschick, E. F. (1969). *Politics and Social Conflict in South India, the Non-Brahman Movement and Tamil Separatism, 1916–1929.* Berkeley and Los Angeles: University of California Press.

(1986). *Tamil Revivalism in the 1930s.* Madras: Cre-A.

Iversen, V., R. Palmer-Jones and K. Sen (2013). "On the Colonial Origins of Agricultural Development in India: A Re-examination of Banerjee and Iyer, 'History, Institutions and Economic Performance'." *The Journal of Development Studies* 49(12): 1631–46.

Iyer, L. (2010). "Direct versus Indirect Colonial Rule in India: Long-Term Consequences." *Review of Economics and Statistics* 92(4): 693–713.

Jackson, Ken (2007). Why Does Ethnic Diversity Affect Public Good Provision? An Empirical Analysis of Water Provision in Africa, mimeo, University of British Columbia, Vancouver, Canada.

Jacobs, A. M. (2009). "How Do Ideas Matter? Mental Models and Attention in German Pension Politics." *Comparative Political Studies* 42(2): 252–79.

(2011). *Process Tracing and Ideational Theories.* Committee on Concepts and Methods, Working Paper Series. International Political Science Association (IPSA).

Jaffrelot, C. and C. Robin (2009). "Towards Jat Empowerment in Rajasthan." In C. Jaffrelot and S. Kumar (eds.), *Rise of the Plebeians? The Changing Face of Indian Legislative Assemblies.* New Delhi: Routledge.

Jamous, R. (1996). "The Meo as a Rajput Caste and a Muslim Community." In C. J. Fuller (ed.), *Caste Today,* pp. 180–201. Delhi: Oxford University Press.

Jayal, N. G. (2013). *Citizenship and Its Discontents: An Indian History.* Cambridge, MA: Harvard University Press.

Jeffrey, R. (1976). *The Decline of Nayar Dominance: Society and Politics in Travancore, 1847–1908.* New York: Holmes & Meier Publishers.

Jenkins, R. (1998). "Rajput Hindutva: Caste Politics, Regional Identity, and Hindu Nationalism in Contemporary Rajasthan." In C. Jaffrelot and T. B. Hansen (eds.), *The BJP and the Compulsions of Politics in India.* Delhi: Oxford University Press.

Jensen, C. and S. E. Skaaning (2015). "Democracy, Ethnic Fractionalization, and the Politics of Social Spending: Disentangling a Conditional Relationship." *International Political Science Review,* 36(4): 457–72.

Jha, A. M. (2005). "Leading a New Pack of Biharis in the IAS." *Times of India.*

Johnston, R., K. Banting, W. Kymlicka, and S. Soroka, (2010). "National Identity and Support for the Welfare State." *Canadian Journal of Political Science* 43(02): 349–77.

Joshi, D. (2007). "Government Performance, Economic Growth and Human Development in China and India." *Political Science Department, University of Washington.*

Kabir, M. (2002). *Growth of Service Sector in Kerala: A Comparative Study of Travancore and Malabar, 1950–51.* Trivandrum: University of Kerala.

(2003). Beyond Philanthropy: The Rockefeller Foundation's Public Health Intervention in Thiruvithamkoor, 1929–1939. CDS working papers, no.350. Trivandrum: CDS.

Kabir, M., and T. N. Krishnan (1993). *Social Intermediation and Health Transition – Lessons from Kerala.* Thiruvananthapuram: Center for Development Studies.

Kalt, J. P. and M. A. Zupan (1984). "Capture and Ideology in the Economic Theory of Politics." *The American Economic Review* 74(3): 279–300.

Kannan, K. P. and K. S. Hari (2002). "Kerala's Gulf Connection: Emigration, Remittances and Their Macroeconomic Impact 1972–2000." *Centre for Development Studies, Trivandrum,* Working Paper No. 328.

Kaplan, G. A., E. R. Pamuk, et al. (1996). "Income Inequality and Mortality in the United States: Analysis of Mortality and Potential Pathways." *British Medical Journal* 312(7041):1253.

Kau, James B. and Paul H. Rubin (1982). *Congressman, Constituents, and Contributors: An Analysis of Determinants of Roll-Call Voting in the House of Representatives.* Springer Science & Business Media. Vol. 4.

Kauneckis, D. and K. Andersson (2008). "Making Decentralization Work: A Cross-National Examination of Local Governments and Natural Resource Governance in Latin America." *Studies in Comparative International Development* 44(1): 23–46.

Kawachi, I. and B. P. Kennedy (1997). "The Relationship of Income Inequality to Mortality: Does the Choice of Indicator Matter?" *Social Science & Medicine* 45(7): 1121–27.

Kawashima, K. (1998). *Missionaries and a Hindu State: Travancore, 1858–1936.* Delhi; New York: Oxford University Press.

Keating, M. (2009). "Social Citizenship, Solidarity and Welfare in Regionalized and Plurinational States." *Citizenship Studies* 13(5): 501–13.

Keating, M. and J. Loughlin(1997). *The Political Economy of Regionalism.* London; Portland, OR: Routledge.

Kedourie, E. (1966). *Nationalism.* London: Hutchinson.

Kellogg, S. (1875). *A Grammar of the Hindi Language.* Allahabad: Am. Pres. Mission Press.

Keys, V. O. (1949). *Southern Politics in State and Nation.* Knoxville: University of Tennessee Press.

Khwaja, A. I. (2009). "Can Good Projects Succeed In Bad Communities?" *Journal of Public Economics* 93(7–8): 899–916.

Kingdon, J. W. (1984). *Agendas, Alternatives, and Public Policies.* Boston: Little, Brown.

Kirk, Jason A. (2011), *India and the World Bank: The Politics of Aid and Influence.* New York: Anthem Press.

Kishwar, M. (1999). *Off the Beaten Track: Rethinking Gender Justice for Indian Women.* New Delhi: Oxford University Press.

Knack, S. and P. Keefer (1997). "Does Social Capital Have an Economic Payoff? A Cross-Country Investigation." *Quarterly Journal of Economics* 112(4): 1251–88.

Knight, D. (2010). "The Accepted Other Within: the Macedonian Sub-Nationalism." *Anthropology Reviews: Dissent and Cultural Politics, Special Issue: Sub State Nationalisms in Contemporary Europe* 2(1).

Kohli, A. (1987). *The State and Poverty in India: The Politics of Reform.* Cambridge; New York: Cambridge University Press.

(1990). *Democracy and Discontent: India's Growing Crisis of Governability.* Cambridge; New York: Cambridge University Press.

(2001). *The Success of India's Democracy.* Cambridge; New York: Cambridge University Press.

Korpi, W. (1983). *The Democratic Class Struggle.* London; Boston: Routledge.

Koshy, M. J. (1972). *Genesis of Political Consciousness in Kerala.* Trivandrum: Kerala Historical Society.

Kothari, R. (1960). *Caste in Indian Politics.* Hyderabad: Orient Blackswan.

(1964). "The Congress 'System' in India." *Asian Survey* 4(12): 1161–73.

Kramer, R. M. and Marilynn B. Brewer (1984). "Effects of Group Identity on Resource Use in a Simulated Commons Dilemma." *Journal of Personality & Social Psychology* 46(5): 1044–57.

Kremer, M., N. Chaudhury, et al. (2005). "Teacher Absence in India: A Snapshot." *Journal of the European Economic Association* 3(2–3): 658–67.

Krishnan, T. N. (1995). "The Route to Social Development in Kerala: Social Intermediation and Public Action, a Retrospective Study, 1960–1993." *World Summit on Social Development.* UNICEF.

Kristensen, I. P. and G. Wawro (2003). Lagging the Dog: The Robustness of Panel Corrected Standard Errors in the Presence of Serial Correlation and Observation Specific Effects. Working paper. Summer Methods Conference.

Kudaisya, G. (2006). *Region, Nation, 'Heartland': Uttar Pradesh in India's Body Politics*. New Delhi: Sage Publications.

(2007). "Region, Nation, 'Heartland'." In S. Pai (ed.), *Political Process in Uttar Pradesh: Identity, Economic Reforms, and Governance*. New Delhi, Pearson Longman, xlviii.

Kumar, A. (2008). *Community Warriors: State, Peasants and Caste Armies in Bihar*. New Delhi; New York: Anthem Press.

(2014). *A Matter of Rats: A Short Biography of Patna*. Durham: Duke University Press.

Kumar, D. (1998). *Colonialism, Property and the State*. New York; Delhi: Oxford University Press.

Kumar, N. (2010). Young People Feel Proud of Being Bihari. Interview by S. Ghose. IBN-Live [Television broadcast]. *CNN-IBN, New Delhi*.

Kumar, S. (1994). *Political Evolution in Kerala: Travancore 1859–1938*. New Delhi, Phoenix.

Kurien, John (1995). "The Kerala Model: Its Central Tendency and the Outlier." *Social Scientist* 70–90.

Kutty, V. R. (2000). "Historical Analysis of the Development of Health Care Facilities in Kerala State, India." *Health Policy and Planning* 15(1): 103–09.

Kymlicka, W. (2002). *Contemporary Political Philosophy: An Introduction*. Oxford; New York: Oxford University Press.

Kymlicka, W. and K. Banting (2006). "Immigration, Multiculturalism, and the Welfare State." *Ethics & International Affairs* 20: 281–304.

Laitin, D. (1986). *Hegemony and Culture: Politics and Religious Change among the Yoruba*. Chicago: University of Chicago Press.

Laitin, D. and D. Posner (2001). "The Implications of Constructivism for Constructing Ethnic Fractionalization Indices." *APSA-CP*: Comparative Politics Newsletter 12.

Laitin, D. (1992). *Language Repertoires and State Construction in Africa*. Cambridge, UK; New York: Cambridge University Press.

Lake, D. and M. Baum (2001). "The Invisible Hand of Democracy: Political Control and Provision of Public Services." *Comparative Political Studies* 34(6): 587–621.

Lal, A. (2006). "Growth with Welfare." *Times of India*, New Delhi.

Lange, M. (2009). *Lineages of Despotism and Development: British Colonialism and State Power*. Chicago: University of Chicago Press.

Lange, M., J. Mahoney and M. Vom Hau (2006). "Colonialism and Development: A Comparative Analysis of Spanish and British Colonies." *American Journal of Sociology* 111(5): 1412–62.

La Porta, R., F. Lopez-de-Silanes, A. Shleifer, and R. W. Vishny (1998). "Law and Finance." *Journal of Political Economy* 106(6): 1113–55.

Lauren, M. M. and M. Bava (1954). "Memorandum Submitted to the States Reorganization Committee, File no. 25/13/54. 2." *National Archives of India, New Delhi*.

Levi-Faur, D. (1997). Economic Nationalism: From Friedrich List to Robert Reich. *Review of International Studies* 23(03): 359–70.

Lieberman, E. (2001). "Causal Inference in Historical Institutional Analysis: A Specification of Periodization Strategies." *Comparative Political Studies* 34(9): 1011–35.

(2009). *Boundaries of Contagion: How Ethnic Politics Have Shaped Government Responses to AIDS*. Princeton: Princeton University Press.

Lieberman, E. and P. Singh (2009). "Measuring State Institutionalization of Ethnic Categories across Time and Space." *Qualitative and Multi-Method Research, Newsletter of the American Political Science Association Organized Section for Qualitative and Multi-Method Research* 7(1): 29–35.

(2012). "Conceptualizing and Measuring Ethnic Politics: An Institutional Complement to Demographic, Behavioral, and Cognitive Approaches." *Studies in Comparative International Development* 47(3): 255–86.

Lieberman, E. S. (2003). *Race and Regionalism in the Politics of Taxation in Brazil and South Africa*. Cambridge, UK; New York: Cambridge University Press.

(2005). "Nested Analysis as a Mixed-Method Strategy for Cross-National Research." *American Political Science Review* 99: 435–52.

Lieberman, E. S. and Gwyneth H. McClendon (2013). "The Ethnicity–Policy Preference Link in Sub-Saharan Africa." *Comparative Political Studies* 46(5): 574–602.

Lieten, G. K. (1994). "On Casteism and Communalism in Uttar Pradesh." *Economic and Political Weekly* 29(14): 777–81.

Lindblom, C. (1959). "The Science of 'Muddling Through'." *Public Administration Review* 19(2): 79–88.

Lipset, S. M. and S. Rokkan (1967). *Party Systems and Voter Alignments: Cross-National Perspectives*. New York: Free Press.

List, F. (1841). *The National System of Political Economy*, English edition (1904). London: Longman.

Lockard, D. (1968). *Toward Equal Opportunity: A Study of State and Local Antidiscrimination Laws*. New York: Macmillan.

Lodrick, D. (1994). "Rajasthan as a Region: Myth or Reality?" In K. Schomer, J. L. Erdman, and L. Rudolph (eds.), *The Idea of Rajasthan: Explorations in Regional Identity*. New Delhi: Manohar Publishers & Distributors; American Institute of Indian Studies, 2 volumes.

Ludden, D. E. (1996). *Contesting the Nation: Religion, Community, and the Politics of Democracy in India*. Philadelphia: University of Pennsylvania Press.

Lynch, J. (2006). *Age in the Welfare State: The Origins of Social Spending on Pensioners, Workers and Children*. Cambridge; New York: Cambridge University Press.

MacPherson, Y. and S. Chamberlain (2013). "Health on the Move: Can Mobile Phones Save Lives?" In A. S. Mahal, B. Debroy and L. Bhandari (eds.), *BBC Media Action. India Health Report, 2010*. Business Standard Books (2010).

Mahoney, J. (2010). *Colonialism and Postcolonial Development: Spanish America in Comparative Perspective*. Cambridge; New York: Cambridge University Press.

Mahoney, J. and D. Rueschemeyer (2003). *Comparative Historical Analysis in the Social Sciences*. Cambridge; New York: Cambridge University Press.

Maioni, A. (2002). "Courts and Healthy Policy: Judicial Policy Making and Publicly Funded Health Care in Canada." *Journal of Health Politics, Policy, and Law* 27(2): 211–38.

Mamdani, M. (1996). *Citizen and Subject: Contemporary Africa and the Legacy of Late Colonialism*. Princeton: Princeton University Press.

(2001). *When Victims Become Killers: Colonialism, Nativism, and the Genocide in Rwanda*. Princeton: Princeton University Press.

Manion, M. (2006). "Democracy, Community, Trust: The Impact of Elections in Rural China." *Comparative Political Studies* 39(3): 301–24.

Manisha (2004). *Profiles of Indian Prime Ministers: From Jawaharlal Nehru to Dr. Manmohan Singh.* New Delhi: Mittal Publications.

Mansbridge, Jane (1990). *Beyond Self-Interest.* 1 edition. Chicago: University Of Chicago Press.

Mansuri, G. and V. Rao (2012). *Localizing Development: Does Participation Work?*, 1 edition. Washington, D.C: World Bank Publications.

Mares, I. (2003). *The Politics of Social Risk: Business and Welfare State Development.* Cambridge: Cambridge University Press.

Mares, Isabela and Matthew E. Carnes (2009). "Social Policy in Developing Countries." *Annual Review of Political Science* 12(1): 93–113.

Mari Bhat, P. N., S. H. Preston, et al. (1984). *Vital Rates in India, 1961–1981.* Washington, DC: National Academy Press.

Markovits, C. (2002). *A History of Modern India, 1480–1950.* London: Anthem.

Marshall, T. H. (1964). *Class, Citizenship, and Social Development; Essays.* Garden City, NY: Doubleday.

Marx, A. W. (1998). *Making Race and Nation: A Comparison of South Africa, the United States, and Brazil.* Cambridge, UK; New York: Cambridge University Press.

Masaldan, P. N. (1967). "Politics in Uttar Pradesh since 1947." In I. Narain (ed.), *State Politics in India.* Meerut: Meenakshi Prakashan, xxxvii.

Mason, A. (2000). *Community, Solidarity, and Belonging: Levels of Community and Their Normative Significance.* Cambridge; New York: Cambridge University Press.

Mathew, E. T. (1999). "Growth of Literacy in Kerala: State Intervention, Missionary Initiatives and Social Movements." *Economic and Political Weekly* 34(39): 2811–20.

Mathur, K. (1972). *Bureaucratic Response to Development: A Study of Block Development Officers in Rajasthan and Uttar Pradesh.* New Delhi: National Publishing House.

Mathur, K. and Shobhita Rajgopal (2011). "No Right to Be Born in Rajasthan." *Economic and Political Weekly* 46(18): 26–27.

McAdams, R. (1982). *Behavioral and Social Science Research: A National Resource.* Washington, D.C.: National Academy Press.

McCrone, D. (1992). *Understanding Scotland: The Sociology of a Stateless Nation.* London; New York: Routledge.

McCrone, D., and L. Paterson. (2002) "The Conundrum of Scottish Independence." *Scottish Affairs* 40 (First Series), no. 1: 54–75.

McEwen, N. (2002). "State Welfare Nationalism: The Territorial Impact of Welfare State Development in Scotland." *Regional & Federal Studies* 12(1): 66–90.

(2003). Welfare Solidarity in a Devolved Scotland. *Workshop 10: The Welfare State and Territorial Politics: An Under-Explored Relationship.* University of Edinburgh European Consortium for Political Research.

(2006). *Nationalism and the State: Welfare and Identity in Scotland and Quebec.* Peter Lang.

McEwen, N. and L. Moreno (2005). *The Territorial Politics of Welfare.* London; New York: Routledge.

McEwen, N. and R. Parry (2005). "Devolution and the Preservation of the United Kingdom Welfare State." In N. McEwen and L. Moreno (eds.), *The Territorial Politics of Welfare.* London; New York: Routledge.

McQuoid, Alexander (2011). "Does Diversity Divide? Public Goods Provision and Soviet Emigration to Israel." Manuscript. Department of Economics, Columbia University, November 12.

Mehrotra, S. (2000). Integrating Economic and Social Policy: Good Practices from High Achieving Countries. *UNICEF Innocenti Working Paper.*

(2007). "Intersections between Caste, Health and Education: Why Uttar Pradesh Is Not Like Tamil Nadu." In S. Pai (ed.), *Political Process in Uttar Pradesh: Identity, Economic Reforms, and Governance.* New Delhi: Pearson Education India.

Mehrotra, S. K. (2006). *The Economics of Elementary Education in India: The Challenge of Public Finance, Private Provision, and Household Costs.* New Delhi; Thousand Oaks, CA: Sage Publications.

Meier, Stephan (2006). *A Survey of Economic Theories and Field Evidence on Pro-Social Behavior.* FRB of Boston Working Paper No. 06-6.

Meister, M. W. (1994). "Art Regions and Modern Rajasthan." In K. Schomer, J. L. Erdman and L. Rudolph (eds.), *The Idea of Rajasthan: Explorations in Regional Identity.* New Delhi: Manohar Publishers & Distributors: American Institute of Indian Studies, 2 volumes.

Mencher, J. (1980). "The Lessons and Non-Lessons of Kerala." *Economic and Political Weekly* 15(41–43): 1781–802.

Menon, M. D. (1994). *Caste, Nationalism and Communism in South India, Malabar 1900–1948.* Cambridge: Cambridge, University Press.

Metz-McDonnell, Erin (2015). "We Chop Together: Ethnic Diversity, Public Goods, and Conciliatory States in Africa." In Prerna Singh and Mathias vom Hau (eds.), *Ethnicity in Time: Politics, History, and Whether Diversity Undermines Public Goods Provision?* Forthcoming as a Special Issue of *Comparative Political Studies.*

Miguel, E. (2004). "Tribe or Nation?: Nation Building and Public Goods in Kenya versus Tanzania." *World Politics* 56(3): 327–62.

Miguel, E. and M. K. Gugerty (2005). "Ethnic Diversity, Social Sanctions, and Public Goods in Kenya." *Journal of Public Economics* 89(11–12): 2325–68.

Mill, J. S. (1875). *Considerations on Representative Government.* London: Longmans, Green, and Co.

Mill, J. S., J. M. Robson, et al. (1990). *Writings on India.* Toronto, Buffalo, London: University of Toronto Press; Routledge.

Miller, D. (1995). *On Nationality.* New York: Clarendon Press.

(1998). *Rethinking Northern Ireland: Culture, Ideology, and Colonialism.* London; New York: Longman.

(2000). *Citizenship and National Identity.* Cambridge, UK: Malden, MA, USA: Polity.

Minorities at Risk Project (2009). *Minorities at Risk Dataset.* College Park, MD: Center for International Development and Conflict Management. Retrieved from http://www.cidcm.umd.edu/mar/data.aspx

Minorities at Risk Project (2014). *Minorities at Risk Dataset (MAR).* College Park, Maryland Center for International Development and Conflict Management, University of Maryland.

Mirza, Rinchan Ali (2014). "Occupation, Diversity and Public Goods: Evidence from Pakistan Through Partition." Unpublished Ph.D. diss. University of Oxford.

Mishra, V. (1995). "Dream of Jharkhand Remains Remote." *Times of India*, September 8, 1995

Montalvo, José and Marta Reynal-Querol (2002). "Why Ethnic Fractionalization? Polarization, Ethnic Conflict and Growth," unpublished, Universitat Pompeu Fabra.

Moore, M. (2003). "Sub-State Nationalism and International Law." *Michigan Journal of International Law* 25: 1319.

Moreno, C. (2005). "Decentralization, Electoral Competition, and Local Government Performance in Mexico." PhD dissertation, Department of Political Science. University of Texas, Austin.

Moreno, L. (2001). *The Federalization of Spain*. London: Frank Cass Ltd.

Moreno, L. and N. McEwen (2003). "The Welfare State and Territorial Politics: An Under-Explored Relationship." *European Council of Political Research, Workshop 10*.

Moreno, L., A. Arriba and A. Serrano (1997). Multiple identities in decentralized Spain: The case of Catalonia. Instituto de Estudios Sociales Avanzados (CSIC) Working Paper 97-06, CSIC.

Morris, M. D. (1979). *Measuring the Conditions of the World's Poor: The Physical Quality of Life*. New York. Pergamon Press.

Mukherjee, R. (2010). Reviving the Administration: Bihar State, India 2005–2009. Princeton University's Innovations for Successful Societies. http://www.princeton .edu/successfulsocieties.

Munck, G. L. and R. Snyder (2007). *Passion, Craft, and Method in Comparative Politics*. Baltimore: Johns Hopkins University Press.

Nag, M. (1989). *Political Awareness as a Factor in Accessibility of Health Services: A Case Study of Rural Kerala and West Bengal*. (1 Dag Hammarskjold Plaza, New York, NY 10017). Population Council.

Nair, K. V. S. (1954). "Memorandum Submitted to the States Reorganization Commission, File no. 25/13/54-SRC. 2." *National Archives of India*, New Delhi.

Nair, P. R. G. (1976). "Education and Socio-Economic Change in Kerala, 1793–1947." *Social Scientist* 4(8): 28–43.

(1981). *Primary Education, Population Growth and Socio-Economic Change: A Comparative Study with Particular Reference to Kerala*. New Delhi: Allied Publishers.

Nair, T. P. S. (1986). "Aiyyankali and Travancore Pulayas. History of Political Development in Kerala." PhD dissertation, Department of Political Science. Trivandrum University of Kerala, Trivandrum.

Nambi Arooran, K. (1980). *Tamil Renaissance and Dravidian Nationalism, 1905–1944*. Madurai: Koodal.

Namboodiripad, E. M. S. (1952). *The National Question in Kerala*. Bombay: People's Publishing House.

Naqvi, Saba. (2005). "Bihar: A Quiet Rising." *Outlook*, November 14.

Narain, I. (1967, 1976). *State Politics in India*. Meerut: Meenakshi Prakashan.

Narain, I. and P. C. Mathur (1989). "The Thousand Year Raj: Regional Isolation and Rajput Hinduism in Rajasthan before and after 1947." In F. R. Frankel and M. S. A. Rao (eds.), *Dominance and State Power in Modern India*. Delhi; New York: Oxford University Press.

Narayan, D. and L. Pritchett (1999). "Cents and Sociability: Household Income and Social Capital in Rural Tanzania." *Economic Development and Cultural Change* 47(4): 871–97.

Nevill, H. R. (1904). *The District Gazetteers of the United Provinces of Agra and Oudh.* Allahabad: Government Press.

Noakes, L. and J. Pattinson, eds. (2013). *British Cultural Memory and the Second World War.* London: Bloomsbury.

Nobles, M. (2000). *Shades of Citizenship: Race and the Census in Modern Politics.* Stanford: Stanford University Press.

North, D. C. (2005). *Understanding the Process of Economic Change.* Princeton: Princeton University Press.

Nossiter, T. J. (1982). *Communism in Kerala: A Study in Political Adaptation.* London: C. Hurst for the Royal Institute of International Affairs.

Nussbaum, M. C. (2001). *Women and Human Development: The Capabilities Approach.* Cambridge; New York: Cambridge University Press.

 (2006). *Frontiers of Justice: Disability, Nationality, Species Membership.* Cambridge, MA: The Belknap Press of Harvard University Press.

Office of the Registrar General and Census Commissioner (1871–2011). Census Reports of India.

Olken, B. A. (2005). *Monitoring Corruption: Evidence from a Field Experiment in Indonesia.* National Bureau of Economic Research (No. w11753).

Olson, M. (1965). *The Logic of Collective Action: Public Goods and the Theory of Groups.* Cambridge, MA: Harvard University Press.

Ostrom, E. (1990). *Governing the Commons: The Evolution of Institutions for Collective Action.* Cambridge; New York: Cambridge University Press.

Packel, D. (2008). "Electoral Institutions and Local Government Accountability: A Literature Review." *The World Bank Social Development Papers, Local Governance and Accountability Series,* 111.

Padmanabhan, P., P. S. Raman and D. V. Mavalankar (2009). "Innovations and Challenges in Reducing Maternal Mortality in Tamil Nadu, India." *Journal of Health, Population, and Nutrition* 27(2): 202.

Page, B. (2002). "The Semi-Sovereign Public." In J. Manza, F. L. Cook and B. Page (eds.), *Navigating Public Opinion.* Oxford; New York: Oxford University Press.

Page, B. I. and R. Y. Shapiro (1983). "Effects of Public Opinion on Policy." *American Political Science Review* 77(1): 175–90.

Pai, S. (2002). *Dalit Assertion and the Unfinished Revolution: The BSP in Uttar Pradesh.* New Delhi: Sage Publications.

Pai, S., ed. (2007). *Political Process in Uttar Pradesh: Identity, Economic Reforms, and Governance.* New Delhi: Pearson Education India.

Pandey, A. (2008). "The Story of the Creation of the State Symbol of Uttar Pradesh." In P. Mahendra and S. Z. H. Jafri (eds.), *Region in Indian History.* New Delhi: Anamika Publishers & Distributors, xiv.

Pandey, G. (1990). *The Construction of Communalism in Colonial North India.* Delhi: Oxford University Press.

Pandey, S. N. (1975). *Education and Social Changes in Bihar, 1900–1921: A Survey of Social History of Bihar from Lord Curzon to Noncooperation Movement.* Varanasi: Motilal Banarsidass Publishers.

Pandian, J. (1987). *Caste, Nationalism and Ethnicity: An Interpretation of Tamil Cultural History and Social Order.* Bombay: Popular Prakasham.

Pandian, M. S. S. (2003). *Brahmin & Non-Brahmin: Genealogies of the Tamil Political Present.* New Delhi: Permanent Black.

Panigrahi, D. N. (2004). *India's Partition: The Story of Imperialism in Retreat.* London; New York: Routledge.

Pargal, S., M. Huq, et al. (1999). "Social Capital in Solid Waste Management: Evidence from Dhaka, Bangladesh." *Social Capital Initiative, The World Bank.* Working Paper No. 16.

Parihar, Rohit. (1999). "Nothing but Embers." *India Today.*

Parsons, T. (1951). *Social System.* London: Routledge.

Paterson, L. (2000). "Social Inclusion and the Scottish Parliament." *Scottish Affairs* 30: 68–77.

Pavković, A. (2000). "Recursive Secessions in Former Yugoslavia: Too Hard a Case for Theories of Secession?" *Political Studies* 48(3): 485–502.

Persson, A. (2012). *State-Building in Ethnically Diverse Societies.* Presented at the workshop, "Building State Capacity: The Other Side of Political Development," Radcliffe Institute, Harvard University, May 4–5.

Peters, E., D. Västfjäll, T., Gärling, and P. Slovic (2006). "Affect and Decision Making: A 'Hot' Topic." *Journal of Behavioral Decision Making* 19(2): 79–85.

Pierson, P. (2001). *The New Politics of the Welfare State.* Oxford: Oxford University Press.

(2004). *Politics in Time: History, Institutions, and Social Analysis.* Princeton: Princeton University Press.

Plümper, T. and V. E. Troeger (2007). "Efficient Estimation of Time-Invariant and Rarely Changing Variables in Finite Sample Panel Analyses with Unit Fixed Effects." *Political Analysis* 15: 124–39.

Pocker Sahib, B., P., U. Sahib, et al. (1954). Memorandum submitted to the States Reorganization Commission, File no. 25/13/54-SRC. 2. *National Archives of India.* New Delhi.

Podestà, F. (2002). "Recent Development in Quantitative Comparative Methodology: The Case of Pooled Time Series Cross-section analysis." *DSS PAPERS SOC* 3-02.

Posner, D. N. (2004). "The Political Salience of Cultural Difference: Why Chewas and Tumbukas Are Allies in Zambia and Adversaries in Malawi." *American Political Science Review* no. 04:529–45.

(2005). *Institutions and Ethnic Politics in Africa.* Cambridge; New York: Cambridge University Press.

Prakash, A. (2001). *Jharkhand: Politics of Development and Identity.* Hyderabad: Orient Blackswan.

Price, P. (1996). "Revolution and Rank in Tamil Nationalism." *Journal of Asian Studies* 55(2): 359–83.

Putnam, R. D. (1993). *Making Democracy Work: Civic Traditions in Modern Italy.* Princeton: Princeton University Press.

(1995). "Bowling Alone: America's Declining Social Capital." *Journal of Democracy* 6(1): 65–78.

Quadagno, J. (1996). *The Color of Welfare: How Racism Undermined the War on Poverty.* New York: Oxford University Press.

Radhakrishnan, P. (1992). "Communal Representation in Tamil Nadu, 1850–1916: The Pre-Non-Brahmin Movement Phase." *Economic and Political Weekly* 31(31).

Rae, J. (1895). *Life of Adam Smith.* London; New York: Macmillan.

Raghavaiyangar, S. (1893). *Memorandum on the Progress of the Madras Presidency during the Last Forty Years of British Administration.* Madras: Printed by the Superintendent, Government Press.

Rahn, W. (2004). "Feeling, Thinking, Being Doing: Public Mood, American National Identity, and Civic Participation." *Annual Meeting of the Midwest Political Science Association.*

Raja, P. R. R. V. (1954). "Memorandum Submitted to the States Reorganization Commission." *National Archives of India.* New Delhi, File no. 25/13/54-SRC. 3.

Rajan, M. C. (2013). "Jaya Goes to War on Lankan Tamils." *The Sunday Standard,* September 1, 2013.

Rajasthan Legislative Assembly Secretariat (1950–2009). *Proceedings of the Rajasthan State Legislative Assembly*: Jaipur.

(2001). *Budget Speeches by Finance Ministers in the Rajasthan Legislative Assembly (1952–80).*

Rajayyan, K. (1982). *History of Tamil Nadu, 1565–1982.* Madurai: Raj Publishers.

Ramachandran, V. and H. Sethi (2000). "Rajasthan Shiksha Karmi Project: An Overall Appraisal: Desk Study Commissioned by SIDA, Embassy of Sweden, New Delhi." *New Education Division Documents.* Stockholm: Education Division at Sida.

Ramachandran, V. K. (1996). "Kerala's Development Achievements: A Review." In J. Dreze and A. Sen (eds.), *Indian Development: Selected Regional Perspectives.* New Delhi: Oxford University Press.

(1998). "On Kerala's Development Achievements." In J. Dreze and A. Sen (eds.), *Indian Development: Selected Regional Perspectives.* Delhi: Oxford University Press, 205–356.

Ramanujan, A. K. (1967). *The Interior Landscape: Love Poems from a Classical Tamil Anthology.* Delhi: Oxford University Press.

Ramaswamy, S. (1993). "Engendering Language: The Poetics of Tamil Identity." *Comparative Studies in Society and History* 35: 683–725.

Ramesh, J. (1999). "Future of Uttar Pradesh: Need for a New Political Mindset." *Economic and Political Weekly* 34(31): 2127–31.

Rammohan, K. T. (2000). "Assessing Reassessment of Kerala Model." *Economic and Political Weekly* 35(15): 1234–36.

Ramusack, B. (1995). "The Indian Princes as Fantasy: Palace Hotels, Palace Museums, and Palace on Wheels." In C. A. Breckenridge (ed.), *Consuming Modernity: Public Culture in a South Asia World.* Minneapolis: University of Minnesota Press.

Rao, K. V. and L. Venkataraman (1976). *State Politics in India,* edited by I. Narain. Meerut: Meenakshi Prakashan, xxxvii.

Rathore, M. S. (2005). "State Level Analysis of Drought Policies and Impacts in Rajasthan, India." *Drought Series Paper No. 6.*

Ray, S. (2006). "The Cost and Financing of Universalising Elementary Education: A Silver Lining in Rajasthan?" In S. K. Mehrotra (ed.), *The Economics of Elementary Education in India: The Challenge of Public Finance, Private Provision, and Household Costs.* New Delhi; Thousand Oaks, CA: Sage Publications.

(2008). "Is Rajasthan Heading Towards Caste War?" *Economic and Political Weekly,* 19–21.

Reddy, K. S. and Dandona, L. (2013). "The Health Sector on the Mend." In N. K. Singh and N. Stern (eds.), *The New Bihar.* India: HarperCollins Publishers.

Renan, E. (1882). *What Is a Nation?* Kessinger Publishing, LLC.

Risley, H. H. and E. A. Gait (1903). Report on the Census of India, 1901. Calcutta: Superintendent of Government Printing.

Robinson, A. L. (2011) "National Identification and Interpersonal Trust in Diverse Societies." Working Paper.

Robinson, F. (1974). *Separatism among Indian Muslims: The Politics of the United Provinces' Muslims, 1860–1923.* London: Cambridge University Press.

Robinson, F. C. R. (1971). "Consultation and Control: the United Provinces' Government and Its Allies, 1860–1906." *Modern Asian Studies* 5(4): 313–36.

Rohlfing, I. (2008). "What You See and What You Get: Pitfalls and Principles of Nested Analysis in Comparative Research." *Comparative Political Studies* 41(11): 1492–1514.

Rostow, W. W. (1990). *The Stages of Economic Growth: A Non-Communist Manifesto.* Cambridge; New York: Cambridge University Press.

Rothstein, Bo. (2011). *The Quality of Government: Corruption, Social Trust and Inequality in Comparative Perspective.* Chicago: University of Chicago Press.

Roy, Arundhati (2008). *The God of Small Things: A Novel.* Reprint edition. New York, NY: Random House Trade Paperbacks.

Rudolph, L. and S. H. Rudolph (1960). "The Political Role of India's Caste Associations." *Pacific Affairs* 33(1): 335.

(1962). *From Princes to Politicians.* Chicago: University of Chicago Press.

Rudolph, S. H. and L. I. Rudolph (1972). *Education and Politics in India; Studies In Organization, Society, and Policy.* Cambridge, MA: Harvard University Press.

Rugh, J. and J. Trounstine (2011). "The Provision of Local Public Goods in Diverse Communities: Analyzing Municipal Bond Elections." *The Journal of Politics* 73(4): 1038–50.

Sachs, J. (2001). *Macroeconomics and Health: Investing in Health for Economic Development: Report of the Commission on Macroeconomics and Health.* World Health Organization.

Sachs, N. (2009). "Experimenting with Identity: Islam, Nationalism and Ethnicity." Paper presented at the Annual Meeting of the American Political Science Association, Toronto.

Saez, L. and A. Sinha (2010). "Political Cycles, Political Institutions and Public Expenditure in India, 1980–2000." *British Journal of Political Science* 40: 91–113.

Saideman, S. M. and R. W. Ayres (2008). *For Kin or Country: Xenophobia, Nationalism, and War.* New York: Columbia University Press.

Sarkar, S. (1997). *Writing Social History,* New York: University of Minnesota.

Schrock-Jacobson, G. (2012). "The Violent Consequences of the Nation, Nationalism and the Initiation of Interstate War." *Journal of Conflict Resolution* 56: 825–52.

Sen, A. (1977). "Rational Fools: A Critique of the Behavioral Foundations of Economic Theory." *Philosophy & Public Affairs* 6(4): 317–44.

(1990). *More Than 100 Million Women Are Missing.* New York Review of Books.

(1990). *Welfare, Preference and Freedom.* Harvard Institute of Economic Research.

(1991). "Reply to 'The Kerala Difference'." *New York Review of Books* 38.

(1999). *Development as Freedom.* New Delhi: Oxford University Press.

(2013) "Bihar: Past, Present and Future." N. K. Singh and N. Stern. *The New Bihar.* India: HarperCollins Publishers.

Shah, G. (2004). *Caste and Democratic Politics in India.* London: Anthem Press.

Shalev, M. (1983). "The Social Democratic Model and Beyond: Two 'Generations' of Comparative Research on the Welfare State." *Comparative Social Research* 6(3): 315–51.

Shandra, J. M., B. London, O. P., Whooley and J. B. Williamson (2004). International Nongovernmental Organizations and Carbon Dioxide Emissions in the Developing World: A Quantitative, Cross-National Analysis. *Sociological Inquiry* 74(4): 520–45.

Shariff, A. and P. K. Ghosh (2000). "Indian Education Scene and the Public Gap." *Economic and Political Weekly* 35(16): 1396–1406.

Sharkansky, I. (1968). *Spending in the American States*. Chicago Rand McNally.

Sharkansky, I. and R. I. Hofferbert (1969). "Dimensions of State. Politics, Economics, and Public Policy." *American Political Science Review* 63: 867–80.

Sharma, A. (1998). *Caste in India*. New Delhi: India Publishers Distributers

Sharma, C. L. (1993). *Ruling Elites of Rajasthan: A Changing Profile*. New Delhi: M.D. Publications Pvt. Ltd.

Sharma, D. (1966). *Rajasthan through the Ages*. Jaipur: Government of Rajasthan.

Sharma, P. (1969). *Political Aspects of States Reorganization in India*. New Delhi: Mohuni Publications.

Sharma, S. (1995). "Drought, Mortality and Social Structure." *International Journal of Environmental Education and Information* 14(1): 85–94.

Sidanius, J., S. Feshbach, et al. (1997). "The Interface between Ethnic and National Attachment: Ethnic Pluralism or Ethnic Dominance?" *Public Opinion Quarterly* 61(1): 102–33.

Singh, A. K. (2007). "The Economy of Uttar Pradesh since the 1990s: Economic Stagnation and Fiscal Crisis." In Sudha Pai (ed.), *Political Process in Uttar Pradesh: Identity, Economic Reforms, and Governance*. New Delhi: Pearson Longman, 273–94.

Singh, B. (1944). "Financial Developments in Travancore (1800–1940)." PhD dissertation. *Department of Economics*, Trivandrum, Travancore University.

Singh, N. K. and N. Stern (2013). *The New Bihar*. India: HarperCollins Publishers.

Singh, P. (2011). "We-ness and Welfare: A Longitudinal Analysis of Social Development in Kerala, India." *World Development* 39(2): 282–93.

Singh, P. and Zubin Shroff (2014). "Different Worlds of Patronage within a Patronage Democracy." Working paper.

Singh, P. and Matthias vom Hau (2014). "Ethnicity, State Capacity, and Development: Reconsidering Causal Connections." In S. Hickey, K. Sen, and B. Bukenya (eds.), *The Politics of Inclusive Development*. Oxford University Press.

   (2015). "Ethnicity in Time: Politics, History, and Whether Diversity Undermines Public Goods Provision?" In *Ethnicity in Time: Politics, History, and Whether Diversity Undermines Public Goods Provision? Forthcoming as a Special Issue of Comparative Political Studies.*

Sinha, A. (1995). "Village Visit Reports." *Compendium of Selected Field Reports of the 60th Foundational Course: Lal Bahadur Shastri National Academy of Administration.*

Sinha, Aseema (2005). *The Regional Roots of Developmental Politics in India: A Divided Leviathan*. Bloomington: Indiana University Press.

Sinnott, R. (2006). "An Evaluation of the Measurement of National, Subnational and Supranational Identity in Crossnational Surveys." *International Journal of Public Opinion* 18(2): 211–23.

Sisson, R. (1966). "Institutionalization and Style in Rajasthan Politics." *Asian Survey* 6(11): 605–13.
 (1969). "Peasant Movements and Political Mobilization: The Jats of Rajasthan." *Asian Survey* 9(12): 946–63.
Sisson, R. and L. L. Shrader (1972). *Legislative Recruitment and Political Integration: Patterns of Political Linkage in an Indian State*. Berkeley, CA: Center for South and Southeast Asian Studies, 12.
Skaaning, S. E. (2010). "Satisfaction with Democracy in Sub-Saharan Africa: Assessing the Effects of System Performance." *African Journal of Political Science and International Relations* 4(5): 164–72.
Skocpol, T. (1992). *Protecting Soldiers and Mothers: The Political Origins of Social Policy in the United States*. Cambridge, MA: Belknap Press of Harvard University Press.
 (1995). *Social Policy in the United States: Future Possibilities In Historical Perspective*. Princeton: Princeton University Press.
Skocpol, T. and E. Amenta (1986). "States and Social Policies." *Annual Review of Sociology* 12(1): 131–57.
Sleeman, J. F. (1973). *The Welfare State: Its Aims, Benefits, Costs*. London: George Allen and Unwin Ltd.
Smelser, N. J. and S. M. Lipset (1966). *Social Structure and Mobility in Economic Development*. Chicago: Aldine.
Smith, A. D. (1987). *The Ethnic Origins of Nations*. Oxford, UK; New York: Blackwell.
 (1991). *National Identity*. London; New York: Penguin.
 (1998). *Nationalism and Modernism: A Critical Survey of Recent Theories of Nations and Nationalism*. New York: Routledge.
Smith, H. and T. Tyler (1996). "Justice and Power: When Will Justice Concerns Encourage the Advantaged to Support Policies Which Redistribute Economic Resources and the Disadvantaged to Willingly Obey the Law?" *European Journal of Social Psychology* 26: 171–200.
Smith, M. and R. Kohn (1998). Nonparametric Seemingly Unrelated Regression. *Monash Econometrics and Business Statistics Working Papers*.
Snehanshu, H. (2014). "Bihari: The Portrait of an Artist." *Bricolage Magazine*.
Snyder, R. (2001). "Scaling Down: The Subnational Comparative Method." *Studies in Comparative International Development* 36(1): 93–110.
Soifer, Hillel (2015). "Regionalism, Ethnic Diversity, and Variation in Public Good Provision by National States." In Prerna Singh and Mathias vom Hau (eds.), *Ethnicity in Time: Politics, History, and Whether Diversity Undermines Public Goods Provision?* Forthcoming as a Special Issue of *Comparative Political Studies*.
Sonntag, S. (1996). "The Political Saliency of Language in Bihar and Uttar Pradesh." *Journal of Commonwealth and Comparative Politics* 34(2): 1–18.
Spratt, P. (1970). *D.M.K. in Power*. Bombay: Nachiketa Publications.
Srivastava, R. S. (2007). "Economic Change among Social Groups in Uttar Pradesh, 1983–2000." In S. Pai (ed.), *Political Process in Uttar Pradesh: Identity, Economic Reforms, and Governance*. New Delhi: Pearson Education India.
Stalin, J. (1954). *The Foundations of Leninism: Concerning Questions of Leninism*. Moscow, Foreign Languages Pub. House.

Stasavage, D. (2005). "Democracy and Education Spending in Africa." *American Journal of Political Science* 49: 343.

States Reorganization Commission (1955). *Report of States Reorganization Commission*: Delhi, Manager of Publications.

Stepan, A. J. Linz, and Y. Yadav. *Crafting State-Nations: India and Other Multinational Democracies*. *1 edition*. Baltimore: Johns Hopkins University Press, 2011.

Stern, R. W. (1988). *The Cat and the Lion: Jaipur State in the British Raj*. Leiden: E.J. Brill.

Stimson, J. A. (1985). "Regression in Space and Time: A Statistical Essay." *American Journal of Political Science* 29(4): 914–47.

Stone, B. S. (1988). "Institutional Decay and the Traditionalization of Politics: The Uttar Pradesh Congress Party." *Asian Survey* 28(10): 1018–30.

Subramanian, N. (1999). *Ethnicity and Populist Mobilization: Political Parties, Citizens, And Democracy in South India*. Delhi: Oxford University Press.

Sundararajan, S. (1989). *March to freedom in Madras Presidency, 1916–1947*. Madras: Lalitha Publications.

Surridge, P. and D. McCrone (1999). "The Scottish Electorate: The 1997 Election and Beyond." In B. Taylor and K. Thomson (eds.), *Scotland and Wales: Nations Again?* Cardiff: University of Wales Press, xlii.

Tajfel, H. (1970). "Experiments in Intergroup Discrimination." *Scientific American* 223(96–102).

Tajfel, H. and J. C. Turner (1986). "The Social Identity Theory of Inter-group Behavior." In S. Worchel and L. W. Austin (eds.), *Psychology of Intergroup Relations*. Chicago: Nelson-Hall.

Tamir, Y. (1993). "Liberal Nationalism." *Studies in Moral, Political, and Legal Philosophy*. From http://site.ebrary.com/lib/princeton/Doc?id=10002098.

Tamil Nadu State Assembly Debates, Official Report (1952). Tamil Nadu Secretariat. Chennai.

Taneja, V. R. (2005). *Socio-Philosophical Approach to Education*. New Delhi: Atlantic Publishers & Distributors.

Task Force on Higher Education and Society (2000). *Higher Education in Developing Countries: Peril and Promise*. Washington, DC: World Bank.

Taylor, M. Z. (2008). Political Decentralization and Technological Innovation: Testing the Innovative Advantages of Decentralized States. *Munich Personal RePEc Archive Paper No. 10996 16*.

Tendler, J. (1989). "What Ever Happened to Poverty Alleviation?" *World Development* 17(7): 1033–44.

Thanickan, J. (2006). "United Kerala Movement: A Descriptive Essay." New Delhi.

Tharakan, M. (1984). "Socio-Economic Factors in Educational Development: Case of Nineteenth Century Travancore." *Economic and Political Weekly* 19 (46): 1913–67.

Thomas, George. (2012). "India's Innocent: Secret Weddings of Child Brides." *Christian Broadcasting Network*.

Thompson, E. P. (1963). *The Making of the English Working Class*. New York: Vintage Books.

Tilak, J. B. G. (1990). The Political Economy of Education in India. Special Studies in Comparative Education no. 24, Comparative Education Center, Graduate School of Education, State University of New York, Buffalo.

Tilly, C. (1985). "War-Making and State Making as Organized Crime." In Peter B. Evans, Dietrich Rueschemeyer and Theda Skocpol (eds.), *Bringing the State Back In*. Cambridge: Cambridge University Press.

Tiryakian, E. A. and R. Rogowski (1985). *New Nationalism of the Developed West: Toward Explanation*. Boston: Allen & Unwin.

Titmuss, R. (1958). *War and Social Policy. Essays on the 'Welfare State'*. London: George Allen and Unwin.

Tiwari, B. N. (2007). "BJP's Political Strategies: Development, Caste and Electoral Discourse." In S. Pai (ed.), *Political Process in Uttar Pradesh: Identity, Economic Reforms, and Governance*. New Delhi: Pearson Education India

Tiwari, L. (1995). *Issues in Indian Politics*. New Delhi: Mittal Publications.

Tomar, K. S. (1998). "BJP Confident of Giving a Drubbing to Congress." *Hindustan Times*.

Transue, J. E. (2007). "Identity Salience, Identity Acceptance, and Racial Policy Attitudes: American National Identity as a Uniting Force." *American Journal of Political Science* 51(1): 78–91.

Tsai, L. (2007). "Solidary Groups, Informal Accountability, and Local Public Goods Provision in Rural China." *American Political Science Review* 101(2): 355–72.

Tsai, L. and Daniel Ziblatt (2012). "The Rise of Subnational and Multilevel Comparative Politics." *Annual Review of Political Science*, forthcoming.

Tyler, Tom R. and Heather J. Smith (1999). "Justice, Social Identity, and Group Processes." In Tom R. Tyler, Roderick M. Kramer and Oliver P. John (eds.), *The Psychology of the Social Self*. Mahwah, NJ: Lawrence Erlbaum Associates, Inc.

UN Country Team in India (2003). India: Situation report on Rajasthan drought, http://reliefweb.int/node/118859.

Unnithan-Kumar, M. (1997). Identity, Gender, and Poverty: New perspectives on Caste and Tribe in Rajasthan. Oxford: Berghahn books.

Varma, P. K. (2013). "A State on the Cusp of a Cultural Renaissance." In N. K. Singh and N. Stern (eds.), *The New Bihar*. India: HarperCollins Publishers.

Varma, U. (1994). *Uttar Pradesh State Gazetteer*. Government of Uttar Pradesh, Department of District Gazetteers.

Varshney, A. (1998a). *Democracy, Development, and the Countryside: Urban-Rural Struggles in India*. Cambridge: Cambridge University Press.

(1998b). "Why Democracy Survives," *Journal of Democracy* 9.3: 36–50.

(2001). "Ethnic Conflict and Civil Society: India and Beyond." *World Politics* 53(3): 362–98.

(2002). *Civic Life and Ethnic Conflict: Hindus and Muslims in India*. New Haven: Yale University Press.

Varshney, A., S. Wilkinson, et al. (2006). "Varshney-Wilkinson Dataset on Hindu-Muslim Violence in India, 1950–1995, Version 2." From http://webapp.icpsr.umich.edu/cocoon/ICPSR-STUDY/04342.xml.

Veliz, C. (1980). *The Centralist Tradition of Latin America*. Princeton: Princeton University Press.

Venugopal, P. (2006). "State Up against New Challenges." *Hindu*. Madras.

Verba, S., K. L. Schlozman, et al. (1995). *Voice and Equality: Civic Voluntarism in American Politics*. Cambridge, MA: Harvard University Press.

Verma, B. M. (1994). *Rural Leadership in a Welfare Society: A Study in Social Status and Role Performance*. New Delhi: Mittal Publications.

Véron, René (2001). "The "New" Kerala Model: Lessons for Sustainable Development." *World Development* 29.4: 601–17.

Vigdor, J. L. (2004). "Other People's Taxes: Nonresident Voters and Statewide Limitation of Local Government." *Journal of Law and Economics* 47(2): 453.

Vohra, R. (2012). *The Making of India: A Political History*. M.E. Sharpe.

Wang, S. and Y. Yao (2007). "Grassroots Democracy and Local Governance: Evidence from Rural China." *World Development* 35(10): 1635–49.

Washbrook, D. (1990). "South Asia, the World System, and World Capitalism." *Journal of Asian Studies* 49: 479–508.

Wawro, G. (2002). "Estimating Dynamic Panel Data Models in Political Science." *Political Analysis* 10(1): 25–48.

Weber, E. (1976). *Peasants into Frenchmen: The Modernization of Rural France, 1870–1914.* Stanford University Press.

Weber, M. (1948). *Essays in Sociology.* New York: Oxford University Press.

Webster, Noah (1789). "An Essay on the Necessity, Advantages, and Practicality of Reforming the Mode of Spelling and of Rendering the Orthography of Words Correspondent to Pronunciation." In *Dissertations on the English Language: With Notes, Historical and Critical, to Which Is Added, by Way of Appendix, an Essay on a Reformed Mode of Spelling, with Dr. Franklin's Arguments on That Subject.* Boston, MA.

Weiner, M. (1967). *Party Building in a New Nation: the Indian National Congress.* Chicago: University of Chicago Press.

(1968). *State Politics in India.* Princeton: Princeton University Press.

(1991). *The Child and the State in India: Child Labor and Education Policy in Comparative Perspective.* Princeton: Princeton University Press.

Wells, Paul (1998). "Quebecers? Canadians? We're proud to Be Both." *The Gazette,* 4 April.

Wildavsky, A. (1987). "Choosing Preferences by Constructing Institutions: A Cultural Theory of Preference Formation." *American Political Science Review* 81(1): 3–22.

Wildavsky, A. B. (1964). *The Politics of the Budgetary Process.* Boston: Little.

Wilensky, H. (1975). *The Welfare State and Equality: Structural and Ideological Roots of Public Expenditures.* Berkeley: University of California Press.

Wilkinson, R. G. (1996). *Unhealthy Societies: The Afflictions of Inequality.* London; New York: Routledge.

Wilkinson, S. (2004). *Electoral Competition and Ethnic Violence in India.* Cambridge; New York: Cambridge University Press.

(2008). "Which Group Identities Lead to Most Violence? In S. N. Kalyvas, I. Shapiro and T. E. Masoud (eds.), *Order, Conflict, and Violence.* Cambridge, UK; New York: Cambridge University Press, xiii.

Wilson, S. E. and D. M. Butler (2007). "Lot More to Do: The Sensitivity of Time-Series Cross-Section Analyses to Simple Alternative Specifications." *Political Analysis* 15(2): 101–23.

Wimmer, A. (2015). "Is Diversity Detrimental? Ethnic Fractionalization, Public Goods Provision, and the Historical Legacies of Stateness." In Prerna Singh and Mathias vom Hau (eds.), *Ethnicity in Time: Politics, History, and Whether Diversity Undermines Public Goods Provision?* Forthcoming as a Special Issue of *Comparative Political Studies.*

Wimmer, A. (2014). "Nation Building. A Long-term Perspective and Global Analysis." *European Sociological Review* 30(6).

Windmiller, M. (1954). *The Left Wing in India.* Berkeley: *University of California Press.*

Witsoe, J. (2013). "Bihar." In A. Kohli and P. Singh (eds.), *Handbook of Indian Politics.* New York: Routledge.

Wolfe, A. and J. Klausen (2000). "Other Peoples." *Prospect* (December).

Wynad Taluk, A. K. C. (1954). "Memorandum Submitted to the States Reorganization Commission. File no. 25/13/54-SRC. 2." *National Archives of India. New Delhi.*

Zerinini-Brotel, J. (1998). "The BJP in Uttar Pradesh: From Hindutva to Consensual Politics?" In C. Jaffrelot and T. B. Hansen (eds.), *The BJP and the Compulsions of Politics in India.* Delhi: Oxford University Press.

Index

Greenfeld, Liah, 29
Gugerty, Mary Kay, 50
Gupta, Shaibal, 180
Guru, Sri Narayan, 83

Harrison, Selig S., 134
health services. *See also* Bihar; Kerala;
    mortality, infant and maternal;
    Rajasthan; Tamil Nadu (TN);
    Uttar Pradesh (UP)
  Communist party, effect on policies, 224
  private provision, 187
  subnationalism, effect on, 224
Hechter, Michael, 56
Heller, Patrick, 19, 48, 56, 138
Herder, Johann G., 194
Herring, Ronald J., 48
Hindu Mahasabha, 92–94
Hiskey, Jonathan T., 49
Hobsbawm, Eric J., 29, 30, 193
Hofferbert, Richard I., 49
Horowitz, Donald L., 52
Huber, Evelyne, 255
Huber, John D., 1
Human Development Index (HDI), 13,
    15, 175
Huntington, Samuel P., 251

identity. *See* collective identity
identity and motivation of groups, 38–39
Immergut, Ellen M., 1, 254
India
  caste system and education, 59–60
  Congress party, 84, 92, 99, 118
  dual self-identification in, 44
  economic growth and social
    development, 47
  education indicators, 15, 206, 215
  health indicators, 4, 9, 14, 21, 48, 124,
    206, 213, 215
  linguistic reorganization of states, 44, 84,
    195, 202
  Ministries of Education and Health, 58
  national government role, 37, 118
  National Policy on Education, 164, 185
  provinces of, 5–9, 16
  provincial government role, 32, 37
  social development across subnational
    states, 206
individuals and national identity,
    250–51, 252
International Social Survey Program (ISSP), 44

Iyer, Lakshmi, 50, 56, 209
Izhavas, 64, 79–82, 83, 86, 113

Jacobs, Alan M., 253–54
Jan Sangh, 157
Jeffrey, Robin, 127
Jharkhand, 177–80
  Jharkhand Mukti Morcha, 179
Johnson, Simon, 1
Joshi, Devin K., 47

Kedourie, Elie, 29
Kerala. *See also* Izhavas; Travancore
  Congress party in, 141
  electoral participation, 139, 159
  Gram Sabha, 139
  health indicators, 19
  infant and maternal mortality, 19, 126, 132,
    139, 164
  lack of civil society organizations, 56
  land redistribution, 252
  literacy and literacy rate, 107, 126,
    132, 139
  low economic growth, high social
    development, 47
  Mahabali as symbol of state, 137
  Malayali culture and language, 81, 86
  princely rule, impact of, 56
  religious diversity, 54
Keys, V.O. Jr., 49
Khan, Syed Ahmed, 91
Khwaja, Asim I., 50
Kisan Sabhas, 102
Klausen, J., 242
Kohli, Atul, 48
Kumar, Nitish, 181–82, 186
Kymlicka, Will, 28, 242

land redistribution, 138
Lange, Matthew K., 56
language. *See* linguistic subnationalism
Lecours, André, 243, 244–47
Levesque, Rene, 244
Levine, Ross, 50
'liberal nationalist' paradigm, 35
linguistic subnationalism. *See also* States
    Reorganization Commission (SRC)
  in the Indian sub-continent, 194–96, 202
    Bangladesh, 195
    Sri Lanka, 195
Linguistic Survey of India, 99
Lipset, Seymour M., 46

Other Books in the Series (*continued from page iii*)